SWAMI VIVEKANANDA

FOR OUR TIMES

Rajiv Sikri, a student of history, politics and international relations, joined the Indian Foreign Service in 1970. In the course of a distinguished career spanning more than three and a half decades, he served in key diplomatic assignments in Moscow (twice), New York, Paris and Kathmandu, and as India's Ambassador to Kazakhstan. He retired as Secretary in the Ministry of External Affairs, Government of India.

Post-retirement, Rajiv Sikri has authored two highly acclaimed books on India's foreign policy, which have been widely appreciated for their depth and insight. He has been closely associated with the Vivekananda International Foundation since its inception and continues to contribute as a member of its Advisory Council.

In addition to his professional pursuits, he is an avid photographer.

SWAMI VIVEKANANDA

FOR OUR TIMES

Edited and compiled by RAJIV SIKRI

Introduction by S. GURUMURTHY

RUPA

Published by
Rupa Publications India Pvt. Ltd 2026
161-B/4, Gulmohar House,
Yusuf Sarai Community Centre,
New Delhi 110049

Sales centres:
Bengaluru Chennai
Hyderabad Kolkata Mumbai

P-ISBN: 978-93-7003-553-9
E-ISBN: 978-93-7003-277-4

First impression 2026

10 9 8 7 6 5 4 3 2 1

Printed in India

For my grandchildren,
Shivan and Dev

CONTENTS

PUBLISHER'S NOTE

There are voices that belong to their moment, and there are voices that transcend it. Swami Vivekananda's belongs to the latter. More than a century after his passing, his words still ring with a startling freshness.

Swamiji spoke of the strength of the spirit, the dignity of service, the harmony of faiths and the infinite potential hidden within every human being. His was a vision that sought to unite the deepest truths of the spirit with the practical challenges of daily life, encouraging individuals to awaken their own inner power while working for the good of all.

Swami Vivekananda for Our Times brings together these reflections in a volume where his words unfold like beams of light, illuminating questions that remain central to human civilization: how to educate, how to believe, how to serve, how to be free.

We gratefully acknowledge **Advaita Ashrama** for granting permission to use excerpts from *The Complete Works of Swami Vivekananda*. Readers are encouraged to explore the full nine-volume set, available through their official website, www.advaitaashrama.org. We also express our sincere appreciation to the **Vivekananda International Foundation** (VIF) for their assistance and support in bringing out this book—particularly to its Chairman, Mr S. Gurumurthy, for encouraging the book right from its inception and then graciously contributing the Introduction—and its Secretary, Ms Anuttama Ganguly, for her constant help and advice.

It is our hope that this volume will serve as a doorway for readers—especially younger generations—to rediscover Swami Vivekananda, engage with his timeless vision, and draw inspiration for building lives, communities and a nation rooted in courage, compassion and confidence.

PREFACE

This is a book by accident, not by design. Twenty-five years ago, I knew little about Swami Vivekananda—a towering personality who was much talked about, but not sufficiently read or understood. It was well known that he had delivered a stirring speech at the Parliament of the World's Religions in Chicago in 1893, which had reportedly created an immediate and powerful impact in the United States. From there, his fame spread to India. Yet there had to be much more to Swami Vivekananda that enabled him, in his relatively short lifespan of less than 40 years, to create an impact on the thinking of leaders like Mahatma Gandhi and Jawaharlal Nehru, inspire Subhas Chandra Bose and become an idol of the Sangh Parivar.

Swami Vivekananda was no ordinary swami. He relished good food (including non-vegetarian dishes), smoked and was at ease in the company of women—many of whom were among his most ardent devotees—while remaining a strict and disciplined *brahmachari*. Had he been merely a swami in ochre robes, no matter how learned or accomplished, he could not have captured the imagination of millions during his lifetime and beyond. Here was a man who was both a staunch disciple of the rustic mystic Ramakrishna Paramahansa and a highly educated, widely travelled aristocrat with a deep understanding of both Indian and Western philosophy. As I embarked on my journey to understand Swami Vivekananda, the question in my mind was: what is it about him that makes him a legendary and respected figure, yet less prominent in the public imagination than many stalwarts of the freedom movement?

It was while I was working in the lonely diplomatic outpost of Almaty in Kazakhstan in the late 1990s that I found both the environment and the time to explore Swami Vivekananda's thoughts in greater depth. His ideas left a strong impression on me, but after I left Almaty, professional preoccupations took precedence. It was only after a couple of decades that I returned to studying Swami Vivekananda, this time with greater focus and determination.

The challenge, however, lies in the fact that—except on a handful of issues—there is no systematic exposition of his thoughts. Most of his ideas were expressed in extempore speeches, letters and conversations rather than in a formal structured format over a decade or so in India and abroad. All these have been compiled in *The Complete Works of Swami Vivekananda* (nine volumes) published by the Advaita Ashrama. While this compilation is an invaluable source, it does not lend itself to easy reading. Swamiji often revisited the same issue in different speeches and writings, months or years apart, in response to changing circumstances and audiences. To gain a comprehensive understanding of his thinking on any issue and to connect the various threads in his words, one must go through his works with a fine-toothed comb.

As I ploughed through his writings, I began taking notes for my own reference. His thoughts are so profound that they demand more than one concentrated reading and ample time for reflection. At that stage, I had no intention of producing a book. It was Shri S. Gurumurthy, Chairman of the Vivekananda International Foundation, who, in a casual conversation about my personal study, suggested publishing a book based on my notes.

In studying Swami Vivekananda, I consciously chose to rely on his original works rather than on secondary material. The available commentaries and writings on him often left me somewhat dissatisfied as I feel that they do not do full justice to his formidable intellect and deep vision. Some tend to be overly hagiographical; others, inordinately abstract; still others focus only on his philosophical discourses. A few try to pigeonhole him or selectively quote him to serve a preconceived agenda. The myriad compilations of his aphorisms make for good quotations, but are mere trailers to the main film.

Two caveats are in order. First, I have not studied other works on Swami Vivekananda that may contain relevant supplementary material. It is also highly likely that many of his utterances were never recorded or transcribed. Second, his views on some issues did evolve over time, shaped by his experiences and learnings during his long sojourns in the West. On some issues, he was tentative or ambiguous, perhaps because he did not have the time to reflect deeply on them. Thus, there is no need to accept his views uncritically—he would have been the last to urge such an approach.

For me, studying Swami Vivekananda was made easier by the fact that his writings and speeches are in, or have been translated into, English—the language in which I am most comfortable reading and reflecting. Moreover, his audience consisted largely of laypeople rather than scholars or philosophers, and his language is simple, strong and often blunt. Swami Vivekananda openly stated that he abhorred hypocrisy. He was especially contemptuous of 'those caste-ridden, superstitious, merciless, hypocritical, atheistic cowards that you find only among the educated Hindus.'[1] He made it clear that his focus was not on being sweet, but on spreading his message to the world.

During his first visit abroad, he held to the view that no country had any special claim on him and that he belonged to the world as much as to India. Yet it is clear that his views evolved upon his return to India in 1897. Although he claimed not to be a chauvinist and professed no belief in politics ('God and truth are the only politics in the world; everything else is trash'),[2] his heart always beat for the poor of India, and his mind was ever set on making India great again.

---

[1] *Vol. 5, Epistles (First Series), The Complete Works of Swami Vivekananda*, LII, p. 96.
[2] *Ibid.*

Swami Vivekananda spoke passionately and eloquently in a conversational, free-flowing style. He understood the importance of accessibility:

'To put the Hindu ideas into English and then make out of dry philosophy and intricate mythology and queer startling psychology, a religion which shall be easy, simple, popular, and at the same time meet the requirements of the highest minds—is a task only those can understand who have attempted it. The dry, abstract Advaita must become living—poetic—in everyday life; out of hopelessly intricate mythology must come concrete moral forms; and out of bewildering Yogi-ism must come the most scientific and practical psychology—and all this must be put in a form so that a child may grasp it. That is my life's work.'[3]

Elsewhere he said: 'My success is due to my popular style—the greatness of a teacher consists in the simplicity of his language.'[4]

I also admire the way he invariably provides detailed reasoning when rejecting what he considered to be false interpretations of religious and social practices or beliefs.

I have put together this compilation on the assumption that there may be many other non-scholars like me who wish to gain a deeper understanding of Swami Vivekananda's thoughts but are daunted by the prospect of having to wade through thousands of pages of his voluminous speeches, letters and writings. To make his insights more accessible, each chapter begins with a brief summary paraphrasing the essence of the quotations that follow.

I hope this compilation helps readers gain a flavour of his thought and encourages them to reflect independently. For those inclined to explore further, the volume number, chapter and sub-chapter headings, and relevant page references from *The Complete Works of Swami Vivekananda* are provided after each quotation, to facilitate direct consultation of the original text.

I have not attempted to interpret Swami Vivekananda's

---

[3]*Ibid*, LVIII, pp. 104–105.

[4]*Ibid*, LIX, p. 106.

thoughts, but leave it to readers to form their own independent judgment.

What prodded me to explore the personality and thoughts of Swami Vivekananda? Looking back over my life, I cannot but be deeply grateful for the many things it has given me over the decades—the privilege of studying in prestigious educational institutions, rich and varied experiences through travel across the world, and a fulfilling professional career. Yet, as I grew older, I increasingly felt that something had been missing from my education and experience.

In the early decades after India's Independence, the dominant national narrative portrayed India as a poor and backward country, inhabited by a meek people given to non-violence. We grew up in an insular society beset by shortages of every kind. For young Indians, the West was the 'promised land', embodying hope, success, and prosperity. My generation, educated within the constricting framework of an inherited colonial template, remained relatively ignorant of our country's vast cultural and spiritual heritage, since our sources of knowledge were confined to what we picked up from family and society.

The Christian community ran the 'best' educational institutions—'best' in the sense that they offered the greatest opportunities for career advancement. In schools and colleges, we were not taught anything about India's cultural and spiritual traditions or about the great personalities from diverse fields in our long history. History teaching relied heavily on the works of British historians and left-oriented Indian scholars. British constitutional history was considered important enough to be included as an optional subject in the civil services competitive examination! In school, French was available as an optional subject, but not Sanskrit.

Among the figures of India's freedom movement, it was Mahatma Gandhi and Jawaharlal Nehru who dominated our mental space. There was no shortage of information about their stellar contributions to the 'non-violent' freedom movement—indeed, there was always a question on Gandhiji's thoughts in the General Knowledge paper of the civil services examination! By contrast, the intellectual and material contributions of giants such as Swami Vivekananda, Lala Lajpat Rai, Bal Gangadhar Tilak, Bipin Chandra Pal, Subhas Chandra Bose, Sardar Patel, Sri Aurobindo, Veer Savarkar, Shaheed Bhagat Singh, Chandrashekhar Azad, and many others to India's freedom struggle received only superficial treatment, if at all, in educational institutions and public discourse.

This neglect could not have been mere oversight. At least in the case of Swami Vivekananda, paeans of praise for him had flowed from the lips and pens of acknowledged stalwarts of our freedom movement—among them Jawaharlal Nehru, Subhas Chandra Bose and Mahatma Gandhi. Nehru observed that Vivekananda came as a tonic to the depressed and demoralized Hindu mind and gave Indians a sense of pride in their inheritance. Subhas Chandra Bose wrote that it was Swami Vivekananda's rich, profound, and full-blooded masculine personality—'reckless in his sacrifice, unceasing in his activity, boundless in his love, profound and versatile in his wisdom, exuberant in his emotions, merciless in his attacks, but yet simple as a child'[5]—that explained his influence on his countrymen, and that 'if he had been alive, I would have been at his feet.'[6] Swami Vivekananda also inspired a key element in Gandhiji's philosophy: the concept of *Daridra Narayana*—God manifested in the hungry and destitute—which Vivekananda coined and Gandhiji later popularized.

This book is a selected compilation of Swami Vivekananda's quotations on three broad themes. The first concerns the nature of religion. Across societies and cultures, religion is often misunderstood and frequently misused for political and social

[5]*Vivekananda: The Great Spiritual Teacher*, Advaita Ashrama, p. 561.
[6]*Ibid.*

ends. It is, all too often, a principal trigger for conflict and war. Hence, it helps to have a clearer and deeper understanding of the true nature of religion and the underlying unity of all faiths.

This logically leads to the second theme of the book: India's philosophical and religious traditions and practices. Religion was the trigger for the Partition of India in 1947—a gut-wrenching and decisive turning point in our modern history. Nearly eight decades later, it remains a core element in the Indian psyche, regardless of faith. Anyone seeking to understand India must understand this powerful force that continues to shape our politics and society.

The third theme is Swami Vivekananda's dream of making India a great country—a remarkable vision at a time when India was still firmly under British rule and there was no organized nationalist movement. All these themes have immense contemporary relevance.

The dedicated band of workers and followers of the Advaita Ashrama, the Ramakrishna Mission and the Vivekananda Kendra have selflessly taken upon themselves the task of spreading awareness of Swami Vivekananda's spiritual message and thoughts on religion. They have done magnificent work, including the construction of the Vivekananda Memorial at Vivekananda Rock.

Sadly, despite the high praise accorded to Swami Vivekananda by the leading lights of India's freedom movement, successive governments over the decades made little effort to popularize his inspiring thoughts on Indian society and nationalism. It is imperative that we keep his message alive and fresh in the minds of Indians across generations. There has, however, been a welcome change with the coming to power of Narendra Modi, who, in his youth, was so inspired by Swami Vivekananda's teachings that he retreated for a couple of years into the Himalayas on a voyage of self-discovery. After his victory in the 2024 general elections, he meditated at the Vivekananda Memorial.

Strength, faith and fearlessness are recurring themes in

Swami Vivekananda's thought. Are these not also the pillars of nation-building implicit in Prime Minister Narendra Modi's vision of a 'Viksit Bharat' by 2047? Should we not turn to Swami Vivekananda to motivate and guide us as we seek to make India once again a great and globally influential country?

India, like every nation, needs inspirational heroes. While many stalwarts of the freedom movement such as Subhas Chandra Bose, Veer Savarkar and Sardar Patel have in recent years been visibly honoured for their contributions, Swami Vivekananda remains somewhat in the background. Although he believed that 'the highest men are calm, silent and unknown,'[7] I firmly believe that Swami Vivekananda deserves wider public recognition—not only as a philosopher, thinker, reformer, internationalist and humanist, but also as a great freedom fighter, richly deserving an elevated place among the giants of the freedom movement.

Although he stayed away from politics, he spoke and wrote on issues that can legitimately be regarded as political. As the person who gave civilizational confidence to Indians and intellectual ballast to the freedom struggle of the 19th century, he set in motion the flywheel that culminated in India's independence. At a time of political divisiveness and competing reassessments of India's freedom fighters, perhaps it is time to recognize Swami Vivekananda as the true intellectual progenitor of India's struggle for independence.

It is my humble suggestion that there would be great gains for our country and society if young minds in schools and colleges were to be made familiar with his glorious thinking and vision.

In conclusion, I would like to express my deep gratitude to the Advaita Ashrama (www.advaitaashrama.org) for their kind permission to use excerpts from *The Complete Works of Swami Vivekananda* for this compilation.

—Rajiv Sikri

---

[7]*Vol. 1, Karma Yoga*, VII, p. 106.

INTRODUCTION

THE WEST-LED WORLD WAKES UP TO SWAMI VIVEKANANDA'S MESSAGE—A CENTURY LATE

I feel extremely privileged and delighted to write the introduction to this critically important book, *Swami Vivekananda for Our Times*.

Thinkers and scholars from diverse domains of knowledge have written on and about Swami Vivekananda. Yet this is perhaps the first book to examine Swamiji's thoughts through the eyes of an expert in international relations—particularly one who has been an integral part of India's domestic polity and foreign relations for most of his career as a diplomat. The author's professional world was shaped by the intellectual frameworks of Karl Marx and Max Weber, whose worldviews as research shows, dominated Indian academic, intellectual and administrative domains for decades. Marx dismissed Indian civilization as semi-barbaric, while Weber regarded it—because of its belief in karma and rebirth—as lacking enterprise and therefore incompatible with the capitalist model of growth. Their ideas undermined, if not delegitimized, the ancient wisdom of non-conflicting spiritual and civilizational nationalism that Swami Vivekananda so powerfully expounded. As post-Independence Indian statecraft and diplomacy came to be rooted in Western thought and models,. the author lived through an era when India's civilizational consciousness had largely gone underground.

The author is, therefore, uniquely suited to write on Swami Vivekananda for three reasons. One, as a career diplomat, he experienced—perhaps painfully—that India's civilizational consciousness, rooted in Swamiji's ideas of global harmony, remained at the margins of Indian diplomacy rather than its core, where it rightly belonged. Two, Swamiji's ideas were not confined to espousing the quintessence of India's spiritual and civilizational values; he was India's first cultural and philosophical ambassador, who showed the world that diverse religions and philosophies could coexist in harmony—an idea totally alien to the colonial and religious Western worldview, yet one whose time has truly come. Three, the author observes that the civilizational consciousness of non-Western nations, long in a state of suspended animation in global geopolitics, is now rising again; and that India's civilizational nationalism—once eclipsed in post-Independence polity—is witnessing a remarkable revival.

Seizing the opportunity the author has kindly given me, I wish to offer a broad overview of the 19th-century world—particularly the West—that Swami Vivekananda addressed through the Parliament of Religions in 1893, the great initiative the West undertook a century ago. I shall also touch upon how the 20th-century West, which led 'the Rest', failed to follow up on that initiative and instead repeated its own violent history—wars and atrocities that cost over 350 million lives before the West finally rediscovered Swami Vivekananda, a century late, at the close of the 20th century.

I also wish to highlight how Swami Vivekananda defined India as a nation of those whose hearts beat to the same spiritual rhythm; how he inspired the Indian freedom movement and helped build the civilizational India that is now rising as a benevolent force in a world of hate and conflict; and how this messenger of universal brotherhood—who gave humanity the concept of 'Vasudhaiva Kutumbakam'—was recognized by great thinkers in India and abroad as a visionary for the world.

The Violent Record of Western History, Ideologies and Worldview

At this point, I feel that, unconstrained by the politically comfortable idea of political correctness—which has killed honest intellectualism in global discourse—some plain speaking is necessary.

That the Western religious and material thoughts, which promoted conflicts, had no conflict-avoidance potential is proved not only by the history of the Dark-Age West but also by that of the modern West. Leave the Dark Ages aside; look instead at the modern age, which the West proudly traces to the Age of Enlightenment. The ideas originating in the modern West shaped the post–World War II order. World War I, which US President Woodrow Wilson—who introduced into geopolitics the concept of world order—declared to be the war to end all wars, ironically sowed the seeds of World War II. Both wars together cost the world 100 million lives and, in financial terms, about US$42 trillion in today's money.

Wars did not end even with the two world wars. They continued during the Cold War period, when warmongers kept finding newer and deadlier weapons of destruction. Their efforts yielded—and continue to yield—sophisticated weapons capable of destroying the world several times over. During the Cold War—when there was no world-scale war—mass killings by religious and political ideologies rooted in the West continued. To a question about how many were killed during the Cold War, Artificial Intelligence answered: 'Estimates for deaths during the Cold War vary widely, ranging from tens of millions to over 100 million, with the high-end estimates often focused on deaths resulting from communist regimes, including executions, man-made famines, and forced labour. Some sources, like *The Black Book of Communism*, claim over 94 million victims, with a significant portion attributed to China and the Soviet Union.

Other estimates suggest that wars fought during this period resulted in up to 20 million deaths.'

It is clear from history that wars do not end wars. With the end of each war begins the preparation for the next. When the mind is perpetually in a state of war, there can be no peace, for the threat of war coexists with an insincere and artificial calm that gives an appearance of false peace. History demonstrates that wars in the West have been a miserable saga of unbridled violence and massacre. The rule of war is encapsulated in the grim maxim *vae victis*–woe to the vanquished—which means that the defeated could expect little mercy. As the *Encyclopaedia Britannica* observes: 'In early history, war appears to have been a matter of almost unrelieved barbarity. Practically no restraints were observed in methods of war; with little discrimination between combatant and non-combatant; and torture, slavery, death, and confiscation of property awaited conquered forces and population.'[1]

The first serious attempt by the West to regulate its barbaric rules of war came only in 1899 at The Hague. Yet neither of the two world wars respected such restraint. Even the staggering loss of life in those wars pales in comparison with the deaths caused by autocratic regimes outside the battlefield. Professor R.J. Rummel, scholar of Indiana, Yale and Hawaii universities, dedicated decades to studying state-sponsored mass killings across the last 2,500 years—a body of work he collectively titled *Power Kills*. He estimated pre-20th-century killings at between 625 million and 1.2 billion, and those of the 20th century alone at 262 million—excluding the casualties of the two world wars.[2]

---

[1]*Encyclopaedia Britannica: Macropaedia—Knowledge in Depth*, 'Warfare, Laws of', 15th ed., vol. 19.

[2]Rummel, R. J., *Power Kills: Democracy as a Method of Nonviolence*, Transaction Publishers, New Brunswick, New Jersey, 1997.

India: An Oasis of Peace and Harmony for 17 Centuries

Rummel's data show that prior to the 13th century, there were virtually no instances of mass killing in India, apart from Emperor Ashoka's Kalinga War, in which some 1,00,000 were killed. Between the 13th and 19th centuries—the period of Islamic invasions and rule—he estimates around 4.5 million deaths. That means, for nearly 1,700 years (BC 5th century–12th century AD), India enjoyed complete peace and harmony.

Peace and economic development are natural companions. It is no coincidence that during this long era of internal stability and external security—underpinned by the statecraft of Kautilya's *Arthashastra*, composed after his encounter with Alexander—India remained the leading economic power in the world for 17 centuries, as demonstrated by independent studies by Paul Bairoch and Angus Maddison.

When blood flowed across much of the world before the 20th century, India stood as an oasis of peace—despite being both the most populous and the most diverse nation on earth. Indeed, if India were placed on one side and the rest of the world on the other, the diversity within India would still surpass that of the rest combined. With such astonishing diversity, how was India—and India alone—a harmonious and peaceful civilization? The answer to this one question should make the violence-ridden, West-led world look to India for a way out.

India's Humane Rules of War

One reason why there was no mass violence in ancient India, and later until the Islamic invasions, is that Hindu philosophers had laid down humane rules even for warfare. Writing on the Hindu rules of war in *The Wonder That Was India*, A. L. Basham observed:[3]

---

[3]Basham, A. L., *The Wonder That Was India: A Survey of the Culture of the Indian Sub-Continent Before the Coming of the Muslims*, Sidgwick & Jackson, London, 1954.

> In no other early civilisation were slaves so few in number, and in no other ancient lawbook are their rights so well protected as in the Arthashastra. No other ancient law giver proclaimed such noble ideals of fair play in battle as did Manu. In all her history of warfare Hindu India has few tales to tell of cities put to sword or the massacre of non combatants. The ghastly sadism of the kings of Assiriya, who flayed their captives alive, is completely without parallel in ancient India. There was sporadic cruelty and oppression no doubt, but in comparison with conditions in other early cultures, it was mild. To us the most striking feature of the ancient Indian civilisation is its humanity.

Why am I citing these rules of war in Hindu India? Because a civilization's worst qualities reveal themselves most starkly in battle. If the rules of war—barbaric elsewhere—were humane in Hindu India, then it needs no seer to see that India's philosophy and way of life were fundamentally different. If, even in war Indian civilization could avoid cruelty, in peace it could never have been violent. This explains why there was no mass violence in India as in other civilizations.

Hindu Religion: A Philosophy, Not an Ideology

Why were there no mass killings in India from ancient times till the invasions, when the rest of the world was soaked in blood? How did ancient and medieval India maintain peace and harmony? The reason lies in the fact that Hinduism is a philosophy, not an ideology.

There is a world of difference between the two. Philosophy concedes that there could be another viewpoint; ideology insists that only it is right and all others are wrong. In a speech on political polarization in the US, former President Bill Clinton—not a philosopher, but a politician—spoke of this critical difference between philosophy and ideology: 'This is a practical country. We have ideals. We have philosophies. But the problem with any ideology is that it gives the answer before you look at the evidence.'[4]

Hinduism, which accepts the legitimacy of all religions, is not an ideological faith like the Abrahamic religions, each of which believes that only it is correct and that others are not merely wrong but deserve to be eliminated. That is why the Abrahamic religions are inherently conflict-prone. In contrast, Hinduism holds that all religions are true—none more or less true than another.

The Strategic World: Ignorant about Hinduism—the Only Non-conflicting Civilization

The strategic world remains largely ignorant of Hinduism. Here is a shocking example of that costly ignorance—both to Hindu civilization and to global peace and harmony. Samuel Huntington shook the world with his famous essay, 'The Clash of Civilizations?', published in *Foreign Affairs* magazine in the summer of 1993. After that essay, he set out on a global quest to study world religions and civilizations before writing his celebrated book *The Clash of Civilizations and the Remaking of World Order*.

In the preface to that book, Huntington wrote:[5]

> [...] I became involved in innumerable seminars and meetings focused on "the clash" with academic, government, business, and other groups across the United States. In addition, I was fortunate to be able to participate in discussions of the article and its thesis in many other

---

[4]Lewis, Waylon, 'Video: President Bill Clinton, on Jon Stewart: "the problem with any ideology is that it gives the answer before you look at the evidence."', *Elephant Journal*, https://tinyurl.com/mmrxk5tm. Accessed on 7 November 2025.

[5]Huntington, Samuel P., *The Clash of Civilizations and the Remaking of World Order*, Simon & Schuster, New York, 1996.

> countries, including Argentina, Belgium, China, France, Germany, Great Britain, Korea, Japan, Luxembourg, Russia, Saudi Arabia, Singapore, South Africa, Spain, Sweden, Switzerland, and Taiwan. These discussions exposed me to all the major civilizations except Hinduism, and I benefitted immensely from the insights and perspectives of the participants in these discussions.

Note the words 'except Hinduism'. The only country he did not visit before writing his book was India. The result was predictable: Huntington was exposed only to exclusive, doctrinally intolerant and conflict-prone religions and civilizations. He remained unaware of the only inclusive, doctrinally tolerant and non-conflicting civilization—the Hindu civilization. Yet even from afar, he observed that only in Hindu civilization were the state and religion separate—a profound truth about Hindu philosophy. Had he engaged directly with Hinduism, he would have realized that it is non-conflicting, unlike all other religions, precisely because it accepts, rather than disputes, the legitimacy of multiple paths.

Against such a backdrop of deficit in global strategic and civilizational discourse, the author of this volume—drawing on his wide experience as a diplomat and policymaker during some of the most turbulent phases of national and global affairs—appears to have felt that what the world most needs today, caught as it is in ideological cobwebs, is Swami Vivekananda's exposition of the non-conflicting Hindu philosophy that can help prevent both religious and civilizational conflict.

From a 'Conflict-free' Post-Cold War Order to a Conflict-prone World

When the Cold War order collapsed, the West declared its political and economic ideologies the ultimate victors over the rest of the world. It deepened the 'one-size-fits-all' post-war order into a quasi–world government through the WTO and its allied institutions. Intellectuals such as Francis Fukuyama even suggested that the victory of the West had ushered in the perfect society—free of all conflict—envisioned by the 18th-century Enlightenment philosopher Georg Wilhelm Friedrich Hegel.

The US, in particular, turned euphoric when the Communist bloc collapsed. Convinced of its invincibility, it began violating all rules of economics and pursued policies that even mocked economies which believed prudence was important. It printed and exported dollars in trillions to pay for its imports and to sustain an extravagant lifestyle, which ultimately did it in. This is a vast subject, but it is enough to say that even the economists who once celebrated such policies later admitted that they burdened the US with a ceaseless current account deficit, weakened its economy, and turned it into the world's most indebted nation. This is now forcing the US to reverse its globalist stance and return to economic nationalism—once dismissed in the 1990s as autarchic and backward.

As the US—and, with it, the West—grew financially weaker, the dream of a conflict-free world proved a mirage. Islamic terror began targeting the US, Europe, India and Russia, while completely destabilizing Islamic nations themselves. The prognosis of thinkers like Samuel Huntington, who warned that the West's universalist approach would provoke civilizational clashes, proved more realistic in understanding the diversity of the world. In less than a decade after the post-war order, instead of a conflict-free world assured by the West, it became a conflict-prone one.

Most Conflicts Today Are Religious—Say Studies

Throughout the 20th century, religion was considered a relic of the past. The secular and scientific world underestimated its enduring power. Yet religion returned through the civilizational resurgence of non-Western nations and, even within the West, through right-wing movements.

Various studies show that most conflicts today are religious in nature. An article on *Modern Diplomacy* notes: 'Religious conflicts have escalated dramatically since the onset of the cold war. Throughout the 1950–1996 periods, religious conflicts constituted 33% or 47% of all conflicts.'[6]

Another study, 'Post-Cold War Civil Conflict and the Role of History and Religion: A Stochastic Search Variable Selection Approach' states:[7]

> We find past conflict constitutes the most powerful predictor of current conflict: Path dependency matters. Also, larger shares of Jewish, Muslim, or Christian citizens are associated with increased conflict, while economic and political factors remain less relevant than colonial origin and religion. [...] in 2019 alone global conflicts and violence caused an economic loss of US $ 14.4 trillion.

Note the absence of Hindus—who constitute one-sixth of the world's population—among the religious groups mentioned in these studies on conflict.

Hans Knippenberg, Professor Emeritus at the University of Amsterdam, in his essay 'A Clash of Religions? Religion, Territory, and Conflict after the Cold War', writes:[8]

> First of all, culture and religion are back in the minds of political scientists and politicians. In geography and other

[6]Shaukat, Amna, 'Religious Conflicts Around the Globe and a Solution', *Modern Diplomacy*, 15 October 2020, https://tinyurl.com/3a68j5d9. Accessed on 27 October 2025.

[7]Jetter, Michael, et al., 'Post-Cold War Civil Conflict and the Role of History and Religion: A Stochastic Search Variable Selection Approach', *Economic Modelling*, Vol. 114, June 2022, https://tinyurl.com/4y7nvm4c. Accessed on 27 October 2025.

[8]Knippenberg, Hans, 'A Clash of Religions? Religion, Territory, and Conflict after the Cold War', *Acta Universitatis Carolinae:Geographica*, Univerzita Karlova, Amsterdam, Vol. 41, no. 1–2, 2006, pp. 49–64, https://tinyurl.com/mt3ka7rm. Accessed on 27 October 2025.

> disciplines, like in political science, there has been a cultural turn. Globalisation has strengthened the consciousness of cultural and religious differences in the world and contributed to a religious revival. On a theoretical level, this means that culture and religion are not just dependent functions of the world economic or political system (Beyer 1994). Culture matters. Religion matters.

A World Economic Forum report dated 25 February 2019 shows that while the number of non-religious armed conflicts moderated between 1975 and 2015, religious and identity-based conflicts rose from 10 per cent to nealry 40 per cent.[9]

Similarly, the Federal Department of Foreign Affairs (FDFA) of Switzerland states:[10]

> The proportion of armed conflicts in which religion plays a role has doubled in the last 40 years—from one third in 1975 to two-thirds in 2017. The main cause of these conflicts is not religion per se, but rather the clash between different world views.

The Fondation pour l'Innovation Politique (Fondapol), a French think tank for European integration and free economy, notes a huge rise in Islamic attacks worldwide. Between 1979 and April 2024, there were 66,872 attacks causing at least 2,49,941 deaths. The pace has been accelerating dramatically:

- 1979–2000: 2,194 attacks and 6,817 deaths
- 2001–2012: 8,265 attacks and 38,187 deaths

[9]'Religious Violence Is on the Rise. What Can Faith-Based Communities Do about It?' *World Economic Forum*, 25 February 2019, https://tinyurl.com/3kxs4be8. Chart data derived from Svensson, Isak, and Desirée Nilsson, *Religion and Armed Conflict (RELAC) Dataset*, Uppsala University, Department of Peace and Conflict Research, 2016. Accessed on 27 October 2025,

[10]'Religion, Politics and Conflicts', *Federal Department of Foreign Affairs (FDFA)*, https://tinyurl.com/ynxfjkuw. Accessed on 27 October 2025.

- 2013–April 2024: 56,413 attacks and 2,04,937 deaths[11]

When sociologists made the West believe that an age of peace, harmony, and prosperity lay ahead, some thinkers—including, surprisingly, theologians—warned against such shallow optimism. They cautioned that unless there was religious peace, there could be no peace among nations.

Dialogue Among Religions a Must for Peace—Says Christian Theologian of the 1990s

Although not widely noticed outside religious and academic circles, around the time Francis Fukuyama was proclaiming the end of all conflicts and unlimited prosperity through globalization—and a few years before Huntington published his sombre prognosis of the clash of civilizations—a renowned Christian theologian, Hans Küng, principal architect of the Second Vatican Council, came out with a formulation tracing religion as the persistent cause of conflict. His view aligned with Huntington's thesis. Hans Küng memorably wrote:[12]

> No peace among the nations without peace among the religions. No peace among the religions without dialogue between the religions. No dialogue between the religions without research into the foundations of the religions.

Küng recognized, like Huntington, that religions have an innate propensity to clash. He concluded that there can be no peace among nations unless there is peace among religions, and no peace among religions without dialogue—one that must reach as deep as the foundations of each faith. Such dialogue, he said, must be secular rather than dogmatic.

---

[11]Reynié, Dominique, et al., editors, *Islamist Terrorist Attacks in the World 1979–2024*, translated by Alice Candy, Fondation pour l'Innovation Politique (Fondapol), 2024, https://tinyurl.com/4txjpwff. Accessed on 27 October 2025.

[12]Küng, Hans, *Christianity: Essence, History, and Future*, Continuum International Publishing Group, New York, 1995.

Vivekananda Suggested Dialogue Among Religions a Century Earlier

Swami Vivekananda was the first to introduce the concept of dialogue among religions, regarding the 1893 Parliament of Religions itself as such a dialogue. However, the dialogue he envisioned was not meant to probe religions critically, as Küng suggested, but to promote mutual acceptance. In his opening address at the 1893 Conference, Vivekananda declared:[13]

> I am proud to belong to a religion which has taught the world both tolerance and universal acceptance. We believe not only in universal toleration, but we accept all religions as true.

Vivekananda's call for mutual acceptance of all religions as true represents a virtue far higher than mere tolerance.

Professor Jeffery D. Long, American author and academic, observed:[14]

> As a disciple of Sri Ramakrishna, Swamiji envisioned and embodied interfaith dialogue in a way that was far more radical than most conceived of it in his time. Even many of the participants in as progressive a body as the Parliament of the World's Religions saw the chief function of interfaith dialogue to be "preparing the way for the reunion of all the world's religions in their true center–Jesus Christ." Swamiji resisted all such parochialism and proposed, in its place, the idea of the world's religions as "different streams having their sources in different places" that "all mingle their water in the sea" that is the shared divinity of all beings. Rather

[13]'Addresses at the Parliament of Religions', *The Complete Works of Swami Vivekananda*, Vol. 1, Advaita Ashrama, 1947.

[14]Long, Jeffery D., 'Swami Vivekananda and the Role of Intercultural Dialogue in Saving Our Human Heritage', *Vedanta*, no. 404, Nov–Dec 2018, https://tinyurl.com/mpevmcpr. Accessed on 28 October 2025.

than insisting on the unique truth of a single cultural source, religion, or authoritative text, Swamiji saw truth as being present everywhere.

Küng's formula for interreligious dialogue, framed a century after Vivekananda, was rational; Vivekananda's, framed a century before, was civilizational. Küng's approach was contextual—shaped by the post-Cold War euphoria and the triumph of liberal democracy and the free market. Vivekananda's approach, in contrast, was transcontextual—rooted in India's eternal values, Sanatana Dharma. He was not confined by the religious or political context of Abrahamic dominance; he transcended it.

Unfortunately, the record of peace and harmony—preached and practised by Hindu philosophy and sustained by its people for millennia—is seldom highlighted, even in Indian discourse, let alone in global geopolitics. India's education system still suffers from colonial hangovers, ensuring that although the country is politically free, it remains intellectually dependent.

Vivekananda Globalized the Concept of Vasudhaiva Kutumbakam

The Hindu philosophy expounded by Swami Vivekananda centres on 'Vasudhaiva Kutumbakam'. *Vasudha* refers not merely to the human world but to Mother Earth herself, inhabited by all living beings—humans, animals and plants—forming one large eco-family. The concept views Mother Earth, with all animate and inanimate existance, as one vast family. Thus, the idea of Vasudhaiva Kutumbakam encompasses not only nations or people but the entire creation—the living and the non-living alke.

This philosophy, which originated in ancient Indian thought and is found in the Vedas over 5,000 years ago, went global through Swami Vivekananda. In his famous address at the World Parliament of Religions in Chicago in 1893, he articulated this concept and captured the world's imagination by commencing his speech with the mesmerizing words, 'Sisters and Brothers of America'—words that themselves symbolized the idea of a global family. He went on to explain how Hindu India had long practised the concept of universal brotherhood:[15]

> I am proud to belong to a nation which has sheltered the persecuted and the refugees of all religions and all nations of the earth. I am proud to tell you that we have gathered in our bosom the purest remnant of the Israelites, who came to Southern India and took refuge with us in the very year in which their holy temple was shattered to pieces by Roman tyranny. I am proud to belong to the religion which has sheltered and is still fostering the remnant of the grand Zoroastrian nation.

The principle of diversity articulated by Vivekananda in the context of human brotherhood is not limited to human beings alone but extends to all animate beings and inanimate things that form part of Mother Earth. The concept of Vasudhaiva Kutumbakam appears in the earliest Hindu scripture, the *Rig Veda*, in the section titled the *Maha Upanishad*. It declares that 'This is ours and that is not' is the outlook of the narrow-minded, while the wise believe that the entire earth is one family.

That India practised this philosophy is evident from the fact that, though it occupies only 2.4 per cent of the world's land area, it is home to 18 per cent of the global human population,[16] 30 per cent of the world's cattle population[17] and 8 per cent of its bioresources.[18] Had Indians not owned, accommodated

[15]'Addresses at the Parliament of Religions', *The Complete Works of Swami Vivekananda*, Vol. 1, Advaita Ashrama, 1947.

[16]NITI Aayog, *GROW Report*, 20 February 2024, https://tinyurl.com/5t4fjyfx. Accessed on 10 November 2025.

[17]'India–Country Profile: Biodiversity Facts', *Convention on Biological Diversity*, https://tinyurl.com/mrxff29z. Accessed on 7 November 2025.

[18]Robinson, T.P., Wint, G. W., Conchedda, G., Van Boeckel, T.P., Ercoli, V., Palamara, E., Cinardi, G., D'Aietti, L., Hay, S.I., and Gilbert, M., 'Mapping the Global Distribution of Livestock', *PLOS ONE*, Vol. 9, No. 5, 2014.

and fostered—not only humans but all other living beings—as part of extended family, guided by their deep ecological and environmental consciousness, such immense diversity of life could not have coexisted on such a small stretch of land. The Hindu concept of Vasudhaiva Kutumbakam is not anthropocentric but ecocentric, embracing the entire creation.

Yet this was not how highly civilized Hindu India was perceived in the wider world, particularly in the US, at the turn of the 19th century when Swami Vivekananda arrived there.

Vivekananda Took the West by Storm in 1893

It is necessary to recall how Swami Vivekananda mesmerized the world with his exposition of the only non-conflicting religious philosophy at the World Parliament of Religions in Chicago in 1893, where he counselled humanity away from hate, bigotry, and violence. I intend to explain this in detail, for it demonstrates how relevant the author's work, *Swami Vivekananda for Our Times*, is today.

I also wish to provide the background to his work by recalling the 19th-century world that convened the great initiative of the World Parliament of Religions—where Vivekananda expounded the Hindu philosophy of not just tolerance but acceptance of all faiths and dialogue among them—and the 20th-century world that failed to follow up on that initiative, repeating its violent history once again. In that century, 100 million were killed in wars and 262 million by intolerant states.[19]

A century later, Harvard University's Religious Pluralism Project recalled the 19th-century initiative and Swami Vivekananda, who—long before Hans Küng—pleaded for harmony among religions as a precondition for peace among peoples.

---

[19]Rummel, R. J., *Power Kills: Democracy as a Method of Nonviolence*, Transaction Publishers, New Brunswick, New Jersey, 1997.

In the 1893 World Parliament of Religions, Swami Vivekananda did not merely address the audience—he spellbound them. He emerged as a global philosopher and thought leader with a single speech, shifting the focus of a Christianity-centred gathering towards harmony among religions. His address—one of the shortest of the Parliament—was electrifying.

Reverend John Henry Barrows, principal organizer of the 1893 Parliament, recorded that when Vivekananda greeted the audience as 'Sisters and Brothers of America', they rose to their feet in rapture, responding with 'a peal of applause that lasted several minutes.'[20]

In an article in the American religious magazine *The Open Court*, titled 'India at the World's Parliament of Religions', J.V. Nash wrote:[21]

> Unfortunately the space now remaining is quite inadequate for suitable discussion of Vivekananda. But my readers will perhaps forgive me, by reason of the fact that in a previous issue of *The Open Court* (December, 1925) I made this Hindu religious genius the subject of a special article. It is entitled "The Message and Influence of Vivekananda," and to it I must refer those who wish a more extensive review of the part which played in the Parliament of Religions.

He continued:[22]

> Coming to Chicago without credentials, representing no particular religious group, never having made a public

[20]Barrows, John Henry, *The World's Parliament of Religions: An Illustrated and Popular Story of the World's First Parliament of Religions, Held in Chicago in Connection with the Columbian Exposition of 1893*, vol. 1, The Parliament Publishing Company, Chicago, 1893.

[21]Nash, J.V., 'India at the World's Parliament of Religions', *The Open Court*, Vol. 47, no. 923, June 1933, pp. 217–230, https://tinyurl.com/467hnh4f. Accessed on 28 October 2025.

[22]*Ibid.*

> address, and without even a prepared speech, he took the Parliament by storm.
>
> [...] When he was introduced he looked upon a yawning audience which had sat through a day of manuscript reading. He hesitated, nervously. Then a sudden access to power and eloquence came upon him, and he began to speak. As by an electric shock the assembly became galvanized into eager attention.
>
> [...] After saluting the audience as "Sisters and Brothers of America," he waited for two minutes until the applause subsided, and then began [...]

Nash also noted:[23]

> Before half a dozen words had left his lips, the great hall was shaking with storms of applause as in a political convention, and when his brief extemporaneous address was concluded everyone began asking, "Who is this brilliant, eloquent, handsome, magnetic young Hindu, the Swami Vivekananda?"
>
> Probably never in any similar gathering did so short a speech create so profound an impact. It consists of only six brief paragraphs.

By failing to follow up the 1893 initiative, the West—which led the world—again lost a century to unprecedented violence and war.

The Second Parliament of Religions, 2018

Nearly a century later, the Parliament of the World's Religions (PWR) was reconstituted in 1989. It took three more decades to convene the second World Parliament of Religions, held in 2018—125 years after the first.

---

[23] *Ibid.*

In connection with the second Parliament, the PWR recalled Vivekananda's message of harmony in the first Parliament, distinguishing it from unity. The idea of harmony among religions or even within religions, had been virtually unknown to the world.

Molly Horan, Communications Director of the PWR, said that its mission statement—'to cultivate harmony among the world's religious and spiritual communities'—is aligned with Vivekananda's message in 1893. She emphasized the congruence between his vision and that of the PWR:[24]

> Swami Vivekananda's message, we feel, speaks in alignment with our mission to promote harmony between the religious and spiritual communities of the world, and to foster their engagement with the guiding institutions to achieve a more just, peaceful and sustainable world. His message echoes in so much of what we do 125 years later, each time we seek to bring people of difference together, whether it be for understanding, reconciliation, and change, or to rally around a common goal.

She added:[25]

> His legacy is intertwined with ours and therefore his birth anniversaries and important anniversaries (such as the 125th anniversary of the 1893 at the 2018 Parliament in Toronto this November) devote prominent attention from us communications-wise.

Horan also spoke of the continuing admiration for Vivekananda's message:[26]

---

[24]Howard, Veena, 'Swami Vivekananda on the World Stage of the Parliament of the World's Religions', *Parliament of the World's Religions*, 2018, https://tinyurl.com/26j8j264. Accessed on 28 October 2025.

[25]*Ibid.*

[26]*Ibid.*

> I would say that that the Parliament is so fortunate to be able to continue to celebrate the legacies of several very important figures sent from religious communities all over the world to speak at the 1893 Parliament, and that there has always been heightened adoration for the PWR as an institution across India and beyond, especially among followers of Swami Vivekananda's teachings throughout the world who celebrate the Parliament every year.

Harvard Universit'sy Religious Pluralism Project (1994)

Harvard University's Religious Pluralism Project, set up in 1994—a century after the first Parliament of Religions and a year after Samuel Huntington's warning of emerging civilizational clashes driven by religion—explained what the exponents of different faiths had attempted in 1893 and how Swami Vivekananda transformed the entire approach to religious pluralism.

Some extracts from the Harvard Pluralism Project illustrate the direction in which the religious world was moving and how Vivekananda reshaped it:[27]

> There were many voices at the 1893 Parliament that stressed not the universals, but the real differences between and within religions. Their voices made clear the difficult tasks that lay ahead and forecast the complex challenges that religious diversity would pose for the 20th century. The Buddhist reformer Anagarika Dharmapala asked the audience in a large lecture hall, "How many of you have read the life of the Buddha?" When only five raised a hand, he scolded, "Five only! 475 million people accept our religion of love and hope. You call yourselves a nation—a great nation—and yet you do not know the history of

[27]'Parliament of Religions, 1893', *The Pluralism Project*, https://tinyurl.com/ycejuyts. Accessed on 28 October 2025.

this great teacher. How dare you judge us!" One of the Buddhists from Japan was equally challenging, pointing to the anti-Japanese feeling he had met in America and deploring the signs that read "No Japanese is allowed to enter here." "If such be the Christian ethics," he said, "We are perfectly satisfied to be heathen."

Of the major speakers, only two were African Americans. Frederick Douglass called the "White City" created for the event a "whitened sepulchre" for blacks. Fannie Barrier Williams declared, "It is a monstrous thing that nearly one-half of the so-called evangelical churches of this country repudiate and haughtily deny fellowship to every Christian lady and gentleman happening to be of African descent." She challenged Christians to take seriously their own religion.

Among the women who spoke was the first ordained as minister in America, Antoinette Brown Blackwell, who declared, "Women are needed in the pulpit as imperatively and for the same reason they are needed in the world—because they are women." And Elizabeth Cady Stanton, who had been working on the Women's Bible, called for a religion that would preach the dignity of all human beings. A new world, she said, would have to build its house with the cellar first, and that meant justice for the poorest.

Finally, despite sentiments of universal fellowship expressed at the Parliament, there were no Native Americans present except as curiosities displayed on the fair's Midway. For many visitors, these Indians were as exotic as Vivekananda. But no native elder or chief was invited to speak at the Parliament. Native American lifeways were not yet seen as a spiritual perspective. Just three years earlier Chief Sitting Bull had been arrested and killed, the Ghost Dance had been suppressed, and 350 Sioux had been massacred at Wounded Knee Creek.

Harvard Project Recalled Swami Vivekananda's Speech 'As the Heavens Above Us'

The Harvard Pluralism Project recalled Swami Vivekananda's address at the 1893 conference in glowing terms:[28]

> It was the first time that many Americans had ever heard Hindus or Buddhists speak in their own voices on behalf of their own faith. Swami Vivekananda, a Hindu, confirmed the vision of universal convergence that had captured the imagination of the planners. Their self-understanding was confirmed, mirrored back to themselves in the presence of this exotic swami from the East who was one of the most popular speakers at the Parliament. One journalist wrote of him: "Vivekananda's address before the Parliament was broad as the heavens above us, embracing the best in all religions, as the ultimate universal religion—charity to all mankind, good works for the love of God, not for fear of punishment or hope of reward."

Harvard Project—Suggestion to Hold the Next World Parliament of Religions on the Banks of the Ganges at Varanasi

The magnetic effect of Vivekananda's exposition of Hinduism led many delegates at the 1893 Parliament of Religions to suggest that the next Parliament be held in India—a land Rudyard Kipling had described as 'uncivilized'. This alone demonstrated how Vivekananda had demolished the racial theories of white supremacy that were dominant at the time. This little-known fact was brought out by the Harvard Pluralism Project, which recalled:[29]

> As the Parliament concluded, many felt that the universalist vision should be sustained. One of the Unitarian conveners

[28] *Ibid.*

[29] *Ibid.*

> suggested that the representatives of the world's traditions convene again in 1900 "on the banks of the Ganges in the ancient city of Benares."

The Project added:[30]

> This was not to be, but there was a meeting in Boston in 1900 of a new group: the International Council of Unitarian and other Liberal Religious Thinkers and Workers. It came to include a few Muslims, Jews, Catholics, and reformist Hindus. Its agenda of international congresses addressed the question of justice for women and the expansion of narrow patriotism to a wider human loyalty. From this seed grew the International Association for Religious Freedom. Two world wars would impede the progress of organized interreligious efforts such as this one, but the wars would, at the same time, underline the importance of interreligious efforts.

Thus, after the 1893 Parliament of Religions, the West—mesmerized by science and industry, obsessed with territorial nationalism and ideological revolutions—lost direction and failed to pursue the interreligious dialogue for harmony that Vivekananda had so powerfully articulated in Chicago.

The UN Awakened to Vivekananda's Message of Unity—Six Decades Late

The core message of Swami Vivekananda at the 1893 meet was that diversity is the law of nature, and that unless diversity is respected, intolerance and violence will prevail. Yet the West—victorious in World War II—imposed a universalist order that rejected all diversities and prescribed a one-size-fits-all approach for the world.

It was more than a century later, and over half a century

---

[30]*Ibid.*

after its own founding, that the United Nations recognized the idea of 'diversity'. The term entered its official vocabulary for the first time in 1994, in the Convention on Biological Diversity, and again in 2001, in the Convention on Cultural Diversity—when the world was still mesmerized by a globalist, homogenizing model of civilization, culture, economy and polity.

At Chicago, Vivekananda had spoken instead of harmony in diversity. His exposition of unity through diversity reflects India's long civilizational history, which stands as living testimony to this truth. If India is placed on one side and the rest of the world on the other, there is more diversity in India than in all other nations combined. India's philosophy and way of life offer humanity a standing assurance that harmony in diversity is the law of nature itself.

Vivekananda–A Moulder of the Modern World

Vivekananda gave not only spiritual leadership to the world but also moral direction to modern civilization. He was regarded as an honour to humanity—one who shook the mightiest minds, a moulder of the modern world, and one of the greatest historical figures of India.

A.L. Basham, the most celebrated of Orientalists, observed:[31]

> [I]t is very difficult to evaluate his importance in the scale of world history. It is certainly far greater than any Western historian or most Indian historians would have suggested at the time of his death. The passing of the years and the many stupendous and unexpected events which have occurred since then suggest that in centuries to come he will be remembered as one of the main moulders of the modern world, especially as far as Asia is concerned, and as one of

[31]Basham, A.L., *The Wonder That Was India: A Survey of the Culture of the Indian Sub-Continent Before the Coming of the Muslims*, Sidgwick & Jackson, London, 1954.

> the most significant figures in the whole history of Indian religion.

Romain Rolland, Nobel Laureate, wrote:[32]

> Vivekananda's words are great music, phrases in the style of Beethoven, stirring rhythms like the march of Handel choruses. I cannot touch these sayings of his, scattered as they are through the pages of books, at thirty years' distance, without receiving a thrill through my body like an electric shock. And what shock, what transports, must have been produced when in burning words they issued from the lips of the hero!

Swami Sivananda Saraswati, a renowned Hindu spiritual leader and founder of the Divine Life Society, said of Vivekananda:[33]

> Swami Vivekananda's powerful personality and his passionate call of service of the poor, is still influencing people all over India and the world.
>
> Swami Vivekananda arrived in America penniless and depending only on God's Grace. After the Parliament he began to receive the homage and hospitality of all America. He lectured at all the important centres. As a true Sannyasin he refused to sell religion for the sake of amassing money. He preached the gospel of unity of faiths and scattered the seeds of purity, knowledge and faith. After his stay of two years in America he toured England and Europe for three months.
>
> The tremendous ovation he received on his return to India in no way took his mind away from his mission of bringing religion to the doors of the poorest. His aim was to awaken the masses by reviving Vedic religion, and to clean

[32]Rolland, Romain, *The Life of Vivekananda and the Universal Gospel*, 1930.

[33]'World Leaders and Spiritual Masters on Swami Vivekananda', *VivekaVani*, https://tinyurl.com/mtvn92xh. Accessed on 10 November 2025.

it of the dross and impurity that had clung to it for so many centuries.

In 1902 Swami Vivekananda entered Mahasamadhi. Six years of discipleship under Sri Ramakrishna had taken him to the realms of God-vision. Seven years of travelling in India had broadened his outlook on life. Nine years of a national and international career were all that were left for him; yet, how filled with glorious work those nine years were!

Swami Vivekananda's gospel was one of hope, faith and strength. He never succumbed to despair, for he knew that India was capable of expansion and growth. His clarion call to the nation was: "Awake, arise, and stop not till the goal is reached."

The American novelist Christopher Isherwood said that Vivekananda was 'one of the very greatest historical figures that India has ever produced.'[34]

William James, the Harvard philosopher and psychologist who had met Swami Vivekananda several times, said:[35]

> The paragon of all monistic systems is the Vedanta philosophy of Hindusthan, and the paragon of Vedantist missionaries was the late Swami Vivekananda who visited our land some years ago. [...] I have been reading some of Vivekananda's addresses [...] [he] is simply a wonder for oratorical power [...] the Swami is an honour to humanity in any case.

Sir John Woodroffe, also known by his pseudonym Arthur Avalon—a British Orientalist whose work helped to awaken

---

[34]Isherwood, Christopher, 'Great Thinkers on Ramakrishna–Vivekananda', *Studies and Interpretation on Sri Ramakrishna and Swami Vivekananda*, Ramakrishna Mission Institute of Culture, https://tinyurl.com/2wkr26ha. Accessed on 10 November 2025.
[35]James, William, 'Great Thinkers on Ramakrishna–Vivekananda', *Studies and Interpretation on Sri Ramakrishna and Swami Vivekananda*, Ramakrishna Mission Institute of Culture, https://tinyurl.com/4xr9ur4w. Accessed on 10 November 2025.

Western interest in Hindu philosophy and Yogic practices—wrote:[36]

> The qualities I most admire in Vivekananda are his activity, manliness and courage. . . . He spoke up and acted. For this, all must honour him, who, whatever be their own religious beliefs, value sincerity, truth and courage, which are the badges of every noble character.

Vivekananda established his credentials as a global thinker through his travels and lectures abroad. His integrative vision—transcending divisions of religion, race, and nation—was appreciated by the greatest minds of his time and continues to inspire many.

Vivekananda—The Builder of Independent India

Swami Vivekananda was not only a philosopher and thought leader of the world but also one of the architects of modern India. A spiritualist and nation-builder, he helped shape India's self-identity and the moral foundations of its freedom struggle. His name evokes ideals of humanism, courage, and a deep sense of national character.

The role of his ideas in inspiring India's movement for independence is universally acknowledged. Celebrated as the patriotic monk of India, his high philosophy and oratory inspired freedom fighters—ranging from violent revolutionaries to non-violent satyagrahis. The stalwarts of the Indian freedom struggle looked upon him with reverence and drew from him their inspiration and strength.

---

[36]'World Leaders and Spiritual Masters on Swami Vivekananda', *VivekaVani*, https://tinyurl.com/mtvn92xh. Accessed on 10 November 2025.

Founder of India's Freedom Movement

No one defined Vivekananda's role more accurately than the great Tamil poet Subrahmanya Bharati, who said:[37]

> It was Swami Vivekananda by whom the [Indian] movements for 'Swarāj' and independence were first had its foundation. [...] He was the great inspirer of patriotism, and the fundamental power behind rousing love for the country. [...] Sri Ramakrishna had shaped Swami Vivekananda and he was the foremost among the creators of modern India.

Bharati was right. Vivekananda was to his spiritual master, Sri Ramakrishna, what Chhatrapati Shivaji was to Saint Ramdas. If Samarth Ramdas was the vision, Shivaji was the action; if Sri Ramakrishna was the vision, Vivekananda was its action.

Inspiration to Freedom Fighters

Historian R.C. Majumdar observed that Vivekananda's ideals gave a spiritual foundation to Indian nationalism:[38]

> Though an ascetic, Vivekananda was a patriot of patriots. The thought of restoring the pristine glory of India by resuscitating among her people the spiritual vitality which was dormant, but not dead, was always the uppermost thought in his mind.

---

[37]Bharati, Subrahmanya, 'Great Thinkers on Ramakrishna–Vivekananda', *Studies and Interpretation on Sri Ramakrishna and Swami Vivekananda*, Ramakrishna Mission Institute of Culture, https://tinyurl.com/k2t6t4vt. Accessed on 10 November 2025.

[38]Majumdar, Ramesh Chandra, 'Great Thinkers on Ramakrishna–Vivekananda', *Studies and Interpretation on Sri Ramakrishna and Swami Vivekananda*, Ramakrishna Mission Institute of Culture, https://tinyurl.com/mtpc68y3. Accessed on 10 November 2025.

Mahatma Gandhi, the face of India's non-violent freedom movement, said:[39]

> I have gone through his works very thoroughly, and after having gone through them, the love that I had for my country became a thousandfold.

C. Rajagopalachari, the first Indian Governor-General of India, remarked: 'Swami Vivekananda saved Hinduism and saved India. [:..] We there owe everything to Swami Vivekananda.'[40]

Rabindranath Tagore declared: 'If you want to know India, study Vivekananda. In him, there is everything positive and nothing negative.'[41]

Maharishi Aurobindo said:[42]

> Vivekananda was a soul of puissance if ever there was one, a very lion among men, but the definite work he has left behind is quite incommensurate with our impression of his creative might and energy.

Jawaharlal Nehru, India's first Prime Minister, was overawed by Vivekananda's personality and dignity, saying that his heart carried fire:[43]

---

[39]Gandhi, M.K., 'Great Thinkers on Ramakrishna–Vivekananda', *Studies and Interpretation on Sri Ramakrishna and Swami Vivekananda*, Ramakrishna Mission Institute of Culture, https://tinyurl.com/aay8keyb. Accessed on 10 November 2025.

[40]Rajagopalachari, C., 'Great Thinkers on Ramakrishna–Vivekananda', *Studies and Interpretation on Sri Ramakrishna and Swami Vivekananda*, Ramakrishna Mission Institute of Culture, https://tinyurl.com/kwp23n57. Accessed on 10 November 2025.

[41]'Rabindranath Tagore On Swami Vivekananda', *VivekaVani*, https://tinyurl.com/2y5s5sk6. Accessed on 10 November 2025.

[42]Ghose, Aurobindo, 'Great Thinkers on Ramakrishna–Vivekananda', *Studies and Interpretation on Sri Ramakrishna and Swami Vivekananda*, Ramakrishna Mission Institute of Culture, https://tinyurl.com/e6zczd7p. Accessed on 10 November 2025.

[43]Nehru, Jawaharlal, 'Great Thinkers on Ramakrishna–Vivekananda', *Studies and Interpretation on Sri Ramakrishna and Swami Vivekananda*, Ramakrishna Mission Institute of Culture, https://tinyurl.com/yfu33dp6. Accessed on 10 November 2025.

> He was no politician in the ordinary sense of the word and yet he was, I think, one of the great founders—if you like, you may use any other word—of the national modern movement of India, and a great number of people who took more or less an active part in that movement in a later date drew their inspiration from Swami Vivekananda. Directly or indirectly he has powerfully influenced the India of today.

Subhas Chandra Bose said:[44]

> [H]e took an active part in inspiring every form of healthy national activity. With him religion was the inspirer of nationalism. He tried to infuse into the new generation a sense of pride in India's past, of faith in India's future and a spirit of self-confidence and self-respect. Though the Swami never gave any political message, every one who came into contact with him or his writings developed a spirit of patriotism and a political mentality.

Bal Gangadhar Tilak, another stalwart of the freedom movement, said:[45]

> [I]t is an undisputed fact that it was Swami Vivekananda who first held aloft the banner of Hinduism as a challenge against the material science of the West. It was Swami Vivekananda who first took on his shoulders this stupendous task of establishing the glory of Hinduism in different countries across the borders. And he, with his erudition, oratorical power, enthusiasm, and inner force, laid that work upon a solid foundation.... Twelve centuries

---

[44]Bose, Subhas Chandra, 'Great Thinkers on Ramakrishna–Vivekananda', *Studies and Interpretation on Sri Ramakrishna and Swami Vivekananda*, Ramakrishna Mission Institute of Culture, https://tinyurl.com/3wurtfdc. Accessed on 10 November 2025.

[45]Tilak, Bal Gangadhar, 'Great Thinkers on Ramakrishna–Vivekananda', *Studies and Interpretation on Sri Ramakrishna and Swami Vivekananda*, Ramakrishna Mission Institute of Culture, https://tinyurl.com/37y6n475. Accessed on 10 November 2025.

> ago Śaṅkārācārya was the only great personality, who not only spoke of the purity of our religion […] but also brought all this into action. Swami Vivekananda is a person of that stature […]

Vinoba Bhave praised Vivekananda for awakening Indians to their inner strength, asserting that he 'pointed out' their 'defects and drawbacks' and taught them to overcome these.[46]

Dr Sarvepalli Radhakrishnan, the second President of India, said that Vivekananda was born in a 'critical period' when the nation and her people were collapsing 'in despair, frustration and hopelessness'; in such circumstances, Vivekananda's teachings gave them 'hope in distress' and taught them to rely on spiritual resources.[47]

Inspired Revolutionaries Too

Swami Vivekananda's thoughts influenced revolutionaries as much as they inspired the leaders of the non-violent national freedom movement.

Kuldip Nayar, in his book *The Martyr Bhagat Singh: Experiments in Revolution*, wrote:[48]

> The Anushilan Samiti, which was formed in Calcutta in 1894, had divided revolutionaries into two categories: those who believed in religion and those who did not. Most revolutionaries of Bengal at that time were influenced by Bankim Chandra Chatterjee and Vivekananda. The Samiti

[46]Bhave, Vinoba, 'Great Thinkers on Ramakrishna–Vivekananda', *Studies and Interpretation on Sri Ramakrishna and Swami Vivekananda*, Ramakrishna Mission Institute of Culture, https://tinyurl.com/3fdvsdz6. Accessed on 10 November 2025.
[47]Radhakrishnan, S., 'Great Thinkers on Ramakrishna–Vivekananda', *Studies and Interpretation on Sri Ramakrishna and Swami Vivekananda*, Ramakrishna Mission Institute of Culture, https://tinyurl.com/3ybd2anx. Accessed on 10 November 2025.
[48]Nayar, Kuldip, *Bhagat Singh: Experiments in Revolution*, Har-Anand Publications, 2000, p. 45.

> members had to read the Hindu scriptures, especially the Gita. Songs and slogans based on Hindu myths inspired Bengal's revolutionaries in the early twentieth century.

Hem Chandra Kanungo, a revolutionary associated with the Anushilan Samiti and an accused along with Aurobindo Ghose in the Alipore Bomb case, said:[49]

> It was Swamiji who first exposed the mean, insidious plot of the British to destroy India politically, morally, culturally and intellectually, so that Indians would remain slaves forever. Hence, you'll find in my article this comment that Swamiji served the nation more as a National Patriot of the first order rather than as a Religious Awakener, as a Prophet of militant nationalism. India's slavery agitated him profoundly. This agony burst forth in his speeches with a dazzling flame of fire. His speeches electrified the whole nation and his complete works served as a continuous stream of inspiration to the whole of India, particularly to the Revolutionaries of Bengal. In fact, every freedom fighter derived strength and inspiration from the Bhagavad-Gita and the speeches and writings of Swami Vivekananda. In our youthful years, these were our constant companions. Whenever the British Police searched the homes of the Revolutionaries, invariably they found copies of Swamiji's speeches, his letters, and the Gita. The Police were thus convinced of the close association of Swamiji with the Indian freedom struggle.
>
> [...] I had the great good fortune to have seen him. I touched his feet. I can still feel his fiery touch as he blessed me on the head and shoulders. Oh! Those few moments with Swamiji are the most unforgettable and enchanting moments of my life, because then I learnt how to love my Motherland Bhartavarsha. Then I felt how terrible and painful it was for my people to live like slaves of the British. I had gone to

[49]Swami Purnatmananda, *I Am India,* Vivekananda Kendra Prakashan Trust, 2012.

him to learn about Religion. But what a remarkable lesson he taught me that day! He opened our eyes to patriotism and nationalism. He set fire to our innermost being. That fire still burns in me today, as brightly as in 1901. That fire is Vivekananda. That fire's other name is Bharatavarsha – the undivided Bharatavarsha extending from the Himalayas to the Indian Ocean. That India had to be freed from the British yoke - but not merely this. India had to establish herself as a Shining Guide and Teacher of Humanity in the arts of Peace, Civilisation and Culture. She had to be made the Queen of all the nations of the earth. This heavy task was given to us young revolutionaries to complete by Swami Vivekananda. It was Swamiji who boldly and fearlessly started this movement for National Resurgence. He gave us the onerous task of advancing and fulfilling the pledge, this dream, this hope, this vision, this destiny. But have we been able to do his bidding? Have we been able to hold aloft his great banner? Why, I have witnessed almost a full century of struggle and achievement. Perhaps, his Spirit will reject us as unworthy, and he will look for his fresh soldiers among the new generation of Indian youths. I was told by Kamakhya Mitra that Swamiji had expressed such hope to Swami Saradananda.

Vivekananda's Idea of India—Spiritual Nationalism

Swami Vivekananda defined the idea of India as 'a gathering up of its scattered spiritual forces', declaring that the Indian nation 'must be a union of those whose hearts beat to the same spiritual tune'. This was his vision of India—an idea he proclaimed with pride before the World Parliament of Religions on 11 September 1893.

His conception of Indian nationalism as Hindu spiritual nationalism clearly inspired Maharishi Aurobindo, Mahatma Gandhi, Jawaharlal Nehru, and even the communist thinker

Rajni Palme Dutt—all of whom recognized that the spirit of the Vedas, Sanatana Dharma and India's sacred pilgrimage centres together defined the civilizational idea of the nation.

'Sanatana Dharma Is Hindu Nationalism'–Maharishi Aurobindo

In his famous Uttarpara Speech (1909), Maharishi Aurobindo declared:[50]

> I say no longer that nationalism is a creed, a religion, a faith; I say it is the Sanatana Dharma which for us is nationalism. This Hindu nation was born with the Sanatana Dharma, with it moves and with it grows. When the Sanatana Dharma declines, then the nation declines, and if the Sanatana Dharma were capable of perishing, with the Sanatana Dharma it would perish. The Sanatana Dharma, that is nationalism.

Indian Nationalism as Hindu Cultural Nationalism–Mahatma Gandhi in *Hind Swaraj*

Mahatma Gandhi, in his treatise *Hind Swaraj*—about which he later said that not even a comma or full stop required change—wrote:[51]

> The English have taught us that we were not one nation before and that it will require centuries before we become one nation. This is without foundation. We were one nation before they came to India. One thought inspired us. Our mode of life was the same. It was because we were

[50]'The Psychology of Indian Nationalism: Part 2', *Renaissance – Sri Aurobindo Society*, https://tinyurl.com/4t2edvdk. Accessed on 12 November 2025.

[51]Gandhi, M. K., *Hind Swaraj or Indian Home Rule*, Navajivan Publishing House, 1938. Originally published by The International Printing Press in 1909.

> one nation that they were able to establish one kingdom. Subsequently they divided us.

He went on to explain:[52]

> I do not wish to suggest that because we were one nation we had no differences, but it is submitted that our leading men travelled throughout India either on foot or in bullock carts. They learned one another's languages and there was no aloofness between them. What do you think could have been the intention of those farseeing ancestors of ours who established Setubandha (Rameshwar) in the South, Jagannath in the East and Hardwar in the North as places of pilgrimage? You will admit they were no fools. They knew that worship of God could have been performed just as well at home. They taught us that those whose hearts were aglow with righteousness had the Ganges in their own homes. But they saw that India was one undivided land so made by nature. They, therefore, argued that it must be one nation. Arguing thus, they established holy places in various parts of India, and fired the people with an idea of nationality in a manner unknown in other parts of the world.
>
> And we Indians are one as no two Englishmen are.

When asked whether the principle of Indian nationalism and unity of the 'pre-Mohammedan period' could still hold after the advent of Mohammedans, Parsis and Christians—and how India could be one nation—given the fact that 'Hindu and Mohammedans are old enemies' and there are irreconcilable differences among them, Mahatma Gandhi replied:[53]

> India cannot cease to be one nation because people belonging to different religions live in it. The introduction of foreigners does not necessarily destroy the nation;

---

[52] *Ibid.*

[53] *Ibid.*

they merge in it. A country is one nation only when such a condition obtains in it. That country must have a faculty for assimilation. India has never been such a country. In reality there are as many religions as there are individuals; but those who are conscious of the spirit of nationality do not interfere with one another's religion. If they do, they are not fit to be considered a nation. If the Hindus believe that India should be peopled only by Hindus, they are living in dreamland. The Hindus, the Mahomedans, the Parsis and the Christians who have made India their country are fellow countrymen, and they will have to live in unity, if only for their own interest. In no part of the world are one nationality and one religion synonymous terms; nor has it ever been so in India.

[…] Should we not remember that many Hindus and Mahomedans own the same ancestors and the same blood runs through their veins? Do people become enemies because they change their religion?

Gandhi's secretary, Mahadev Desai, wrote in the Preface to *Hind Swaraj* that 'when [Gopal Krishna] Gokhale saw the translation, on his visit to South Africa in 1912, he thought it so crude and hastily conceived that he prophesied that Gandhiji himself would destroy the book after spending a year in India.' But Gandhiji never changed his view.

In 1938 Gandhi said, '[…] after the stormy thirty years […] I have seen nothing to make me alter the views expounded in it.'[54]

In 1939 he wrote, '*Hind Swaraj* has undergone many editions and I had the pleasure, therefore, of having to re-read it carefully. The reader may know that I could not revise a single idea.'[55]

---

[54]*Ibid.*

[55]Tendulkar, D.G., *Mahatma: Life of Mohandas Karamchand Gandhi*, vol. 5 (1938–1940), Vithalbhai K. Jhaveri and D.G. Tendulkar, Bombay, 1953, p. 239.

In a letter dated 5 October 1945 to Pandit Nehru, he reiterated: 'I have said that I fully stand by the kind of governance which I have described in *Hind Swaraj*. It is not just a way of speaking. My experience has confirmed the truth of what I wrote in 1909.'[56]

This is important, for although Gandhi is celebrated in India, his idea of India is not widely known.

The Vedas Give Us the Spirit of Freedom

The colonial rulers of India—and many English intellectuals—used to taunt the leaders of the Indian freedom movement, most of whom were English-educated. They claimed that colonial education had instilled in Indians the spirit of freedom, implying that the freedom movement itself was a gift from the rulers. Without this education, they suggested, Indians would have been content to remain slaves.

Rajni Palme Dutt, founder of the Communist Party of Great Britain, rebutted this claim in his Marxist treatise *India Today*:[57]

> [I]f the Indian bourgeoisie had been educated only in the Sanscrit Vedas, in monastic seclusion from every other current of thought, they would have assuredly found in the Sanscrit Vedas the inspiring principles and slogans for their struggle.'

Even a communist—who would normally dismiss the past as irrelevant and anti-revolutionary—acknowledged that the Hindu *Vedas* contained philosophical principles capable of inspiring a revolutionary spirit of freedom.

[56]'Letter to Jawaharlal Nehru, 5 October 1945,' *The Collected Works of Mahatma Gandhi*, vol. 81, Publications Division, Government of India, New Delhi, 1958, pp. 319–320.

[57]Dutt, Rajni Palme, *India Today*, Victor Gollancz Ltd, London, 1940, p. 271, https://tinyurl.com/4sbz2vvf. Accessed on 28 October 2025.

Vivekananda's Hindu Nationalism Was Not Against Anyone

Jawaharlal Nehru accepted Vivekananda's conception of Hindu nationalism as the foundation of India's identity. In *Glimpses of World History*, he wrote:[58]

> A famous disciple of Ramakrishna was Swami Vivekananda, who very eloquently and forcibly preached the gospel of nationalism. This was not in any way anti-Muslim or anti-anyone else. Vivekananda's nationalism was Hindu nationalism, and it had its roots in the Hindu religion and culture.

He added:[59]

> It was not easy [...] to draw a sharp line between this Hindu nationalism and true nationalism. The two overlapped, as India is the only home of the Hindus and they form a majority there.

Writing in *Foreign Affairs* magazine, Nehru observed: 'Indian background and unity is essentially cultural; not religious in the narrow sense of the word.'[60]

And in his lecture at the Ramakrishna Mission in 1949, he said:[61]

> Our nationalism must not be a narrow nationalism. Swami Vivekananda, though a great nationalist, never preached anything else. His was a kind of nationalism which automatically slipped into Indian nationalism which was part of internationalism.

---

[58]Nehru, Jawaharlal, *Glimpses of World History*, Jawaharlal Nehru Memorial Fund, New Delhi, 1982, p. 437.

[59]*Ibid*, p. 720.

[60]Nehru, Jawaharlal, 'The Unity of India', *Foreign Affairs*, 1 Jan 1938, https://tinyurl.com/46dk6hpm. Accessed on 28 October 2025.

[61]'On Sri Ramakrishna', *Prabuddha Bharata*, Ramakrishna Mission, May 1949, pp. 196–199, https://tinyurl.com/yp72cnxt. Accessed on 28 October 2025.

Nehru Changed His Views Post-independence

After Independence, Jawaharlal Nehru changed his views on Hindu nationalism and began to equate it with Hindu communalism. He declared that 'communalism of the majority is far more dangerous than the communalism of the minority', as the former can wear the 'garb' of nationalism.[62] He observed that while Muslim communalism might appear stronger and more intense, it lacked the capacity to dominate Indian society or foster fascism—dangers that, in his view, could arise only from Hindu communalism. Hence, he cautioned that the greater vigilance and resistance must be directed towards majoritarian communalism.

Nehru thus reduced the vast, inclusive Hindu philosophy to a narrow notion of communalism. Fortunately, after a long civilizational struggle, India's polity returned to Swami Vivekananda's idea of India through the landmark Supreme Court judgment of 1995.

The Supreme Court of India: Hinduism, Hindutva and the National Ethos

In 1995, the Supreme Court of India, drawing on earlier Constitution Bench decisions, ruled that Hinduism and Hindutva are not narrow or fundamentalist concepts. This historic judgment reaffirmed Swami Vivekananda's vision of Hindu cultural nationalism—an idea Nehru himself had endorsed in 1935 before later departing from it for political reasons. The Court held:[63]

> [No] precise meaning can be ascribed to the terms 'Hindu', 'Hindutva' and 'Hinduism'; and no meaning in the abstract

[62] 'Communalism of the Majority', *Deccan Herald*, 9 January 2020, https://tinyurl.com/ycxna8h4. Accessed on 10 November 2025.

[63] *Dr Ramesh Yeshwant Prabhoo v. Shri Prabhakar Kashinath Kunte and Others*. 1996 AIR 1113; 1996 SCC (1) 130; JT 1995 (8) 609; 1995 SCALE (7) 1, Supreme Court of India, 11 December 1995.

can confine it to the narrow limits of religion alone, excluding the content of Indian culture and heritage. It is also indicated that the term `Hindutva' is related more to the way of life of the people in the sub- continent. It is difficult to appreciate how in the face of these decisions the term `Hindutva' or `Hinduism' per se, in the abstract, can be assumed to mean and be equated with narrow fundamentalist Hindu religious bigotry [...]

Ordinarily, Hindutva is understood as a way of life or a state of mind and it is not to be equated with, or understood as religious Hindu fundamentalism.

[...] it cannot be doubted, particularly in view of the Constitution Bench decisions of this Court that the words `Hinduism' or `Hindutva' are not necessarily to be understood and construed narrowly, confined only to the strict Hindu religious practices unrelated to the culture and ethos of the people of India, depicting the way of life of the Indian people. Unless the context of a speech indicates a contrary meaning or use, in the abstract these terms are indicative more of a way of life of the Indian people and are not confined merely to describe persons practising the Hindu religion as a faith.

Considering the terms `Hinduism' or `Hindutva' per se as depicting hostility, enmity or intolerance towards other religious faiths or professing communalism, proceeds from an improper appreciation and perception of the true meaning of these expressions emerging from the detailed discussion in earlier authorities of this Court.

The Court cited the *Encyclopaedia Britannica* to explain what constitutes Hindus and Hinduism and how it differs from other religions:[64]

In principle, Hinduism incorporates all forms of belief and

---

[64]*Ibid.*

> worship without necessitating the selection or elimination of any. The Hindu is inclined to revere the divine in every manifestation, whatever it may be, and is doctrinally tolerant, leaving others tolerant, leaving others - including both Hindus and non-Hindus - whatever creed and worship practices suit them best. A Hindu may embrace a non-Hindu religion without ceasing to be a Hindu, and since the Hindu is disposed to think synthetically and to regard other forms of worship, strange gods, and divergent doctrines as inadequate rather than wrong or objectionable, he tends to believe that the highest divine powers complement each other for the well-being of the world and mankind. Few religious ideas are considered to be finally irreconcilable. The core of religion does not even depend on the existence or non-existence of God or on whether there is one god or many. Since religious truth is said to transcend all verbal definitions, it is not conceived in dogmatic terms. Hinduism is then both a civilization and a conglomerate of religions, with neither a beginning, a founder, nor a central authority, hierarchy, or organization. Every attempt at a specific definition of Hinduism has proved unsatisfactory in one way or another, the more so because the finest Indian scholars of Hinduism, including Hindus themselves, have emphasized different aspects of the whole.

The Court also cited Dr S. Radhakrishnan's 'The Hindu View of Life' (based on the lectures he delivered at the Oxford University in 1925):[65]

> The Hindu civilization is so called, since its original founders or earliest followers occupied the territory drained by the Sindhu (the Indus) river system corresponding to the North West Frontier Province and the Punjab. This is recorded in the Rig Veda, the oldest of the Vedas, the Hindu

[65]*Ibid.*

> scriptures which give their name to this period of Indian history. The people on the Indian side of the Sindhu were called Hindu by the Persian and the later western invaders.
>
> […] That is the genesis of the word "Hindu". When we think of the Hindu religion[, we] find it difficult, if not impossible, to define Hindu religion or even adequately describe it. Unlike other religions in the world, the Hindu religion does not claim any one prophet; it does not worship any one God; it does not subscribe to any one dogma; it does not believe in any one philosophic concept; it does not follow any one set of religious rites or performances; in fact, it does not appear to satisfy the narrow traditional features of any religion or creed. It may broadly be described as a way of life and nothing more.

On that basis, the Court observed:[66]

> [T]he usual tests which can be applied in relation to any recognised religion or religious creed in the world turn out to be inadequate in dealing with the problem of Hindu religion. Normally, any recognised religion or religious creed subscribes to a body of set philosophic concepts and theological beliefs. Does this test apply to the Hindu religion?
>
> In answering this question, we would base ourselves mainly on the exposition of the problem by Dr. Radhakrishnan in his work on Indian philosophy. […] Unlike other countries, India can claim that philosophy in ancient India was not an auxiliary to any other science or art, but always held a prominent position of independence. … "In all the fleeting centuries of history", says Dr. Radhakrishnan, 'in all the vicissitudes through which India has passed, a certain marked identity is visible. It has held fast to certain psychological traits which constitute its

[66] *Ibid.*

> special heritage, and they will be the characteristic marks of the Indian people so long as they are privileged to have a separate existence".

The Court concluded:[67]

> The term 'Hindu', according to Dr. Radhakrishnan, had originally a territorial and not a credal significance. It implied residence in a well-defined geographical area.

The Court also cited Justices A. M. Ahmadi and P. S. Bharucha as precedent, who had observed in an earlier case:[68]

> Hinduism is a tolerant faith. It is that tolerance that has enabled Islam, Christianity, Zoroastrianism, Judaism, Buddhism, Jainism an[d] Sikhism to find shelter and support upon this land.

The judgment further noted:[69]

> It is somewhat remarkable that this broad sweep of Hindu religion has been eloquently described by Toynbee. Says Toynbee: "When we pass from the plane of social practice to the plane of intellectual outlook, Hinduism too comes out well by comparison with the religions and ideologies of the South- West Asian group. In contrast to these Hinduism has the same outlook as the pre-Christian and pre-Muslim religions and philosophies of the Western half of the world. Like them, Hinduism takes it for granted that there is more than one valid approach to truth and to salvation and these different approaches are not only compatible with each other, but are complementary.

To conclude: Swami Vivekananda's Hindu wor expounded at the 1893 Parliament of the World's

[67] *Ibid.*

[68] *Ibid.*

[69] *Ibid.*

described by contemporary media as 'broad as the heavens above us'—has since been recognized by Harvard University's Religious Pluralism Project and commemorated at the Second Parliament of the World's Religions in 2018. Many of the West's great minds have regarded Vivekananda as a builder of the modern world and an honour to humanity. His philosophy of unity and harmony in diversity, and his worldview grounded in that philosophy, remain even more relevant today than when he first spoke in 1893.

Swami Vivekananda defined the idea and identity of India, inspired the Indian freedom movement, and motivated both revolutionaries and moderates among its leaders. He gave the world India's ancient message of universal brotherhood and Vasudhaiva Kutumbakam, and urged interreligious harmony and dialogue. When it comes to the philosophical basis for religious plurality, even Harvard's Religious Pluralism Project has had to look to India. Swami Vivekananda gave humanity the formula for religious and civilizational harmony.

As the World Turns to Swami Vivekananda

The West-led world order is awakening—belatedly—to Swami Vivekananda's civilizational message delivered at Chicago in 1893. Harvard University's Religious Pluralism Project recalled him a full century later, recognizing his idea of religious pluralism and the equal validity of all faiths—concepts the West had never heard of. Around the same time, the celebrated Catholic theologian Hans Küng proposed inter-religious dialogue as a means to prevent violence and achieve peace—a century after Swami Vivekananda had urged dialogue among religions to overcome bigotry and hatred and avert the wars and violence that had long ravaged humanity. Later still, the United Nations recognized that the world is culturally diverse and cannot be confined within a 'one-size-fits-all' Western framework, affirming that cultural diversity must form the basis of human and economic development. These are unmistakable signs that the world is at last grasping the essence of Vivekananda's resounding call for dialogue and harmony among diverse faiths and civilizations.

Throughout the 20th century, however, the West-led world—mesmerized by transient material ideologies—ignored his message. To borrow Swami Vivekananda's own words, it 'lived a few hours of exultant and exuberant dominance and of a wicked national life, and then vanished like ripples on the face of the waters.' This neglect cost humanity dearly: two world wars and unending conflicts that claimed over hundred millions of lives.

India, as a living embodiment of unity in diversity, bears a profound responsibility to carry forward Swami Vivekananda's message in a world now awakening to its past blunders and moving closer to his vision. Prime Minister Narendra Modi has repeatedly invoked Vivekananda's message in both national and global forums. The most consequential audience for this message is the strategic community—those who mediate between geopolitics, which drives the world order, and the world's cultural and civilizational diversity.

Swami Vivekananda's philosophy provides the overarching framework for this reconciliation and the way forward. The author's work, *Swami Vivekananda for Our Times*, is therefore a critical and timely contribution to the global strategic discourse—one that urgently needs to integrate Swami Vivekananda's vision into the world narrative, now largely shaped by powerful national and international establishments influenced by the strategic community.

And Finally

I thought this background to *Swami Vivekananda for Our Times*—though long—would enrich readers' understanding of the strenuous and meticulous work of the author.

Swami Vivekananda lived for just 39 years and died as a youthful monk. A Vivekananda who is bald, grey-haired or worn out by age is unthinkable. Vivekananda is Vivekananda only because he looks young even today. He is ever a youth—to inspire young India forever—and for that reason, he died young.

In that short life, he travelled to the West and the East by long journeys—not by air, as now, but by routes that took him months. He travelled extensively by ship, bus, train and even on foot, for five years as a *parivrajak*—one he knows neither where the next meal will come from nor where he will sleep. He lived thus in India for five years, from 1888 until 1893, when he reached Chicago. He was always on the move.

During his travels, he met hundreds of great men and women, discussed the mightiest and subtlest ideas with them, delivered hundreds of speeches across the world, and wrote thousands of pages of essays, commentaries, and letters. All those discussions, speeches, and writings are in his *Collected Works*, which run to over 5,000 pages. The author has distilled the essence of that massive corpus into a relatively short, readable text.

Swami *Vivekananda for Our Times* is not a précis of the massive *Collected Works* of Swami Vivekananda. The author has dissected and digested Vivekananda's message into nine distinct subjects, presented as nine chapters:

1. Essential Elements of Religion
2. Understanding and Realizing God
3. Incarnations, Messengers, Gurus
4. Diversity, Tolerance, Inter-faith Harmony
5. Principal Elements of Vedanta
6. The Soul and Reincarnation
7. Buddha and Buddhism
8. Leveraging India's Strengths
9. Overcoming India's Weaknesses

This enables seekers of Swami Vivekananda's message to find each theme in one place and at one go. The contents of these nine chapters are scattered across the 5,000 pages of the *Collected Works*; it would have required enormous effort to comb through that vast material to cull and collect not only the ideas but also the powerful words of Vivekananda himself.

To recall Romain Rolland, who said, 'I cannot touch these sayings of his', the author has produced a work that perfectly fulfils Rolland's dictum—touching Vivekananda's words without diminishing their power. The book is not merely a thematic dissection of Swami Vivekananda's thoughts but a presentation in his very own stirring and irreplaceable words.

The author deserves to be congratulated for this strenuous and meticulous work. I commend it not only to the strategic community to which the author belongs but also to public intellectuals, think tanks, educational institutions, parliamentarians, and judges. It should be circulated beyond India so that the modern world—with its rickety global order, trapped in context and short-termism, and clueless about how to take the next step—may be guided by the decontextualized and eternal message of Swami Vivekananda.

—S. Gurumurthy
Chairman, Vivekananda International Foundation

Part I

WHAT IS RELIGION?

Chapter 1

ESSENTIAL ELEMENTS OF RELIGION

Religion has three aspects, viz. philosophy, mythology and ritual. The mainspring of the strength of every race lies in its spirituality. Religious thought is in man's very constitution. Religion begins with man's dissatisfaction with the present state of things, and the search for freedom and the way out of this world. Children are born optimists, but the rest of life is a continuous disillusionment. Not one ideal can be fully attained nor can one thirst be quenched. So, people go on trying to solve the riddle, and religion has taken up the task. There is certainly an element of reason in religion, seeing that religion is a fundamental feature of humanity, present in all societies around the world across the ages. The inevitability of death compels man to search for the meaning of life. The fear of God is the beginning of religion, and traces of fear will remain with us until we know what God is.

Why is man not satisfied with the pleasures of this world? Life would be a desert if we cannot know the beyond. When the world is the end and God the means to attain that end, that is material. When God is the end and the world is only the means to attain that end, spirituality has begun. The inquiry into the beyond is religion, and it is this that makes the difference between man and an animal. Take religion away from human society, and what will remain is a forest of brutes.

Should religion be based on faith and belief, or should we try to understand it through reason? The same methods of investigation that are applied to other sciences should be applied to religion too. All religions of the book—and they encompass the majority of the world's population—are based on truths that are the results of the experiences of a few chosen persons a long time ago and are impossible at the present time. Thus, religion has come to be based on belief. But if there has been one experience in this world in any particular branch of knowledge, it follows that that experience has been possible many times before and will be repeated eternally. How can it be said that man has a soul if one cannot feel it, or that there is a God unless one can see Him? The fact that someone in some age saw God doesn't help anyone in realizing God except to the extent that it may excite and urge a person to do the same. Just as the holy teachers found their light, every person has to find his own light. Moreover, neither the New Testament nor the Koran can be the arbiter in a quarrel between them. There must be some independent authority, and that cannot be any book, but something that is universal. What can be more universal than reason? If, following his reason, a person becomes an atheist, that's all right; it's better to be an atheist than a hypocrite.

At the same time, religion is beyond reasoning and the plane of the intellect. It belongs to the supersensuous plane. Religion consists in actual perception and realization, not in talk, theories or intellectual consent. Nor is it sectarianism. Religion is a question of being and becoming, not of believing. Religion is useless if it does not make you realize God. Unfortunately, many people, in the name of what may be called religious liberalism, are feeding their idle curiosity with a continuous succession of different ideals. For them, religion is merely a sort of intellectual opium-eating. For others, religion has become a hobby, a fashion, or a mere social necessity.

Religion is the greatest motive power to realize the infinite energy that is within every human being. It builds character, makes for everything that is good and great, and brings peace to others and oneself. Love, charity and unselfishness are the key features of true religiosity. All religions claim that there is unity within us. Knowledge means finding this unity. One must feel the oneness of human life. Where shall we go to find God if we cannot see Him in our own hearts and in every living being? Love everyone, especially the poor, the miserable and the weak. True religion is positive, not negative. It is not merely refraining from evil, but in doing noble deeds.

Ceremonials, external observances, as well as food habits, are only aids to internal purity. It is better to have internal purity alone when minute attention to external observances is not practicable. However, rituals and symbols should not be ignored. As it is very difficult for most people to comprehend abstract ideas, they can be of great help in keeping the mind fixed on God. Image worship and nature worship are not wrong, but they are only the lowest forms of worship. External worship is only a symbol of internal worship. Internal worship and purity are the real things. The practice of going to temples is not essential to religion. Neither are local customs. Thus, all the external manifestations of religion—be they idols, temples, churches, books, rituals, music, superstitions, symbols, dogmas, doctrines, scriptures, etc.—do not constitute the essence of religion. They are only supports or pegs on which to hang religion; merely the means and not the end. They are only the kindergarten of religion, the first steps to make the spiritual child strong enough to take higher steps. They are merely hedges to protect a tender plant that must be broken down to ensure that the plant becomes a tree. These must be eventually given up if one is to become truly religious.

It is absurd to imagine that all knowledge can be confined to a book! No book has ever created God, but

God has inspired all the great books. And no book has ever created a soul. We may study all the books and become great intellectuals, but that does not mean that we have developed at all spiritually. Religion is in us. Books and teachers can only help us to find it, and even without them we can get all truth within. Learning and scholarship are not a condition for spiritual growth. An illiterate man can be perfectly religious. On the other hand, books are responsible for the persecution and fanaticism that we see in the world.

Priestcraft by its very nature is cruel and heartless. Priests make people believe that God can be approached and known only through them. The priests lure and threaten people, confuse them and make them their slaves. Religion is made easy for ordinary people—the priest does everything! Of course, the priest has a vested interest in perpetuating this state of affairs because it is a question of his livelihood.

“

Superstition is a great enemy of man, but bigotry is worse. Why does a Christian go to church? Why is the cross holy? Why is the face turned toward the sky in prayer? Why are there so many images in the Catholic Church? Why are there so many images in the minds of Protestants when they pray? My brethren, we can no more think about anything without a mental image than we can live without breathing. By the law of association, the material image calls up the mental idea and *vice versa*. This is why the Hindu uses an external symbol when he worships. He will tell you, it helps to keep his mind fixed on the Being to whom he prays. He knows as well as you do that the image is not God, is not omnipresent.

We naturally connect our idea of holiness with the image of a church, a mosque, or a cross. The Hindus have associated the idea of holiness, purity, truth, omnipresence, and such other ideas with different images and forms. But with this difference that while some people devote their whole lives to their idol of a church and never rise higher, because with them religion means an intellectual assent to certain doctrines and doing good to their fellows, the whole religion of the Hindu is centred in realisation. Man is to become divine by realising the divine. Idols or temples or churches or books are only the supports, the helps, of his spiritual childhood; but on and on he must progress.

The Hindus have discovered that the absolute can only be realised, or thought of, or stated, through the relative, and the images, crosses and crescents are simply so many symbols—so many pegs to hang the spiritual ideas on. It is not that this help is necessary for every one, but those that do not need it have no right to say that it is wrong. Nor is it compulsory in Hinduism.

Idolatry in India does not mean anything horrible. It is not the mother of harlots. On the other hand, it is the attempt of undeveloped minds to grasp high spiritual traits.

Vol. 1, Addresses at the Parliament of Religions,
Paper on Hinduism, pp. 15–18

Whatever may be the position of philosophy, whatever may be the position of metaphysics, so long as there is such a thing as death in the world, so long as there is such a thing as weakness in the human heart, so long as there is a cry going out of the heart of man in his very weakness, there shall be a faith in God.

Vol. 1, Addresses at the Parliament of Religions,
Buddhism, the Fulfilment of Hinduism, p. 22

In every religion there are three parts: philosophy, mythology, and ritual. Philosophy, of course, is the essence of every religion; mythology explains and illustrates it by means of the more or less legendary lives of great men, stories and fables of wonderful things, and so on; ritual gives to that philosophy a still more concrete form, so that everyone may grasp it—ritual is in fact concretised philosophy. This ritual is Karma; it is necessary in every religion, because most of us cannot understand abstract spiritual things until we grown much spiritually. It is easy for men to think that they can understand anything; but when it comes to practical experience, they find that abstract ideas are often very hard to comprehend. Therefore symbols are of great help, and we cannot dispense with the symbolical method of putting things before us. From time immemorial symbols have been used by all kinds of religions. In one sense we cannot think but in symbols; words themselves are symbols of thought. In another sense everything in the universe may be looked upon as a symbol. The whole universe is a symbol, and God is the essence behind.

Every thought in the mind has a form as its counterpart. This is called in Sanskrit philosophy Nama-Rupa—name and form. It is as impossible to create by convention a system of symbols as it is to create a language. In the world's ritualistic symbols we have an expression of the religious thought of humanity. It is easy to say that there is no use of rituals and temples and all such paraphernalia; every baby says that in modern times. But it must be easy for all to see that those who worship inside a temple are in many respects different from those who will not worship there. Therefore the association of particular temples, rituals and other concrete forms with particular religions has a tendency to bring into the minds of the followers of those religions the thoughts for which those concrete things stand as symbols; and it is not wise to ignore rituals and symbology altogether.

Vol. 1, Karma-Yoga, Chapter V,
We Help Ourselves, Not the World, pp. 72–74

Each soul is potentially divine. The goal is to manifest this Divinity within by controlling nature, external and external. Do this either by work, or worship, or psychic control, or philosophy—by one, or more, or all of these—and be free. This is the whole of religion. Doctrines, or dogmas, or rituals, or books, or temples, or forms, are but secondary details.

Vol. 1, Raja-Yoga, Preface, p. 124

Religion, as it is generally taught all over the world, is said to be based upon faith and belief, and in most cases consists only of different sets of theories, and that is the reason why we find all religions quarrelling with one another. These theories, again, are based upon belief. One man says there is a great Being sitting above the clouds and governing the whole universe, and he asks me to believe that solely on the authority of his assertion. In the same way, I may have my own ideas, which I am asking others to believe, and if they ask a reason, I cannot give them any. This is why religion and metaphysical philosophy have a bad name nowadays [...] Nevertheless, there is a basis of universal belief in religion, governing all the different theories and all the varying ideas of different sects in different countries. Going to their basis we find that they also are based upon universal experiences.

If you analyse all the various religions of the world, you will find that these are divided into two classes, those with a book and those without a book. Those with a book are the strongest, and have the largest number of followers. Those without books have mostly died out, and the few new ones have very small following. Yet, in all of them we find one consensus of opinion, that the truths they teach are the results of the experiences of particular persons [...] The teachers all saw God; they all saw their own souls, they saw their future, they saw their eternity, and what they saw they preached. Only there is this difference that by most of these religions especially in modern times, a peculiar claim is made, namely, that these experiences are impossible at the present day; they were only possible with a few men, who were the first founders of the religions that subsequently bore their names. At the present time these experiences have become obsolete, and therefore we have now to take religion on belief.

This I entirely deny. If there has been one experience in this world in any particular branch of knowledge, it absolutely follows that that experience has been possible millions of times before, and will be repeated eternally. Uniformity is the rigorous law of nature; what once happened can happen again. The teachers of the science of Yoga [...] declare that religion is not only based upon the experience of ancient times, but that no man can be religious until he has the same perceptions himself. Yoga is the science which teaches us how to get these perceptions [...] What right has a man to say he has a soul if he does not feel it, or that there is God if he does not see Him? If there is a God we must see Him; if there is a soul we must perceive it; otherwise it is better not to believe. It is better to be an outspoken atheist than a hypocrite.

Vol. 1, Raja-Yoga, Introductory, pp. 125–127

Clinging to books only degenerates the human mind. Was there ever a more horrible blasphemy than the statement that all the knowledge of God is confined to this or that book? How dare men call God infinite, and yet try to compress Him within the covers of a little book! Millions of people have been killed because they did not believe what the books said, because they would not see all the knowledge of God within the covers of a book. Of course this killing and murdering has gone by, but the world is still tremendously bound up in a belief in books.

Vol. 1, Raja-Yoga, Dhyana and Samadhi, pp. 185–186

Religion does not consist in doctrines or dogmas. It is not what you read, nor what dogmas you believe that is of importance, but what you realise. There are those who teach that this can be gained by the mumbling of words. But no great Master ever taught that external forms were necessary for salvation. The power of attaining it is within ourselves. We live and move in God. Creeds and sects have their parts, but they are for children, they last but temporarily. Books never make religion, but religions make books. We must not forget that. No book ever created God, but God inspired all the great books. And no book ever created a soul. The end of all religions is the realising of God in the soul. That is the one universal religion. If there is one universal truth in all religions, I place it here—in realising God.

A man may believe in all the churches in the world, he may carry in his head all the sacred books ever written, he may baptise himself in all the rivers of the earth, still, if he has no perception of God, I would class him with the rankest atheist. And a man may have never entered a church or a mosque, nor performed any ceremony, but if he feels God within himself and is thereby lifted above the vanities of the world, that man is a holy man, a saint, call him what you will. As soon as a man stands up and says that he is right or his church is right, and all others are wrong, he is himself all wrong. He does not know that upon the proof of all the others depends the proof of his own. Love and charity for the whole human race, that is the test of true religiousness. I do not mean the sentimental statement that all men are brothers, but that one must feel the oneness of human life.

So far as they are not exclusive, I see that the sects and creeds are all mind; they are all grand. They are all helping men towards the real religion [...] Though all religions are essentially the same, they must have the varieties of form produced by dissimilar circumstances among different nations [...]

Until your religion makes you realise God, it is useless. He who only studies books for religion reminds one of the fable of the ass which carried a heavy load of sugar on its back, but did not know the sweetness of it.

The man who is frightened into religion has no religion at all.

Vol. 1, Lectures and Discourses, Soul, God and Religion, pp. 345–327

Is religion to justify itself by the discoveries of reason, through which every other science justifies itself? Are the same methods of investigation, which we apply to sciences and knowledge outside, to be applied to the science of Religion? In my opinion this must be so, and I am also of the opinion that the sooner it is done the better. If a religion is destroyed by such investigations, it was then all the time useless, unworthy superstition; and the sooner it goes the better. I am thoroughly convinced that its destruction would be the best thing that could happen. All that is dross will be taken off, no doubt, but the essential parts of religion will emerge triumphant out of this investigation. Not only will it be made scientific—as scientific, at least, as any of the conclusions of physics or chemistry—but will have greater strength, because physics or chemistry has no internal mandate to vouch for its truth, which religion has.

The proof of religion depends on the truth of the constitution of man, and not on any books. These books are the outgoings, the effects of man's constitution; man made these books. We are yet to see the books that made man.

Vol. 1, Lectures and Discourses, Reason and Religion, pp. 367–369

Priestcraft is in its nature cruel and heartless. That is why religion goes down where priestcraft arises.

Vol. 1, Lectures and Discourses, Vedanta and Privilege, p. 426

The vast mass of mankind are never thinkers. Even if they try to think, the effects of the vast mass of superstitions on them is terrible. The moment they weaken, one blow comes, and the backbone breaks into twenty pieces. They can only be moved by lures and threats. They can never move their own accord. They must be frightened, horrified, or terrorised, and they are your slaves forever. They have nothing else to do but to pay and obey. Everything else is done by the priest [...] How much easier religion becomes! You see, you have nothing to do. Go home and sit quietly. Somebody is doing the whole thing for you. Poor, poor animals! [...] In every country it is the priest who is conservative, for two reasons—because it is his bread and because he can only move with the people. All priests are not strong [...] They are the servants of the congregation who pay them. God does not pay them. So blame yourselves before blaming the priests. You can only get the government and the priesthood you deserve and no better.

Vol. 1, Lectures and Discourses, The Gita I, pp. 450–455

Get rid of the idea that religion consists in doctrines [...] Religion means realisation, nothing else. It does not matter whether one approaches the destination in a carriage with four horses, in an electric car, or rolling on the ground. The goal is the same.

If you [can realise Brahman] by standing on your head, or on one foot, or by worshipping five thousand gods with three heads each—welcome to it! Do it any way you can! Nobody has the right to say anything. Therefore, Krishna says, if your method is better and higher, you have no business to say that another man's method is bad, however wicked you may think it.

Religion is [a matter of] growth, not a mass of foolish words [...] No man's seeing God can help you the least bit except that it may excite you and urge you to do the same thing. That is the whole value of the ancients' example. Nothing more. [Just] signposts on the way. No man's seeing God can save another man. You have to see God yourself. All these people fighting about what God's nature is—whether He has three heads in one body or five heads in six bodies. Have you seen God? No [...] And they do not believe they can ever see Him. What fools we mortals be! Sure, lunatics!

Vol. 1, Lectures and Discourses, The Gita III, pp. 468–469

[Religion] is not a doctrine, [not] a rule. It is a process. That is all. [Doctrines and rules] are all for exercise. By that exercise we get strong and at last break the bonds and become free. Doctrine is of no use except for gymnastics […] Through exercise the soul becomes perfect. That exercise is stopped when you say, 'I believe.'

Vol. 1, Lectures and Discourses, Mohammed, p. 484

Throughout the history of the world, we find that man is trying to grasp the abstract through thought-forms, or symbols. All the external manifestations of religion—bells, music, rituals, books, and images—come under this head […] From time to time, there have been reformers in every religion who have stood against all symbols and rituals. But vain has been their opposition […] It is vain to preach against the use of symbols, and why should we preach against them? There is no reason why man should not use symbols […] If, therefore, anyone says that symbols, rituals and forms are to be kept forever, he is wrong; but if he says that these symbols and rituals are a help to the growth of the soul, in its low and undeveloped state, he is right.

In almost every religion these are the three primary things which we have in the worship of God—forms or symbols, names, God-men […] Temples or churches, books or forms, are simply the kindergarten of religion, to make the spiritual child strong enough to take higher steps; and these first steps are necessary if he wants religion. With the thirst, the longing for God, comes real devotion, real Bhakti.

Do you think that all this mass of people in the world want God, and cannot get Him? That cannot be. What want is there without its object outside? […] He, therefore, in whom this desire is awakened, will reach the goal. We want everything but God. This is not religion that you see all around you. My lady has furniture in her parlour, from all over the world, and now it is the fashion to have something Japanese; so she buys a vase and puts it in her room. Such is religion with the vast majority; they have all sorts of things for enjoyment, and unless they add a little flavour of religion, life is not all right, because society would criticise them. Society expects it; so they must have some religion. This is the present state of religion in the world.

Vol. 2, Bhakti or Devotion, pp. 38–45

In all the ancient religions which have come down to us at the present day, we find one claim made—that they are all supernatural, that their genesis is not, as it were, in the human brain, but that they have originated somewhere outside of it. Two theories have gained acceptance amongst modern scholars. [...] One party maintains that ancestor worship is the beginning of religious ideas; the other, that religion originates in the personification of the powers of nature.

The real germ of religion [is] the struggle to transcend the limitations of the senses. [...] The first idea of immortality man may well get through dreams. [...] These dreams are not verified by their waking states[...] during the dream state it is not that man has a fresh existence, but simply that he recapitulates the experiences of the awakened state. [...] Man continued inquiring more deeply into the different stages of the mind and discovered higher states than either the waking or the dreaming. This state of things we find in all the organised religions of the world, called either ecstasy or inspiration. In all organised religions, their founders, prophets, and messengers are declared to have gone into states of mind that were neither waking nor sleeping, in which they came face to face with a new series of facts relating to what is called the spiritual kingdom. [...]Thus, a tremendous statement is made by all religions: that the human mind, at certain moments, transcends not only the limitations of the senses, but also the power of reasoning.

Man is man so long as he is struggling to rise above nature, and this nature is both internal and external...It is grand and good to know the laws that govern the stars and planets; it is infinitely grander and better to know the laws that govern the passions, the feelings, the will, of mankind. This conquering of the inner man, understanding the secrets of the subtle workings that are within the human mind, and knowing its wonderful secrets, belong entirely to religion.

The mainspring of the strength of every race lies in its spirituality, and the death of that race begins the day that spirituality wanes and materialism gains ground.

The lower types of humanity in all nations find pleasure in the senses, while the cultured and the educated find it in thought, in philosophy, in arts and sciences. Spirituality is a still higher plane. The subject being infinite, that plane is the highest, and the pleasure there is the highest for those who can appreciate it.

Religion is the greatest motive power for realising that infinite energy which is the birthright and nature of every man. In building up character, in making for everything that is good and great, in bringing peace to others and peace to one's own self, religion is the highest motive power and, therefore, ought to be studied from that standpoint.

Vol. 2, Jnana Yoga, The Necessity of Religion, pp. 57-67

It is a significant fact that all religions, without one exception, hold that man is a degeneration of what he was, whether they clothe this in mythological words, or in the clear language of philosophy, or in the beautiful expression of poetry.

Vol. 2, Jnana Yoga, The Real Nature of Man, p. 72

Religion begins with a tremendous dissatisfaction with the present state of things, with our lives, and hatred, an intense hatred, for this patching up of life, an unbounded disgust for fraud and lies.

All these various manifestations of religion, in whatever shape and form they have come to mankind, have this one common central basis. It is the preaching of freedom, the way out of this world.

Vol. 2, Jnana Yoga, Maya and Freedom, pp. 123-124

Religion is not in books and temples. It is an actual perception. Only the man who has actually perceived God and soul has religion.

We are all atheists; let us confess it. Mere intellectual assent does not make us religious…we are all in the dark; religion is to us a mere intellectual assent, a mere talk, a mere nothing. We often consider a man religious who can talk well. But this is not religion…when you see religion and God in a more intense sense than you see this external world, nothing will be able to shake your belief. Then you have real faith.

Vol. 2, Jnana Yoga, Realisation, pp. 163-165

The one great idea that…comes out through masses of superstition in every country and in every religion, is the one luminous idea that man is divine, that divinity is our nature.

Vol. 2, Jnana Yoga, The Freedom of the Soul, p. 193

Why is it that everyone says, 'Do good to others?' Where is the explanation? Why is it that all great men have preached the brotherhood of mankind, and greater men the brotherhood of all lives? Because whether they were conscious of it or not, behind all that, through all their irrational and personal superstitions, was peering forth the eternal light of the Self denying all manifoldness, and asserting that the whole universe is but one. Again, the last word gave us one universe, which through the senses we see as matter, through the intellect as souls, and through the spirit as God.

Vol. 2, Jnana Yoga, The Atman, pp. 252-253

Where shall we go to find God if we cannot see Him in our own hearts and in every living being? […] This seems to many to be a terrible contradiction to the traditional God who lives behind a veil somewhere and whom nobody ever sees. The priests only give us an assurance that if we follow them, listen to their admonitions, and walk in the way they mark out for us—then when we die, they will give us a passport to enable us to see the face of God! What are all these heaven ideas but simply modifications of this nonsensical priestcraft? Of course, the impersonal idea is very destructive; it takes away all trade from the priests, churches and temples.

Those who worship God through ceremonials and forms, however crude we may think them to be, are not in error. It is the journey from truth to truth, from lower truth to higher truth.

Vol. 2, Practical Vedanta and Other Lectures,
Practical Vedanta Part II, pp. 320-327

Why religions should claim that they are not bound to abide by the standpoint of reason, no one knows... Neither the New Testament nor the Koran can be the arbiter in a quarrel between them. There must be some independent authority, and that cannot be any book, but something which is universal; and what is more universal than reason? It has been said that reason is not strong enough; it does not always help us to get at the Truth; many times it makes mistakes, and, therefore, the conclusion is that we must believe in the authority of a church! That was said to me by a Roman Catholic, but I could not see the logic of it. On the other hand I should say, if reason be so weak, a body of priests would be weaker, and I am not going to accept their verdict, but I will abide by my reason, because with all its weakness there is some chance of my getting at truth through it; while, by the other means, there is no such hope at all. We should, therefore, follow reason and also sympathise with those who do not come to any sort of belief, following reason. For it is better that mankind should become atheist by following reason than blindly believe in two hundred millions of gods on the authority of anybody.

Vol. 2, Practical Vedanta and Other Lectures,
Practical Vedanta III, pp. 335-336

True religion never changes. Religion is realisation; not talk, nor doctrine, nor theories, however beautiful they may be. It is being and becoming, not hearing or acknowledging; it is the whole soul becoming changed into what it believes. That is religion.

Vol. 2, Practical Vedanta and Other Lectures,
The Ideal of a Universal Religion, p. 396

There was never a human race which did not have a religion and worship some sort of God or gods. Whether the God or gods existed or not is no question; but what is the analysis of this psychological phenomenon? Why is all the world trying to find, or seeking for a God? Why? Because in spite of all this bondage, in spite of nature and this tremendous energy of law grinding us down, never allowing us to turn to any side—wherever we go, whatever we want to do, we are thwarted by this law, which is everywhere—in spite of all this, the human soul never forgets its freedom and is ever seeking it. The search for freedom is the search of all religions; whether they know it or not, whether they can formulate it well or ill, the idea is there. Even the lowest man, the most ignorant, seeks for something which has power over nature's laws. He wants to see a demon, a ghost, a god—somebody who can subdue nature, for whom nature is not almighty, for whom there is no law.

Vol. 2, Practical Vedanta and Other Lectures, The Open Secret, p. 400

The farthest that all religions can see is the existence of a spiritual entity. So no religion can teach beyond this point. In every religion there is the essential truth and non-essential casket in which this jewel lies. The believing in the Jewish book or the Hindoo book is non-essential. Circumstances change, the receptacle is different; but the central truth remains. The essentials being the same, the educated people of every community retains the essentials [...] Superstition gets the better of religion. All the religions are good since the essentials are the same. Each man should have the perfect exercise of his individuality but these individualities form a perfect whole.

Vol. 2, Reports in American Newspapers, Religious Harmony, p. 483

Essentially, however, religion belongs to the supersensuous and not to the sense plane. It is beyond all reasoning and is not on the plane of intellect. It is a vision, an inspiration, a plunge into the unknown and unknowable, making the unknowable more than known, for it can never be 'known.' This search has been in the human mind, as I believe, from the very beginning of humanity. There cannot have been human reasoning and intellect in any period of the world's history without this struggle, this search beyond [...] I shall try to bring before you the Hindu theory that religions do not come from without, but from within. It is my belief that religious thought is in man's very constitution, so much so that it is impossible for him to give up religion until he can give up his mind and body, until he can give up thought and life. As long as a man thinks, this struggle must go on, and so long man must have some form of religion. Thus we see various forms of religion in the world.

The great question of all questions at the present time is this: Taking for granted that the known and the knowable are bounded on both sides by the unknowable and the infinitely unknown, why struggle for that infinite unknown? Why shall we not be content with the known? Why shall we not rest satisfied with eating, drinking, and doing a little good to society? This idea is in the air [...] But fortunately we *must* inquire into the beyond. This present, this expressed, is only one part of that unexpressed [...] Thus man finds himself driven to a study of the beyond. Life will be a desert, human life will be vain, if we cannot know the beyond. It is very well to say: be contented with the things of the present. The cows and the dogs are, and so are all animals; and that is what makes them animals. So if man rests content with the present and gives up all search into the beyond, mankind will have to go back to the animal plane again. It is religion, the inquiry into the beyond, that makes the difference between man and an animal. Well has it been said that man is the only animal that naturally looks upwards; every other animal naturally looks down. That looking upward and going upward and seeking perfection are what is called religion, and the sooner a man begins to go higher, the sooner he raises himself towards this idea of truth as salvation.

Religion does not live on bread, does not dwell in a house. Again and again you hear this objection advanced: 'What good can religion do? Can it take away the poverty of the poor?' Supposing it cannot, would that prove the untruth of religion? [...] We must not judge of higher things from a low standpoint. Everything must be judged by its own standard and the infinite must be judged by the standard of infinity. Religion permeates the whole of man's life, not only the present, but the past, present, and future. It is, therefore, the eternal relations between the eternal soul and the eternal God. Is it logical to measure its value by its action upon five minutes of human life? Certainly not. These are all negative arguments. Now comes the question: Can religion really accomplish anything? It can. It brings to man eternal life. It has made man what he is, and will make of this human animal a god. That I what religion can do. Take religion from human society and what will remain? Nothing but a forest of brutes.

One question more: What is the goal? [...] You must end where you begin: and as you began in God, you must go back to God. What remains? Detail work. Through eternity you have to do the detail work. Yet another question: Are we to discover new truths of religion as we go on? Yea and nay. In the first place, we cannot know more of religion, it has all been known. In all religions of the world you will find it claimed that there is a unity within us. Being one with divinity, there cannot be any further progress in that sense. Knowledge means finding this unity [...] The next question is: Can such a unity be found? In India the attempt has been made from the earliest times to reach a science of religion and philosophy, for the Hindus do not separate these as is customary in Western countries. We regard religion and philosophy as but two aspects of one thing which must equally be grounded in reason and scientific truth.

Vol. 3, Lectures and Discourses, Unity, the Goal of Religion, pp. 1–5

Forms and ceremonials, though absolutely necessary for the progressive soul, have no other value than taking us on to that state in which we feel the most intense love to God.

Vol. 3, Bhakti-Yoga, Definition of Bhakti, p. 33

Religion, which is the highest knowledge and the highest wisdom, cannot be bought, nor can it be acquired from books.

Vol. 3, Bhakti-Yoga, Qualifications of the Aspirant and the Teacher, p. 52

Of the principal religions of the world, we see Vedantism, Buddhism and certain forms of Christianity freely using images; only two religions, Mohammedanism and Protestantism, refuse such help. Yet the Mohammedans use the grave of their saints and martyrs almost in the place of images; and the Protestants, in rejecting all concrete helps to religion, are drifting away every year farther and farther from spirituality.

Vol. 3, Bhakti-Yoga, Worship of Substitutes and Images, p. 61

The tender plant of spirituality will die if exposed too early to the action of a constant change of ideas and ideals. Many people, in the name of what may be called religious liberalism, may be seen feeding their idle curiosity with a continuous succession of different ideals. With them, hearing new things grows into a kind of disease, a sort of religious drink-mania. They want to hear new things just by way of getting a temporary nervous excitement, and when one such exciting influence has had its effect on them, they are ready for another. Religion is with these people a sort of intellectual opium-eating, and there it ends.

Vol. 3, Bhakti-Yoga, The Chosen Ideal, p. 63

We must always remember that external practices have value only as helps to develop internal purity. It is better to have internal purity alone when minute attention to external observances is not practicable. But woe unto the man and woe unto the nation that forgets the real, internal, spiritual essentials of religion and mechanically clutches with death-like grasp at all external forms and never lets them go.

Vol. 3, Bhakti-Yoga, The Method and the Means, p. 68

It is in love that religion exists, and not in ceremony, in the pure and sincere live in the heart. Unless a man is pure in body and mind, his coming into a temple and worshipping Shiva is useless. The prayers of those that are pure in mind and body will be answered by Shiva, and those that are impure and yet try to teach religion to others will fail in the end. External worship is only a symbol of internal worship; but internal worship and purity are the real things. Without them, external worship would be of no avail [...] This is the gist of all worship—to be pure and do good to others [...] You must be pure and help anyone who comes to you, as much as lies in your power [...] Selfishness is the chief sin, thinking of ourselves first [...] Unselfishness is the test of religion.

Vol. 3, Lectures from Colombo to Almora, Address at the Rameswaram Temple on Real Worship, pp. 141–143

And the only religion that ought to be taught is the religion of fearlessness. Either in this world or the world of religion, it is true that fear is the sure cause of degradation and sin. It is fear that brings misery, fear that brings death, fear that breeds evil. And what causes fear? Ignorance of our nature.

Vol. 3, Lectures from Colombo to Almora, Reply to the Address of Welcome at Paramakudi, p. 160

Various are the customs all over India, but they are local. The greatest mistake made is that ignorant people always think that this local custom is the essence of our religion [...] You have always to remember that because a little social custom is going to be changed you are not going to lose your religion. Not at all. Remember these customs have already been changed. There was a time in this very India when, without eating beef, no Brahmin would remain a Brahmin; you read in the Vedas how, when a Sannyasin, a king or a great man came into a house, the best bullock was killed, how in time it was found that as we were an agricultural race, killing the best bulls meant annihilation of the race. Therefore the practice was stopped, and a voice was raised against the killing of cows.

Vol. 3, Lectures from Colombo to Almora, Reply to the Address of Welcome at Madura, pp. 173–174

It has become a trite saying that idolatry is wrong [...] why? Nobody knows. Because some hundreds of years ago some man of Jewish blood happened to condemn it? That is, he happened to condemn everybody else's idols except his own. If God is represented in any beautiful form or any symbolic form, said the Jew, it is awfully bad; it is sin. But if He is represented in the form of a chest, with two angels sitting on each side, and a cloud hanging over it, it is the holy of holies. If God comes in the form of a dove, it is holy. But if He comes in the form of a cow, it is heathen superstition; condemn it! That is how the world goes. That is why the poet says, 'What fools we mortals be!' How difficult it is to look through each other's eyes, and that is the bane of humanity. That is the basis of hatred and jealousy, of quarrel and of fight.

Vol. 3, Lectures from Colombo to Almora, My Plan of Campaign, p. 218

Not belief in doctrines, not going to thousands of temples, nor bathing in all the rivers in the world, but becoming the Rishi, the Mantra-drashta—that is freedom, that is salvation.

Vol. 3, Lectures from Colombo to Almora, The Sages of India, pp. 253–255

The Self is not to be reached by too much talking, not even by the highest intellects, not even by the study of the scriptures. The scriptures themselves say so. Do you find in any other scripture such a bold assertion as that—not even by the study of the Vedas will you reach the Atman? You must open your heart. Religion is not going to church, or putting marks on the forehead, or dressing in a peculiar fashion; you may paint yourselves in all the colours of the rainbow, but if the heart has not been opened, if you have not realised God, it is all vain. If one has the colour of the heart, he does not want any external colour. That is the true religious realisation. We must not forget that colours and all these things are good so far as they help; so far they are all welcome. But they are apt to degenerate and instead of helping they retard, and a man identifies religion with externalities. Going to the temple becomes tantamount to spiritual life. Giving something to a priest becomes religious life. These are dangerous and pernicious, and should be at once checked. Our scriptures declare again and again that even the knowledge of the external senses is not religion. That is religion which makes us realise the Unchangeable One, and that is the religion for everyone.

Vol. 3, Lectures from Colombo to Almora, The Work Before Us, p. 283

You may eat what you like. If food alone would purify the Sattva, then feed the monkey with milk and rice all its life; would it become a great Yogi? Then the cows and the deer would be great Yogis. As has been said, 'If it is by bathing much that heaven is reached, the fishes will get to heaven first. If by eating vegetables a man gets to heaven, the cows and the deer will get to heaven first.'

Vol. 3, Lectures from Colombo to Almora, The Vedanta in All its Phases, pp. 338–339

This external worship of images has, however, been described in all our Shastras as the lowest of all forms of worship. But that does not mean that it is a wrong thing to do. Despite the many iniquities that have found entrance into the practices of image-worship as it is in vogue now, I do not condemn it. Ay, where would I have been if I had not been blessed with the dust of the holy feet of that orthodox, image-loving Brahmin! Those reformers who preach against image-worship, or what they denounce as idolatry—to them I say, 'Brothers, if you are fit to worship God-without-form discarding all external help, do so, but why do you condemn others who cannot do the same?

Vol. 3, Lectures from Colombo to Almora, The Religion We Are Born In, p. 460

You will be astonished if I tell you that, according to the old ceremonials, he is not a good Hindu who does not eat beef. On certain occasions he must sacrifice a bull and eat it. That is disgusting now. However they may differ from each other in India, in that they are all one—they never eat beef. The ancient sacrifices and the ancient gods, they are all gone: modern India belongs to the spiritual part of the Vedas.

Vol. 3, Buddhistic India, p. 536

What is the use of writing a book either to prove or disprove God? What does it matter to most people whether there is a God or not? The majority of men work just like a machine with no thought of God and feeling no need of Him [...] But there are some who get a little awakening [...] By reading books we become parrots; no one becomes learned by reading books. If a man reads but one word of love, he indeed becomes learned [...] This quickening impulse which comes from outside cannot be received from books; the soul can receive impulse only from another soul, and from nothing else. We may study books all our lives, we may become very intellectual, but in the end we find we have not developed at all spiritually.

Vol. 4, Addresses on Bhakti-Yoga, The First Steps, pp. 18–21

All the worship that you have seen in any country in the world, or in any religion, is regulated by love. There is a good deal that is simple ceremony; there is also a good deal, which, though not ceremony, is still not love, but a lower state. Yet these ceremonies are necessary. The external part of Bhakti is absolutely necessary to help the soul onward. Man makes a great mistake when he thinks that he can at once jump to the highest state. If a baby thinks he is going to be an old man in a day, he is mistaken; and I hope you will always bear in mind this one ideal, that religion is neither in books, nor in intellectual consent, nor in reasoning. Reason, theories, documents, doctrines, books, religious ceremonies, are all *helps* to religion; religion itself consists in *realisation[...]* To be religious you have first to throw books overboard. The less you read of books, the better for you; do one thing at a time[...] You must bear in mind that religion does not consist in talk, or doctrines, or books, but in realisation; it is not learning, but *being.* No amount of doctrines or philosophies or ethical books, that you may have stuffed into your brain, will matter much, only what you *are* and what you have *realised.* So we have to realise religion, and this realisation of religion is a long process.

Vol. 4, Addresses on Bhakti-Yoga, The Need of Symbols, pp. 33–35

One of the great advantages of a book is that it crystallises everything in tangible and convenient form, and is the handiest of all idols. Just put a book on an altar and everyone sees it; a good book everyone reads. I am afraid I may be considered partial. But, in my opinion, books have produced more evil than good. They are accountable for many mischievous doctrines. Creeds all come from books, and books are alone responsible for the persecution and fanaticism in the world. Books in modern times are making liars everywhere.

The next thing to be considered is the Pratima, or image, the use of images. All over the world you will find images in some form or other [...] One sect thinks a certain form is the right sort of image, and another thinks it is bad [...] This is the defect of image-worship. Yet these seem to be necessary stages.

I believe in thinking independently. I believe in becoming entirely free from the holy teachers; pay all reverence to them, but look at religion as an independent research. I have to find my light, just as they found theirs. Their finding the light will not satisfy us at all. You have to *become* the Bible, and not follow it, except as paying reverence to it as a light on the way, as a guidepost, a mark: that is all the value it has. But these images and other things are quite necessary. You may try to concentrate your mind, or even to project any thought. You will find that you naturally form images in your mind. You cannot help it. Two sorts of persons never require an image—the human animal who never thinks of any religion, and the perfected being who has passed through these stages. Between these two points all of us require some sort of ideal, outside and inside. It may be in the form of a departed human being, or of a living man or woman. This is clinging to personality and bodies, and is quite natural. We are prone to concretise. How could we be here if we did not concretise?

Vol. 4, Addresses on Bhakti-Yoga, The Chief Symbols, pp. 44–45

For all the devilry that religion is blamed with, religion is not at all in fault: no religion ever persecuted men, no religion ever burnt witches, no religion ever did any of these things. What then incited people to do these things? Politics, but never religion; and if such politics takes the name of religion, whose fault is it? So when each man stands and says, 'My Prophet is the only true Prophet,' he is not correct—he knows not the alpha of religion. Religion is neither talk, nor theory, nor intellectual consent. It is realisation in the heart of our hearts; it is touching God; it is feeling, realising that I am a spirit in relation with the Universal Spirit and all Its great manifestations. If you have really entered the house of the Father, how can you have seen His children and not known them? And if you do not recognise them, you have not entered the house of the Father. The mother recognises her child in any dress and knows him however disguised. Recognise all the great, spiritual men and women in every age and country, and see that they are not really at variance with one another.

Vol. 4, Lectures and Discourses, The Great Teachers of the World, pp. 125–126

Our temples are not churches in your sense of the word, they are not places for public worship; for, properly speaking, there is no such thing as public worship in India. Temples are erected mostly by rich persons as a meritorious religious act. If a man has much property, he wants to build a temple. In that he puts a symbol or an image of an Incarnation of God, and dedicates it to worship in the name of God. The worship is akin to that which is conducted in Roman Catholic churches, very much like the mass, reading certain sentences from the sacred books, waving a light before the image, and treating the image in every respect as we treat a great man. That is all that is done in the temple. The man who goes to a temple is not considered thereby a better man than he who never goes. More properly, the latter is considered the more religious man, for religion in India is to each man his own private affair.

Vol. 4, Lectures and Discourses, My Master, pp. 163–164

Religion is not talk, or doctrines, or theories; nor is it sectarianism. Religion cannot live in sects and societies. It is the relation between the soul and God; how can it be made into a society? It would then degenerate into business, and wherever there are business and business principles in religion, spirituality dies. Religion does not consist in erecting temples, on building churches, or attending public worship. It is not to be found in books, or in words, or in lectures, or in organisations.

Vol. 4, Lectures and Discourses, My Master, pp. 179–180

Impress upon your children that true religion is positive and not negative, that it does not consist in merely refraining from evil, but in a persistent performance of noble deeds. True religion comes not from the teaching of men or the reading of books; it is the awakening of the spirit within us, consequent upon pure and heroic action.

Vol. 4, Lectures and Discourses, Indian Religious Thought, p. 190

When it was discovered that 'I and my Father are one,' the last word was said of religion. Then there only remained detail work. In true religion there is no faith or belief in the sense of blind faith. No great preacher ever preached that. That only comes with degeneracy. Fools pretend to be followers of this or that spiritual giant and, although they may be without power, endeavour to teach humanity to believe blindly. Believe what? To believe blindly is to degenerate the human soul. Be an atheist if you want, but do not believe in anything unquestioningly. Why degrade the soul to the level of animals? You not only hurt yourselves thereby, but you injure society, and make danger for those that come after you. Stand up and reason out, having no blind faith. Religion is a question of being and becoming, not of believing. This is religion, and when you have attained in that you have religion. Before that you are no better than animals. 'Do not believe in what you have heard,' says the great Buddha, 'do not believe the doctrines because they have been handed down to you through generations; do not believe in anything because it is followed blindly by many; do not believe because some old sage makes a statement; do not believe in truths to which you have become attached by habit; do not believe merely on the authority of your teachers and elders. Have deliberation and analyse, and when the result agrees with reason and conduces to the good of one and all, accept it and live up to it.'

Vol. 4, Lectures and Discourses, The Claims of Religion, pp. 216–217

External purity is very easy and all the world rushes towards it [...] The people who do external, superficial things are so self-righteous [...] Bathing, and dress, and food regulation—all these have their proper value when they are complementary to the spiritual.

Vol. 4, Lectures and Discourses, Concentration, p. 222

About vegetarian diet I have to say this—first, my Master was a vegetarian; but if was given meat offered to the Goddess, he used to hold it up to his head. The taking of life is undoubtedly sinful; but so long as vegetable food is not made suitable to the human system through progress in chemistry, there is no other alternative but meat-eating. So long as man shall have to live a Rajasika (active life under circumstances like the present, there is no other way except through meat-eating. It is true that the Emperor Asoka saved the lives of millions of animals by the threat of the sword; but is not the slavery of a thousand years more dreadful than that? Taking the life of a few goats as against the inability to protect the honour of one's own wife and daughter, and to save the morsels for one's children from robbing hands—which of these is more sinful? Rather let those belonging to the upper ten, who do not earn their livelihood by manual labour, not take meat; but the forcing of vegetarianism upon those who have to earn their bread by labouring day and night is one of the causes of the loss of our national freedom. Japan is an example of what good and nourishing food can do.

Vol. 4, Translations of Writings: Prose and Poems, The Education that India Needs, pp. 486–487

I do not believe in a God or religion which cannot wipe the widow's tears or bring a piece of bread to the orphan's mouth. However sublime be the theories, however well spun may be the philosophy—I do not call it religion so long as it is confined to books and dogmas.

Do you love your fellow men? Where should you go to seek for God—are not all the poor, the miserable, the weak, Gods? Why not worship them first? Why go to dig a well on the shores of the Ganga? Believe in the omnipotent power of love.

Vol. 5, Epistles (First Series), XXI, pp. 50–52

My son, I believe in God, and I believe in man. I believe in helping the miserable. I believe in going even to hell to save others. Rituals are the kindergarten of religion. They are absolutely necessary for the world as it is now; only we shall have to give people newer and fresher rituals.

Vol. 5, Interviews, The Abroad and the Problems at Home. pp. 216–217

Religion is realising, and I shall call you a worshipper of God when you have become able to realise the Idea. Before that it is the spelling of words and no more. It is this power of realisation that makes religion; no amount of doctrines or philosophies, or ethical books that you may have stuffed into your brain, will matter much—only what you *are* and what you have *realised.*

Through fanaticism and bigotry a religion can be propagated very quickly, no doubt, but the preaching of that religion is firm, based on solid ground, which gives everyone liberty to his opinions and thus uplifts him to a higher path, though this process is slow.

Vol. 5, Notes from Lectures and Discourses, On Bhakti-Yoga, pp. 265–267

Which do you think is the higher—the end or the means? Surely, the means can never be higher than the end, because the means to realise the same end must be numerous, as they vary according to the temperament or mental capacities of individual followers. The counting of beads, meditation, worship, offering oblations in the sacred fire—all these and such other things are the limbs of religion; they are but means.

Vol. 5, Conversations and Dialogues (Recorded by Disciples), XII, p. 386

Religion is not a thing of imagination but of direct perception. [...] The downfall of a religious sect begins from the day that the worship of the rich enters into it. [...] Any sect that may help you to realise God is welcome. Religion is the realising of God. [...] An atheist can be charitable but not religious. But the religious man must be charitable. [...] It is the cultured among a community that are the real custodians of religion and philosophy in their purest form.

Vol. 5, Sayings and Utterances, 48/51/71/72/81, pp. 414–418

Realisation of religion is the only way. Each one of us will have to discover. Of what use are these books, then, these Bibles of the world? They are of great use, just as maps are of a country. I have seen maps of England all my life before I came here, and they were great helps to me informing some sort of conception of England. Yet, when I arrived in this country, what a difference between the maps and the country itself! These books are only the maps, the experiences of past men, as a motive power to us to dare to make the same experiences and discover in the same way, if not better. This is the first principle of Vedanta, that realisation is religion, and he who realises it is the religious man [...] In this realisation, again, we shall be helped very much by these books, not only as guides, but as giving instructions and exercises; for every science has its own particular method of investigation [...] Every science has its own method of learning, and religion has to be learnt in the same way. It has its own methods, and here is something we can learn, and must learn, from all the ancient prophets of the world, every one who has found something, who has realised religion. They will give us the methods, the particular methods, through which alone we shall be able to realise the truths of religion. They struggled all their lives, discovered particular methods of mental culture, bringing the mind to a certain state, the finest perception, and through that they perceive the truths of religion. To become religious, to perceive religion, feel it, to become a prophet, we have to take these methods and practices them; and then if we find nothing, we shall have the right to say, 'There is nothing in religion, for I have tried and failed.'

Vol. 6, Lectures and Discourses, The Methods and Purpose of Religion, pp. 14–15

Formal worship is one of the stages we have to pass through. Therefore, instead of crusading against it, let us take the best in worship and study its underlying principles. Of course, the lowest form of worship is what is known as [tree and stone worship]. Every crude, uncultured man will take up anything and add to it some ideas of his own; and that will help him. He may worship a bit of bone, or stone—anything. In all these crude states of worship man has never worshipped a stone as a stone, a tree as a tree [...] In this case, man conceived the stone as spirit or the tree as spirit. He imagined that some part of that Being resides in the stone or the tree, that the stone or the tree has a soul. Tree worship and serpent worship always go together. There is the tree of knowledge. There must always be the tree, and the tree is somehow connected with the serpent. These are the oldest forms of worship [...] A higher state in formal worship is that of images of ancestors and God. People make images of men who have died and imaginary images of God. Then they worship those images. Still higher is the worship of saints, of good men and women who have passed on. Men worship their relics. [They feel that] the presence of saints is somehow in the relics, and that they will help them [...] these are all low states of worship and yet worship. We all have to pass through them. It is only from an intellectual standpoint that they are not good enough. In our hearts we cannot get rid of them.

There is still a higher order of formal worship—the world of symbolism. The forms are still there, but they are neither trees, nor [stones], nor images, nor relics of saints. They are symbols [...] Some people take it into their heads to see nothing in symbols […] [Others want] all sorts of abracadabra. If you tell them plain, simple truths, they will not accept them. Human nature being [what it is], the less they understand the better—the greater man [they think] you are. In all ages in every country such worshippers are deluded by certain diagrams and forms […] In wanting to get spiritual power through [all this abracadabra] there is fear, fear of life. I do not mean that sort of symbolism. But there is some truth in symbolism. There cannot be any falsehood without some truth behind it. There cannot be any imitation without something real. There is the symbolic form of worship in the different religions. There are fresh, vigorous, poetic, healthy symbols. Think of the marvellous power the symbol of the cross has had upon millions of people! Think of the symbol of the crescent. Think of the magnetism of this one symbol! Everywhere there are good and great symbols in the world. They interpret the spirit and bring about certain conditions of the mind; as a rule we find they create a tremendous power of faith and love.

Learning has no place in religion; for the majority, learning is a block in the way. […] The whole of religion is our own inner perception. […] The only value of knowledge is in the strengthening, the disciplining, of the mind.

We pray for material things. To attain some end we worship God with shopkeeping worship. Go on and pray for food and clothes! Worship is good. Something is better than nothing […] A very rich young man becomes ill, and then to get rid of his disease he begins to give to the poor. That is good, but it is not religion yet, not spiritual religion. It is all on the material plane. What is material, and what is not? When the world is the end and God the means to attain that end, that is material. When God is the end and the world is only the means to attain that end, spirituality has begun […] Formal worship is a low state of worship when you worship God as a means to the end, which is this life and this world […] So what does it mean? You say, 'Lord, give me my bread, my money! Heal my diseases! Do this and that!' Every time you say that, you are hypnotising yourselves with the idea, 'I am matter, and this matter is the goal.' Every time you try to fulfil a material desire, you tell yourselves that you are the body, that you are not spirit [...] Yet this form of worship is all right. Go on! To pray for something is better than nothing. These are the stages through which we pass. These are the first lessons. Gradually, the mind begins to think of something higher than the senses, the body, the enjoyments of this world. How does man do it? First he becomes a thinker. When you think upon a problem, there is no sense enjoyment there, but the exquisite delight of thought [...] Thus, working through the plane of the senses, you get more and more entry into the other regions, and then this world falls away from you. You get one glimpse of that spirit, and then your senses and your sense-enjoyments, your clinging to the flesh, will all melt away from you. Glimpse after glimpse will come from the realm of spirit. You will have finished Yoga, and spirit will stand revealed as spirit. Then you will begin the worship of God as spirit. Then you will begin to understand that worship is not to gain something.

Vol. 6, Lectures and Discourses, Formal Worship, pp. 60–69

The fear of God is the beginning of religion, but the love of God is the end of religion. All fear has died out.

Vol. 6, Lectures and Discourses, Divine Love, p. 71

The God of Infinite Love and the object of Love sublime and infinite are painted blue. Krishna is painted blue, so also Solomon's God of Love. It is a natural law that anything sublime and infinite is associated with blue colour. Take a handful of water, it is absolutely colourless. But look at the deep wide ocean; it is as blue as anything. Examine the space near you; it is colourless. But look at the infinite expanse of the sky; it is blue.

Vol. 6, Notes of Class Talks and Lectures, Notes Taken Down in Madras 1892-93, p. 106

Morality is a relative term. Is there anything like absolute morality in this world? The idea is a superstition. We have no right to judge every man in every age by the same standard. Every man, in every age, in every country is under peculiar circumstances. If the circumstances change, ideas also must change. Beef-eating was once moral. The climate was cold, and the cereals were not much known. Meat was the chief food available. So in that age and clime, beef was in a manner indispensable. But beef-eating is held to be immoral now.

Vol. 6, Notes of Class Talks and Lectures, Notes Taken Down in Madras 1892-93, p. 109

We are asked: What good is your Religion to society? Society is made a test of truth. Now this is very illogical. Society is only a stage of growth through which we are passing. We might just as well judge the good or utility of a scientific discovery by its use to the baby. It is simply monstrous. If the social state were permanent, it would be the same as if the baby remained a baby [...] there can be no perfect society. Man must and will grow out of such early stages. Society is good at a certain stage, but it cannot be our ideal; it is a constant flux. The present mercantile civilisation must die, with all its pretensions and humbug [...] What the world wants is thought-power through individuals [...] The world needs people who are mad with the love of God. You must believe in yourself, and then you will believe in God [...] We need to have three things; the heart to feel, the brain to conceive, the hand to work.

Vol. 6, Notes of Class Talks and Lectures, Lessons on Bhakti-Yoga, On Doing Good to the World, p. 144

Children are born optimists, but the rest of life is a continuous disillusionment; not one ideal can be fully attained, not one thirst can be quenched. So on they go trying to solve the riddle, and religion has taken up the task.

Vol. 6, Notes of Class Talks and Lectures, Mother-Worship, p. 146

It won't do to live on abstract ideas merely. These festivals and the like are also necessary; for then only, these ideas will spread gradually among the masses. You see, Hindus have got their festivals throughout the year, and the secret of it is to infuse the great ideals of religion gradually into the minds of the people. It has also its drawback, though. For people in general miss their inner significance and become so much engrossed in externals that no sooner are these festivities over than they become their old selves again. Hence it is true that all these form the outer covering of religion, which in a way hide real spirituality and self-knowledge.

Vol. 6, Conversations and Dialogues, IV, p. 467

Churches, doctrines, forms, are the hedges to protect the tender plant, but they must later be broken down that the plant may become a tree. So the various religions, Bibles, Vedas, dogmas—all are just tubs for the little plant; but it must get out of the tub.

Vol. 7, Inspired Talks, 23 June 1895, pp. 6–7

Real religion is one, but we quarrel with the forms, the symbols, the illustrations.

Vol. 7, Inspired Talks, 29 June 1895, p. 20

Temples have no hold on the Hindu religion; if they were all destroyed, religion would not be affected a grain. A man must only build a house for 'God and guests,' to build for himself would be selfish; therefore he erects temples as dwelling places for God.

Vol. 7, Inspired Talks, 1 July 1895, p. 23

Generally speaking, human religion begins with fear [...] Traces of fear will remain with us until we get knowledge, know what God is.

Vol. 7, Inspired Talks, 3 July 1895, p. 27

Books cannot teach God, but they can destroy ignorance; their action is negative.

Vol. 7, Inspired Talks, 16 July 1895, p. 53

Luther drove a nail into religion when he took away renunciation and gave us morality instead. Atheists and materialists can have ethics, but only believers in the Lord can have religion.

Vol. 7, Inspired Talks, 31 July 1895, pp. 80–81

Books suggest the inner light and the method of bringing that out, but we can only understand them when we have earned the knowledge ourselves. When the inner light has flashed for you, let the books go, and look only within. You have in you all and a thousand times more than is in all the books. Never lose faith in yourself, you can do anything in this universe. Never weaken, all power is yours. If religion and life depend upon books or upon the existence of any prophet whatsoever, then perish all religion and books! Religion is in us. No books or teachers can do more than help us to find it, and even without them we can get all truth within. You have gratitude for books and teachers without bondage to them; and worship your Guru as God, but do not obey him blindly; love him all you will, but think for yourself. No blind belief can save you, work out your own salvation. Have only one idea of God—that He is an eternal help.

Vol. 7, Inspired Talks, 1 August 1895, pp. 85–86

Practising the concrete forms of religion is easy and attracts the masses; but really there is nothing in the external.

Vol. 7, Inspired Talks, 5 August 1895, p. 101

Religion is not the outcome of the weakness of human nature; religion is not here because we fear a tyrant; religion is love, unfolding, expanding, growing.

Vol. 7, Notes of Class Talks and Lectures, The Destiny of Man, p. 421

Priests believe that there is a God, but that this God can be approached and know only through them. People can enter the Holy of Holies only with the permission of the priests. You must pay them, worship them, place everything in their hands. Throughout the history of the world, this priestly tendency has cropped up again and again—this tremendous thirst for power, this tiger-like thirst, seems a part of human nature. The priests dominate you, lay down a thousand rules for you. They describe simple truths in roundabout ways. They tell you stories to support their own superior position. If you want to thrive in this life or go to heaven after death, you have to pass through their hands. You have to perform all kinds of ceremonies and rituals. All this has made life so complicated and has so confused the brain that if I give you plain words, you will go home unsatisfied. You have become thoroughly befuddled. The less you understand, the better you feel! The prophets have been giving warnings against the priests and their superstitions and machinations; but the vast mass of people have not yet learnt to heed these warnings—education is yet to come to them.

Vol. 8, Lectures and Discourses, Buddha's Message to the World, pp. 93–94

We attend lectures and read books, argue and reason about God and soul, religion and salvation. These are not spirituality, because spirituality does not exist in books or in theories or in philosophies. It is not in learning or reasoning, but in actual inner growth [...] The man who cannot write even his own name can be perfectly religious, and the man with all the libraries of the world in his head may fail to be. Learning is not a condition of spiritual growth; scholarship is not a condition. The touch of the Guru, the transmittal of spiritual energy, will quicken your heart. Then will begin the growth. That is the real baptism by fire.

Vol. 8, Lectures and Discourses, Discipleship, p. 114

Religion nowadays has become a mere hobby and fashion. People go to church like a flock of sheep. They do not embrace God because they need Him. Most persons are unconscious atheists who self-complacently think that they are devout believers.

Vol. 8, Notes of Class Talks and Lectures, The Love of God-II, p. 203

Many of us do not believe in any form of idolatry; but they have no right to object when others do it, because that would break the first principle of our religion. Again, God can only be known in and through man.

Vol. 8, Epistles (Fourth Series), XV, p. 298

The world in general must have some form. In fact, in the ordinary sense religion is philosophy concretised through rituals and symbols.

Vol. 8, Epistles (Fourth Series), LVII, p. 356

Ceremonials and symbols etc. have no place in our religion which is the doctrine of the Upanishads, pure and simple. Many people think the ceremonials etc. help them in realising religion. I have no objection. Religion is that which does not depend upon books or teachers or prophets or saviours, and that which does not make us dependent in this or in any other lives upon others. In this sense Advaitism of the Upanishads is the only religion. But saviours, books, prophets, ceremonials etc. have their places. They may help many as Kali worship help me in my *secular work*. They are welcome.

Vol. 8, Epistles (Fourth Series), CLXXXI, p. 523

The vast mass of mankind is born in some church or temple of [some religious] form and never comes out of it. Why? Have these forms helped the growth of spirituality? If through these forms we step onto the highest platform of love, where forms vanish and all these sectarian ideas go away, how is it that the vast majority of men are always grovelling in some form or another? They are all atheists; they do not want any religion [...] Do you mean to say that those women who go to churches to show their dresses will ever have religion or will come out of forms? [...] Do you mean to say that those men who go to church to look at the beautiful faces of women will ever have religion? Those who have certain social religions—because society required that they shall belong to Mr. So-and-so's church or because that was their father's church—will they ever have religion? [...] If you want to play the fool all your life with all these churches and foolish organisations, you will have them and have to live in them all your lives [...] That drill business in the temples and churches—kneeling down at a certain time, standing at ease, and all that drill nonsense, all mechanical, with the mind thinking of something else—all this has nothing to do with real religion.

Vol. 9, Lectures and Discourses, Bhakti-Yoga, pp. 231–232

Always remember this, that whenever a religious system gains ground with the people at large, it has a strong economic side to it. It is the economic side of a religion that finds lodgement with the people at large, and never its spiritual, or philosophic, side. If you should preach the grandest philosophy in the streets for a year, you would not have a handful of followers. But you could preach the most arrant nonsense, and if it had an economic element, you would have the whole people with you.

Vol. 9, Notes of Lectures and Classes, The Gita-I, p. 277

”

Chapter 2

UNDERSTANDING AND REALIZING GOD

God is Almighty, and All-merciful. As the universe is without beginning and without end, so is God. He is love itself. One must love God. What is love? Love knows no bargaining and no fear. Love is always the giver, never the taker. It is always the highest ideal. God has no desires. If He desires, He cannot be God. His nature is unselfishness. Just as the universe is without beginning and without end, so is God. God has no purpose, because if that were so, He would be nothing better than a man, and He would be bound by it.

We must want God, but that happens when our wants and needs have gone beyond the narrow limits of the physical universe. One should give up all desires. This does not mean that you should not have all that you want, only that you should have no sense of proprietorship, because all belongs to God. Don't be attached to money. Hold it merely as a custodian for what is God's, for God is the only Giver, and all the men in the world are only shopkeepers. Name, fame and money are a terrible bondage. Be unselfish. Give love, give help, give service, give any little thing you can, but do so unconditionally, without any bartering, without any conditions. The mind can never turn towards God unless the desire for wealth and lust has gone. Possessions, learning, beauty, etc. are of practical value so long as they help us to achieve the goal of freedom.

The idea of freedom is the only true idea of salvation—freedom from everything, the senses, whether of pleasure or pain, from good as well as evil—and, more than this, freedom from death. This means that we must get away from life, because where there is life there will be death. The main thing is to want God. We want everything except God, because our ordinary wants are supplied by the external world. It is only when our necessities have gone beyond the external world that we want a supply from the internal, from God. Don't make the world the end and God the means. Today, God is being abandoned by the world because He does not seem to be doing enough for the world. So, people say, 'Of what good is He?' Shall we look upon God as a mere municipal authority?

One cannot realize God without renunciation. The test of progress is the amount of renunciation. In any case, it is a fallacy to believe that a time will come when all the miseries of life will cease, and only its joys and pleasures will remain, and this earth will become a heaven. The idea of heaven after death, where the good live a life of eternal happiness, is a vain dream. Whatever anyone is doing is only in the hope of gaining that Supreme Bliss. One will get hard knocks along the way, and it may take many incarnations to do so. Those who never rise higher than hedonistic pleasures need many more births and reincarnations to feel even the faintest necessity of anything higher.

There are various ways of reaching God. They do not conflict with one another. Different methods will suit different people. Choose your own path to realize God, depending on your nature. This is the theory of Ishta, and that way which is ours we call our own Ishta. For a worker or an active man, the path is that of unselfishness and good deeds (Karma-Yoga); for the emotional man, that of devotion and love (Bhakti-Yoga); for the mystic, that of control of the mind (Raja-Yoga); and for the philosopher, that of knowledge and reasoning (Jnana-Yoga). These different methods are not steps that necessarily have to be taken one after another.

For most people, the path of Jnana-Yoga is very difficult. It is the highest but most difficult path. Many persons get an intellectual grasp of it, but very few attain realization. It is the Yoga for the strong, for those who are neither mystical nor devotional, but rational. They want to realize God by pure reason, to believe in nothing till they know it. The first thing is to get rid of fear. A Jnana-Yogi desires nothing, except to know. He has perfect restraint of the senses, and an intense desire for freedom. Mind control is essential for this path. Only people with exceptional minds and tremendous will can follow this path. Jnana-Yoga involves, first, hearing the truth, namely, that the Atman is the only reality and that everything else is Maya; second, reasoning upon this philosophy from all points of view; and third, giving up all further argumentation and realizing the truth.

Raja-Yoga is the instrument of religious inquiry, and is the method of investigation of religion. The chief parts are Pranayama, concentration and meditation. (Swami Vivekananda has given a detailed exposition of Raja-Yoga in his well-known and widely read book *Raja-Yoga*.)

Most people are Karma-yogis or Bhakti-yogis. Karma-Yoga is purifying the mind by means of work. Any work that is done, whether good or bad, must result in a good or bad effect. If work is done with the intention of enjoyment, it does not purify the mind. Therefore, all work should be done without any desire to enjoy the fruits thereof. One has to work unselfishly, without any desire to go to heaven, or gain name or fame or any other benefit in this world. There is no such thing as fate. Our lives are the result of our previous actions, our Karma. Good karma creates non-attachment and purifies the mind. However, each soul is not absolutely bound down by this past Karma; one ray of Divine Light can free him, and reveal to him his true nature.

As long as you see the external world, it is impossible to avoid a Personal God and a personal soul. Ordinary mortals cannot do without a Personal God. Just as a man cannot satisfy his hunger by the simple knowledge or sight of food, so a man cannot be satisfied by the knowledge or even the perception of God until love comes; therefore, love is the highest. Religion should be joyful. Asceticism cannot make us holy. Bhakti, or worship of love in some form or another, is the easiest, most pleasant and most natural way of man. The teaching of Bhakti is to make religion practical and to bring it from its high philosophical flights into the everyday lives of common people. That is the reason for the existence of the Puranas. Bhakti is the easiest way of worship. But one must have a strong thirst or desire, a mad longing, in order to realize God. Of course, this takes a long time. Religion begins when you begin to circle inwards. Anything that will help a person to attain spirituality in the material world is welcome, so long as it is moral. In all religions, prayers are not to God, but to gods. The Personal God worshipped by the Bhakta is not separate or different from the Brahman; only, the Brahman is too much of an abstraction to be loved and worshipped. We cannot know Brahman. Hence, the Bhakta chooses the relative aspect of Brahman, viz. Ishvara, the Supreme Ruler, which is the highest possible reading of the Absolute by the human mind.

Don't ask for a 'comfortable' religion. Comfort is no test of truth. On the contrary, truth is far from being 'comfortable.' One should not pray to God for trivial things that would make our lives more comfortable but for higher things, such as how to get beyond the limitations of this universe. Our explanation of the universe is only from the point of view of beings with five senses; they cannot comprehensively explain the entire universe.

Scriptures do not make us religious. Religion is attained

neither by hearing, nor by seeing or thinking. No one can make a spiritual man of you. You have to teach yourself. Your growth must come from inside. One has to follow one's heart to realize God, because the heart goes beyond the intellect and reaches what is called inspiration. Just as the intellect is the instrument of knowledge, so is the heart the instrument of inspiration. The intellect is only an inactive secondary help that is necessary to check mistakes; God can be seen only through the heart.

Nobody has seen God or has had God in his consciousness. The proof of God lies in direct perception. God is beyond our senses and our consciousness. God is in everything—in the good and in the bad, in life and in death. Where shall we go to find God if we cannot see Him in our own hearts and in every living being? He can be seen in the awesome beauty and manifestations of nature. But if you cannot see Him in everything, see Him in one thing, in that thing you like best, and then see Him in another. It is a long and perilous struggle, but you should not despair. Take your time and you will achieve your end. He who comes face to face with God, who sees God in everything, has become a Rishi. Everyone seeking salvation must pass through the stage of being a Rishi.

The more good that we do to others the more our hearts will be purified. Therefore, one should study holy and good things; respect our forefathers; help all living beings; be truthful, straightforward, righteous; show pity and compassion; not be selfish; practice Ahimsa; and be cheerful without excessive merriment.

Religion is a growth that each one of us must personally experience. Records of great spiritual men of the past do us no good except to urge us onward to do the same, to experience religion ourselves. If God came to anyone, He will also come to me. He can also speak to me today, otherwise how can I know that He has not died? I will go to God direct; let Him talk to me. Belief cannot be a basis for connecting with God—that is atheism and blasphemy.

"

What is His nature? He is everywhere, the pure and formless One, the Almighty and the All-merciful [...] And how to worship Him? Through love.

Vol. 1, At the Parliament of Religions, Paper on Hinduism, p. 11

To be an ideal householder is a much more difficult task than to be an ideal Sannyasin; the true life of work is indeed as hard as, if not harden than, the equally true life of renunciation.

Vol. 1, Karma-Yoga, Chapter III, The Secret of Work, p. 62

Unselfishness is God. One may live on a throne, in a golden palace, and be perfectly unselfish; and then he is in God. Another may live in a hut and wear rage, and have nothing in the world; yet, if he is selfish, he is intensely merged in the world.

Our various Yogas do not conflict with each other; each of them leads us to the same goal and makes us perfect. Only each has to be strenuously practised. The whole secret is in practising. First you have to hear, then think, and then practise. This is true of every Yoga [...] Are you unselfish? That is the question. If you are, you will be perfect without reading a single religious book, without going into a single church or temple. Each one of our Yogas is fitted to make man perfect even without the help of the others, because they have all the same goal in view. The Yogas of work, of wisdom, and of devotion are all capable of serving as direct and independent means for the attainment of Moksha.

Vol. 1, Karma-Yoga, Chapter VI, Non-Attachment is Complete Self-Abnegation, pp. 87–93

It is an impossible and childish desire to make the whole of infinite existence conform to the limited and conditioned existence which we know. When a man says that he will have again and again this same thing which he is having now, or, as I sometimes put it, when he asks for a *comfortable* religion, you may know that he has become so degenerate that he cannot think of anything higher than what he is now; he is just his little present surroundings and nothing more. He has forgotten his infinite nature, and his whole idea is confined to these little joys, and sorrows, and heart-jealousies of the moment. He thinks that this finite thing is the infinite; and not only so, he will not let this foolishness go. He clings on desperately unto Trishna, and the thirst after life, what the Buddhists call Tanha and Tissa. There may be millions of kinds of happiness, and beings, and laws, and progress and causation, all acting outside the little universe that we know; and, after all, the whole of this comprises but one section of our infinite nature. To acquire freedom we have to get beyond the limitations of this universe; it cannot be found here [...] But it is a most difficult thing to give up the clinging to this universe; few ever attain to that. There are two ways to do that mentioned in our books. One is called the 'Neti, Neti' (not this, not this), the other is called 'Iti' (this); the former is the negative, and the latter is the positive way. The negative way is the most difficult. It is only possible to the men of the very highest, exceptional minds and gigantic wills [...] But such people are very rare. The vast majority of mankind choose the positive way, the way through the world, making use of all the bondages themselves to break those very bondages [...] The former way of obtaining non-attachment is by reasoning, and the latter is through work and experience. The first is the path of Jnana-Yoga, and is characterised by the refusal to do any work; the second is that of Karma-Yoga, in which there is no cessation from work.

Vol. 1, Karma-Yoga, Chapter VII, Freedom, pp. 97–98

Karma-Yoga therefore is a system of ethics and religion intended to attain freedom through unselfishness, and by good works. The Karma-Yogi need not believe in any doctrine whatsoever. He many not believe even in God, may not ask what his soul is, nor think of any metaphysical speculation. He has got his own special aim of realising selflessness; and he has to work it out himself.

Vol. 1, Karma-Yoga, Chapter VIII, The Ideal of Karma-Yoga, p. 111

In all sensible religions, they never allow prayers to God; they allow prayers to gods. That is quite natural. The Roman Catholics pray to the saints; that is quite good. But to pray to God is senseless. To ask God to give you a breath of fresh air, to send down a shower of rain, to make fruits grow in your garden, and so on, is quite unnatural [...] Unto Him we must go for higher things. A fool indeed is he who, resting on the banks of the Ganga, digs a little well for water; a fool indeed is he who, living near a mine of diamonds, digs for bits of crystal. And indeed we shall be fools if we go to the Father of all mercy, for trivial earthly things. Unto Him, therefore, we shall go for light, for strength, for love.

Vol. 1, Lectures and Discourses, Reason and Religion, p. 379

Religion is not attained through the ears, nor through the eyes, nor yet through the brain. No scriptures can make us religious. We may study all the books that are in the world, yet we may not understand a word of religion or of God. We may study all the books that are in the world, yet we may not understand a word of religion or of God. We may talk all our lives and yet may not be the better for it; we may be the most intellectual people the world ever saw, and yet we may not come to God at all. On the other hand, have you not seen what irreligious men have been produced from the most intellectual training? It is one of the evils of your Western civilisation that you are after intellectual education alone, and take no care of the heart. It only makes men ten times more selfish, and that will be your destruction. When there is a conflict between the heart and the brain, let the heart be followed, because intellect has only one state, reason, and within that, intellect works, and cannot go beyond. It is the heart which takes one to the highest plane, which intellect can never reach; it goes beyond intellect, and reaches to what is called inspiration. Intellect can never become inspired; only the heart when it is enlightened becomes inspired. An intellectual, heartless man never becomes an inspired man. It is always the heart that speaks in the man of love; it discovers a greater instrument than intellect can give you, the instrument of inspiration. Just as the intellect is the instrument of knowledge, so is the heart the instrument of inspiration.

It is not at all necessary to be educated or learned to get to God. A sage once told me, 'To kill others one must be equipped with swords and shields, but to commit suicide a needle is sufficient; so to teach others, much intellect and learning are necessary, but not so for your own self-illumination.' Are you pure? If you are pure, you will reach God.

Follow the heart. A pure heart sees beyond the intellect; it gets inspired; it knows things that reason can never know, and whenever there is conflict between the pure heart and the intellect, always side with the pure heart, even if you think what your heart is doing is unreasonable.

The great truths about atoms, and the finer elements, and the fine perceptions of men, were discovered ages ago by men who never saw a telescope, or a microscope, or a laboratory. How did they know all these things? It was through the heart; they purified the heart. It is open to us to do the same today; it is the culture of the heart, really, and not that of the intellect that will lessen the misery of the world.

The field of religion is beyond our senses, beyond even our consciousness. We cannot *sense* God. Nobody has seen God with his eyes or ever will see; nobody has God in his consciousness. I am not conscious of God, nor you, nor anybody. Where is God? Where is the field of religion? It is beyond the senses, beyond consciousness [...] What is the proof of God? Direct perception, Pratyaksha. The proof of this wall is that I perceive it. God has been perceived that way by thousands before, and will be perceived by all who want to perceive Him. But this perception is no sense-perception at all; it is supersensuous, superconscious, and all this training is needed to take us beyond the senses.

Vol. 1, Lectures and Discourses, Steps to Realisation, pp. 412–416

The knowledge of man is the highest knowledge, and only by knowing man can we know God. This is also a fact that the knowledge of God is the highest knowledge, and knowing God alone we can know man. Apparently contradictory though these statements may appear, they are the necessity of human nature.

God is not to be made, for He already exists.

Vol. 1, Lectures and Discourses, Privilege, pp. 433–434

The highest worship is that of the man who loves God for God's sake. [The question may be asked:] 'Why should there be so much sorrow if there is a God?' The worshipper replies!. '[...] There is misery in the world but because of that I do not cease to love God. I do not worship Him to take away my [misery]. I love Him because He is love itself.'

If you are strong, take up the Vedanta philosophy and be independent. If you cannot do that, worship God; if not, worship some image. If you lack strength even to do that, do some good works without the idea of gain. Offer everything you have unto the service of the Lord.

Vol. 1, Lectures and Discourses, Krishna, pp. 440–443

Each one thinks his method is best. Very good! But remember, it may be good for you. One food which is very indigestible to one is very digestible to another. Because it is good for you, do not jump to the conclusion that your method is everybody's method, that Jack's coat fits John and Mary. All the uneducated, uncultured, unthinking men and women have been put into that sort of strait jacket! Think for yourselves. Become atheists! Become materialists! That would be better. Exercise the mind! [...] What right have you to say that this man's method is wrong? It may be wrong for you. That is to say, if you undertake the method, you will be degraded; but that does not mean that he will be degraded.

Vol. 1, Lectures and Discourses, The Gita III, p. 470

The greatest religion is to be true to your own nature. Have faith in yourselves! If you do not exist, how can God exist, or anybody else? Wherever you are, it is this mind that perceives even the Infinite. I see God, therefore He exists. If I cannot think of God, He does not exist [for me].

Vol. 1, Lectures and Discourses, Mohammed, p. 483

The moment you want Him, that moment you get Him.

Do not say 'God.' Do not say 'Thou.' Say 'I.'

Vol. 1, Lectures and Discourses, The Soul and God, pp. 498–500

Until you have that thirst, that desire, you cannot get religion, however you may struggle with your intellect, or your books, or your forms. Until that thirst is awakened in you, you are no better than any atheist; only the atheist is sincere, and you are not.

As soon as a man begins to believe there is a God, he becomes mad with longing to get to Him. Others may go their way, but as soon as a man is sure that there is a much higher life than that which he is leading here, as soon as he feels sure that the senses are not all, that this limited, material body is as nothing compared with the immortal, eternal, undying bliss of the Self, he becomes mad until he finds out this bliss for himself. And this madness, this thirst, this mania, is what is called the 'awakening' to religion and when that has come, a man is beginning to be religious. But it takes a long time. All these forms and ceremonies, these prayers and pilgrimages, these books, bells, candles, and priests, are the preparations: they take off the impurities from the soul. And when the soul has become pure, it naturally wants to get to the mine of all purity, God Himself.

The world is full of the talk of love, but it is hard to love. Where is love? How do you know that there is love? The first test of love is that it knows no bargaining. So long as you see a man love another only to get something from him, you know that that is not love; it is shopkeeping. Wherever there is any question of buying and selling, it is not love. So, when a man prays to God, 'Give me this, and give me that,' it is not love. How can it be? I offer you a prayer, and you give me something in return; that is what it is, mere shopkeeping.

The first test of love is that it knows no bargaining. Love is always the giver, never the taker.

The second test is that love knows no fear. So long as man thinks of God as a Being sitting above the clouds, with rewards in one hand and punishments in the other, there can be no love. Can you frighten one into love? [...] So the children of God never see in Him a punisher or a rewarder. It is only people who have never tasted of love that fear and quake.

The third is a still higher test. Love is always the highest ideal. When one has passed through the first two stages, when one has thrown off all shopkeeping, and cast off all fear, one then begins to realise that love is always the highest ideal.

Vol. 2, Bhakti or Devotion, pp. 45–49

There is one set of ideas in our mind which is always struggling to get outside through the channels of the senses, and behind that, although it may be thin and weak, there is an infinitely small voice which says, do not go outside. The two beautiful Sanskrit words for these phenomena are Pravritti and Nivritti, 'circling forward' and 'circling inward.' It is the circling forward which usually governs our actions. Religion begins with this circling inward. Religion begins with this 'do not.' Spirituality begins with this 'do not.' When the 'do not' is not there, religion has not begun. And this 'do not' came, causing men's ideas to grow, despite the fighting gods which they had worshipped.

Vol. 2, Jnana-Yoga, Maya and the Evolution of the Conception of God, pp. 108–109

In life and in death, in happiness and in misery, the Lord is equally present. The whole world is full of the Lord. Open your eyes and see Him. This is what Vedanta teaches.

It is He who is in the child, in the wife, and in the husband; it is He who is in the good and in the bad; He is in the sin and in the sinner; He is in life and in death. A tremendous assertion indeed! Yet that is the theme which the Vedanta wants to demonstrate, to teach, and to preach. This is just the opening theme.

The cause of all miseries from which we suffer is desire.

We all understand that desires are wrong, but what is meant by giving up desires? How could life go on? It would be the same suicidal advice, killing the desire and the man too. The solution is this. Not that you should not have property, not that you should not have things which are necessary and things which are even luxuries. Have all that you want, and more, only know the truth and realise it. Wealth does not belong to anybody. Have no idea of proprietorship, possessorship. You are nobody, nor am I, nor anyone else. All belongs to the Lord.

When we have given up desires, then alone shall we be able to read and enjoy this universe of God. Then everything will become deified.

Have the desire to live a long life of helpfulness, of blissfulness and activity on this earth. Thus working, you will find the way out.

Work incessantly, holding life as something deified, as God Himself, and knowing that this is all we have to do, this is all we should ask for. God is in everything, where else shall we go to find Him?

'This Self is first to be heard, then to be thought upon, and then meditated upon.' Everyone can see the sky, even the very worm crawling upon the earth sees the blue sky, but how very far away it is! So it is with our ideal. It is far away, no doubt, but at the same time we know that we must have it.

Never mind failures; they are quite natural, they are the beauty of life [...] hold the ideal a thousand times, and if you fail a thousand times, make the attempt once more.

The ideal of man is to see God in everything. But if you cannot see Him in everything, see Him in one thing, in that thing which you like best, and then see Him in another. So on you can go. There is infinite life before the soul. Take your time and you will achieve your end.

This is another great theme of the Vedanta, this Oneness of life, this Oneness of everything. [...] If you go below the surface, you find that Unity between man and man, between races and races, high and low, rich and poor, gods and men, and men and animals. If you go deep enough, all will be seen as only variations of the One, and he who has attained to this conception of Oneness has no more delusion.

Vol. 2, Jnana-Yoga, God in Everything, pp. 146–153

We see this universe as human beings, and our God is our human explanation of the universe. [...] Our explanation of the universe is not the whole of the solution. Neither does our conception cover the whole of the universe. [...] We only know the universe from the point of view of beings with five senses. Suppose we obtain another sense, the whole universe must change for us. [...] Our senses are limited, very limited indeed; and within these limitations exists what we call our universe; and our God is the solution of that universe, but that cannot be the solution of the whole problem. But man cannot stop there. He is a thinking being and wants to find a solution which will comprehensively explain all the universes.

At best, the external world is but one part of the whole of phenomena. There are other parts, the mental, the moral, and the intellectual—the various planes of existence—and to take up only one, and find a solution of the whole out of that one, is simply impossible [...]. We first, therefore, want to find somewhere a centre from which, as it were, all the other planes of existence start, and standing there we should try to find a solution. That is the proposition. And where is that centre? It is within us. The ancient sages penetrated deeper and deeper until they found that in the innermost core of the human soul is the centre of the whole universe.

The question whether there is a God or not can never be proved by argument, for the arguments are as much on one side as on the other. But if there is a God, He is in our own hearts. Have you ever seen Him?

Here is a beautiful figure. Picture the Self to be the rider and this body the chariot, the intellect to be the charioteer, mind the reins, and the senses the horses. He whose horses are well broken, and whose reins are strong and kept well in the hands of the charioteer (the intellect) reaches the goal which is the state of Him, the Omnipresent. But the man whose horses (the senses) are not controlled, nor the reins (the mind) well managed, goes to destruction. The Atman in all beings does not manifest Himself to the eyes or the senses, but those whose minds have become purified and refined realise Him. Beyond all sound, all sight, beyond form, absolute, beyond all taste and touch, infinite, without beginning and without end, even beyond nature, the Unchangeable; he who realises Him, frees himself from the jaws of death. But it is very difficult. It is, as it were, walking on the edge of a razor; the way is long and perilous, but struggle on, do not despair. Awake, arise, and stop not till the goal is reached.

Religion is possible only for those who have finished with these lower things. We must have our own experiences, must have our full run. It is only when we have finished this run that the other world opens.

The enjoyments of the senses sometimes assume another phase which is dangerous and tempting. You will always hear the idea—in very old times, in every religion—that a time will come when all the miseries of life will cease, and only its joys and pleasures will remain, and this earth will become a heaven. That I do not believe. This earth will always remain this same world. It is a most terrible thing to say, yet I do not see my way out of it.

Vol. 2, Jnana-Yoga, Realisation, pp. 155–171

The flowers that we see all around us are beautiful, beautiful is the rising of the morning sun, beautiful are the variegated hues of nature. The whole universe is beautiful, and man has been enjoying it since his appearance on earth. Sublime and awe-inspiring are the mountains; the gigantic rushing rivers rolling towards the sea, the trackless deserts, the infinite ocean, the starry heavens—all these are awe-inspiring, sublime, and beautiful indeed. The whole mass of existence that we call nature has been acting on the human mind since time immemorial. It has been acting on the thought of man, and as its reaction has come out the question: What are these, whence are they?

All the scriptures say, 'In Him we live and move and have our being.' That is why all the scriptures preach that we come from God and go back to God. Do not be frightened by theological terms; if terms frighten you, you are not fit to be philosophers. This cosmic intelligence is what the theologians call God.

All the various forms of cosmic energy, such as matter, thought, force, intelligence and so forth are simply the manifestations of that cosmic intelligence, or, as we shall call it henceforth, the Supreme Lord. Everything that you see, feel or hear, the whole universe is His creation, or to be a little more accurate, is His projection; or to be still more accurate, is the Lord Himself. It is He who is shining as the sun and the stars. He is the mother earth. He is the ocean Himself. He comes as gentle showers, He is the gentle air that we breathe in, and He it is who is working as force in the body. He is the speech that is uttered, He is the man who is talking. He is the audience that is here. He is the platform on which I stand, He is the light that enables me to see your faces. It is all He. [...] In one word, we are born of Him, we live in Him, and unto Him we return.

Vol. 2, Jnana-Yoga, The Cosmos, The Macrocosm, pp. 203–211

Nothing can be evolved which is not already there.

The whole of this life which slowly manifests itself evolves itself from the protoplasm to the perfected human being—the Incarnation of God on earth—the whole of this series is but one life, and the whole of this manifestation must have been involved in that very protoplasm. This whole life, this very God on earth, was involved in it and slowly came out, manifesting itself slowly, slowly, slowly. The highest expression must have been there in the germ state in minute form; therefore this one force, this whole chain, is the involution of that cosmic life which is everywhere. It is this one mass of intelligence which, from the protoplasm up to the most perfected man, is slowly and slowly uncoiling itself. Not that it grows. Take off all ideas of growth from your mind. With the idea of growth is associated something coming from outside, something extraneous, which would give the lie to the truth that the Infinite which lies latent in every life is independent of all external conditions. It can never grow; It was always there, and only manifests Itself.

Vol. 2, Jnana-Yoga, Immortality, pp. 227–228

So long as there is desire or want, it is a sure sign that there is imperfection. A perfect, free being cannot have any desire. God cannot want anything. If He desires, He cannot be God. He will be imperfect. So all the talk about God desiring this and that, and becoming angry and pleased by turns is babies' talk, but means nothing. Therefore it has been taught by all teachers, 'Desire nothing, give up all desires and be perfectly satisfied.'

Vol. 2, Jnana-Yoga, The Atman: its Bondage and Freedom, p. 261

It is through the heart that the Lord is seen, and not through the intellect.

Intellect is necessary, for without it we fall into crude errors and make all sorts of mistakes. Intellect checks these; but beyond that, do not try to build anything upon it. It is an inactive, secondary help; the real help is feeling, love. Do you feel for others? If you do, you are growing in oneness. If you do not feel for others, you may be the most intellectual giant ever born, but you will be nothing; you are but dry intellect, and you will remain so. And if you feel, even if you cannot read any book and do not know any language, you are in the right way. The Lord is yours.

Vol. 2, Practical Vedanta and Other Lectures,
Practical Vedanta: Part I, pp. 306–307

Even people who are thought to be great thinkers get disgusted at the idea of the Impersonal God. But to me it seems so absurd to think of God as an embodied man. Which is the higher idea, a living God, or a dead God? A God whom nobody sees, nobody knows, or a God Known? The Impersonal God is a living God, a principle. The difference between personal and impersonal is this, that the personal is only a man, and the impersonal idea is that He is the angel, the man, the animal, and yet something more which we cannot see, because impersonality includes all personalities, is the sum total of everything in the universe, and infinitely more besides.

Where shall we go to find God if we cannot see Him in our own hearts and in every living being?

The Vedanta says there is nothing that is not God.

The worship of a God in heaven and all these things are not bad, but they are only steps towards the Truth and not the Truth itself.

Do you not remember what the Bible says, 'If you cannot love your brother whom you have seen, how can you love God whom you have not seen?' If you cannot see God in the human face, how can you see him in the clouds, or in images made of dull, dead matter, or in mere fictitious stories of our brain? I shall call you religious from the day you begin to see God in men and women, and then you will understand what is meant by turning the left cheek to the man who strikes you on the right. When you see man as God, everything, even the tiger, will be welcome. Whatever comes to you is but the Lord, the Eternal, the Blessed One, appearing to us in various forms, as our father, and mother, and friend, and child—they are our own soul playing with us.

Vol. 2, Practical Vedanta and Other Lectures,
Practical Vedanta: Part II, pp. 319–326

The whole mass of the universe, taken as a unit, cannot move. In regard to what will it move? It cannot be said to change. With regard to what will it change? So the whole is the Absolute; but within it every particle is in a constant state of flux and change. It is unchangeable and changeable at the same time, Impersonal and Personal in one. This is our conception of the universe, of motion and of God, and that is what is meant by 'Thou art That.'

Vol. 2, Practical Vedanta and Other Lectures,
Practical Vedanta: Part III, p. 338

None can teach you; none can make a spiritual man of you. You have to teach yourself; your growth must come from inside.

In society we see so many different natures [...] First, there is the active man, the worker (karma yogi) [...] then there is the emotional man who loves the sublime and the beautiful to an excessive degree (bhakti yogi) [...] then there is the mystic whose mind wants to analyse its own self, to understand the workings of the human mind (raja yogi) [...] then there is the philosopher who wants to weigh everything and use his intellect even beyond the possibilities of all human philosophy (jnana yogi). A religion, to satisfy the largest proportion of mankind, must be able to supply food for all these various types of minds; and where this capability is wanting, the existing sects all become one-sided.

Vol. 2, Practical Vedanta and Other Lectures, The Ideal of a Universal Religion, pp. 385–386

All these beautiful things that we see in nature are very good, but that is not the way to see God. We must learn how to turn the eyes inwards.

Vol. 2, Practical Vedanta and Other Lectures, The Way to Blessedness, p. 411

All the forms and phases of Vedanta, either dualistic, or qualified-monistic, or monistic, first take this position that God is not only the instrumental, but also the material cause of this universe, that everything which exists is He. The second step in Vedanta is that these souls are also a part of God, one spark of that Infinite Fire [...] So far so good, but it does not satisfy. What is meant by a part of the Infinite? The Infinite is indivisible; there cannot be parts of the Infinite. The Absolute cannot be divided. What is meant, therefore, by saying that al these sparks are from Him? The Advaitist, the non-dualistic Vedantist, solves the problem by maintaining that there is really no part; that each soul is really not a part of the Infinite, but actually *is* the Infinite Brahman.

You cannot see your own face except in a mirror, and so the Self cannot see its own nature until It is reflected, and this whole universe therefore is the Self trying to realise Itself.

Vol. 3, Lectures and Discourses, The Free Soul, pp. 7–8

It has always to be understood that the Personal God worshipped by the Bhakta is not separate or different from the Brahman. All is Brahman, the One without a second; only the Brahman, as unity or absolute, is too much of an abstraction to be loved and worshipped; so the Bhakta chooses the relative aspect of Brahman, that is Ishvara, the Supreme Ruler.

Ishvara is the highest manifestation of the Absolute Reality or, in other words, the highest possible reading of the Absolute by the human mind. Creation is eternal, and so also is Ishvara.

Vol. 3, Bhakti-Yoga, The Philosophy of Ishvara, p. 37

To men who never rise higher than eating, drinking, begetting progeny, and dying, the only gain is in sense enjoyments; and they must wait and go through many more births and reincarnations to learn to feel even the faintest necessity for anything higher.

Vol. 3, Bhakti-Yoga, Spiritual Realisation, the Aim of Bhakti-Yoga, p. 43

There are two ideas of God in our scriptures—the one, the personal; and the other, the impersonal. The idea of the Personal God is that He is the omnipresent creator, preserver, and destroyer of everything, the eternal Father and Mother of the universe, but One who is eternally separate from us and from all souls; and liberation consists in coming near to Him and living in Him. Then there is the other idea of the Impersonal, where all those adjectives are taken away as superfluous, as illogical and there remains an impersonal, omnipresent Being who cannot be called a knowing being, because knowledge only belongs to the human mind. He cannot be called a thinking being, because that is a process of the weak only. He cannot be called a reasoning being, because reasoning is a sign of weakness. He cannot be called a creating being because none creates except in bondage. What bondage has He? None works except for the fulfilment of desires; what desires as He? None works except it be to supply some wants; what wants has He? In the Vedas it is not the word 'He' that is used, but 'It', for 'He' would make an invidious distinction, as if God were a man. 'It', the impersonal, is used, and this impersonal 'It' is preached. This system is called the Advaita.

It is only through the idea of the Impersonal God that you can have any system of ethics. In every nation the truth has been preached from the most ancient time—love your fellow-beings as yourselves [...] But no reason was forthcoming, no one knew the reason why it would be good to love other beings as ourselves. And the reason, why, is there in the idea of the Impersonal God; you understand it when you learn that the whole world is one—the oneness of the universe—the solidarity of all life—that in hurting anyone I am hurting myself, in loving anyone I am loving myself.

Vol. 3, Lectures from Colombo to Almora, Vedantism, pp. 128–129

As long as you see the external world, to avoid a Personal God and a personal soul is arrant lunacy. But there may be times in the lives of sages when the human mind transcends as it were its own limitations, when man goes even beyond nature [...] There the human soul transcends all limitations, and then and then alone flashes into the human soul the conception of monism: I and the whole universe are one; I and Brahman are one. And this conclusion you will find has not only been reached through knowledge and philosophy, but parts of it through the power of love.

He who realises transcendental truth, he who realises the Atman in his own nature, he who comes face to face with God, sees God alone in everything, has become a Rishi. And there is no religious life for you until you have become a Rishi. Then alone religion begins for you, now is only the preparation. Then religion dawns upon you, now you are only undergoing intellectual gymnastics and physical tortures. We must, therefore, remember that our religion lays down distinctly and clearly that everyone who wants salvation must pass through the stage of Rishihood—must become a Mantra-drastha, must see God. That is salvation; that is the law laid down by our scriptures.

Vol. 3, Lectures from Colombo to Almora,
The Work Before Us, pp. 281–284

What vain gods shall we go after and yet cannot worship the god that we see all around us, the Virat? When we have worshipped this, we shall be able to worship all other gods. Before we can crawl half a mile, we want to cross the ocean like Hanuman! It cannot be. Everyone going to be a Yogi, everyone going to meditate! It cannot be [...] What is needed is Chittashuddhi, purification of the heart. And how does that come? The first of all worship is the worship of the Virat—of those all around us. Worship It. Worship is the exact equivalent of the Sanskrit word, and no other English word will do. These are all our gods—men and animals; and the first gods we have to worship are our countrymen. These we have to worship, instead of being jealous of each other and fighting each other. It is the most terrible karma for which we are suffering, and yet it does not open our eyes!

Vol. 3, Lectures from Colombo to Almora,
The Future of India, p. 301

The ordinary man cannot do without a personal God to worship; if he does not worship a God in nature, he has to worship either a God in the shape of a wife, or a child, or a father, or a friend, or a teacher, or somebody else; and the necessity is still more upon women than men [...] We may talk, therefore, of an Impersonal Being and so forth, but so long as we are ordinary mortals, God can be seen in man alone. Our conception of God and our worship of God are, naturally, therefore, human. 'This body, indeed, is the greatest temple of God.' So we find that men have been worshipped throughout the ages, and although we may condemn or criticise some of the extravagances which naturally follow, we find at once that the heart is sound, that in spite of these extravagances, in spite of this going into extremes, there is an essence, there is a true, firm core, a backbone, to the doctrine that is preached [...] There is an essence which ought not to be lost, a reason for the existence of the Puranas, and that is the teaching of Bhakti is to make religion practical, to bring religion from its high philosophical flights into the everyday lives of our common human beings.

Everything that is conducive to the attainment of this spirituality in the material world, therefore, is to be taken hold of and brought to the use of man to evolve the spiritual being [...] If anything helps him to attain to that ideal of spirituality, welcome, so long as it is moral, because anything immoral will not help, but will only retard.

Vol. 3, Lectures from Colombo to Almora, Bhakti, pp. 387–389

People who have done a little better Karma and get a better state of mind, when they die, look upon it as Svarga and see Indra's and so forth. People still higher will see it, the very same thing, as Brahma-Loka, and the perfect ones will neither see the earth nor the heavens, nor any Loka at all. The universe will have vanished, and Brahman will be in its stead.

Can we know this Brahman? [...] Here is this universe, and even admitting that it is Brahman, can we know it? No! No! You must understand this one thing again very clearly. Again and again this doubt will come to you: If this is Brahman, how can we know it? 'By what can the knower be known?' How can the knower be known? The eyes see everything; can they see themselves? They cannot. The very fact of knowledge is a degradation. Children of the Aryans, you must remember this, for herein lies a big story. All the Western temptations that come to you, have their metaphysical bases on that one thing—there is nothing higher than sense-knowledge. In the East, we say in our Vedas that this knowledge is lower than the thing itself, because it is always a limitation. When you want to know a thing, it immediately becomes limited by your mind [...] Can you thus limit Him who is the substance of all knowledge, Him who is the Sakshi, the witness, without whom you cannot have any knowledge, Him who has no qualities, who is the Witness of the whole universe, the Witness in our own souls?

This idea we have to understand: 'How to know the knower?' The knower cannot be known, because if it were known, it will not be the knower. If you look at your eyes in a mirror, the reflection is no more your eyes, but something else, only a reflection.

Vol. 3, Lectures from Colombo to Almora, The Vedanta, pp. 417–419

He who wants to love God must get rid of extreme desires; desire nothing except God. This world is good so far as it helps one to go to the higher world. The objects of the senses are good so far as they help us to attain higher objects. We always forget that this world is a means to an end, not an end in itself. If this were the end we should be immortal here in our physical body; we should never die. But we see people every moment dying around us, and yet, foolishly, we think we shall never die; and from that conviction we come to think that this life is the goal. That is the case with ninety-nine per cent of us. This notion should be given up at once. This world is good so far as it is a means to perfect ourselves; and as soon as it has ceased to be so, it is evil. So wife, husband, children, money and learning are good so long as they help us forward, but as soon as they cease to do that, they are nothing but evil.

The mind should always go towards God [...] Instead of hearing foolish things, we must hear about God; instead of talking foolish words, we must talk of God. Instead of reading foolish books, we must read good ones which tell of God. The greatest aid to this practice of keeping God in memory is, perhaps, music.

The memory of God will not come to the selfish man. The more we come out and do good to others, the more our hearts will be purified, and God will be in them [...] First, study. A man must study every day something holy and good. Secondly, worship of God, angels, or saints, as it may be. Third, our duty to our forefathers. Fourth, our duty to human beings [...] The first of everything should go to the poor; we have only a right to what remains [...] Fifth, our duty to the lower animals [...] One portion of the food cooked in a household belong to the animals also [...] Then there is Kalyana, purity, which comprises the following: Satya, truthfulness [...] Arjava, straightforwardness, rectitude [...] Daya, pity, compassion [...] Ahimsa, not injuring any being by thought, word or deed [...] Dana, charity [...] the next is Anavasada, not desponding, cheerfulness. Despondency is not religion, whatever else it may be [...] The man who always feels miserable will never come to God [...] God is not to be reached by the weak. You must be strong; you have infinite strength within you. How else will you conquer anything? How else will you come to God? At the same time you must avoid excessive merriment, Uddharsha, as it is called. A mind in that state never becomes calm; it becomes fickle. Excessive merriment will always be followed by sorrow.

Vol. 4, Addresses on Bhakti-Yoga, The Preparation, pp. 7–11

Religion is not for the many, that is impossible. A sort of knee-drill, standing up and sitting down, may be suited for the many; but religion is for the few. There are in every country only a few hundreds who can be, and will be, religious. The others cannot be religious, because they will not be awakened, and they do not want to be. The chief thing is to *want* God. We want everything except God, because our ordinary wants are supplied by the external world; it is only when our necessities have gone beyond the external world that we want a supply from the internal, from God. So long as our needs are confined within the narrow limits of this physical universe, we cannot have any need for God; it is only when we have become satiated with everything here that we look beyond for a supply. It is only when the need is there that the demand will come. Have done with this child's play of the world as soon as you can, and then you will feel the necessity of something beyond this world, and the first step in religion will come.

Unfortunately, too often we make the world the end and God the means. We find people going to church and saying, 'God, give me such and such; God, heal my disease.' They want nice healthy bodies; and because they hear that someone will do this work for them, they go and pray to Him. It is better to be an atheist than to have such an idea of religion.

Vol. 4, Addresses on Bhakti-Yoga, The First Steps, pp. 18–21

We are by our present constitution limited and bound to see God as man [...] Two classes of men do not worship God as man—the human brute who has no religion, and the Paramahamsa (highest Yogi) who has gone beyond humanity, who has thrown off his mind and body and gone beyond the limits of nature [...] The extremely ignorant do not worship God, not being developed enough to feel the need for so doing. Those that have attained the highest knowledge also do not worship God—having realised and become one with God. God never worships God. Between these two poles of existence, if anyone tells you he is not going to worship God as man, take care of him. He is an irresponsible talker, he is mistaken; his religion is for frothy thinkers, it is intellectual nonsense.

Therefore it is absolutely necessary to worship God as man, and blessed are those races which have such a 'God-man' to worship. Christians have such a God-man in Christ. That is the natural way to see God; see God in man. All our ideas of God are concentrated there. The great limitation Christians have is that they do not heed other manifestations of God besides Christ.

He was a manifestation of God; so was Buddha; so were some others, and there will be hundreds of others. Do not limit God anywhere. Pay all the reverence that you think is due to God, to Christ; that is the only worship we can have. God cannot be worshipped; He is the immanent Being of the universe. It is only to His manifestation as man that we can pray. It would be a very good plan, when Christians pray, to say, 'in the name of Christ.' It would be wise to stop praying to God, and only pray to Christ.

Vol. 4, Addresses on Bhakti-Yoga, The Teacher of Spirituality, pp. 30–31

Religion is a long, slow process. We are all of us babies here; we may be old, and have studied all the books in the universe, but we are all spiritual babies. We have learnt the doctrines and dogmas, but realised nothing in our lives. We shall have to begin now in the concrete, through forms and words, prayers and ceremonies; and of these concrete forms there will be thousands; one form need not be for everybody. Some may be helped by images, some may not. Some require an image outside, others one inside the brain. The man who puts it inside says, 'I am a superior man. When it is inside it is all right; when it is outside, it is idolatry, I will fight it.' When a man puts an image in the form or a church or a temple, he thinks it is holy; but when it is in a human form, he objects to it!

So there are various forms through which the mind will take this concrete exercise; and then, step by step, we shall come to the abstract understanding, abstract realisation. Again, the same form is not for everyone; there is one form that will suit you, and another will suit somebody else, and so on. All forms, though leading to the same goal, may not be for all of us. Here is another mistake we generally make. My ideal does not suit you; and why should I force it on you? My fashion of building churches or reading hymns does not suit you; why should I force it on you? Go into the world and every fool will tell you that his form is the only right one, that every other form is diabolical, and he is the only chosen man ever born in the universe. But in fact, all these forms are good and helpful. Just as there are certain varieties in human nature, so it is necessary that there should be an equal number of forms in religion; and the more there are, the better for the world.

The final idea is that my religion cannot be yours, or yours mine. Although the goal and the aim are the same, yet each one has to take a different road, according to the tendencies of his mind; and although these roads are various, they must all be true, because they lead to the same goal. It cannot be that one is true and the rest not. The choosing of one's own road is called in the language of Bhakti, Ishta, the chosen way.

Vol. 4, Addresses on Bhakti-Yoga, The Need of Symbols, pp. 36–37

That way, which your nature makes it absolutely necessary for you to take, is the right way. Each one of us is born with a peculiarity of nature as the result of our past existence. Either we call it our own reincarnated past experience or a hereditary past; whatever way we may put it, we are the result of the past—that is absolutely certain, thorough whatever channels that past may have come. It naturally follows that each one of us is an effect, of which our past has been the cause; and as such, there is a peculiar movement, a peculiar train, in each one of us; and therefore each one will have to find way for himself. This way, this method, to which each of us is naturally adapted, is called the 'chosen way.' This is the theory of Ishta, and that way which is ours we call our own Ishta. For instance, one man's idea of God is that He is the omnipotent Ruler of the universe. His nature is perhaps such. He is an overbearing man who wants to rule everyone; he naturally finds God an omnipotent Ruler. Another man, who was perhaps a schoolmaster, and severe, cannot see any but a just God, a God of punishment, and so on. Each one sees God according to his own nature; and this vision, conditioned by our own nature is our Ishta.

This theory of Ishta, therefore, means allowing a man to choose his own religion. One man should not force another to worship what he worships.

The *real* work of religion must be one's own concern. I have an idea of my own, I must keep it sacred and secret, because I know that it need not be your idea. Secondly, why should I create a disturbance by wanting to tell everyone what my idea is? Other people would come and fight me. They cannot do so if I do not tell them; but if I go about telling them what my ideas are, they will all oppose me. So what is the use of talking about them? This Ishta should be kept secret, it is between you and God. All theoretical portions of religion can be preached in public and made congregational, but higher religion cannot be made public.

But I must warn you that you do not misconstrue my words into the formation of secret societies. If there were a devil, I would look for him within a secret society—as the invention of secret societies. They are diabolical schemes. The Ishta is *sacred*, not secret. But in what sense? Why should I not speak of my Ishta to others? Because it is my own most holy thing. It may help others, but how do I know that it will not rather hurt them?

Vol. 4, Addresses on Bhakti-Yoga, The Ishta, pp. 52–57

Wherever there is love, wherever there is a spark of joy, know that to be a spark of His presence because He is joy, blessedness, and love itself. Without that, there cannot be any love.

Vol. 4, Lectures and Discourses, The Great Teachers of the World, p. 129

Here is the ideal. When a man has no more self in him, no possession, nothing to call 'me' or 'mine,' has given himself entirely, destroyed himself as it were—in that man is God himself; for in him self-will is gone, crushed out, annihilated. That is the ideal man. We cannot reach that stage yet; yet, yet us worship the ideal, and slowly struggle to reach the ideal, though, maybe, with faltering steps. It may be tomorrow, or it may be a thousand years hence; but that ideal has to be reached. For it is not only the end, but also the means. To be unselfish, perfectly selfless, is salvation itself; for the man within dies, and God alone remains.

Vol. 4, Lectures and Discourses, Christ, the Messenger, p. 150

Learn humility, because he (my Master) had found that the one idea in all religions is, 'not me, but Thou' and he who says, 'not me,' the Lord fills his heart. The less of this little 'I' the more of God there is in him. That he found to be the truth in every religion of the world and he set himself to accomplish this.

Vol. 4, Lectures and Discourses, My Master, p. 174

What good is it, if we acknowledge in our prayers that God is the Father of us all, and in our daily lives do not treat every man as our brother? Books are only made so that they may point the way to a higher life; but no good results unless the path is trodden with unflinching steps!

Vol. 4, Lectures and Discourses, Indian Religious Thought, p. 191

What is the power in the human mind which says, 'It is good to do good,' which unfolds before us in glorious view the grandeur of the soul, the beauty of goodness, the all-attractive power of goodness, the infinite power of goodness? That is what we call God. Is it not?

Vol. 4, Lectures and Discourses, The Claims of Religion, p. 205

What is practical religion, then? To get to that state—freedom, the attainment of freedom. And this world, if it helps us on to that goal, [is] all right; if not—if it begins to bind one more layer on the thousands already there, it becomes an evil. Possessions, learning, beauty, everything else—as long as they help us to that goal, they are of practical value. When they have ceased helping us on to that goal of freedom, they are a positive danger. What is practical religion then? Utilise the things of this world and the next just for one goal—the attainment of freedom. Every enjoyment, every ounce of pleasure is to be bought by the expenditure of the infinite heart and mind combined.

Vol. 4, Lectures and Discourses, The Practice of Religion, p. 241

God, though everywhere, can be known to us in and through human character. No character was ever so perfect as Ramakrishna's, and that should be the centre round which we ought to rally, at the same time allowing everybody to regard him in his own light, either as God, saviour, teacher, model, or great man, just as he pleases.

Vol. 4, Writings: Prose and Poems, What We Believe In, p. 356

There is no purpose in view with God, because if there were some purpose, He would be nothing better than a man. Why should He need any purpose? If He had any, He would be bound by it.

The real happiness is God. Love is God, freedom is God; and everything that is bondage is not God.

Vol. 5, Notes from Lectures and Discourses,
Law and Freedom, pp. 287–288

The ultimate goal of all mankind, the aim an end of all religions, is but one—reunion with God [...] But while the aim is one, the method of attaining may vary with the different temperaments of men.

Both the goal and the methods employed for reaching it are called Yoga, a word derived from the same Sanskrit root as the English 'yoke', meaning 'to join', to join us to our reality, God. There are various such Yogas, or methods of union—but the chief ones are—Karma-Yoga, Bhakti-Yoga, Raja-Yoga, and Jnana-Yoga.

Every man must develop according to his own nature. As every science has its methods, so has every religion. The methods of attaining the end of religion are called Yoga by us, and the different forms of Yoga that we teach are adapted to the different natures and temperaments of men. We classify them in the following way, under four heads:

Karma-Yoga—The manner in which a man realises his own divinity through works and duty.

Bhakti-Yoga—The realisation of the divinity through devotion to, and love of, a Personal God.

Raja-Yoga—The realisation of the divinity through the control of mind.

Jnana-Yoga—The realisation of a man's own divinity through knowledge.

These are all different roads leading to the same centre—God. Indeed, the varieties of religious beliefs are an advantage, since all faiths are good, so far as they encourage man to lead a religious life. The more sects there are, the more opportunities there are for making successful appeals to the divine instinct in all men.

Vol. 5, Notes from Lectures and Discourses, The Goal and Methods of Realisation, p. 292

Ponder over it, and you will see that whatever anyone is doing, he is doing in the hope of gaining that Supreme Bliss. Only, not everyone is conscious of it and so cannot understand it. That Supreme Bliss fully exists in all, from Brahma down to the blade of grass. You are also that undivided Brahman. This very moment you can realise if you think yourself truly and absolutely to be so. It is all mere want of direct perception. That you have taken service and work so hard for the sake of your wife also shows that the aim is ultimately to attain to that Supreme Bliss of Brahman. Being again and again entangled in the intricate maze of delusion and hard hit by sorrows and afflictions, the eye will turn of itself to one's own real nature, the Inner Self. It is owing to the presence of this desire for bliss in the heart that man, getting hard shocks one after another, turns his eye inwards—to his own Self. A time is sure to come to everyone, without exception, when he will do so—to one it may be in this life, to another, after thousands of incarnations.

Vol. 5, Conversations and Dialogues, XIII, p. 393

(Q: Shri Ramakrishna used to say, Swamiji, that a man cannot progress far towards religious realisation unless he first relinquishes Kama-Kanchana (lust and greed). If so, what will become of householders? For their whole minds are set on these two things.

It is true that the mind can never turn to God until the desire for lust and wealth has gone from it, be the man a householder or a Sannyasin. Know this for a fact, that as long as the mind is caught in these, so long true devotion, firmness and Shraddha (faith) can never come.

(Q: Where will the householders be, then? What way are they to follow?)

To satisfy our smaller desires and have done with them forever, and to relinquish the greater ones by discrimination—that is the way. Without renunciation, God can never be realised [...] Sannyasins are at least struggling to make themselves ready for renunciation, whereas householders are in this matter like boatmen who work at their oars while the boat lies at anchor. Is the desire for enjoyment ever appeased? It increases ever and ever.

(Q: But was not Shri Ramakrishna wont to say, 'All these attachments vanish through the grace of God when one prays to Him?)

Yes, it is so, no doubt, through His mercy, but one needs to be pure first before one can receive His mercy—pure in thought, word, and deed; then it is that His grace descends on one.

(Q: But of what necessity is grace to him who can control himself in thought, word and deed? For then he would be able to develop himself in the path of spirituality by means of his own exertions!

The Lord is very merciful to him whom He sees struggling heart and soul for Realisation. But remain idle, without any struggle, and you will see that His grace will never come.

Vol. 5, Notes from Lectures and Discourses, XIV - From the Diary of a Disciple, Shri Sharat Chandra Chakravarty, pp. 396–398

This world is the great gymnasium where we come to make ourselves strong. [...] You have to grow from inside out. None can teach you, none can make you spiritual. There is no other teacher but your own soul. [...] Have charity towards all beings. Pity those who are in distress. Love all creatures. Do not be jealous of anyone. Look not to the faults of others.

Vol. 5, Sayings and Utterances, 16/20/28, p. 410

Whether men understand it or not, they are impelled by that power behind to become unselfish. That is the foundation of all morality. It is the quintessence of all ethics, preached in any language, or in any religion, or by any prophet in the world.

Vol. 6, Lectures and Discourses, The Methods and Purpose of Religion, p. 5

The book from which to learn religion is your own mind and heart.

Vol. 6, Notes of Class Talks and Lectures, Religion and Science, p. 81

Religion comes with intense self-sacrifice. Desire nothing for yourself. Do all for others.

Vol. 6, Notes of Class Talks and Lectures, Religion is Self-Abnegation, p. 83

The idea of heaven must pass away. The idea of heaven after death where the good live a life of eternal happiness is a vain dream, without a particle of meaning or sense in it. Wherever there is happiness there must follow unhappiness sometime. Wherever there is pleasure there must be pain. This is absolutely certain, every action has its reaction somehow.

The idea of freedom is the only true idea of salvation—freedom from everything, the senses, whether of pleasure or pain, from good as well as evil. More than this even, we must be free from death; and to be free from death, we must be free from life. Life is but a dream of death. Where there is life, there will be death; so get away from life if you would be rid of death.

Vol. 6, Notes of Class Talks and Lectures, How to Become Free, p. 93

The idea of renunciation and sacrifice is in all religions as a means to reach God.

Vol. 6, Notes of Class Talks and Lectures, The Design Theory, p. 98

Religion is a growth. Each one must experience it himself. The Christians believe that Jesus Christ died to save man. With you it is belief in a doctrine, and this belief constitutes your salvation. With us doctrine has nothing whatever to do with salvation. Each one may believe in whatever doctrine he likes; or in no doctrine. What difference does it make to you whether Jesus Christ lived at a certain time or not? What has it to do with you that Moses saw God in the burning bush? The fact that Moses saw God in the burning bush does not constitute your seeing Him, does it? If it does, then the fact that Moses ate is enough for you; you ought to stop eating. One is just as sensible as the other. Records of great spiritual men of the past do us no good whatever except that they urge us onward to do the same, to experience religion ourselves. Whatever Christ or Moses or anybody else did does not help us in the least, except to urge us on.

Each one has a special nature peculiar to himself, which he must follow and through which he will find his way to freedom. Your teacher should be able to tell you what your particular path in nature is and to put you in it. He should know by your face where you belong and should be able to indicate it to you. You should never try to follow another's path, for that is his way, not yours. When that path is found, you have nothing to do but fold your arms, and the tide will carry you to freedom. Therefore when you find it, never swerve from it. Your way is the best for you, but that is no sign that it is the best for others.

Vol. 6, Notes of Class Talks and Lectures, Spirit and Nature, pp. 98–99

Every worship consists of prayer in the highest form. For a man who cannot make Dhyana or mental worship, Puja or ceremonial worship is necessary.

Vol. 6, Notes of Class Talks and Lectures, Notes Taken Down in Madras 1892–93, p. 110

Bhakti is intense love for God. It is the nectar of love, getting which man becomes perfect, immortal and satisfied for ever; getting which man desires no more, does not become jealous of anything, does not take pleasure in vanity; knowing which man becomes filled with spirituality, becomes calm, and finds pleasure only in God. It cannot be used to fill any desire, itself being the check to all desires.

Vol. 6, Notes of Class Talks and Lectures, Narada-Bhakti-Sutras, Chapter I, pp. 150–151

Bhakti is greater than Karma, greater than Jnana, greater than Yoga (Raja-Yoga), because Bhakti itself is its result, because Bhakti is both the means and the end (fruit).

As a man cannot satisfy his hunger by simple knowledge or sight of food, so a man cannot be satisfied by the knowledge or even the perception of God until love comes; therefore love is the highest.

Vol. 6, Notes of Class Talks and Lectures, Narada-Bhakti-Sutras, Chapter II, pp. 151–152

These, however, the Masters have said about Bhakti: one who wants this Bhakti must give up sense-enjoyments and even the company of people; day and night he must think about Bhakti and nothing else; he must go where they sing or talk of God; the principal cause of Bhakti is the mercy of a great (or free) soul; meeting with a great soul is hard to obtain, and never fails to save the soul; through the mercy of God we get such Gurus.

Evil company is always to be shunned; because it leads to lust and anger, illusion, forgetfulness of the goal, destruction of the will (lack of perseverance), and destruction of everything.

He gets across Maya who gives up all attachment, serves the great ones, lives alone, cuts the bondages of this world, goes beyond the qualities of nature, and depends upon the Lord for even his living.

He who gives up the fruits of work, he who gives up all work and the dualism of joy and misery, who gives up even the scriptures, gets that unbroken love for God.

Vol. 6, Notes of Class Talks and Lectures, Narada-Bhakti-Sutras, Chapter III, p. 152

Bhakti is the easiest way of worship. It is its own proof and does not require any other. Its nature is peace and perfect bliss. Bhakti never seeks to injure anyone or anything, not even the popular modes of worship;

Conversation about lust, or doubt of God or about one's enemies must not be listened to. Egotism, pride, etc. must be given up. If those passions cannot be controlled, place them upon God, and place all your actions on Him.

Vol. 6, Notes of Class Talks and Lectures, Narada-Bhakti-Sutras, Chapter IV, p. 153

The only way of getting our divine nature manifested is by helping others to do the same.

Vol. 6, Epistles (Second Series), LXXI, p. 319

In the world take always the position of the giver. Give everything and look for no return. Give love, give help, give service, give any little thing you can, but *keep out barter*. Make no conditions, and none will be imposed. Let us give out of our own bounty, just as God gives to us. The Lord is the only Giver, all the men in the world are only shopkeepers. Get His cheque, and it must be honoured everywhere.

Vol. 7, Inspired Talks, 19 June 1895, p. 5

Know you are the Infinite, then fear must die. Say ever, 'I and my Father are one.

Vol. 7, Inspired Talks, 23 June 1895, p. 7

After every happiness comes misery; they may be far apart or near. The more advanced the soul, the more quickly does one follow the other. *What we want is neither happiness nor misery*. Both make us forget our true nature; both are chains—one iron, one gold; behind both is the Atman, who knows neither happiness nor misery. These are *states* and states must ever change; but the nature of the Soul is bliss, peace, unchanging. We have not to get it, we have it; only wash away the dross and see it.

Vol. 7, Inspired Talks, 25 June 1895, p. 11

Knowing is only relative; we can be God, but never *know* Him. Knowledge is a lower state; Adam's fall was when he came to 'know.'

Today God is being abandoned by the world because He does not seem to be doing enough for the world. So they say, 'Of what good is He?' Shall we look upon God as a mere municipal authority?

Vol. 7, Inspired Talks, 27 June 1895, p. 17

So long as the 'skin sky' surrounds man, that is, so long as he identifies himself with his body, he cannot see God.

Vol. 7, Inspired Talks, 7 July 1895, p. 36

It is impossible to find God outside of ourselves. Our own souls contribute all the divinity that is outside of us. We are the greatest temple. The objectification is only a faint imitation of what we see within ourselves.

Concentration of the powers of the mind is our only instrument to help us see God. If you know one soul (your own), you know all souls, past, present, and to come. The will concentrates the mind, certain things excite and control this will, such as reason, love, devotion, breathing. The concentrated mind is a lamp that shows us every corner of the soul.

No one method can suit all. These different methods are not steps necessary to be taken one after another. Ceremonials are the lowest form; next God external, and after that God internal. In some cases gradation may be needed, but in many only one way is required. It would be the height of folly to say to everyone, 'You must pass through Karma and Bhakti before you can reach Jnana.'

Stick to your reason until you reach something higher; and you will know it to be higher, because it will not jar with reason. The stage beyond consciousness is inspiration (Samadhi); but never mistake hysterical trances for the real thing. It is a terrible thing to claim this inspiration falsely, to mistake instinct for inspiration. There is no external test for inspiration, we know it ourselves; our guardian against mistake is negative—the voice of reason. All religion is going beyond reason, but reason is the only guide to get there. Instinct is like ice, reason is the water, and inspiration is the subtlest form or vapour; one follows the other.

Hold your money merely as custodian for what is God's. Have no attachment for it. Let name and fame and money go; they are a terrible bondage.

Vol. 7, Inspired Talks, 20 July 1895, pp. 59-60

Religion gives you nothing new; it only takes off obstacles and let you see your Self. Sickness is the first great obstacle; a healthy body is the best instrument. Melancholy is an almost insuperable barrier. If you have once known Brahman, never after can you be melancholy. Doubt, want of perseverance, mistaken ideas are other obstacles.

Vol. 7, Inspired Talks, 21 July 1895, p. 62

To attain liberation through work, join yourself to work but without desire, looking for no result. Such work leads to knowledge, which in turn brings emancipation. To give up work before you *know*, leads to misery. Work done for the Self gives no bondage.

Vol. 7, Inspired Talks, 23 July 1895, p. 63

What you only grasp intellectually may be overthrown by a new argument; but what you realise is yours forever. Talking, talking religion is but little good. Put God behind everything—man, animal, food, work; make this a habit.

Vol. 7, Inspired Talks, 29 July 1895, p. 77

In Bhakti-yoga the first essential is to want God honestly and intensely. We want everything but God, because our ordinary desires are fulfilled by the external world. So long as our needs are confined within the limits of the physical universe, we do not feel any need for God; it is only when we have had hard blows in our lives and are disappointed with everything here that we feel the need for something higher; then we seek God.

Bhakti differs from your Western idea of religion in that Bhakti admits no elements of fear, no Being to be appeased or propitiated. There are even Bhaktas who worship God as their own child, so that there may remain no feeling even of awe or reverence. There can be no fear in true love, and so long as there is the least fear, Bhakti cannot even begin. In Bhakti there is also no place for begging or bargaining with God. The idea of asking God for anything is sacrilege to a Bhakta. He will not pray for health or wealth or even to go to heaven.

So it goes without saying that the first task in becoming a Bhakta is to give up all desires of heaven and so on. Such a heaven would be like this place, this earth, only a little better. The Christian idea of heaven is a place of intensified enjoyment. How can that be God? All this desire to go to heaven is a desire for enjoyment. This has to be given up. The love of the Bhakta must be absolutely pure and unselfish, seeking nothing for itself either here or hereafter.

Vol. 7, Inspired Talks, 31 July 1895, pp. 83–84

Until we realise God for ourselves, we can know nothing about Him. Each man is perfect by his nature; prophets have manifested this perfection, but it is potential in us. How can we understand that Moses saw God unless we too see Him? If God ever came to anyone, He will come to me. I will go to God direct; let Him talk to me. I cannot take belief as a basis; that is atheism and blasphemy. If God spake to a man in the deserts of Arabia two thousand years ago, He can also speak to me today, else how can I know that He has not died? Come to God any way you can; only come. But in coming do not push anyone down.

Vol. 7, Inspired Talks, 4 August 1895, p. 97

It will not do merely to listen to great principles. You must apply them in the practical field, turn them into constant practice. What will be the good of cramming the high sounding dicta of the scriptures? You have first to grasp the teachings of the Shastras, and then to work them out in practical life. Do you understand? This is called practical religion.

Vol. 7, Conversations and Dialogues, II, p. 117

Realisation of the truth is the essential thing. Whether you bathe in the Ganga for a thousand years or live on vegetable food for a like period, unless it helps towards the manifestation of the Self, know that it is all of no use. If on the other hand, any one can realise the Atman, without the observance of outward forms, then that very non-observance of forms is the best means. But even after the realisation of Atman, one should observe outward forms to a certain extent for setting an example to the people.

The test of progress is the amount of renunciation. Know that to be the goal. Each distinct creed is but a way to the Truth. The test of progress is the amount of renunciation that one has attained. Where you find the attraction for lust and wealth considerably diminished, to whatever creed he may belong, know that his inner spirit is awakening. The door of Self-realisation has surely opened for him. On the contrary, if you observe a thousand outward rules and quote a thousand scriptural texts, still if it has not brought the spirit of renunciation in you, know that your life is in vain.

Vol. 7, Conversations and Dialogues, XVII, pp. 210–211

The object of Jnana-Yoga is the same as that of Bhakti and Raja Yogas, but the method is different. This is the Yoga for the strong, for those who are neither mystical nor devotional, but rational. As the Bhakti-Yogi works his way to complete oneness with the Supreme through love and devotion, so the Jnana-Yogi forces his way to the realisation of God by the power of pure reason. He must be prepared to throw away all old idols, all old beliefs and superstitions, all desire for this world or another, and be determined only to find freedom. Without Jnana (knowledge), liberation cannot be ours. It consists in knowing what we really are, that we are beyond fear, beyond birth, beyond death. The highest good is the realisation of the Self. It is beyond sense, beyond thought. The *real* 'I' cannot be grasped. It is the eternal subject and can never become the object of knowledge, because knowledge is only of the related, not of the Absolute.

The first thing to be got rid of by him who would be a Jnani is fear. Fear is one of our worst enemies. Next, believe in nothing until you *know* it. Constantly tell yourself, 'I am not the body, I am not the mind, I am not thought, I am not even consciousness; I am the Atman. When you can throw away all, only the true Self will remain.

The Jnana-Yogi must be as intense as the narrowest sectarian, yet as broad as the heaven. He must absolutely control his mind, be able to be a Buddhist or a Christian, to have the power to consciously divide himself into all these different ideas and yet hold fast to the eternal harmony.

Vol. 8, Lectures And Discourses, Discourses on Jnana-Yoga, I, pp. 3–5

Religion should be the most joyful thing in the world, because it is the best. Asceticism cannot make us holy. Why should a man who loves God and who is pure be sorrowful? He should be like a happy child, be truly a child of God. The essential thing is religion is making the heart pure; the Kingdom of Heaven is within us, but only the pure in heart can see the King.

Jnana is 'creedlessness,' but that does not mean that it despises creeds. It only means that a stage above and beyond creeds has been gained. The Jnani seeks not to destroy, but to help all.

Vol. 8, Lectures and Discourses, Discourses on Jnana-Yoga, II, pp. 7–8

Jnana teaches that the world should be given up, but not on that account to be abandoned. To be *in* the world, but not *of* it, is the true test of the Sannyasin. The idea of renunciation has been in some form common to nearly all religions. Jnana demands that we look upon all alike, that we see only 'sameness.'

The Jnani has to come out of all forms, to get beyond all rules and books, and be his own book. Bound by forms, we crystallise and die. Still, othe Jnani must never condemn those who cannot yet rise above forms. He must never even think of another, 'I am holier than thou.'

These are the marks of the true Jnana-Yogi: (1) He desires nothing, save to know. (2) All his senses are under perfect restraint [...] (3) He knows that all but the One is unreal. (4) He has an intense desire for freedom. With a strong will, he fixes his mind on higher things and so attains peace.

The Jnani has to be free from all forms; he is neither a Hindu, a Buddhist, not a Christian, but he is all three. All action is renounced, given up to the Lord; then no action has power to bind. The Jnani is a tremendous rationalist; he denies everything. He tells himself day and night, 'There are no beliefs, no sacred words, no heaven, no hell, no creed, no church—there is only the Atman.' When everything has been thrown away until what cannot be thrown away is reached, that is the Self. The Jnani takes nothing for granted; he analyses by pure reason and force of will, until he reaches Nirvana which is the extinction of all relativity. No description or even conception of this state is possible. Jnana is never to be judged by any earthly result.

Vol. 8, Lectures and Discourses, Discourses on Jnana-Yoga, III, pp. 9–11

'Comfort' is no test of truth; on the contrary, truth is often far from being 'comfortable.' If one intends to really find truth, one must not cling to comfort. It is hard to let go, but the Jnani *must* do it. He must become pure, kill out all desires and cease to identify himself with the body. Then and then only, the higher truth can shine in his soul. Sacrifice is necessary, and this immolation of the lower self is the underlying truth that has made sacrifice a part of all religions. All the propitiatory offerings to the gods were but dimly understood types of the only sacrifice that is of any real value, the surrender of the apparent self, through which alone we can realise the higher Self, the Atman. The Jnani must not try to preserve the body, nor even wish to do so. He must be strong and follow truth, though the universe fall.

If there is a God, *all* can find Him. No one needs to be told it is warm; each one can discover it for himself. So it should be with God. He should be a fact in the consciousness of men.

Vol. 8, Lectures and Discourses, Discourses on Jnana-Yoga, IV, pp. 14–15

Until we give up the world manufactured by the ego, never can we enter the Kingdom of Heaven. None ever did, none ever will. To give up the world is to utterly forget the ego, to know it not at all, living in the body but not being ruled by it. This rascal ego must be obliterated [...] The more we sink the 'little self,' the more God comes. Let us get rid of the little 'I' and let only the great 'I' live in us. Our best work and our greatest influence is when we are without a thought of self.

Vol. 8, Lectures and Discourses, Discourses on Jnana-Yoga, VIII, p. 31

If you want to be spiritual, you must renounce. This is the real test. Give up this world—this nonsense of the senses. There is only one real desire: to know what is true, to be spiritual. No more materialism, no more this egoism, I must become spiritual. Strong, intense must be the desire. If a man's hands and feet were so tied that he could not move and then if a burning piece of charcoal were placed on his body, he would struggle with all his power to throw it off. When I shall have that sort of extreme desire, that restless struggle, to throw off this burning world, then the time will have come for me to glimpse the Divine Truth.

Shri Krishna says in the Gita (VII.16): 'four classes of people worship Me: the distressed, the seeker of material things, the inquirer, and the knower of truth.' People who are in distress approach God for relief. If they are ill, they worship Him to be healed; if they lose their wealth, they pray to Him to get it back. There are other people who ask Him for all kinds of things, because they are full of desires—name, fame, wealth, position and so on. They will say, 'O Virgin Mary, I will make an offering to you if I get what I want. If you are successful in granting my prayer, I will worship God and give you a part of everything.' Men not so material as that, but still with no faith in God, feel inclined to know about Him. They study philosophies, read scriptures, listen to lectures, and so on. They are the inquirers. The last class are those who worship God and know Him. All these four classes of people are good, not bad. All of them worship Him.

Vol. 8, Lectures and Discourses, Discipleship, pp. 118–120

What is immortality? How few reply, 'It is this very existence of ours!' Most people think this is all mortal and dead—that God is not here, that they will become immortal by going to heaven. They imagine that they will see God after death. But if they do not see Him here and now, they will not see Him after death.

It is evident then that until we realise ourselves as the Absolute, we cannot attain to deliverance. Yet there are various ways of attaining to this realisation. These methods have the generic name of Yoga (to join, to join ourselves to our reality). These Yogas, though divided into various groups, can principally be classed into four; and as each is only a method leading indirectly to the realisation of the Absolute, they are suited to different temperaments.

Karma-Yoga is purifying the mind by means of work. Now if any work is done, good or bad, it must produce as a result a good or bad effect; no power can stay it, once the cause is present. Therefore good action producing good Karma, and bad action, bad Karma, the soul will go on in eternal bondage without ever hoping for deliverance. Now Karma belongs only to the body or the mind, never to the Atman (Self); only it can cast a veil before the Atman. The veil cast by bad Karma is ignorance. Good karma has the power to strengthen the moral powers. And thus it creates non-attachment; it destroys the tendency towards bad Karma and thereby purifies the mind. But if the work is done with the intention of enjoyment, it then produces only that very enjoyment and does not purify the mind or Chitta. Therefore all work should be done without any desire to enjoy the fruits thereof. All fear and all desire to enjoy here or hereafter must be banished forever by the Karma Yogi. Moreover, this Karma without desire of return will destroy the selfishness, which is the root of all bondage. The watchword of the Karma-Yogi is 'not I, but Thou,' and no amount of self-sacrifice is too much for him. But he does this without any desire to go to heaven, or gain name or fame or any other benefit in this world. Although the explanation and rationale of this unselfish work is only in Jnana-Yoga, yet the natural divinity of man makes him love all sacrifice simply for the good of others, without any ulterior motive, whatever his creed or opinion. Again, with many the bondage of wealth is very great; and Karma-Yoga is absolutely necessary for them as breaking the crystallisation that has gathered round their love of money.

Next is Bhakti-Yoga. Bhakti or worship or love in some form or other is the easiest, pleasantest, and most natural way of man. The natural state of this universe is attraction; and that is surely followed by an ultimate disunion. Even so, love is the natural impetus of union in the human heart; and though itself a great cause of misery, properly directed towards the proper object, it brings deliverance. The object of Bhakti is God. Love cannot be without a subject and an object. The object of love again must be at first a being who can reciprocate our love. Therefore the God of love must be in some sense a human God. He must be a God of love. Aside from the question whether such a God exists or not, it is a fact that to those who have love in their heart this Absolute appears as a God of love, as personal.

The lower forms of worship, which embody the idea of God as a judge or punisher or someone to be obeyed through fear, do not deserve to be called love, although they are forms of worship gradually expanding into higher forms. We pass on to the consideration of love itself. We will illustrate love by a triangle, of which the first angle at the base is fearlessness. So long as there is fear, it is not love. Love banishes all fear. A mother with her baby will face a tiger to save her child. The second angle is that love never asks, never begs. The third or the apex is that love loves for the sake of love itself. Even the idea of object vanishes. Love is the only form in which love is loved. This is the highest abstraction and the same as the Absolute.

Next is Raja-Yoga. This Yoga fits in with every one of these Yogas. It fits inquirers of all classes with or without any belief, and it is the real instrument of religious inquiry. As each science has its particular method of investigation, so is this Raja-Yoga the method of religion. This science also is variously applied according to various constitutions. The chief parts are the Pranayama, concentration, and meditation. For those who believe in God, a symbolical name, such as Om or other sacred words received from a Guru, will be very helpful. Om is the greatest, meaning the Absolute. Meditating on the meaning of these holy names while repeating them is the chief practice.

Next is Jnana-Yoga. This is divided into three parts. First: hearing the truth—that the Atman is the only reality and that everything else is Maya (relativity). Second: reasoning upon this philosophy from all points of view. Third: giving up all further argumentation and realising the truth. This realisation comes from (1) being certain that Brahman is real and everything else is unreal; (2) giving up all desire for enjoyment; (3) controlling the senses and the mind; (4) intense desire to be free. Meditating on this reality always and reminding the soul of its real nature are the only ways in this Yoga. It is the highest, but most difficult. Many persons get an intellectual grasp of it, but very few attain realisation.

Vol. 8, Writings: Prose and Poems, Four Paths of Yoga, pp. 152–155

If God had spoken to Christ, Mohammed, and the Rishis of the Vedas, why did He not speak also to him, one of his children? 'Indeed, he does speak to me,' the Swami continued, 'and to all His children. We see Him all around us and are impressed continually by the boundlessness of His love, and from that love we draw the inspiration for our well-being and well-doing.

Vol. 8, Notes of Class Talks and Lectures, The Love of God-I, p. 200

There is no such thing as fate. Our lives are the result of our previous actions, our Karma. And it naturally follows that having been ourselves the makers of our Karma, we must also be able to unmake it. The whole gist of Jnana-Yoga is to show humanity the method of undoing this Karma.

Knowledge will remove all misery. Knowledge will make us free. What knowledge? Chemistry? Physics? Astronomy? Geology? They help us a little, just a little. But the chief knowledge is that of your own nature. 'Know thyself.' You must know what you are, what your real nature is. You must become conscious of that infinite nature within. Then your bondages will burst.

How to know ourselves? the question remains now. There are various ways to know this Self, but in Jnana-Yoga it takes the help of nothing but sheer intellectual reasoning. Reason alone, intellect alone, rising to spiritual perception, shows what we are. There is no question of believing. Disbelieve everything—that is the idea of the Jnani. Believe nothing and disbelieve everything—that is the first step. Dare to be a rationalist. Dare to follow reason wherever it leads you.

This method can be followed only by the boldest. Do not think that the man who believes in no church or belongs to no sect, or the man who boasts of his unbelief, is a rationalist. Not at all. In modern times it is rather bravado to do anything like that.

To be a rationalist requires more than unbelief. You must be able not only to reason, but also to follow the dictates of your reason.

The first obstruction to our following reason is our unwillingness to go to truth. We want truth to come to us. In all my travels, most people told me: 'Oh, that is not a comfortable religion you talk about. Give us a comfortable religion!'

Vol. 9, Lectures and Discourses, The First Step Towards Jnana, pp. 213–216

This giving not up your own seat is what is called Nishtha. It is not that one should hate, or even criticise, the ideals of other people; he knows they are all right. But at the same time, he must stick to his own ideal very strictly.

Take up one idea, your Ishta, and let the whole soul be devoted to it.

Of course, at the same time, we must always remember that we must recognise the Ishta of others and respect them—the other ideas of God—or else worship will degenerate into fanaticism.

Vol. 9. Lectures and Discourses, Bhakti-Yoga, pp. 223–225

This idea of one being held down fast by past Karma, or work, is all nonsense. No matter how dense one may be, or how bad, one ray of light will dissipate it all. A bale of cotton, however large, will be utterly destroyed by a spark. If a room has been dark for untold ages, a lamp will end it all. So with each soul, however benighted he may be, he is not absolutely bound down by this past Karma to work for ages to come. 'One ray of Divine Light will free him, reveal to him his true nature.'

Vol. 9, Notes of Lectures and Classes, The Gita, p. 276

”

Chapter 3

INCARNATIONS, MESSENGERS, GURUS

There are no special messengers of God. There never were, and never can be any such messengers. Great souls like Krishna, Jesus or Buddha are already free, but they take a human embodiment out of their own free will to help mankind. God is everywhere, but we can only see Him if he takes a human form. The characters and methods of great souls are mysterious and we must not judge them. These great souls are merely signposts on the way, but we cling to them and never want to move. Instead of thinking for ourselves, we want others to think for us. All great teachers of the world have declared that they came not to destroy but to fulfil. Patiently, slowly and surely, they went on applying their remedies not by denouncing and frightening people, but by gently and kindly leading them upwards. Sadly, this is frequently not understood, because their sympathy, patience and forbearance are seen as an unworthy compromise with existing popular opinions. Yet the movers and shakers of the world always have a spiritual background. People worship Incarnations like Jesus and Buddha because they are the perfect manifestations of the eternal Self. They represent God Himself in the form of man. These Avatars of Ishvara can transmit spirituality with a touch, even a mere wish. They are the highest manifestations of God through man. We cannot see God except through them.

The overwhelming majority of people require a Personal God. Only two classes of men do not worship God as man—

one, those who are extremely ignorant, because they are not developed enough to feel the need for doing so; and, two, those who have attained the highest knowledge and who have realized and become one with God. Instead of, and better than, the vain imaginations of a Personal God are living Gods on earth like Shri Krishna, Jesus and Buddha. These Messengers come with a mission and a message. They never reason what they teach, but speak directly because they see the Truth, and have a unique intense faith in themselves. They are conscious of their divinity. All their knowledge comes during a state of superconsciousness, during times in their lives when they are apparently unconscious of the external world.

Recognize all the great spiritual men and women in every age and country, and see that they are not really at variance with one another. Each of these great Messengers was destined to play only a part. None of them was born to rule the world forever, and none has yet succeeded in doing so. Each one has come to preach a great idea. Krishna's message is work, duty and non-attachment to the results of work. Buddha's message is unselfishness, and the evanescence and misery of the world. Christ's message is 'Be ready, for the Kingdom of Heaven is at hand,' or, in other words, do not delay, leave nothing for tomorrow, and get ready for the final event which may overtake you any time. Mohammed was the Prophet of equality, of the brotherhood of all Muslims, regardless of race or colour.

Neither Buddha nor Christ was perfect, but they are to be judged by their virtues, never by their defects. Jesus fell short because he did not always live up to his own highest ideal and, above all, did not give woman an equal place with man—not one was made an apostle.

It is wrong to believe that there can be only one Prophet or one Incarnation. Other and greater Prophets will come in this world, but instead of looking forward to that, it is better to take the old message, supplement it with what you have realized yourself, and become a Prophet unto others. Do not trust teachers who say that they have seen but you cannot. All the prophets and teachers can do is to give the spark that brings out spiritual truths in a person.

The idea of privilege is the bane of human life and the privilege of spirituality is the most tyrannical. All knowledge is in the soul, but it has not been manifested; perhaps because of the absence of the right opportunity or environment. In order to accelerate spiritual growth, every person needs a Guru or teacher. There is nothing higher and holier than the knowledge that is transmitted by a spiritual teacher. As soon as the soul earnestly desires to have religion, a Guru must appear, and does appear. Find the teacher, serve him as a child, open your heart to his influence, see in him God manifested. We should let go of any idea that we possess any spiritual wisdom and surrender ourselves completely to the guidance of the Guru. But there are dangers. There should be a real thirst for knowledge—and perseverance. Momentary emotions should not be mistaken for real religious yearning. Moreover, one should be careful in the choice of the Guru. It should not be a case of the blind leading the blind. A true Guru must know the spirit of the scriptures, be sinless, and have no ulterior or selfish motive for money, name or fame. The custom of hereditary Gurus, as in Bengal, is questionable. Those who twist and torture texts are not real Gurus. Generally, religion is not taught as a science of experience; but there is a small group of men, called mystics, who teach religion from experience.

"

The idea of privilege is the bane of human life [...] There is the privilege of wealth [...] There is the still subtler and more powerful privilege of intellect [...] And the last of all, and the worst, because the most tyrannical, is the privilege of spirituality. If some persons think they know more of spirituality, of God, they claim a superior privilege over everyone else [...] Where is the claim to privilege? All knowledge is in every soul, even in the most ignorant; he has not manifested it, but perhaps he has not had the opportunity, the environments were not perhaps suitable to him. When he gets the opportunity, he will manifest it. The idea that one man is born superior to another has no meaning in the Vedanta; that between two nations one is superior and the other inferior has no meaning whatsoever. Put them in the same circumstances, and see whether the same intelligence comes out or not. Before that you have no right to say that one nation is superior to another. And as to spirituality, no privilege should be claimed here. It is a privilege to serve mankind, for this is the worship of God. God is here, in all these human souls. He is the soul of man. What privilege can men ask? There are no special messengers of God, never were, and never can be. All beings, great or small, are equally manifestations of God; the difference is only in the manifestation [...] If the pride of spirituality enters into you, woe unto you. It is the most awful bondage that ever existed. Neither can wealth nor any other bondage of the human heart bind the soul so much as this. 'I am purer than others' is the most awful idea that can ever enter into the human heart. In what sense are you pure? The God in you is the God in all. If you have not known this, you have known nothing. How can there be difference? It is all one. Every being is the temple of the Most High; if you can see that, good, if not, spirituality has yet to come to you.

Vol. 1. Lectures and Discourses, Vedanta and Privilege, pp. 423–429

There are a great many similarities in the teachings of the New Testament and the Gita. The human thought goes the same way [...] I will find you the answer in the words of Krishna himself: *'Whenever virtue subsides and irreligion prevails, I come down. Again and again, I come. Therefore, whenever thou seest a great soul struggling to uplift mankind, know that I am come, and worship [...]'*

At the same time, if he comes as Jesus or as Buddha, why is there so much schism? The preachings must be followed! A Hindu devotee would say: These are the great souls; they are already free. And though free, they refuse to accept their liberation while the whole world is suffering. They come again and again, take a human embodiment and help mankind. They know from their childhood what they are and what they come for [...] They do not come through bondage like we do [...] They come out of their own free will, and cannot help having tremendous spiritual power. We cannot resist it. The vast mass of mankind is dragged into the whirlpool of spirituality, and the vibration goes on and on because one of these [great souls] gives a push. So it continues until all mankind is liberated and the play of this planet is finished. Glory unto the great souls whose lives we have been studying! They are the living gods of the world. They are the persons whom we ought to worship. If He comes to me, I can only recognise Him if He takes a human form. He is everywhere, but do we see Him? We can only see Him if He takes the limitation of man [...] If men and [...] animals are manifestations of God, these teachers of mankind are leaders, are Gurus.

Vol. 1, Lectures and Discourses, Krishna, p. 444–445

The characters of great souls are mysterious, their methods past our finding out. We must not judge them. Christ may judge Mohammed. Who are you and I? Little babies. What do we understand of these great souls? Mohammedanism] came as a message for the masses […] The first message was equality […] There is one religion—love. No more question of race, colour, [or] anything else. Join it! That practical quality carried the day […] The great message was perfectly simple. Believe in one God, the creator of heaven and earth. All was created out of nothing by Him. Ask no questions […] Their temples are like Protestant churches […] no music, no paintings, no pictures. A pulpit in the corner; on that lies the Koran. The people all stand in line. No priest, no person, no bishop […] The man who prays must stand at the side of the audience. Some parts are beautiful […]

These [great souls] are signposts on the way. That is all they are […] We cling to them; we never want to move. We do not want to think; we want others to think for us. The messengers fulfil their mission. They ask to be up and doing. A hundred years later we cling to the message and go to sleep.

Vol. 1, Lectures and Discourses, Mohammed, pp. 482–484

Remember the words of Christ: 'Ask, and it shall be given you; seek, and ye shall find; knock, and it shall be opened unto you.' These words are literally true, not figures or fiction. They were the outflow of the heart's blood of one of the greatest sons of God who have ever come to this world of ours; words which came as a fruit of realisation, from a man who had felt and realised God himself; who had spoken with God, lived with God, a hundred times more intensely than you or I see this building.

Vol. 2, Bhakti or Devotion, p. 44

The world-movers, men who bring, as it were, a mass of magnetism into the world, whose spirit works in hundreds and in thousands, whose life ignites others with a spiritual fire—such men, we always find, have that spiritual background. Their motive power came from religion.

Vol. 2, Jnana-Yoga, The Necessity of Religion, pp. 66–67

All the great teachers of the world have declared that they came not to destroy but to fulfil. Many times this has not been understood, and their forbearance has been thought to be an unworthy compromise with existing popular opinions. Even now, you occasionally hear that these prophets and great teachers were rather cowardly and dared not say and do what they thought was right; but that was not so. Fanatics little understand the infinite power of love in the hearts of these great sages who looked upon the inhabitants of this world as their children. They were the real fathers, the real gods, filled with infinite sympathy and patience for everyone; they were ready to bear and forbear. They knew how human society should grow, and patiently, slowly, surely, went on applying their remedies, not by denouncing and frightening people, but by gently and kindly leading them upwards step by step.

Vol. 2, Jnana-Yoga, Maya and the Evolution of the Conception of God, pp. 116–117

The perfect man is the highest reflection of that Being who is both subject and object. That is why man instinctively worships everything, and how perfect men are instinctively worshipped as God in every country. You may talk as you like, but it is they who are bound to be worshipped. That is why men worship Incarnations, such as Christ or Buddha. They are the most perfect manifestations of the eternal Self. They are much higher than all the conceptions of God that you or I can make.

Vol. 3, Lectures and Discourses, The Free Soul, pp. 8–9

This inadequacy of books to quicken spiritual growth is the reason why, although almost every one of us can *speak* most wonderfully on spiritual matters, when it comes to action and the living of a truly spiritual life, we find ourselves so awfully deficient. To quicken the spirit, the impulse must come from another soul. The person from whose soul such impulse comes is called the Guru—the teacher; and the person to whose soul the impulse is conveyed is called the Shishya—the student […] As soon as the soul earnestly desires to have religion, the transmitter of the religious force *must* and does appear to help that soul. When the power that attracts the light of religion in the receiving soul is full and strong, the power which answers to that attraction and sends in light does come as a matter of course. There are, however, certain great dangers in the way. There is, for instance, the danger to the receiving soul of mistaking momentary emotions for real religious yearning […] There are still greater dangers in regard to the transmitter, the Guru. There are many who, though immersed in ignorance, yet, in the pride of their hearts, fancy they know everything, and not only do not stop there, but offer to take others on their shoulders; and thus the blind leading the blind, both fall into the ditch.

Vol. 3, Bhakti-Yoga, The Need of Guru, pp. 45–47

How are we to know a teacher, then? […] When a teacher of men comes to help us, the soul will instinctively know that truth has already begun to shine upon it […] The teachers whose wisdom and truth shine like the light of the sun are the very greatest the world has known, and they are worshipped as God by the major portion of mankind. But we may get help from comparatively lesser ones also; only we ourselves do not possess intuition enough to judge properly of the man from whom we receive teaching and guidance; so there ought to be certain tests, certain conditions, for the teacher to satisfy, as there are also for the taught.

The conditions necessary for the taught are purity, a real thirst after knowledge, and perseverance. No impure soul can be really religious. Purity in thought, speech and act is absolutely necessary for anyone to be religious. As to the thirst after knowledge, it is an old law that we all get whatever we want. None of us can get anything other than what we fix or hearts upon. To pant for religion truly is a very difficult thing, not at all so easy as we generally imagine. Hearing religious talks or reading religious books is no proof yet of a real want felt in the heart; there must be a continuous struggle, a conscious fight, an unremitting grappling with our lower nature, till the higher want is actually felt and the victory is achieved. It is not a question of one or two days, of years, or of lives; the struggle may have to go on for hundreds of lifetimes. The success sometimes may come immediately, but we must be ready to wait patiently even for what may look like an infinite length of time. The student who sets out with such a spirit of perseverance will surely find success and realisation at last.

In regard to the teacher, we must see that he knows the spirit of the scriptures [...] The teacher who deals too much in words and allows the mind to be carried away by the force of words loses the spirit. It is the knowledge of the *spirit* of the scriptures alone that constitutes the true religious teacher [...] The second condition necessary in the teacher is—sinlessness [...] What religion can an impure man teach? The *sine qua non* of acquiring spiritual truth for one's self or for imparting it to others is the purity of heart and soul [...] The third condition is in regard to the motive. The teacher must not teach with any ulterior selfish motive—for money, name or fame; his work must be simply out of love, out of pure love for mankind at large [...] When you see that in your teacher these conditions are fulfilled, you are safe; if they are not, it is unsafe to allow yourself to be taught by him, for there is the great danger that, if he cannot convey goodness to your heart, he may convey wickedness [...] We cannot be taught to love, appreciate and assimilate religion everywhere and by everybody [...] Without faith, humility, submission and veneration in our hearts towards our religious teacher, there cannot be any growth of religion in us; and it is a significant fact that, where this kind of relation between the teacher and the taught prevails, there alone gigantic spiritual men are growing;

while in those countries which have neglected to keep up this kind of relation the religious teacher has become a mere lecturer, the teacher expecting his five dollars and the person taught expecting his brain to be filled with the teacher's words, and each going his own way after this much has been done.

Vol. 3, Bhakti-Yoga, Qualifications of the Aspirant and the Teacher, pp. 47–52

Higher and nobler than all ordinary ones are another set of teachers, the Avatars of Ishvara, in the world. They can transmit spirituality with a touch, even with a mere wish. The lowest and the most degraded characters become in one second saints at their command. They are the Teachers of all teachers, the highest manifestations of God through man. We cannot see God except through them. We cannot help worshipping them; and indeed they are the only ones we are bound to worship. No man can really see God except through these human manifestations. If we try to see God otherwise, we make for ourselves a hideous caricature of Him and believe the caricature of Him and believe the caricature to be no worse than the original [...] Whenever we try to think of God as He is in His absolute perfection, we invariably meet with the most miserable failure, because as long as we are men, we cannot conceive Him as anything higher than man. The time will come when we shall transcend our human nature and know Him as He is; but as long as we are men, we must worship Him in man and as man.

Vol. 3, Bhakti-Yoga, Incarnate Teachers and Incarnation, pp. 53–54

There is no man or woman who can claim to have created the Vedas. They are the embodiment of eternal principles; sages discovered them; and now and then the names of these sages are mentioned—just their names, we do not even know who or what they were. In many cases we do not know who their fathers were, and almost in every case we do not know when and where they were born. But what cared they, these sages, for their names? They were the preachers of principles, and they themselves, so far as they went, tried to become illustrations of the principles they preached. At the same time, just as our God is an Impersonal and yet a Personal God, so is our religion a most intensely impersonal one—a religion based on principles—and yet with an infinite scope for the play of persons; for what religion gives you more Incarnations, more prophets and seers, and still waits for infinitely more? The *Bhagavata* says that Incarnations are infinite, leaving ample scope for as many as you like to come. Therefore, if any one or more of these persons in India's religious history, any one or more of these Incarnations, and any one or more of our prophets are proved not to have been historical, it does not injure our religion at all; even then it remains firm as ever, because it is based upon principles, and not upon persons.

Vol. 3, The Mission of the Vedanta, p. 183

From the very earliest times, our sages have been feeling conscious of this fact that the vast majority of mankind require a personality. They must have a Personal God in some form or other. The very Buddha who declared against the existence of a Personal God had not died fifty years before his disciples manufactured a Personal God out of him. The Personal God is necessary, and at the same time we know that instead of and better than vain imaginations of a Personal God, which in ninety nine cases out of hundred are unworthy of human worship, we have in this world, living and walking in our midst, living Gods, now and then. These are more worthy of worship than any imaginary God, any creation of our imagination, that is to say, any idea of God which we can form. Shri Krishna is much greater than any idea of God which we can form. Shri Krishna is much greater than any idea of God you or I can have. Buddha is a much higher idea, a more living an idolised idea, than the ideal you or I can conceive of in our minds; and therefore it is that they always command the worship of mankind even to the exclusion of all imaginary deities. This our sages knew and therefore left it open to all Indian people to worship such great personages, such Incarnations. *Nay, the greatest of these Incarnations goes further: 'Whenever an extraordinary spiritual power is manifested by external man, know that I am there; it is from Me that that manifestation comes.'* That leaves the door open for the Hindu to worship the Incarnations of all the countries in the world [...] Ours, as I have said, is the universal religion. It is inclusive enough, it is broad enough to include all the ideals.

Vol. 3, Lectures from Colombo to Almora, The Sages of India, p. 251

There is a peculiar custom in Bengal, which they call Kula-Guru, or hereditary Guruship. 'My father was your Guru, now I shall be your Guru. My father was the Guru of your father, so shall be yours.' What is a Guru? Let us go back to the Shrutis—'He who knows the secret of the Vedas,' not bookworms, not grammarians, not Pandits in general, but he who knows the meaning [...] 'an ass laden with a load of sandalwood knows only the weight of the wood, but not its precious qualities;' so are these Pandits. We do not want such. What can they teach if they have no realisation?

The Guru is not the man who twists and tortures texts—'Different ways of throwing out words, different ways of explaining texts of the scriptures, these are for the enjoyment of the learned, not for freedom.'

Shrotriya, he who knows the secret of the Shrutis, Avrijina, the sinless, and Akamahata, unpierced by desire—he who does not want to make money by teaching you—he is the Shanta, the Sadhu, who comes as the spring which brings the leaves and blossoms to various plants but does not ask anything from the plant, for its very nature is to do good. It does good that there it is. Such is the Guru.

'Who has himself crossed this terrible ocean of life, and

without any idea of gain to himself, helps others also to cross the ocean. This is the Guru, and mark that none else can be a Guru.'

Vol. 3, Lectures from Colombo to Almora, The Vedanta in All its Phases, pp. 345–346

There is nothing higher and holier than the knowledge which comes to the soul transmitted by a spiritual teacher. If a man has become a perfect Yogi it comes by itself, but it cannot be got in books [...] Find the teacher, serve him as a child, open your heart to his influence, see in him God manifested. Our attention should be fixed on the teacher as the highest manifestation of God; and as the power of attention concentrates there, the picture of the teacher as man will melt away; the frame will vanish, and the real God will be left there [...] Such teachers are few in number, no doubt in this world, but the world is never altogether without them. The moment it is absolutely bereft of these, it will cease to be, it will become a hideous hell and will just drop. These teachers are the fair flowers of human life and keep the world going; it is the strength that is manifested from these hearts of life that keeps the bounds of society intact.

Beyond these is another set of teachers, the Christs of the world. These Teachers of all teachers represent God himself in the form of man. They are much higher; they can transmit spirituality with a touch, with a wish, which makes even the lowest and most degraded characters saints in one second. Do you not read of how they used to do these things? These are not the teachers about whom I was speaking; they are the Teachers of all teachers, the greatest manifestations of God to man; we cannot see God except through them. We cannot help worshipping them, and they are the only beings we are bound to worship.

Two classes of men do not worship God as man—the human brute who has no religion, and the Paramahamsa (highest Yogi) who has gone beyond humanity, who has thrown off his mind and body and gone beyond the limits of nature. All nature has become his Self. He has neither mind nor body, and can worship God as God, as can a Jesus or a Buddha. They did not worship God as man. The other extreme is the human brute [...] The extremely ignorant do not worship God, not being developed enough to feel the need for so doing. Those that have attained the highest knowledge also do not worship God—having realised and become one with God. God never worships God. Between these two poles of existence, if anyone tells you he is not going to worship God as man, take care of him. He is an irresponsible talker, he is mistaken; his religion is for frothy thinkers, it is intellectual nonsense.

Therefore it is absolutely necessary to worship God as man, and blessed are those races which have such a 'God-man' to worship. Christians have such a God-man in Christ; therefore cling close to Christ; never give up Christ. That is the natural way to see God; see God in man. All our ideas of God are concentrated there. The great limitation Christians have is that they do not heed other manifestations of God besides Christ. He was a manifestation of God; so was Buddha; so were some others, and there will be hundreds of others. Do not limit God anywhere. Pay all the reverence that you think is due to God, to Christ; that is the only worship we can have. God cannot be worshipped; he is the immanent Being of the universe. It is only to His manifestation as man that we can pray. It would be a very good plan, when Christians pray, to say, 'in the name of Christ.' It would be wise to stop praying to God, and only pray to Christ. God understands human failings and becomes a man to do good to humanity. 'Whenever virtue subsides and immorality prevails, then I come to help mankind,' says Krishna. He also says, 'Fools, not knowing that I, the Omnipotent and Omnipresent God of the universe, have taken this human form, deride Me and think that cannot be.' Their minds have been clouded with demonical ignorance, so they cannot see in Him the Lord of the universe.

These great Incarnations of God are to be worshipped. Not only so, they alone can be worshipped; and on the days of their birth, and on the days when they went out of this world, we ought to pay more particular reverence to them. In worshipping Christ I would rather worship Him just as He desires; on the day of His birth I would rather worship Him by fasting than by feasting—by praying. When these are thought of, these great ones, they manifest themselves in our souls, and they make us like unto them. Our whole nature changes, and we become like them.

Vol. 4, Addresses on Bhakti-Yoga, The Teacher of Spirituality, pp. 28–32

There never was a great religion or a great teacher that formed secret societies to preach God's truth.

Vol. 4, Addresses on Bhakti-Yoga, The Ishta, p. 57

Man has an idea that there can be only one religion, that there can be only one Prophet, and that there can be only one Incarnation; but that idea is not true. By studying the lives of all these great Messengers, we find that each, as it were, was destined to play a part, and a part only; that the harmony consists in the sum total, and not in one note. [...] So, not any one of these Prophets is born to rule the world forever. None has yet succeeded and none is going to be the ruler forever. Each only contributes a part; and, as to that part, it is true that in the long run every Prophet will govern the world and its destinies.

Would to God that all of us were so developed that we would not require any example, would not require any person. But that we are not; and, naturally, the vast majority of mankind have put their souls at the feet of these extraordinary personalities, the Prophets, the Incarnations of God—Incarnations worshipped by the Christians, by the Buddhists, and by the Hindus. The Mohammedans from the beginning stood against any such worship. They would have nothing to do with worshipping the Prophets or the Messengers, or paying any homage to them; but, practically, instead of one Prophet, thousands upon thousands of saints are being worshipped.

In the history of mankind [...] there come these Messengers, and that from their very birth their mission is found and formed. The whole plan is there, laid down; and you see them swerving not one inch from that. Because they come with a mission, they come with a message, they do not want to reason. Did you ever hear or read of these great Teachers, or Prophets, reasoning out what they taught? No, not one of them did so. They speak direct. Why should they reason? They see the Truth. And not only do they see it but they show it [...] in these great Teachers you will always find this sign: that they have intense faith in themselves. Such intense faith is unique, and we cannot understand it. [...] When they speak, the world is bound to listen. When they speak, each word is direct; it bursts like a bombshell [...] Sometimes they do not speak at all, but yet they convey the Truth from mind to mind. They come to give. They command, they are the Messengers; you have to receive the Command. Do you not remember in your own scriptures the authority with which Jesus speaks? [...] It runs through all his utterances, that tremendous faith in his own message. That you find in the life of all these great giants whom the world worships as its Prophets.

These great Teachers are the living Gods on this earth. Whom else should we worship? I try to get an idea of God in my mind, and I find what a false little thing I conceive; it would be a sin to worship that God. I open my eye and look at the actual life of these great ones of the earth. They are higher than any conception of God that I could ever form [...] all my best attempts at forming an idea of God would fail in every case [...] What wonder that I should fall at the feet of these men and worship them as God [...] Talking about God and the Impersonal, and this and that, is all very good; but these man-Gods are the real Gods of all nations and all races. These divine men have been worshipped and will be worshipped so long as man is man [...] The purpose and intent of what I have to say to you is this, that I have found it possible in my life to worship all of them, and to be ready for all that are yet to come [...] Recognise all the great, spiritual men and women in every age and country, and see that they are not really at variance with one another.

These great Messengers and Prophets are great and true. Why? Because each one has come to preach a great idea. Take the Prophets of India, for instance. They are the oldest of the founders of religion. We take, first, Krishna. You who have read the Gita see all through the book that the one idea is non-attachment. Remain unattached. The heart's love is due to only One. To whom? To Him who never changeth. Who is that One? It is God. Do not make the mistake of giving the heart to anything that is changing, because that is misery [...] Wherever there is love, wherever there is a spark of joy, know that to be a spark of His presence because He is joy, blessedness, and love itself. Without that there cannot be love [...] Krishna strikes another note as a teacher of intense activity. Work, work, work day and night, says the Gita. You may ask, 'Then, where is peace? If all through life I am to work like a cart-horse and die in harness, what am I here for? Krishna says, 'Yes, you will find peace. Flying from work is never the way to find peace.' Throw off your duties if you can, and go the top of a mountain; even there the mind is going—whirling, whirling, whirling [...] Therefore Krishna teaches us not to shirk our duties, but to take them up manfully, and not think of the result. The servant has no right to question. The soldier has no right to reason. Go forward and do not pay too much attention to the nature of the work you have to do. Ask your mind if you are unselfish. If you are, never mind anything, nothing can resist you! Plunge in! Do the duty at hand. And when you have done this, by degrees you will realise the Truth: 'Whosoever in the midst of intense activity finds intense peace, whosoever in the midst of the greatest peace finds the greatest activity, he is a Yogi, he is a great soul, he has arrived at perfection.' Now, you see that the result of this teaching is that all the duties of the world are sanctified. There is no duty in this world which we have any right to call menial; and each man's work is quite as good as that of the emperor on his throne.

Listen to Buddha's message—a tremendous message. It has a place in our heart. Says Buddha, 'Root out selfishness, and everything that makes you selfish. Have neither wife, child, nor family. Be not of the world; become perfectly unselfish.' [...] As soon as selfish desires arise, as soon as some selfish pursuit is followed, immediately the whole man, the real man, is gone: he is like a brute, he is a slave, he forgets his fellow men.

We find that Krishna's message has also a place for us. Without that message we cannot move at all [...] On the other hand, there is a corner in the heart for the other message: Time flies; this world is finite and all misery. With your good food, nice clothes, and your comfortable home, O sleeping man and woman, do you ever think of the millions that are starving and dying? Think of the great fact that it is all misery, misery, misery! Note the first utterance of the child: when it enters into the world, it weeps. That is the fact—the child weeps. This is a place for weeping! If we listen to the Messenger, we should not be selfish.

Behold another Messenger, He of Nazareth. He teaches, 'Be ready, for the Kingdom of Heaven is at hand.' I have pondered over the message of Krishna, and am trying to work without attachment, but sometimes I forget. Then, suddenly, comes to me the message of Buddha: 'Take care, for everything in the world is evanescent, and there is always misery in this life.' I listen to that, and I am uncertain which to accept. Then again comes, like a thunderbolt, the message: 'Be ready, for the Kingdom of Heaven is at hand.' Do not delay a moment. Leave nothing for tomorrow. Get ready for the final event, which may overtake you immediately, even now. That message, also, has a place, and we acknowledge it. We salute the Messenger, we salute the Lord.

And then comes Mohammed, the Messenger of equality. You ask, 'What good can there be in his religion? If there were no good, how could it live? The good alone lives, that alone survives; because the good alone is strong, therefore it survives [...] How could Mohammedanism have lived, had there been nothing good in its teaching? There is much good. Mohammed was the Prophet of equality, of the brotherhood of man, the brotherhood of all Mussulmans.

So we see that each Prophet, each Messenger, has a particular message. When you first listen to that message, and then look at his life, you see his whole life stands explained, radiant [...] Mohammed by his life showed that amongst Mohammedans there should be perfect equality and brotherhood. There was not question of race, caste, creed, colour, or sex [...] there you see the greatness of the Mohammedan beyond other races, showing itself in equality, perfect equality regardless of race or colour.

Will other and greater Prophets come? Certainly they will come in this world. But do not look forward to that. I should better like that each one of you became a Prophet of this real New Testament, which is made up of all the Old Testaments. Take all the old messages, supplement them with your own realisations, and become a Prophet unto others. Each one of these Teachers has been great; each has left something for us; they have been our Gods. We salute them, we are their servants; and, all the same, we salute ourselves; for if they have been Prophets and children of God, we also are the same. They reached their perfection, and we are going to attain ours now.

Vol. 4, Lectures and Discourses, The Great Teachers of the World, pp. 120–134

The impulsions from the plane of unconsciousness are what we call instinct, and when the same impulsions come from the plane of consciousness we call it reason. But there is a still higher plane, superconsciousness in man. This is apparently the same as unconsciousness, because it is beyond the plane of consciousness, but it is above consciousness and not below it. It is not instinct, it is inspiration. There is proof of it. Think of all these great prophets and sages that the world has produced, and it is well known how there will be times in their lives, moments in their existence, when they will be apparently unconscious of the external world; and all the knowledge that subsequently comes out of them, they claim, was gained during this state of existence.

Vol. 4, Lectures and Discourses, The Claims of Religion, p. 212

The one thing necessary is to be stripped of our vanities—the sense that we possess any spiritual wisdom—and to surrender ourselves completely to the guidance of our Guru. The Guru only knows what will lead us towards perfection. The Guru only knows what will lead us towards perfection. We are quite blind to it. We do not know anything.

Vol. 5, Notes from Lectures and Discourses, Who is a Real Guru?, p. 258

In Vedanta the chief advantage is that it was not the work of one single man; and therefore, unlike Buddhism, or Christianity, or Mohammedanism, the prophet or teacher did not entirely swallow up or overshadow the principles. The principles live, and the prophets, as it were, form a secondary group, unknown to Vedanta. The Upanishads speak of no particular prophet, but they speak of various prophets and prophetesses. Of course, I do not mean that it is bad that these prophets should take religious hold of a nation but it certainly is very injurious if the whole field of principles is lost sight of. We can very much agree as to principles, but not very much as to persons. The persons appeal to our emotions; and the principles, to something higher, to our calm judgement. Principles must conquer in the long run for that is the manhood of man. Emotions many times drag us down to the level of animals [...] That is the reason that, though these great personalities and prophets are tremendous motive powers for good, at the same time their lives are altogether dangerous when they lead to the disregard of the principles they represent. That has always led to fanaticism, and has deluged the world in blood. Vedanta can avoid this difficulty, because it has not one special prophet. It has many Seers, who are called Rishis or sages. Seers—that is the literal translation—those who see these truths, the Mantras. The word Mantra means 'thought out,' cogitated by the mind; and the Rishi is the seer of these thoughts. They are neither the property of particular persons, nor the exclusive property of any man or woman, however great he or she may be; nor even the exclusive property of the greatest spirits—the Buddhas or Christs—whom the world has produced. They are as much the property of a Buddha, and as much the property of the smallest worm that crawls as of the Christ, because they are universal principles. They were never created. These principles have existed throughout time; and they will exist. They are non-create—uncreated by any laws which science teaches us today. They remain covered and become discovered, but are existing through all eternity in nature. If Newton had not been born, the law of gravitation would have remained all the same and would have worked all the same. It was Newton's genius which formulated it, discovered it, brought it into consciousness, made it a conscious thing to the human race. So are these religious laws, the grand truths of spirituality. They are working all the time. If all the Vedas and the Bibles and the Korans did not exist at all, if seers and prophets had never been born, yet these laws would exist. They are only held in abeyance, and slowly but surely would work to raise the human race, to raise human nature. But they are the prophets who see them, discover them, and such prophets are discoverers in the field of spirituality. As Newton and Galileo were the prophets of physical science, so are they prophets of spirituality. They can claim no exclusive right to any one of these laws; they are the common property of all nature.

Vol. 6, Lectures and Discourses, The Methods and Purpose of Religion, pp. 7–9

Experience is the only source of knowledge. In the world, religion is the only science where there is no surety, because it is not taught as a science of experience. This should not be. There is always, however, a small group of men who teach religion from experience. They are called mystics, and these mystics in every religion speak the same tongue and teach the same truth.

Vol. 6, Notes of Class Talks and Lectures, Religion and Science, p. 81

Shri Krishna was God, incarnated to save mankind. Gopi-Lila (his disport with the cowherd maids) is the acme of the religion of love in which individuality vanishes and there is communion. It is in this Lila that Shri Krishna shows what he preaches in the Gita: 'Give up every other tie for me.' Go and take shelter under Vrindavana-Lila to understand Bhakti. On this subject a great number of books is extant. It is the religion of India. The larger number of Hindus follow Shri Krishna. (6.110–111)

Shri Krishna is the God of the poor, the beggar, the sinner, the son, the father, the wife, and of everyone. He enters intimately into all our human relations and makes everything holy and in the end brings us to salvation. He is the God who hides himself from the philosopher and the learned and reveals himself to the ignorant and the children. He is the God of faith and love and not of learning. With the Gopis, love and God were the same thing—they knew Him to be love incarnate.

Vol. 6, Notes of Class Talks and Lectures, Notes Taken Down in Madras 1892–93, pp. 110–111

These Incarnations (Krishna, Buddha, Jesus, Ramakrishna) are always conscious of their own divinity; they know it from their birth. They are like the actors, whose play is over, but who, after their work is done, return to please others. These great Ones are untouched by aught of earth; they assume our form and our limitations for a time in order to teach us; but in reality they are never limited, they are ever free [...]

Vol. 9, Inspired Talks, 19 June 1895, p. 4

Prophets preach, but the Incarnations like Jesus, Buddha, Ramakrishna, can give religion; one glance, one touch is enough. That is the power of the Holy Ghost, the 'laying on of hands'; the power was actually transmitted to the disciples by the Master—the 'chain of Guru-power.' That, the real baptism, has been handed down for untold ages.

Obey the scriptures until you are strong enough to do without them; then go beyond them. Books are not an end-all. Verification is the only proof of religious truth. Each must verify for himself; and no teacher who says, 'I have seen, but *you* cannot, is to be trusted, only that one who says, 'You can see too.' All scriptures, all truths are Vedas in all times, in all countries; because these truths are to be *seen*, and any one may discover them.

Vol. 7, Inspired Talks, 24 June 1895, pp. 8–9

Individuals who are to get freedom in this life have to live thousands of years in one lifetime. They have to be ahead of their times, but the masses can only crawl. Thus, we have Christs and Buddhas.

Vol. 7, Inspired Talks, 2 August 1895, p. 89

If Jesus Christ was not perfect, then the religion bearing his name falls to the ground. If he was perfect, then we too can become perfect.

Vol. 8, Lectures and Discourses, Discourses on Jnana-Yoga, V, p. 17

The great teachers are like bubbles as they begin—here one, there one; but in the end every creature has to be a bubble and escape. Creation, ever new, will bring new water and go through the process all over again. Buddha and Christ are the two greatest 'bubbles' the world has known. They were great souls who having realised freedom helped others to escape. Neither was perfect, but they are to be judged by their virtues, never by their defects. Jesus fell short, because he did not always live up to his own highest ideal; and above all, because he did not give woman an equal place with man. Woman did everything for him, yet not one was made an apostle. This was doubtless owing to his Semitic origin.

Vol. 8, Lectures and Discourses, Discourses on Jnana-Yoga, VII, p. 28

You cannot learn spiritual truths from my lectures. If you have learnt anything, I was only the spark that brought it out, made it flash. That is all the prophets and teachers can do. All this running after help is foolishness.

Vol. 8, Lectures and Discourses, Is Vedanta the Future Religion?, p. 131

Jesus Christ was God—the Personal God become man. He has manifested Himself many times in different forms and these alone are what you can worship. God in His absolute nature is not to be worshipped. Worshipping such God would be nonsense. We have to worship Jesus Christ, the human manifestation, as God. You cannot worship anything higher than the manifestation of God. The sooner you give up the worship of God separate from Christ, the better for you. Think of the Jehovah you manufacture and of the beautiful Christ. Any time you attempt to make a God beyond Christ, you murder the whole thing. God alone can worship God. It is not given to man, and any attempt to worship Him beyond His ordinary manifestations will be dangerous to mankind. Keep close to Christ if you want salvation; He is higher than any God you can imagine. If you think Christ was a man, do not worship Him; but as soon as you can realise that He is God, worship Him. Those who say He was a man and then worship Him commit blasphemy; there is no halfway house for you; you must take the whole strength of it. 'He that hath seen the Son hath seen the Father,' and without seeing the Son, you *cannot* see the Father. It would be only tall talk and frothy philosophy and dreams and speculations. But if you want to have a hold on spiritual life, cling close to God as manifest in Christ.

Philosophically speaking, there was no such human being living as Christ or Buddha; we saw God through them. In the Koran, Mohammed again and again repeats that Christ was never crucified, it was a semblance; no one could crucify Christ.

Vol. 8, Notes of Class Talks and Lectures,
The Divine Incarnation or Avatara, p. 190

”

Chapter 4

DIVERSITY, TOLERANCE, INTER-FAITH HARMONY

Religions have brought tremendous blessings as well as enormous horrors to mankind. Religion has brought peace and love, but also engendered hatred. It has produced brotherhood as well as enmity. It has created charitable institutions and hospitals and also spilled blood. It is important to break down the barriers between different religions in the world. There have been recurrent efforts to bring about harmony among various religions, which have mostly failed. Yet, there is need for a universal religion that has no location in place or time, that embraces everyone, that recognizes divinity in every human being, and that helps humanity to realize its own true, divine nature. Unity in variety is the plan of the universe. In an increasingly interconnected world, religion should be universal. This does not mean that there should be one universal philosophy, mythology or ritual. It is enough to recognize the natural necessity of variation; to learn that truth can be expressed in many ways, each of which is true. There should be an interchange of ideas between different races, by sending teachers to each other in order to educate humanity in the different religions of the world, with the objective of helping, sympathizing and enlightening, instead of abusing and fault-finding with other religions.

However, religious unity cannot come by the triumph of one religion and the destruction of others. It is wrong to try to convert people of other faiths to a particular religion.

People need to assimilate the spirit of the other religions, preserve their individuality and grow according to their own law of growth. In essence, all religions are sacred. They are different expressions of the same truth and teach the same foundational principles. They are not contradictory or antagonistic, but supplementary. All religions teach that the soul is eternal, but that its lustre has been dimmed and can be restored by the knowledge of God. If one were to look at the great spiritual men and women in every age and country, one can see that they are not really at variance with one another. All forms of religion, high or low, are just different stages towards God. In all religions we travel from a lesser to a higher truth, never from error to truth. Religion can manifest itself as work, devotion, mysticism, philosophy, and so on. Since people have different natures, the same religious truth requires different adaptations.

If God intended that people should follow one religion, why have so many religions come up and continue to exist? Even the proselytizing religions, viz. Christianity, Islam and Buddhism, are split into various branches. This makes it clear that none of them is fit to be the religion of the whole of mankind. If the claims of a religion that it has all the truth and that God has given it all this truth in a certain book were true, why are there, even in one religion, so many sects with their own interpretations of the same text? How can contradictory opinions be true at the same time? It is good that there are so many sects. The more sects there are, the better it is, because one religion cannot fit all circumstances. Multiple sects frustrate the tendency towards rigid sameness. Spiritual ideas must come in a language that you understand. But when sects have disputes and fights, it shows that they don't know anything about religion. All quarrels and disputes about religion, which are always over the husks and not the kernel, simply show that spirituality is not present. The religion of many liberal sects degenerates into a kind of politico-social club life. Sectarian conflicts reek of arrogance and create narrow-mindedness.

Religions should be inclusive, without any religion claiming that it has all the truth and that the others are wrong. How can one say that the whole of morality, ethics, spirituality and religion can be true from the sanction of one person only? How can anyone believe in God and yet think that only a handful of men are the guardians of truth for the rest of humanity? One universal religion would be dangerous and degenerating to man. What is needed is neither contempt nor a condescending, patronising, or niggardly expression of goodwill towards other religions but rather mutual esteem and respect. This will require all sides to make concessions. It is not enough to practise tolerance, which means that I think that you are wrong but I am allowing you to live. The watchword should be acceptance, and not exclusion. Admittedly, it will be difficult to bring harmony into religion. Do not try to disturb the faith of any man. If possible, give him a push upwards, but do not destroy what he has. Do not try to find defects in other religions. A true Christian is a true Hindu, and a true Hindu is a true Christian.

Organized religions do more harm than good, because they engender hate for other religions. The profound and noble ideas of Christianity, which some say is the direct offspring of Buddhism, have been distorted. The assertion that Christianity must be the only true religion of the world because Christian nations are prosperous is not sustainable, because the prosperity of Christian nations has been based on the conquest of other lands by bloodshed. The belief that converting to Christianity 'saves' people is mere superstition; if this were true, there would be no wickedness in Christian countries! Instead of sending missionaries to 'save' the souls of the heathen, why don't Christians do anything to save people from starvation? It is an insult to starving people to offer them religion. Christians talk of universal brotherhood, but non-Christians must go to hell! The Christian idea of heaven is a place of intensified enjoyment. How can that be God? In some places, Christian children are taught to call the Hindus 'vile' and 'wretches', and to hate non-Christians. 'Practical Christianity', that involves charity and doing good works, is not fundamental to religion. It is just kindergarten religion, and is often a cover for seeking name and fame. Baptism, that involves sprinkling some water over you, or dipping you in water while muttering formulas, is not true baptism if you remain the same. If you receive real baptism, you know you are not the body but the spirit. One other weakness of Christianity is that it has one set of rules for all. Christ was a Sannyasin, and his religion is fit for Sannyasins, for those people who hunger for righteousness and aim at perfection; its moral values are impossible and impracticable for householders.

As for Islam, so much blood has been shed and cruelty imposed on other people in the name of religion. The Muslims advanced with the Koran in one hand and the sword in the other. Islam does talk of equality and brotherhood, but it is only for the Muslims! Islam is also the only religion that has completely broken down the idea of the priest. The leader of prayer stands with his back to the people, and only the reading of the Koran may take place from the pulpit. For India, there is need for both the Vedanta brain of Hinduism and the body of Islam.

All religions originated in Asia, but even here, all religions except those of India, never went beyond the idea of God in heaven. People in the East look inward for all that is great and good. When they worship, they close their eyes and try to find God within. In the West, people look up outside to find God. For the Westerners, their religious books have been inspired; whereas with the Asians, their books have been expired, like the breath of God out of the hearts of sages. It is noteworthy that it is only religions having their own scriptures that have survived. Whereas Christianity cannot stand without Christ, Islam without Mohammed and Buddhism without Buddha, India's philosophy does not depend on any personality for its truth.

"

I am a Hindu. I am sitting in my own little well and thinking that the whole world is my little well. The Christian sits in his little well and thinks the whole world is his well. The Mohammedan sits in his little well and thinks that is the whole world. I have to thank you of America for the great attempt you are making to break down the barriers of this little world of ours, and hope that, in the future, the Lord will help you to accomplish your purpose.

Vol. 1, At the Parliament of Religions, Why We Disagree, p. 5

If there is ever to be a universal religion, it must be one which will have no location in place or time; which will be infinite like the God it will preach, and whose sun will shine upon the followers of Krishna and of Christ, on saints and sinners alike; which will not be Brahminic or Buddhistic, Christian or Mohammedan, but the sum total of all these, and still have infinite space for development; which in its catholicity will embrace in its infinite arms, and find a place for, every human being [...] It will be a religion which will have no place for persecution or intolerance in its polity, which will recognise divinity in every man and woman, and whose whole scope, whose whole force, will be created in aiding humanity to realise its own true, divine nature.

Vol. 1, At the Parliament of Religions, Paper on Hinduism, p.19

Christians must always be ready for good criticism, and I hardly think that you will mind if I make a little criticism. You

Christians, who are so fond of sending out missionaries to save the soul of the heathen—why do you not try to save their bodies from starvation? In India, during the terrible famines, thousands died from hunger, yet you Christians did nothing. You erect churches all through India, but the crying evil in the East is not religion—they have religion enough—but it is bread that the suffering millions of burning India cry out for with parched throats. They ask us for bread, but we give them stones. It is an insult to a starving people to offer them religion; it is an insult to a starving man to teach him metaphysics. In India a priest that preached for money would lose caste and be spat upon by the people. I came here to seek aid for my impoverished people, and I fully realised how difficult it was to get help for heathens from Christians in a Christian land.

Vol. 1, At the Parliament of Religions/ Religion not the Crying Need of India, p. 20

Much has been said of the common ground of religious unity. I am not going just now to venture my own theory. But if anyone here hopes that this unity will come by the triumph of any one of the religions and the destruction of the others, to him I say, 'Brother, yours is an impossible hope.' Do I wish that the Christian would become Hindu? God forbid. Do I wish that the Hindu or Buddhist would become Christian? God forbid [...] the Christian is not to become a Hindu or Buddhist, nor a Hindu or a Buddhist to become a Christian. But each must assimilate the spirit of the others and yet preserve his individuality and grow according to his own law of growth. If the Parliament of Religions has shown anything to the world it is this: It has proved that holiness, purity and charity are not the exclusive possession of any church in the world, and that every system has produced men and women of the most exalted character. In the face of this evidence, if anybody dreams of the exclusive survival of his own religion and the destruction of the others, I pity him from the bottom of my heart, and point out to him that upon the banner of every religion will soon be written, in spite of resistance: 'Help and not Fight,' 'Assimilation and not Destruction,' 'Harmony and Peace and not Dissension.'

Vol. 1, At the Parliament of Religions, Address at the Final Session, p. 24

By the study of different religions we find that in essence they are one. When I was a boy, this scepticism reached me, and it seemed for a time as if I must give up all hope of religion. But fortunately for me I studied the Christian religion, the Mohammedan, the Buddhistic, and others, and what was to my surprise to find that the same foundation principles taught by my religion were also taught by all religions.

And another fact I find in the study of the various religions of the world is that there are three different stages of ideas with regard to the soul and God. In the first place, all religions admit that, apart from the body which perishes, there is a certain part or something which does not change like the body, a part that is immutable, eternal, that never dies; but some of the later religions teach that although there is a part of us that never dies, it had a beginning. But anything that has a beginning must necessarily have an end. We—the essential part of us—never had a beginning, and will never have an end.

All the different religions which grew among different nations under varying circumstances and conditions had their origin in Asia, and the Asiatics understand them well. When they came out from the motherland, they got mixed up with errors. The most profound and noble ideas of Christianity were never understood in Europe, because the ideas and images used by the writers of the Bible were foreign to it [...] Through all the myths and mythologies by which it is surrounded it is no wonder that the people get very little of the beautiful religion of Jesus, and no wonder that they have made of it a modern shopkeeping religion.

We find that all religions teach the eternity of the soul, as well as that its lustre has been dimmed, and that its primitive purity is to be regained by the knowledge of God.

I do not deprecate the existence of sects in the world. Would to God there were twenty millions more, for the more there are, there will be a greater field for selection. What I do object to is trying to fit one religion to every case. Though all religions are essentially the same, they must have the varieties of form produced by dissimilar circumstances among different nations. We must each have our own individual religion, individual so far as the externals of it go.

Vol. 1, Lectures and Discourses, Soul, God and Religion, pp. 317–326

Truth has always been universal [...] If one religion is true, all the others must be true.

The idea of an objective God is not untrue—in fact, every idea of God, and hence every religion, is true, as each is but a different stage in the journey, the aim of which is the perfect conception of the Vedas. Hence, too, we not only tolerate, but we Hindus accept every religion, praying in the mosque of the Mohammedans, worshipping before the fire of the Zoroastrians, and kneeling before the cross of the Christians, knowing that all the religions, from the lowest fetishism to the highest absolutism, mean so many attempts of the human soul to grasp and realise the infinite, each determined by the conditions of its birth and association, and each of them marking a stage of progress. We gather all these flowers and bind them with the twine of love, making a wonderful bouquet of worship.

Vol. 1, Lectures and Discourses, The Hindu Religion, pp. 329–332

The goal of all religions is the same, but the language of the teachers differs. The attempt is to kill the false 'I,' so that the real 'I,' the Lord, will reign.

Vol. 1, Lectures and Discourses, What is Religion?, p. 342

We have to learn yet that all religions, under whatever name they may be called, either Hindu, Buddhist, Mohammedan, or Christian, have the same God, and he who derides any one of these derides his own God.

Vol. 1, Lectures and Discourses, Vedic Religious Ideals, p. 350

The moment you believe in any book as the eternal word, as sacred, no more can you question [...] Because, if you believe in the Bible as the word of God, you have no right to judge at all. The moment you judge, you think you are higher than the Bible. Then what is the use of the Bible to you?

Vol. 1, Lectures and Discourses, The Gita I, p. 453

If you want to be religious, enter not the gate of any organised religions. They do a hundred times more evil than good because they stop the growth of each one's individual development [...] Religion is only between you and your God, and no third person must come between you. Think what these organised religions have done! What Napoleon was more terrible than those religious persecutions? If you and I organise, we begin to hate every person. It is better not to love, if loving only means hating others. That is no love. That is hell! If loving your own people means hating everybody else, it is the quintessence of selfishness and brutality, and the effect is that it will make you brutes. Therefore, better die working out your own natural religion than following another's natural religion, however great it may appear to you.

Vol. 1, Lectures and Discourses, The Gita III, p. 474

All the superior religions had their growth between the Ganga and the Euphrates [...] Outside of India we will find no further development of religion beyond this idea of God in heaven. That was the highest knowledge ever obtained outside of India. There is the local heaven where he is and [where] the faithful shall go when they die [...] As far as I have seen, we should call it a very primitive idea [...] Mumbo jumbo in Africa [and] God in heaven—the same. He moves the world, and of course his will is being done everywhere.

Vol. 1, Lectures and Discourses, The Soul and God, p. 491

The very fact of these disputations and fighting among sects shows that they do not know anything about religion. Religion to them is a mere mass of frothy words, to be written in books. Each one hurries to write a big book, to make it as massive as possible, stealing his materials from every book he can lay his hands upon, and never acknowledging his indebtedness. Then he launches this book upon the world, adding to the disturbance that is already existing there.

Vol. 2, Bhakti or Devotion, p. 44

Religion must be studied on a broader basis than formerly. All narrow, limited, fighting ideas of religion have to go. All sect ideas and tribal or national ideas of religion must be given up. That each tribe or nation should have its own particular God and think that every other is wrong is a superstition that should belong to the past. All such ideas must be abandoned. As the human mind broadens, its spiritual steps broaden too. The time has already come when a man cannot record a thought without its reaching to all corners of the earth; by merely physical means, we have come into touch with the whole world; so the future religions of the world have to become as universal, as wide. The religious ideals of the future must embrace all that exists in the world and is good and great and, at the same time, have infinite scope for further development. All that was good in the past must be preserved; and the doors must be kept open for future additions.

Religions must also be inclusive, and not look down with contempt upon one another because their particular ideals of God are different. [...] And when religions have become thus broadened, their power for good will have increased a hundred-fold.

Religions, having tremendous power in them, have often done more injury to the world than good, simply on account of their narrowness and limitations. Even at the present time we find many sects and societies, with almost the same ideas, fighting each other, because one does not want to set forth those ideas in precisely the same way as another. Therefore, religions will have to broaden. Religious ideas will have to become universal, vast, and infinite; and then alone we shall have the fullest play of religion, for the power of religion has only just begun to manifest in the world. It is sometimes said that religions are dying out, that spiritual ideas are dying out of the world. To me it seems that they have just begun to grow. The power of religion, broadened and purified, is going to penetrate every part of human life. So long as religion was in the hands of a chosen few or of a body of priests, it was in temples, churches, books, dogmas, ceremonials, forms and rituals. But when we come to the real, spiritual, universal concept, then, and then alone, religion will become real and living; it will come into our very nature, live in our every movement, penetrate every pore of our society, and be infinitely more a power for good than it has ever been before.

What is needed is a fellow-feeling between the different types of religion, seeing that they all stand or fall together, a fellow-feeling which springs from mutual esteem and mutual respect, and not the condescending, patronising, niggardly expression of goodwill, unfortunately in vogue at the present time with many. And, above all, this is needed between types of religious expression coming from the study of mental phenomena—unfortunately, even now laying exclusive claim to the name of religion—and those expressions of religion whose heads, as it were, are penetrating more into the secrets of heaven though their feet are clinging to earth, I mean the so-called materialistic sciences. To bring about this harmony, both will have to make concessions, sometimes very large, nay more, sometimes painful, but each will find itself the better for the sacrifice and more advanced in truth.

Vol. 2, Jnana-Yoga, The Necessity of Religion, pp. 67–69

In this country (England) it is very difficult to become a pessimist. Everyone tells me how wonderfully the world is going on, how progressive; but what he himself is, is his own world. Old questions arise: Christianity must be the only true religion of the world, because Christian nations are prosperous! But that assertion contradicts itself, because the prosperity of the Christian nation depends on the misfortune of non-Christian nations. There must be some to prey on. Suppose the whole world were to become Christian, then the Christian nations would become poor, because there would be no non-Christian nations for them to prey upon. Thus the argument kills itself.

Vol. 2, Jnana-Yoga/ Maya and Illusion, pp. 94–95

The more selfish a man, the more immoral he is. And so also with race. That race which is bound down to itself has been the most cruel and the most wicked in the whole world. There has not been a religion that has clung to this dualism more than that founded by the Prophet of Arabia, and there has not been a religion which has shed so much blood and been so cruel to other men. In the Koran there is the doctrine that a man who does not believe these teachings should be killed; it is a mercy to kill him! And the surest way to get to heaven, where there are beautiful houris and all sorts of sense-enjoyments is by killing these unbelievers. Think of the bloodshed there has been in consequence of such beliefs!

In the religion of Christ there was little of crudeness; there is very little difference between the pure religion of Christ and that of the Vedanta. You find there the idea of oneness; but Christ also preached dualistic ideas to the people in order to give them something tangible to take hold of, to lead them up to the highest ideal. The same Prophet who preached, 'Our Father which art in heaven,' also preached, 'I and my Father are one,' and the same Prophet knew that through the 'Father in heaven' lies the way to the 'I and my Father are one.' There was only blessing and love in the religion of Christ; but as soon as crudeness crept in, it was degraded into something not much better than the religion of the Prophet of Arabia. It was crudeness indeed—this fight for the little self, this clinging on to the 'I,' not only in this life, but also in the desire for its continuance even after death. This they declare to be unselfishness; this the foundation of morality! Lord help us, if this be the foundation of morality!

Vol. 2, Practical Vedanta and Other Lectures,
Practical Vedanta: Part IV, p. 353

We find that though there is nothing that has brought to man more blessings than religion, yet at the same time, there is nothing that has brought more horror than religion. Nothing has made for more peace and love than religion; nothing has engendered fiercer hatred than religion. Nothing has made the brotherhood of man more tangible than religion; nothing has bred more bitter enmity between man and man than religion. Nothing has built more charitable institutions, more hospitals for men, and even for animals, than religion; nothing has deluged the world with more blood than religion. We know, at the same time, that there has always been an undercurrent of thought; there have been always parties of men, philosophers, students of comparative religion who have tried and are still trying to bring about harmony in the midst of all these jarring and discordant sects. As regards certain countries, these attempts have succeeded, but as regards the whole world, they have failed.

Now leaving aside dogmatic study, and taking a common-sense view of the thing, we find at the start that there is a tremendous life-power in all the great religions of the world. Some may say that they are ignorant of this, but ignorance is no excuse [...] Now, those of you that watch the movement of religious thought all over the world are perfectly aware that not one of the great religions of the world has died; not only so, each one of them is progressive. Christians are multiplying, Mohammedans are multiplying, the Hindus are gaining ground, and the Jews are also increasing, and by their spreading all over the world and increasing rapidly, the fold of Judaism is constantly expanding.

Only one religion of the world—an ancient, great religion—has dwindled away, and that is the religion of Zoroastrianism, the religion of the ancient Persians. Under the Mohammedan conquest of Persia about a hundred thousand of these people came and took shelter in India and some remained in ancient Persia. Those that were in Persia, under the constant persecution of the Mohammedans, dwindled down till there are at most only ten thousand; in India there are about eighty thousand of them, but they do not increase. Of course, there is an initial difficulty; they do not convert others to their religion. And then, this handful of persons living in India, with the pernicious custom of cousin marriage, do not multiply. With this single exception, all the great religions of the world are very ancient, not one has been formed at the present time, and that every religion of the world owes its origin to the country between the Ganga and the Euphrates; not one great religion has arisen in Europe, not one in America, not one; every religion is of Asiatic origin and belongs to that part of the world. If what the modern scientists say is true, that the survival of the fittest is the test, these religions prove by their still living that they are yet fit for some people. There is a reason why they should live, they bring good to many. Look at the Mohammedans, how they are spreading in some places in Southern Asia, and spreading like fire in Africa. The Buddhists are spreading all over Central Asia, all the time. The Hindus, like the Jews, do not convert others; still gradually, other races are coming within Hinduism and adopting the manners and customs of the Hindus and falling into line with them. Christianity, you all know, is spreading—though I am not sure that the results are equal to the energy put forth. The Christians' attempt at propaganda has one tremendous defect—and that is the defect of all Western institutions. Preaching has always been the business of the Asiatics. The Western people are grand in organisation, social institutions, armies, governments, etc.; but when it comes to preaching religion, they cannot come near the Asiatic, whose business it has been all the time, and he knows it, and he does not use too much machinery.

This then is a fact in the present history of the human race, that all these religions exist and are spreading and multiplying. Now, there is a meaning, certainly, to this; and had it been the will of an All-wise and All-merciful Creator that one of these religions should exist and the rest should die, it would have become a fact long, long ago. If it were a fact that only one of these religions is true and all the rest are false, by this time it would have covered the whole ground. But this is not so; not one has gained all the ground. All religions sometimes advance—sometimes decline [...] If the claims of a religion that it has all the truth and God has given it all this truth in a certain book were true, why are there so many sects? Fifty years do not pass before there are twenty sects founded upon the same book. If God has put all the truth in certain books, He does not give us those books in order that we may quarrel over texts. That seems to be the fact. Why is it? Even if a book were given by God which contained all the truth about religion, it would not serve the purpose because nobody could understand the book. Take the Bible, for instance, and all the sects that exist amongst Christians; each one puts its own interpretation upon the same text, and each says that it alone understand that text and all the rest are wrong. So with every religion. There are many sects among the

Mohammedans and among the Buddhists, and hundreds among the Hindus. Now, I bring these facts before you in order to show you that any attempt to bring all humanity to one method of thinking in spiritual things has been a failure and always will be a failure [...] If you and I and all who are present here were to think exactly the same thoughts, there would be no thoughts for us to think.

And why should everybody think just as we do? I do not see any reason. If I am a rational man, I should be glad they do not think just as I do. I do not want to live in a grave-like land; I want to be a man in a world of men. Thinking beings must differ; difference is the first sign of thought. If I am a thoughtful man, certainly I ought to like to live amongst thoughtful persons where there are differences of opinion.

Then arises the question: How can all these varieties be true? If one thing is true, its negation is false. How can contradictory opinions be true at the same time? This is the question which I intend to answer. But I will first ask you: Are all the religions of the world really contradictory? I do not mean the external forms in which great thoughts are clad. I do not mean the different buildings, languages, rituals, books, etc. employed in various religions, but I mean the internal soul of every religion. Every religion has a soul behind it, and that soul may differ from the soul of another religion; but are they contradictory? Do they contradict or supplement each other?—that is the question. I took up the question when I was quite a boy, and have been studying it all my life. Thinking that my conclusion may be of some help to you, I place it before you. I believe that they are not contradictory; they are supplementary. Each religion, as it were, takes up one part of the great universal truth, and spends its whole force in embodying and typifying that part of the great truth. It is, therefore, addition, not exclusion. That is the idea.

We are all looking at truth from different standpoints, which vary according to our birth, education, surroundings and so on. We are viewing truth, getting as much of it as these circumstances will permit, colouring the truth with our own heart, understanding it with our own intellect, and grasping it with our own mind. We can only know as much of truth as is related to us, as much of it as we are able to receive. This makes the difference between man and man, and occasions sometimes even contradictory ideas; yet we all belong to the same great universal truth.

And that universal religion about which philosophers and others have dreamed in every country already exists. It is here. As the universal brotherhood of man is already existing, so also is universal religion [...] If the priests and other people that have taken upon themselves the task of preaching different religions simply cease preaching for a few moments, we shall see it is there. They are disturbing it all the time, because it is to their interest. You see that priests in every country are very conservative. Why is it so? There are very few priests who lead the people; most of them are led by the people and are their slaves and servants. If you say it is dry, they say it is so; if you say it is black, they say it is black. If the people advance, the priests must advance. They cannot lag behind. So, before blaming the priests—it is the fashion to blame the priest—you ought to blame yourselves. You only get what you deserve. What would be the fate of a priest who wants to give you new and advanced ideas and lead you forward? His children would probably starve, and he would be clad in rags. He is governed by the same worldly laws as you are [...] Of course, there are exceptional souls, not cowed down by public opinion. They see the truth and truth alone they value.

The greater the number of sects, the more chance of people getting religion [...] Not only must you have the spiritual ideas, but they must come to you according to your own method. They must speak your own language, the language of your soul, and then alone they will satisfy you. When the man comes who speaks my language and gives truth in my language, I at once understand it and receive it for ever. This is a great fact.

Now from this we see that there are various grades and types of human minds and what a task religions take upon them! A man brings forth two or three doctrine and claims that his religion ought to satisfy all humanity [...] Therefore, we at once see why there has been so much narrow-mindedness, the part always claiming to be the whole; the little, finite unit always laying claim to the infinite. Think of little sects, born within a few hundred years out of fallible human brains, making this arrogant claim of knowledge of the whole of God's infinite truth! Think of the arrogance of it! If it shows anything, it is this, how vain human beings are. And it is not wonder that such claims have always failed, and by the mercy of the Lord, are always destined to fail. In this line the Mohammedans were the best off; every step forward was made with the sword—the Koran in one hand and the sword in the other: 'Take the Koran, or you must die; there is no alternative!' You know from history how phenomenal was their success; for six hundred years nothing could resist them, and then there came a time when they had to cry halt. So will it be with other religions if they follow the same methods [...] We see that these sects did not succeed in what they started out to do, which was a great blessing. Just think if one of those fanatical sects had succeeded all over the world, where would man be today? Now, the Lord be blessed that they did not succeed! Yet, each one represents a great truth; each religion represents a particular excellence—something which is its soul.

The fact that all these old religions are living today proves that they must have kept their mission intact; in spite of all their mistakes, in spite of all difficulties, in spite of all quarrels, in spite of all the incrustation of forms and figures, the heart of every one of them is sound—it is a throbbing, beating, living heart. They have not lost, any one of them, the great mission they came for. And it is splendid to study that mission. Take Mohammedanism, for instance. Christian people hate no religion in the world so much as Mohammedanism. They think it is the very worst form of religion that ever existed. As soon as a man becomes a Mohammedan, the whole of Islam receives him as a brother with open arms, without making any distinction, which no other religion does [...] Just think of that: Islam makes its followers all equal—so that, you see, is the peculiar excellence of Mohammedanism. In many places in the Koran, you find very sensual ideas of life. Never mind. What Mohammedanism comes to preach to the world is this practical brotherhood of all belonging to their faith. That is the essential part of the Mohammedan religion; and all the other ideas about heaven and of life etc. are not Mohammedanism. They are accretions.

With the Hindus you will find one national idea—spirituality. In no other religion, in no other sacred books of the world, will you find so much energy spent in defining the idea of God. They tried to define the ideal of soul so that no earthly touch might mar it. The spirit must be divine; and spirit understood as spirit must not be made into a man.

With the Christians, the central idea that has been preached by them is the same: 'Watch and pray, for the kingdom of Heaven is at hand'—which means, purify your minds and be ready! And that spirit never dies. You recollect that the Christians are, even in the darkest days, even in the most superstitious Christian countries, always trying to prepared themselves for the coming of the Lord, by trying to help others, building hospitals, and so on. So long as the Christians keep to that ideal, their religion lives.

Our watchword, then, will be acceptance, and not exclusion. Not only tolerance, for so-called tolerance is often blasphemy, and I do not believe in it. I believe in acceptance. Why should I tolerate? Toleration means that I think that you are wrong and I am just allowing you to live. Is it not blasphemy to think that you and I are allowing others to live? I accept all religions that were in the past, and worship with them all; I worship God with every one of them, in whatever form they worship Him. I shall go to the mosque of the Mohammedan; I shall enter the Christian's church and kneel before the crucifix; I shall enter the Buddhistic temple, where I shall take refuge in Buddha and in his Law. I shall go into the forest and sit down in meditation with the Hindu, who is trying to see the Light which enlightens the heart of every one. Not only shall I do these, but I shall keep my heart open for all that may come in the future. Is God's book finished? Or is it still a continuous revelation going on? It is a marvellous book—these spiritual revelations of the world. The Bible, the Vedas, the Koran, and all other sacred books are but so many pages, and an infinite number of pages remain yet to be unfolded. I would leave it open for all of them.

Vol. 2, Practical Vedanta and Other Lectures, The Way to the Realisation of a Universal Religion, pp. 360–374

Religion is the highest plane of human thought and life, and herein we find that the workings of these two forces have been most marked. The intensest love that humanity has ever known has come from religion, and the most diabolical hatred that humanity has known has also come from religion. The noblest words of peace that the world has ever heard have come from men on the religious plane, and the bitterest denunciation that the world has ever known has been uttered by religious men. The higher the object of any religion and the finer its organisation, the more remarkable are its activities. No other human motive has deluged the world with blood so much as religion; at the same time, nothing has brought into existence so many hospitals and asylums for the poor; no other human influence has taken such care, not only of humanity, but also of the lowest of animals, as religion has done. Nothing makes us so cruel as religion, and nothing makes us so tender as religion. Yet out of the midst of this din and turmoil, this strife and struggle, this hatred and jealousy of religions and sects, there have arisen, from time to time, potent voices, drowning all this noise—making themselves heard from pole to pole, as it were—proclaiming peace and harmony. Will it ever come?

To bring harmony into religion must always be difficult. Yet we will consider this problem of the harmony of religions. In every religion there are three parts—I mean in every great and recognised religion. First there is the philosophy, which presents the whole scope of that religion, setting forth its basic principles, the goal and the means of reaching it. The second part is mythology, which is philosophy made concrete. It consists of legends relating to the lives of men, or of supernatural beings, and so forth. It is the abstractions of philosophy concretised in the more or less imaginary lives of men and supernatural beings. The third part is the ritual. This is still more concrete and is made up of forms and ceremonies, various physical attitudes, flowers and incense, and many other things that appeal to the senses. In these consists the ritual. You will find that all recognised religions have these three elements. Some lay more stress on one, some on another.

Now let us take into consideration the first part, philosophy. Is there one universal philosophy? Not yet. Each religion brings out its own doctrines and insists upon them being the only true ones. And not only does it do that, but it thinks that he who does not believe in them must go to some horrible place. Some will even draw the sword to compel others to believe as they do. This is not through wickedness, but through a particular disease of the human brain called fanaticism. They are very sincere, these fanatics, the most sincere of human beings; but they are quite as irresponsible as other lunatics in the world. This disease of fanaticism is one of the most dangerous of all diseases. All the wickedness of human nature is roused by it. Anger is stirred up, nerves are strung high, and human beings become like tigers.

Is there any mythological similarity, is there any mythological harmony, any universal mythology accepted by all religions? Certainly not. All religions have their own mythology, only each of them say, 'My stories are not mere myths' […] Nobody in the world, as far as I have seen, is able to make out the fine distinction between history and mythology, as it exists in the brains of these persons. All such stories, to whatever religion they may belong, are really mythological, mixed up occasionally, it may be, with a little history.

Next come the rituals. One sect has one particular form of ritual and thinks that is holy, while the rituals of another sect are simply arrant superstition. If one sect worship a peculiar sort of symbol, another sect says, 'Oh, it is horrible!' […] So even in rituals there is no universal symbol, which can command general recognition and acceptance. Where then is any universality? How is it possible then to have a universal form of religion? That, however, already exists. And let us see what it is.

We all hear about universal brotherhood, and how societies stand up especially to preach this […] Mohammedans talk of universal brotherhood, but what comes out of that in reality? Why, anybody who is not a Mohammedan will not be admitted into the brotherhood; he will more likely have his throat cut. Christians talk of universal brotherhood; but anyone who is not a Christian must go to that place where he will be eternally barbecued. And so we go on in this world in our search for universal brotherhood and equality. When you hear such talk in the world, I would ask you to be a little reticent, to take care of yourselves, for, behind all this talk is often the intensest selfishness […] So those who are *really* workers, and *really* feel at heart the universal brotherhood of man, do not talk much, do not make little sects for universal brotherhood; but their acts, their movements, their whole life, show out clearly that they in truth possess the feeling of brotherhood for mankind, that they have love and sympathy for all. They do not speak, they *do* and they *live*. This world is too full of blustering talk. We want a little more earnest work, and less talk.

So far we see that it is hard to find any universal features in regard to religion, and yet we know that they exist. We are all human beings, but are we all equal? Certainly not. Who says we are equal? Only the lunatic. Are we equal in our brains, in our powers, in our bodies? [...] Yet we know that the doctrine of equality appeals to our heart. We are all human beings; but some are men, and some are women. Here is a black man, there is a white man; but all are men, all belong to one humanity. Various are our faces; I see no two alike, yet we are all human beings. Where is this one humanity? I find a man or a woman, either dark or fair; and among all these faces I know that there is an abstract humanity which is common to all. I may not find it when I try to grasp it, to sense it, to actualise it, yet I know for certain that it is there. If I am sure of anything, it is of this humanity which is common to us all. It is through this generalised entity that I see you as a man or a woman. So it is with this universal religion, which runs through all the various religions in the form of God; it must and does exist through eternity. 'I am the thread that runs through all these pearls,' and each pearl is a religion or even a sect thereof. Such are the different pearls, and the Lord is the thread that runs through all of them; only the majority of mankind are entirely unconscious of it.

Unity in variety is the plan of the universe. We are all men, and yet we are all distinct from one another. As a part of humanity I am one with you, and as Mr. So-and-so I am different from you. As a man you are separate from the woman; as a human being, you are one with the woman. As a man, you are separate from the animal, but as living beings, man, woman, animal, and plant are all one; and as existence, you are one with the whole universe. That universal existence is God, the ultimate Unity in the universe. In Him we are all one. At the same time, in manifestation, these differences must always remain. In our work, in our energies, as they are being manifested outside, these differences must always remain. We find then that if by the idea of a universal religion it is meant that one set of doctrines should be believed in by all mankind, it is wholly impossible. It can never be, there can never be a time when all faces will be the same. Again, if we expect that there will be one universal mythology, that is also impossible; it cannot be. Neither can there be one universal ritual. Such a state of things can never come into existence; if it ever did, the world would be destroyed, because variety is the first principle of life [...] The unity of sameness can come only when this universe is destroyed, otherwise such a thing is impossible. Not only so, it would be dangerous to have it. We must not wish that all of us should think alike. There would then be no thought to think.

What then do I mean by the ideal of a universal religion? I do not mean any one universal philosophy, or any one universal mythology, or any one universal ritual held alike by all; for I know that this world must go on working, wheel within wheel, this intricate mass of machinery, most complex, most wonderful. What can *we* do then? We can make it run smoothly, we can lessen the friction, we can grease the wheels, as it were. How? By recognising the natural necessity of variation. Just as we have recognised unity by our very nature, so we must also recognise variation. We must learn that truth may be expressed in a hundred thousand ways, and that each of these ways is true as far as it goes. We must learn that the same thing can be viewed from a hundred different standpoints, and yet be the same thing [...] Even so is it with the Lord. Through high philosophy or low, though the most exalted mythology or the grossest, through the most refined ritualism or arrant fetishism, every sect, every soul, every nation, every religion, consciously or unconsciously, is struggling upward, towards God; every vision of truth that man has, is a vision of Him and of none else.

So far it is all right theoretically. But is there any way of practically working out this harmony in religions? [...] So far, all the plans of religious harmony that have been tried, while proposing to take in all the various views of religion, have, in practice, tried to bind them all down to a few doctrines, and so have produced more new sects, fighting, struggling, and pushing against each other.

I also have my little plan. I do not know whether it will work or not, and I want to present it to you for discussion. What is my plan? In the first place I would ask mankind to recognise this maxim, 'Do not destroy.' Iconoclastic reformers do no good to the world. Break not, pull not anything down, but build. Help, if you can; if you cannot, fold your hands and stand by and see things go on. Do not injure, if you cannot render help. Say not a word against any man's convictions so far as they are sincere. Secondly, take man where he stands, and from there give him a lift. If it be true that God is the centre of all religions, and that each of us is moving towards Him along one of these radii, then it is certain that all of us *must* reach that centre. And at the centre, where all the radii meet, all our differences will cease; but until we reach there, differences there must be. All these radii converge to the same centre. One, according to his nature, travels along one of these lines, and another, along another; and if we all push onward along our own lines, we shall surely come to the centre, because 'All roads lead to Rome.'

Vol. 2, Practical Vedanta and Other Lectures, The Ideal of a Universal Religion, pp. 375–385

If there were not different religions no one religion would survive. The Christian needs his selfish religion. The Hindoo needs his own creed. Those which were founded on a book still stand. Why could not the Christian convert the Jew? Why could they not make the Persians Christians? Why not so with the Mohammedans? Why cannot any impression be made upon China or Japan? The Buddhists, the first missionary religion, have double the converts of any other religion and they did not use the sword. The Mohammedans used the most force, and they number the least of the three great missionary religions. The Mohammedans have had their day. Every day you read of Christian nations acquiring land by bloodshed. What missionaries preach against this? Why should the most bloodthirsty nations exalt an alleged religion which is not the religion of Christ? The Jews and the Arabs were the fathers of Christianity, and how have they been persecuted by the Christians! The Christians have been weighed in the balance in India and found wanting. The speaker did not wish to be unkind, but he wanted to show Christians how they looked in other eyes. The missionaries who preach the burning pit are regarded with horror. The Mohammedans rolled wave after wave over India, waving the sword, and today where are they?

Vol. 2, Reports in American Newspapers, Religious Harmony, pp. 482–483

The Hindoo's view of life is that we are here to learn; the whole happiness of life is to learn; the human soul is here to love learning and get experience. I am able to read my Bible better by your Bible, and you will learn to read your Bible the better by my Bible. If there is but one religion to be true, all the rest must be true. The same truth has manifested itself in different forms, and the forms are according to the different circumstances of the physical or mental nature of the different nations [...] We believe in both a personal and impersonal God, and that same time we believe in all the religions that were, all the religions that are, and all the religions that will be in the world. We also believe we ought not only tolerate these religions, but to accept them.

Vol. 2, Reports in American Newspapers, The Hindu View of Life, pp. 499–500

'In religion.' he said, 'she (India) has exerted a great influence on Christianity, as the very teachings of Christ would [could] be traced back to those of Buddha. He showed by quotations from the works of European and American scientists the many points of similarity between Buddha and Christ. The latter's birth, his seclusion from the world, the number of his apostles, and the very ethics of his teachings are the same as those of Buddha, living many hundred years before him. 'Is it mere chance,' the lecturer asked, 'or was Buddha's religion but the foreshadowing of that of Christ? The majority of your thinkers seem to be satisfied in the latter explanation, but there are some bold enough to say that Christianity is the direct offspring of Buddhism. The majority of your thinkers seem to be satisfied in the latter explanation, but there are some bold enough to say that Christianity is the direct offspring of Buddhism just as the earliest heresy in the Christian religion—the Monecia [Manichaean] heresy—is now universally regarded as the teaching of a sect of Buddhists. But there is more evidence that Christianity is founded in Buddhism. We find it in recently discovered inscriptions from the reign of Emperor Oshoka [Asoka] of India, about 300 B.C., who made treaties with all the Grecian kings, and whose missionaries discriminated [disseminated?] in those very parts, where, centuries after, Christianity flourished, the principles of the Buddhistic religion. Thus it is explained, why you have our doctrine of trinity, of incarnation of God, and of our ethics, and why the service in our temples is so much alike to that in your present Catholic churches, from the mass to the chant and benediction. Buddhism had all these long before you. Now use your own judgment on these premises—we Hindoos stand ready to be convinced that yours is the earlier religion, although we had ours some three hundred years before yours was even thought of.'

Vol. 2, Reports in American Newspapers, India's Gift to the World, pp. 510–511

We find, as a rule, that liberal and sympathetic sects lose the intensity of religious feeling, and in their hands religion is apt to degenerate into a kind of politico-social club life. On the other hand, intensely narrow sectaries, whilst displaying a very commendable love of their own ideals, are seen to have acquired every particle of that love by hating everyone who is not of exactly the same opinions as themselves.

Vol. 3, Bhakti-Yoga, The Chosen Ideal, p. 62

Under the circumstances existing in India, naturally many sects must appear. As a fact, we find that there are so many sects in India, and at the same time we know this mysterious fact that these sects do not quarrel with each other. The Shaivite does not say that every Vaishnavite is going to be damned, nor the Vaishnavite that every Shaivite will be damned. The Shaivite says, this is my path, and you have yours; at the end we must come together. They all know that in India. This is the theory of Ishta. It has been recognised in the most ancient times that there are various forms of worshipping God. It is also recognised that different natures require different methods. Your method of coming to God may not be my method, possibly it might hurt me. Such an idea as that there is but one way for everybody is injurious, meaningless, and entirely to be avoided. Woe unto the world when everyone is of the same religious opinion and takes to the same path. Then all religions and all thought will be destroyed. Variety is the very soul of life. When it dies out entirely, creation will die. When this variation in thought is kept up, we must exist; and we need not quarrel because of that variety. Your way is very good for you, but not for me. My way is good for me, but not for you. My way is called in Sanskrit, my 'Ishta.' Mind you, we have no quarrel with any religion in the world. We have each our Ishta. But when we see men coming and saying, 'This is the only way' and trying to force it on us in India, we have a word to say; we laugh at them. For such people who want to destroy their brothers because they seem to follow a different path towards God—for them to talk of love is absurd. Their love does not count for much. How can they preach of love who cannot bear another man to follow a different path from their own? If that is love, what is hatred?

Vol. 3, Lectures from Colombo to Almora, Vedantism, pp. 131–132

The world is waiting for this grand idea of universal tolerance. It will be a great acquisition to civilisation. Nay, no civilisation can long exist unless this idea enters into it. No civilisation can grow unless fanaticism, bloodshed, and brutality stop. No civilisation can begin to lift up its head until we look charitably upon one another; and the first step towards that much-needed charity is to look charitably and kindly upon the religious convictions of others. Nay more, to understand that not only should we be charitable, but positively helpful to each other, however different our religious ideas and convictions may be. And that is exactly what we do in India.

Vol. 3, Lectures from Colombo to Almora,
The Mission of the Vedanta, pp. 187–188

How is it possible that one person as Mohammed or Buddha or Christ, can be taken up as the one type for the whole world, nay, that the whole of morality, ethics, spirituality, and religion can be true only from the sanction of that one person, and one person alone? Now, the Vedantic religion does not require any such personal authority. Its sanction is the eternal nature of man, its ethics are based upon the eternal spiritual solidarity of man, already existing, already attained and not to be attained.

Vain are your fights and your quarrels; have you seen God whom you want to preach? If you have not seen, vain is your preaching; you do not know what you say; and if you have seen God, you will not quarrel, your very face will shine.

Vol. 3, Lectures from Colombo to Almora, The Sages of India, pp. 250–254

If you deny the authority of the Vedas, you are a Nastika. Therein lies the difference between the scriptures of the Christians or the

Buddhists and ours; theirs are all Puranas, and not scriptures, because they describe the history of the deluge, and the history of kings and reigning families, and record the lives of great men, and so on [...] I was told once by a Christian missionary that their scriptures have a historical character, and therefore are true, to which I replies, 'Mine have no historical character and *therefore* they are true; yours being historical, they were evidently made by some man the other day. Yours are man-made and mine are not; their non-historicity is in their favour.' Such is the relation of the Vedas with all the other scriptures at the present day.

Vol. 3, Lectures from Colombo to Almora, The Vedanta in All its Phases, pp. 333–334

The peculiar tendencies with which a person is born must remain with him [...] We should let a person go the way he intends to go, but if we try to force him into another path, he will lose what he has already attained and will become worthless [...] This life is very important and it, therefore, ought to be guided in the way one's tendency prompts him [...] If God wished that people should follow one religion, why have so many religions sprung up?

Vol. 3, Lectures from Colombo to Almora, Bhakti, pp. 358–359

There is at once an irreconcilable difference between all that is Western and Eastern. The Eastern is looking inward for all that is great and good. When we worship, we close our eyes and try to find God within. The Western is looking up outside for his God. To the Western their religious books have been inspired, while with us our books have been expired; breath-like they came, the breath of God, out of the hearts of sages they sprang.

Vol. 3, Lectures from Colombo to Almora, The Common Bases of Hinduism, p. 375

Only those religions which had one or many scriptures of their own as their basis advanced by leaps and bounds and survive to the present day notwithstanding all the persecution and repression hurled against them. The Greek religion, with all its beauty, died out in the absence of any scripture to support it; but the religion of the Jews stands undiminished in its power, being based upon the authority of the Old Testament. The same is the case with the Hindu religion, with its scripture, the Vedas, the oldest in the world.

Vol. 3, Lectures from Colombo to Almora, The Religion We Are Born In, p. 455

We who have come from the east have sat here day after day and have been told in a patronising way that we ought to accept Christianity because Christian nations are the most prosperous. We look about us and we see England the most prosperous Christian nation in the world, with her foot on the neck of 250 million Asiatics. We look back into history and see that the prosperity of Christian Europe began with Spain. Spain's prosperity began with the invasion of Mexico. Christianity wins its prosperity by cutting the throats of its fellow men. At such a price the Hindu will not have prosperity.

Vol. 3, Reports in American Newspapers, At the Parliament of Religions, Cantankerous Remarks, p. 474

Recognise all the great spiritual men and women in every age and country, and see that they are not really at variance with one another. Wherever there has been actual religion—this touch of the Divine, the soul coming in direct sense-contact with the Divine—there has always been a broadening of the mind which enables it to see the light everywhere. Now, some Mohammedans are the crudest in this respect, and the most sectarian. Their watchword is: 'There is one God, and Mohammed is His Prophet.' Everything beyond that not only is bad, but must be destroyed forthwith; at a moment's notice, every man or woman who does not exactly believe in that must be killed; everything that does not belong to this worship must be immediately broken; every book that teaches anything else must be burnt. From the Pacific to the Atlantic, for five hundred years blood ran all over the world. That is Mohammedanism! Nevertheless, among these Mohammedans, wherever there was a philosophic man, he was sure to protest against these cruelties. In that he showed the touch of the Divine and realised a fragment of the truth; he was not playing with religion; for it was not his father's religion he was talking, but spoke the truth direct like a man.

Vol. 4, Lectures and Discourses, The Great Teachers of the World, p. 126

All forms of religion, high or low, are just different stages toward that eternal state of Light, which is God Himself. Some embody a lower view, some a higher and that is all the difference. Therefore the religions of the unthinking masses all over the world must be, and have always been, of a God who is outside of the universe, who lives in heaven, who governs from that place, who is a punisher of the bad and a rewarder of the good, and so on. As man advanced spiritually, he began to feel that God was omnipresent, that He must be in him, that He must be everywhere, that He was not a distant God, but clearly the Soul of all souls. As my soul moves my body, even so is God the mover of my soul. Soul within soul. And a few individuals who had developed enough and were pure enough, went still further, and at last found God. As the New Testament says, 'Blessed are the pure in heart, for they shall see God.' And they found at last that they and the Father were one.

Vol. 4, Lectures and Discourses, Christ, the Messenger, pp. 147–148

The second idea that I learnt from my Master, and which is perhaps the most vital, is the wonderful truth that the religions of the world are not contradictory or antagonistic. They are but various phases of one eternal religion. That one eternal religion is applied to different planes of existence, is applied to the opinions of various minds and various races. There never was my religion or yours, my national religion or your natural religion; there never existed many religions, there is only the one. One infinite religion existed all through eternity and will ever exist, and this religion is expressing itself in various countries in various ways. Therefore we must respect all religions and we must try to accept them all as far as we can. Religions manifest themselves not only according to race and geographical position, but according to individual powers. In one man religion is manifesting itself as intense activity, as work. In another it is manifesting itself as intense devotion, in yet another as mysticism, in others as philosophy, and so forth. It is wrong when we say to others, 'Your methods are not right.'

To learn this central secret that the truth may be one and yet many at the same time, that we may have different visions of the same truth from different standpoints, is exactly what must be done. Then instead of antagonism to anyone, we shall have infinite sympathy with all. Knowing that as long as there are different natures born in this world, the same religious truth will require different adaptations, we shall understand that we are bound to have forbearance with each other.

One man says, because his is the oldest religion, it is the best; another makes the same claim, because his is the latest. We have to recognise that each of them has the same saving power as the other. What you have heard about their difference, whether in the temple or in the church, is a mass of superstition. The same God answers all; and it is not you, or I, or any body of men that is responsible for the safety and salvation of the least bit of the soul; the same Almighty God is responsible for all. I do not understand how people declare themselves to be believers in God, and at the same time think that God has handed over to a little body of men all truth, and that they are the guardians of the rest of humanity. How can you call that religion?

Do not try to disturb the faith of any man. If you can, give him something better; if you can, get hold of a man where he stands and give him a push upwards; do so, but do not destroy what he has.

Vol. 4, Lectures and Discourses, My Master, pp. 180–183

One of the chief distinctions between the Hindu and the Christian religions is that the Christian religion teaches that each human soul had its beginning at its birth into this world, whereas the Hindu religion asserts that the spirit of man is an emanation of the Eternal Being, and had no more a beginning than God Himself.

Vol. 4, Lectures and Discourses, Indian Religious Thought, p. 188–189

Every day we hear in this country (USA) about practical Christianity—that a man has done some good to his fellow beings. Is that all [...] Charity is great, but the moment you say it is all, you run the risk of running into materialism. It is not religion. It is no better than atheism—a little less [...] You Christians, have you found nothing else in the Bible than working for fellow creatures, building [...] hospitals? [...] here stands a shopkeeper and says how Jesus would have kept the shop! Jesus would neither have kept a saloon, nor a shop, nor have edited a newspaper. That sort of practical religion is good, not bad; but it is just kindergarten religion. It leads nowhere.

Vol. 4, Lectures and Discourses, The Practice of Religion, pp. 238–239

It is not true that I am against any religion. It is equally untrue that I am hostile to the Christian missionaries in India. But I protest against certain of their methods of raising money in America [...] What have the Hindus done to the disciples of Christ that every Christian child is taught to call the Hindus 'vile' and 'wretches' and the most horrible devils on earth? Part of the Sunday School education for children here consists in teaching them to hate everybody who is not a Christian, and the Hindus especially, so that, from their very childhood they may subscribe their pennies to the missions. If not for truth's sake, for the sake of the morality of their own children, the Christian missionaries ought not to allow such things going on. Is it any wonder that such children grow up to be ruthless and cruel men and women? [...] Look again at the books published in Madras against the Hindu religion. If a Hindu writes one such line against the Christian religion, the missionaries will cry fire and brimstone.

Vol. 4, Writings: Prose and Poems, Reply to the Madras Address, pp. 344–345

Although strictly speaking there are no absolutely racial religions, yet it may be said that, of this group, the Vedic, the Mosaic, and the Avestic religions are confined to the races to which they originally belonged; while the Buddhistic, the Christian and the Mohammedan religions have been from their very beginning spreading religions. The struggle will be between the Buddhists and Christians and Mohammedans to conquer the world, and the racial religions also will have unavoidably to join in the struggle. Each one of these religions, racial or spreading, has been already split into various branches and has undergone vast changes consciously or unconsciously to adapt itself to varying circumstances. This very fact shows that not one of them is fitted alone to be the religion of the entire human race. Each religion being the effect of certain peculiarities of the race it sprang from, and being in turn the cause of the intensification and preservation of those very peculiarities, not one of them can fit the universal human nature. Not only so, but there is a negative element in each. Each one helps the growth of a certain part of human nature, but represses everything else which the race from which it sprang had not. Thus, one religion to become universal would be dangerous and degenerating to man.

It seems to be true that the solidarity of the human race, social as well as religious, with a scope for infinite variation, is the plan of nature; and if the line of least resistance is the true line of action, it seems to me that this splitting up of each religion into sects is the preservation of religion by frustrating the tendency to rigid sameness, as well as the clear indication to us of the line of procedure.

The end seems, therefore, to be not destruction but a multiplication of sects until each individual is a sect unto himself. Again, a background of unity will come by the fusion of all the existing religions into one grand philosophy. In the mythologies or the ceremonials, there never will be unity, because we differ more in the concrete than in the abstract. Even while admitting the same principle, men will differ as to the greatness of each of his ideal teacher. So, by this fusion will be found out a union of philosophy as the basis of union, leaving each at liberty to choose his teacher or his form as illustrations of that unity. This fusion is what is naturally going on for thousands of years; only, by mutual antagonism, it has been woefully held back. Instead of antagonising, therefore, we must help all such interchange of ideas between different races, by sending teachers to each other, so as to educate humanity in all the various religions of the world; but we must insist, as the great Buddhist Emperor of India, Asoka, did in the second century before Christ, not to abuse others or to try to make a living out of others' faults; but to help, to sympathise, and to enlighten.

Vol. 4, Writings: Prose and Poems, Fundamentals of Religion, pp. 375–377

The Christianity that is preached in India is quite different from what one sees here (USA); you will be astonished to hear, Dharmapala, that I have friends in this country amongst the clergy of the Episcopal and even Presbyterian churches, who are as broad, as liberal, and as sincere as you are in your own religion. The real spiritual man is broad everywhere. His love forces him to be so. Those to whom religion is a trade are forced to become narrow and mischievous by their introduction into religion of the competitive, fighting and selfish methods of the world.

Vol. 5, Epistles (First Series), XXVII, pp. 59–60

I refer each individual to his own experiences, and where reference is made to books, the latter are procurable, and may be studied by each one for himself [...] I teach only the Self, hidden in the heart of every individual and common to all [...] I propound a philosophy which can serve as a basis to every possible religious system in the world, and my attitude towards all of them is one of extreme sympathy—my teaching is antagonistic to none. I direct my attention to the individual, to make him strong, to teach him that he himself is divine, and I call upon men to make themselves conscious of this divinity within. That is really the ideal—conscious or unconscious—of every religion.

Vol. 5, Interviews, An Indian Yogi in London, pp. 187–188

All religions are different expressions of the same truth; all march on or die out. They are the radii of the same truth, the expression that variety of minds requires.

Vol. 5, Interviews, India's Mission, p. 191

All forms of religion have an essential and a non-essential part. If we strip from them the latter, there remains the real basis of all religion, which all forms of religion possess in common. Unity is behind them all. We may call it God, Allah, Jehovah, the Spirit, Love; it is the same unity that animates all life, from its lowest form to its noblest manifestation in man. It is on this unity that we need to lay stress, whereas in the West, and indeed everywhere, it is on the non-essential that men are apt to lay stress. They will fight and kill each other for these forms, to make their fellows conform. Seeing that the essential is love of God and love of man, this is curious, to say the least.

Vol. 5, Interviews, India and England, p. 197

In all religions we travel from a lesser to a higher truth, never from error to truth. There is a Oneness behind all creation, but minds are very various. 'That which exists is One, sages call It variously.' What I mean is that one progresses from a smaller to a greater truth. The worst religions are only bad readings of the truth. One gets to understand bit by bit. Even devil-worship is but a perverted reading of the ever-true and immutable Brahman. Other phases have more or less of the truth in them. No form of religion possesses it entirely.

Vol. 5, Interviews, Indian Missionary's Mission to England p. 202

Our philosophy does not depend upon any personality for its truth. Thus Krishna did not teach anything new or original to the world, nor does Ramayana profess which is not contained in the Scriptures. It is to be noted that Christianity cannot stand without Christ, Mohammedanism without Mohammed, and Buddhism without Buddha.

Vol. 5, Interviews, With the Swami Vivekananda at Madura, p. 207

A true Christian is a true Hindu, and a true Hindu is a true Christian.

Vol. 5, Sayings and Utterances, 57, p. 415

No form of religion will do for all [...] any system which seeks to destroy individuality is in the long run disastrous.

Let each one therefore give his message; but find not the defects in other religions.

Vol. 6, Notes of Class Talks and Lectures, Religion is Realisation, p. 82

The Christian idea of a practical religion is in doing good works—worldly utility. What good is utility? Judged from a utilitarian standpoint, religion is a failure. Every hospital is a prayer that more people may come there. What is meant by charity? Charity is not fundamental. It is really helping on the misery of the world, not eradicating it. One looks for name and fame and covers his efforts to obtain them with the enamel of charity and good works. He is working for himself under the pretext of working for others. Every so-called charity is an encouragement of the very evil it claims to operate against.

Vol. 6, Notes of Class Talks and Lectures, The Practice of Religion, p. 101

Christ was a Sannyasin, and his religion is essentially fit for Sannyasins only. His teachings may be summed up as: 'Give up;' nothing more—being fit for the favoured few. 'Turn the other cheek also!'—impossible, impracticable! The Westerners know it. It is meant for those who hunger and thirst after righteousness, who aim at perfection. 'Stand on your rights,' is the rule for ordinary men. One set of moral values cannot be preached to all—Sadhus and householders.

Vol. 6, Notes of Class Talks and Lectures, Notes Taken Down in Madras 1892–93, p. 109

The fault with all religions like Christianity is that they have one set of rules for all.

Vol. 6, Notes of Class Talks and Lectures, Notes Taken Down in Madras 1892–93, p. 120

Never quarrel about religion. All quarrels and disputations concerning religion simply show that spirituality is not present. Religious quarrels are always over the husks. When purity, when spirituality goes, leaving the soul dry, quarrels begin, and not before.

Vol. 6, Notes of Class Talks and Lectures, The Power of the Mind, p. 127

My Master used to say that these names, as Hindu, Christian etc., stand as great bars to all brotherly feelings between man and man. We must try to break them down first. They have lost all their good powers and now only stand as baneful influences under whose black magic even the best of us behave like demons.

Vol. 6, Epistles (Second Series), LXI, p. 301

On the other hand, my experience is that if ever any religion approached to this equality in an appreciable manner, it is Islam and Islam alone. Therefore, I am firmly persuaded that without the help of practical Islam, theories of Vedantism, however fine and wonderful they may be, are entirely valueless to the vast mass of mankind. We want to lead mankind to the place where there is neither the Vedas, nor the Bible, nor the Koran; yet this has to be done by harmonising the Vedas, the Bible and the Koran. Mankind ought to be taught that religions are but the varied expression of THE RELIGION, which is Oneness, so that each may choose that path that suits him best. For our own motherland a junction of the two great systems, Hinduism and Islam—Vedanta brain and Islam body—is the only hope. I see in my mind's eye the future perfect India rising out of this chaos and strife, glorious and invincible, with Vedanta brain and Islam body.

Vol. 6, Epistles (Second Series), CXLII, pp. 415–416

The three missionary religions are the Buddhist, Mohammedan, and Christian. The three older ones, Hinduism, Judaism and Zoroastrianism, never sought to make converts. Buddhists never killed, but converted three-quarters of the world at one time by pure gentleness.

Vol. 7, Inspired Talks, 11 July 1895, p. 43

The Christian idea of heaven is a place of intensified enjoyment. How can that be God? All this desire to go to heaven is a desire for enjoyment. This has to be given up.

Vol. 7, Inspired Talks, 31 July 1895 p. 84

I have not one word to say against any religion or founder of religion in the world—whatever you may think of our religion. All religions are sacred to me. Secondly, it is a misstatement that I said that missionaries do not learn our vernaculars. I will stick to my statement that few, if any, of them, pay any attention to Sanskrit; nor is it true that I said anything against any religious body—except that I do insist on my statement that India can never be converted to Christianity, and further I deny that the conditions of the lower classes are made any better by Christianity, and add that the majority of South Indian Christians are not only Catholics, but what they call themselves, caste Christians, that is, they stick close to their castes, and I am thoroughly persuaded that if the Hindu society gives up its exclusive policy, ninety per cent of them would rush back to Hinduism with all its defects.

Vol. 7, Epistles (Third Series), XV, p. 460–461

Some years ago one of your Christian teachers, a friend of mine, said, 'You believe in Christ?' 'Yes,' I answered, 'but perhaps with a little more reverence.' 'Then why don't you be baptised?' How could I be baptised? By whom? Where is the man who can give true baptism? What is baptism? Is it sprinkling some water over you, or dipping you in water, while muttering formulas? Baptism is the direct introduction into the life of the spirit. If you receive real baptism, you know you are not the body but the spirit. Give me that baptism if you can. If not, you are not Christians. Even after the so-called baptism which you received, you have remained the same. What is the sense of merely saying you have been baptised in the name of the Christ? Mere talk, talk—ever disturbing the world with your foolishness! *'Ever steeped in the darkness of ignorance, yet considering themselves wise and learned, the fools go round and round, staggering to and fro like the blind led by the blind.* (Katha Upanishad I.ii.5) Therefore do not say you are Christians; do not brag about baptism and things of that sort. Of course there is true baptism—there was baptism in the beginning when the Christ came to the earth and taught. The illumined souls, the great ones that come to earth from time to time, have the power to reveal the Supernal Vision to us. This is true baptism.

Vol. 8, Lectures and Discourses, Discipleship, pp. 114–115

Certain things are necessary to make a religion. First of all, there is the book. The power of the book is simply marvellous! Whatever it be, the book is the centre round which human allegiance gathers. Not one religion is living today but has a book. With all its rationalism and tall talk, humanity still clings to the books. In your country (USA) every attempt to start a religion without a book has failed. In India sects rise with great success, but within a few years they die down, because there is no book behind them. So in every other country. Study the rise and fall of the Unitarian movement. It represents the best thought of your nation. Why should it not have spread like the Methodist, Baptist, and other Christian denominations? Because there was no book. On the other hand, think of the Jews. A handful of men, driven from one country to another, still hold together, because they have a book. Think of the Parsees—only a hundred thousand in the world. About a million are all that remain of the Jains in India. And do you know that these handfuls of Parsees and Jains still keep on just because of their books? The religions that are living at the present day—every one of them has a book. The second requisite, to make a religion, is veneration for some person. He is worshipped either as the Lord of the world or as the great Teacher. Men must worship some embodied man! They must have the Incarnation of the prophet or the great leader. You find it in every religion today. Hindus and Christians—they have Incarnations: Buddhists, Mohammedans and Jews have prophets. But it is all about the same—all their veneration twines round some person or persons. The third requisite seems to be that a religion, to be strong and sure of itself, must believe that it alone is the truth; otherwise it cannot influence people.

Vol. 8, Lectures and Discourses, Is Vedanta the Future Religion?, pp. 122–123

Here comes a Christian man and he says, 'You are all doomed; but if you believe in this doctrine, Christ will help you out.' If this were true—but of course it is nothing but superstition—there would be no wickedness in the Christian countries.

Vol. 8, Lectures and Discourses, Is Vedanta the Future Religion?, p. 132

The Imitation of Christ is a cherished treasure of the Christian world. This great book was written by a Roman Catholic monk. 'Written', perhaps, is not the proper word. It would be more appropriate to say that each letter of the book is marked deep with the heart's blood of the great soul who had renounced all for his love of Christ. That great soul whose words, living and burning, have cast such a spell for the last four hundred years over the hearts of myriads of men and women; whose influence today remains as strong as ever and is destined to endure for all time to come; before whose genius and Sâdhâna (spiritual effort) hundreds of crowned have bent down in reverence; and before whose matchless purity the jarring sects of Christendom, whose name is legion, have sunk their differences of centuries in common veneration to a common principle—that great soul, strange to say, has not thought fit to put his name to a book such as this [...] We happen to be the subjects of a Christian government now. Through its favour it has been our lot to meet Christians of so many sects, native as well as foreign. How startling the divergence between their profession and practice! Here stands the Christian missionary preaching: 'Sufficient unto the day is the evil thereof. Take no thought for the morrow'—

and then busy soon after, making his pile and framing his budget for ten years in advance! There he says that he follows him who 'hath not where to lay his head,' glibly talking of the glorious sacrifice and burning renunciation of the Master, but in practice going about like a gay bridegroom fully enjoying all the comforts the world can bestow! Look where we may, a true Christian nowhere do we see. The ugly impression left on our mind by the ultra-luxurious, insolent, despotic, barouche-and-brougham-driving Christians of the Protestant sects will be completely removed if we but once read this great book with the attention it deserves.

Vol. 8, Writings: Prose and Poems, A Preface to the Imitation of Christ, pp. 159–160

With all your brags and boastings, where has your Christianity succeeded without the sword? Show me one place in the whole world. One, I say, throughout the history of the Christian religion—one; I do not want two. I know how your forefathers were converted. They had to be converted or killed; that was all. What can you do better than Mohammedanism, with all your bragging? 'We are the only one!' and why? 'Because we can kill others.' The Arabs said that; they bragged. And where is the Arab now? He is the bedouin. The Romans used to say that, and where are they now? Blessed are the peace-makers; they shall enjoy the earth. Such things tumble down; it is built upon sands; it cannot remain long.

Vol. 8, Notes of Class Notes and Lectures, Hindus and Christians, pp. 212–213

We do not only tolerate but accept every religion, and with the Lord's help I am trying to preach it to the whole world.

Vol. 8, Epistles (Fourth Series), XV, p. 299

Mohammedanism is the only religion that has completely broken down the idea of the priest. The leader of prayer stands with his back to the people, and only the reading of the Koran may take place from the pulpit. Protestantism is an approach to this.

Vol. 9, Excerpts from Sister Nivedita's Book: Notes of Some Wanderings with the Swami Vivekananda, Chapter VIII: The Temple of Pandrenthan, p. 377

”

Part II

RELIGION AND PHILOSOPHY IN INDIA

Chapter 5

PRINCIPAL ELEMENTS OF VEDANTA

The Vedas are neither books nor the utterances of persons, but the accumulated treasury of spiritual laws that have existed throughout time. They were never written, never created. When we say that the Vedas are beginningless and eternal, it means that the law or truth revealed by them to man is permanent and changeless. They do not owe their authority to anybody. The real study is 'that by which we realize the Unchangeable.' This means neither reading nor believing nor reasoning, but superconscious perception or Samadhi. Vedanta lays down the principles, maps out for us the goal, and then teaches us the various methods by which we can arrive at the goal. Man can take up any method he likes, and if it turns out to be not suitable, another method may be tried. One peculiarity of the Vedas is that they repeatedly declare that you must go beyond them; they were written just for the child-mind, and when you have grown, you must go beyond them. The study of the Vedas is secondary.

All inquiries of the Vedanta philosophy have to be inside us. As the Hindu sages were not satisfied with their attempts to explain the universe by studying the external world, they sought the answers in the internal world by analysing the mind to find the truth within themselves. The Vedas have been discovered by different persons (Rishis) in different times. The Rishi is the Mantra-drastha, the seer of thought. Rishis are not limited by time, space, sex or race. To get the knowledge of the Vedas, the Rishis had to go beyond the senses. The Vedas contain the essence of all religion. They were divided into branches, and each branch was put into the heads of certain priests and families and kept alive by memory. Unfortunately, the major portion of the Vedas has disappeared, either because these families died out, or were killed under foreign persecution, or, somehow, became extinct. However, one failing of the Rishis is that while enjoining people to do certain things, they never cared to explain the reasons for doing so, under the pretext that the people could not have understood their real meaning. They were selfish in not wanting others to come up to the level of their knowledge. They feared losing their own privilege and prestige over others. Their Adhikarivada, their attempt to make a compromise between the real, eternal truths and the nonsensical prejudices of the people, resulted in the grand truths being buried under heaps of rubbish which were held as real truths.

The Vedas are not properly arranged, and the thoughts, it seems, have been jotted down. The Vedas are divided mainly into two portions: the Karma-kanda, which deals with hymns and rituals, and the Jnana-kanda (which includes the Upanishads), which deals with philosophical and spiritual treatises that are called the Vedanta, also called the Shrutis. The Upanishads, comprising more than a hundred books, were not necessarily composed as a separate portion of the Vedas; many are interspersed among the rituals and, occasionally, the hymns. The Upanishads can be regarded as the Bible of India. The essential elements of the Upanishads are belief in God, the law of Karma, and condemnation of rituals. The philosophic teaching of the Upanishads gives up the idea of going to heaven, for the highest heaven is in our own souls and places do not signify anything.

The Gita is a commentary on the Upanishads. It is like a bouquet of the most beautiful flowers of spiritual truths collected from the Upanishads. The reconciliation of the different paths of Dharma, and work without desire or attachment—these are the two special characteristics of the Gita. But in the Gita, one cannot study the rise of spiritual ideas or trace them to their source. To do that, one must study the Vedas.

Next to the Vedanta come the Smritis, which are also books written by sages, similar to the scriptures of other religions. But they are not the final authority, and if there is anything in a Smriti that contradicts the Vedas, it is to be rejected. These Smritis, mainly regulating the manners and customs of the nation, were changed from time to time.

Below the Smritis are the Puranas, written in Sanskrit—the language of the people of that time—meant for ordinary people who could not understand philosophy, and which use the descriptions of the lives of saints, kings, great men and historical events in order to illustrate the eternal principles of religion. The Puranas were intended to educate mankind, and the sages who constructed them contrived to find some historical personages, superimposed upon them all the best and worst qualities as they wanted, and laid down the rules of morals for the conduct of mankind. Then there are the Tantras, which are very much like the Puranas in some respects.

The Maya of the Vedanta is not a theory, but a simple statement of fact—it is what we are and what we see around us. Everything that has name and form and is bound by the laws of time, space and causation is Maya. This mixture of life and death, good and evil, knowledge and ignorance; this clinging to life; the beliefs that we will never die, that there will be only good and no evil, and that there will be only material prosperity and not misery—all this is Maya. Everything is rushing towards one goal, viz. destruction. The whole struggle is to get rid of this clinging on to time, space and causation. One approach is to indulge in sense pleasures, to make hay while the sun shines, and to be hopeful and positive. While this approach provides a very good motive power for our lives, the danger is that we may give up the struggle in despair. In the midst of sorry and suffering, there is a small voice that has been ringing through all ages, through every country and in every heart, urging people to come to God. This is called religion.

All the orthodox systems of philosophy accept the Vedanta as their foundation, and accept the Vedas as eternal revelations of truth, even as they have their own interpretations. However, even the heterodox systems like Buddhism and Jainism quote the Vedanta as authority when it suits them. Of the three orthodox divisions, viz. the Sankhyas, the Naiyayikas, and the Mimamsakas, the former two, although they existed as philosophical schools, failed to form any sect. The one sect that now really covers India is that of the later Mimamsakas or the Vedantists. Their philosophy is called Vedantism. 'Vedanta' does not mean only the Advaita system, but refers also to the Sutras of Vyasa, which are the consummation of all the preceding systems of philosophy.

Among the Vedantists, there are three principal variations. These are the dualistic (Dvaita), the qualified non-dualistic (Vishishtadvaita), and the non-dualistic (Advaita). They represent the three stages of spiritual growth in man. Each one is necessary. All three systems agree on three points, viz. belief in God, in the Vedas as the revealed word of God, and in cycles that are the result of one primal force (Prana) acting on one primal matter (Akasha).

The dualist philosophy (Dvaita) avers that God, who is the creator of the universe and its ruler, is eternally separate from nature and the human soul. Each one of us is an individual, eternally separate from God and nature. Nature and the souls become manifested and change, but God remains the same. He has human attributes, but He is infinitely greater than man. All good qualities are attributed to Him. Dualists also believe that whatever material things a man wants he will get sooner or later by praying to one of the gods, angels or perfected beings; but if he wants salvation, he must worship God. Another concept is that beyond this universe, there is a place full of happiness and good only, and when that place is reached, there will be no more necessity of being born and reborn. The overwhelming majority of Indians are dualists, since dualism naturally appeals to those who are less educated, who have been persecuted for millennia in every country, and whose idea of salvation is, understandably, freedom from the fear of punishment.

The qualified non-dualist school (Vishishtadvaita) says that we are all individuals, but not separate from God. If the universe is the effect and God the material cause of the universe, the whole universe must be God Himself. God, nature and the soul are one. God is, as it were, the Soul, and nature and souls are the body of God. Like the dualists, the qualified non-dualists say that the soul is by nature pure, but through its own deeds it becomes impure. What we are now trying to do is to remanifest the intelligence, purity and power that are natural to the soul.

The Advaitist believes that not only is God the creator, He is also the created. God is eternally creating, and life is eternal. That which all ignorant people see as the universe does not really exist. Brahman is the only real thing in the universe; everything else is unreal, manifested and manufactured out of Brahman by the power of Maya. There is only one Existence, in which we dream all these various dreams. Everything is that One; the difference being only in degree, not in kind. There is neither nature, nor God, nor the universe—only that one Infinite Existence, out of which, through name and form, all these are manufactured. There is only one Being, and every soul is that Being in full, not a part of that Being. There is only one Soul in the universe that reflects itself through a multiplicity of mirrors, appearing as so many different souls. Just as you cannot see your own face except in a mirror, so the Self cannot see its own nature until It is reflected, and this whole universe is the Self trying to realize itself. It neither comes nor goes, is neither born nor dies, nor does it reincarnate. All these heavens and earths and places only exist in our imagination; they do not exist in reality, have never existed in the past, and will never exist in the future. Creation is without beginning or end. The sum total of cosmic energy is always the same. There was never a time when there was no creation. The non-dualistic philosophy (Advaita) is non-destructive. It does not seek to disturb anyone's faith, and includes all degrees of religious development. The Advaitists have no quarrel with the dualists. Though the best and greatest men that have been born in the world have worked with a high impersonal idea, the Advaita philosophy is too abstruse and too elevated to be the religion of the masses.

In the Vedas, there are apparently contradictory ideas. Some texts are entirely dualistic, while others are entirely monistic. It is foolish to attempt to prove that the whole of the Vedas is either dualistic or non-dualistic. They are both, since both dualistic and monistic conceptions are necessary for the evolution of the mind.

The Vedanta preaches the ideal—that man is divine ('Thou art That')—and that this ideal can be realized by everyone. If there is a God, all can find Him. It teaches men to have faith in themselves first. Anyone who does not believe in himself and in the glory of his own soul is an atheist. The Vedanta recognizes no sin, only errors or mistakes. In the long run, everything is going to be all right. There is no concept of

Satan or hell. The greatest error is to think that one is weak or impure. Everything–infinite purity, freedom, love and power–is already ours, and this can be realized by man in all possible conditions of life.

Whether it is high philosophy, idolatry, mythology, agnosticism or atheism–all have a place in the Hindu religion. Man travels not from error to truth, but from lower to higher truths. To the masses that could not conceive of anything higher than a Personal God, Jesus said, 'Pray to your Father in heaven.' To others who could grasp a higher idea, he said, 'I am the vine, ye are the branches,' but to his disciples, to whom he revealed himself more fully, he proclaimed the highest truth, 'I and my Father are One.'

While the Vedanta is impersonal and does not owe its origin to any person or prophet, it is not against the philosophies that do build themselves around certain persons. Hence, there is no antagonism between the Vedanta and any other system in the world. It claims that man is divine, and everything that is strong, good and powerful in human nature is the outcome of that divinity. Ethics and morality, which is based on love and sympathy, is a manifestation of the oneness of human nature. The Vedanta also posits that we must allow everybody their own opinion because the goal is the same.

The Vedanta not only believes in universal toleration, but accepts all religions as true. Everyone is trying to reach the same goal in different ways and under different circumstances, which sometimes creates apparent contradictions. The Vedanta is not antagonistic to anything, though it does not compromise or give up the truths that it considers fundamental. A Hindu never says that Hindus alone will be saved. Hindus are always for punishing their own bodies, never for killing others. Before the Muslims came to India, religious persecution was unknown. Jews, Parsees and

Christians sought refuge, lived and flourished peacefully in India. Hindus experienced religious persecution only as practised by foreigners on themselves. Throughout its history, there has been freedom of religious thought in India.

There are certain principles of Hinduism. These are: the belief that the Vedas are eternal teachings that reveal the secrets of religion; the belief in God, even though there may be differences in the conception of God; the belief in the doctrine of Karma and the transmigration of the soul; the rejection of the belief that the world was created out of nothing and is going to be destroyed; the belief that man is not just a gross material body but also a finer body, the mind, as well as something beyond; viz., the Atman, which inhabits body after body until it becomes free (the theory of Samsara). Hindus have no sense of blasphemy. Nor do they have any artificial respect for prophets or books, or for hypocritical piety. The Hindu religion is suited to all grades of religious aspirations and progress. It contains all the ideals in their perfect form. For example, the idea of Shanta or blessedness is to be found in Vashishtha; that of love in Krishna; that of duty in Ram and Sita; that of intellect in Shukadeva. One should study the characters of these and of other ideal individuals, and adopt the one that they find the most suitable.

“

I am proud to belong to a religion which has taught the world both tolerance and universal acceptance. We believe not only in universal toleration, but we accept all religions as true. I am proud to belong to a nation which has sheltered the persecuted and the refugees of all religions and all nations on earth.

The present convention (Parliament of Religions in Chicago), which is one of the most august assemblies ever held, is in itself a vindication, a declaration to the world of the wonderful doctrine preached in the Gita: '*Whosoever comes to Me, through whatsoever form, I reach him; all men are struggling through paths which in the end lead to me.*'

Vol. 1, At the Parliament of Religions, Response to Welcome, pp. 3–4

From the high spiritual flights of the Vedanta philosophy, of which the latest discoveries of science seem like echoes, to the low ideas of idolatry with its multifarious mythology, the agnosticism of the Buddhists, and the atheism of the Jains, each and all have a place in the Hindu's religion.

By the Vedas, no books are meant. They mean the accumulated treasury of spiritual laws discovered by different persons in different times. Just as the law of gravitation existed before its discovery, and would exist if all humanity forgot it, so is it with the laws that govern the spiritual world. The moral, ethical, and spiritual relations between soul and soul and between individual spirits and the Father of all spirits were there before their discovery, and would remain even if we forgot them. The discoverers of these laws are called Rishis, and we honour them as perfect beings [...] some of the very greatest of them were women.

The Vedas teach us that creation is without beginning or end. Science is said to have proved that the sum total of cosmic energy is always the same. Then, if there was a time when nothing existed, where was all this manifested energy? Some say it was in a potential form in God. In that case God is sometimes potential and sometimes kinetic, which would make Him mutable. Everything mutable is a compound, and everything compound must undergo that change which is called destruction. So God would die, which is absurd. Therefore there never was a time when there was no creation.

To a Hindu, man is not travelling from error to truth, but from truth to truth, from lower to higher truth. To him all the religions, from the lowest fetishism to the highest absolutism, mean so many attempts of the human soul to grasp and realise the Infinite, each determined by the conditions of its birth and association, and each of these marks a stage of progress; and every soul is a young eagle, soaring higher and higher, gathering more and more strength, till it reaches the Glorious Sun.

The Hindus have their faults, they sometimes have their exceptions; but mark this, they are always for punishing their own bodies, and never for cutting the throats of their neighbours. If the Hindu fanatic burns himself on the pyre, he never lights the fire of Inquisition. And even this cannot be laid at the door of his religion any more than the burning of witches can be laid at the door of Christianity. To the Hindu, then, the whole world of religions is only a travelling, a coming up, of different men and women, through various conditions and circumstances, to the same goal. Every religion is only evolving a God out of the material man, and the same God is the inspirer of all of them. Why, then, are there so many contradictions? They are only apparent, says the Hindu. The contradictions come from the same truth adapting itself to the varying circumstances of different natures.

I challenge the world to find, throughout the whole system of Sanskrit philosophy, any such expression as that the Hindu alone will be saved and not others.

Vol. 1, At the Parliament of Religions, Paper on Hinduism, pp. 6–18

The Hindus found their creed upon the ancient Vedas, a word derived from Vid, 'to know.' These are a series of books which, to our minds, contain the essence of all religion; but we do not think they alone contain the truths. They teach us the immortality of the soul.

Vol. 1, Lectures and Discourses, The Hindu Religion, p. 329

'Ekam Sat Vipra Bahudha Vadanti—That which exists is One; sages call It by various names.' Tremendous results have followed from that one verse [...] India is the only country where there never has been a religious persecution, where never was any man disturbed for his religious faith. Theists or atheists, monists, dualists, monotheists are there and always live unmolested. Materialists were allowed to preach from the steps of Brahminical temples, against the gods, and against God Himself; they went preaching all over the land that the idea of God was a mere superstition, and that gods, and Vedas, and religion were simply superstitions invented by the priests for their own benefit, and they were allowed to do this unmolested [...] Before the Mohammedan wave came into India, it was never known what religious persecution was; the Hindus had only experienced it as made by foreigners on themselves. And even now it is a patent fact how much Hindus have helped to build Christian churches, and how much readiness there is to help them. There never has been bloodshed.

A ruler of the universe does not explain the universe, and much less an external ruler, one outside of it. He may be a moral guide, the greatest power in the universe, but that is no explanation of the universe; and the first question that we find now arising, assuming proportions, is the question about the universe: 'Whence did it come?' 'How did it come?' 'How does it exist?'

The Aryan mind had so long been seeking an answer to the question from outside. They questioned everything they could find, the sun, the moon, and stars, and they found all they could in this way. The whole of nature at best could teach them only of a personal Being who is the Ruler of the universe; it could teach nothing further. In short, out of the external world we can only get the idea of an architect, that which is called the Design Theory. It is not a very logical argument, as we all know; there is something childish about it, yet it is the only little bit of anything we can know about God from the external world, that this world required a builder. But this is no explanation of the universe.

But fortunately these Hindu sages were not the people to be knocked on the head; they wanted to get a solution, and now we find that they were leaving the external for the internal [...] Thus we find that the minds of the ancient Aryan thinkers had begun a new theme. They found out that in the external world no search would give an answer to their question. They might seek in the external world for ages, but there would be no answer to their questions. So they fell back upon this other method; and according to this, they were taught that these desires of the senses, desires for ceremonials and externalities have caused a veil to come between themselves and the truth, and that this cannot be removed by any ceremonial. They had to fall back on their own minds and analyse the mind to find the truth in themselves. The outside world failed and they turned back upon the inside world, and then it became the real philosophy of the Vedanta; from here the Vedanta philosophy begins. It is the foundation stone of Vedanta philosophy. As we go on, we find that all its inquiries are inside.

It (Vedanta philosophy) is not one book, or the work of one man. Vedanta is the name of a series of books written at different times. Sometimes in one of these productions there will be fifty different things. Neither are they properly arranged; the thoughts, as it were, have been jotted down. Sometimes in the midst of other extraneous things, we find some wonderful idea. But one fact is remarkable: that these ideas in the Upanishads would be always progressing.

Vol. 1, Lectures and Discourses, Vedic Religious Ideals, pp. 348–356

The Vedanta philosophy, as it is generally called at the present day, really comprise all the various sects that now exist in India. Thus there have been various interpretations, and to my mind they have been progressive, beginning with the dualistic or Dvaita and ending with the non-dualistic or Advaita. The word Vedanta literally means the end of the Vedas—the Vedas being the scriptures of the Hindus.

The Vedas are divided mainly into two portions: the Karma-kanda and the Jnana-kanda—the work-portion and the knowledge portion. To the Karma-kanda belong the famous hymns and the rituals of the Brahmanas. Those books which treat of spiritual matters apart from ceremonials are called Upanishads. The Upanishads belong to the Jnana-kanda, or knowledge-portion. It is not that all the Upanishads were composed as a separate portion of the Vedas. Some are interspersed among the rituals, and at least one is in the Samhita, or hymn-portion. Sometimes the term Upanishad is applied to books which are not included in the Vedas—e.g. the Gita; but as a rule it is applied to the philosophical treatises scattered through the Vedas. These treatises have been collected, and are called the Vedanta.

Sometimes in the West by the Vedas are meant only the hymns and rituals of the Vedas. But at the present time these parts have almost gone out of use, and usually by the word Vedas in India, the Vedanta is meant. All our commentators, when they want to quote a passage from the scriptures, as a rule, quote from the Vedanta, which has another technical name with the commentators—the Shrutis.

The Vedanta, then, practically forms the scriptures of the Hindus, and all systems of philosophy that are orthodox have to take it as their foundation. Even the Buddhists and Jains, when it suits their purpose, will quote a passage from the Vedanta as authority. All schools of philosophy in India, although they claim to have been based upon the Vedas, took different names for their systems. The last one, the system of Vyasa, took its stand upon the doctrines of the Vedas more than the previous systems did, and made an attempt to harmonise the preceding philosophies, such as the Sankhya and the Nyaya, with the doctrines of the Vedanta [...] In general there are three sorts of commentators in India now; from their interpretations have arisen three systems of philosophy and sects. One is the dualistic, or Dvaita; a second is the qualified non-dualistic, or Vishishtadvaita; and a third is the non-dualistic, or Advaita [...] All the Vedantists agree on three points. They believe in God, in the Vedas as revealed and in cycles. The belief about cycles is as follows: All matters throughout the universe is the outcome of one primal matter called Akasha; and all force, whether gravitation, attraction or repulsion, or life, is the outcome of one primal force called Prana. Prana acting on Akasha is creating or projecting the universe. At the beginning of a cycle, Akasha is motionless, unmanifested. Then Prana begins to act, more and more, creating grosser and grosser forms out of Akasha—plants, animals, men, stars, and so on. After an incalculable time this evolution ceases and involution begins, everything being resolved back through finer and finer forms into the original Akasha and Prana. Both can be resolved into a third thing called Mahat—the Cosmic Mind. This Cosmic Mind does not create Akasha and Prana, but changes itself into them.

Vol. 1, Lectures and Discourses, The Vedanta Philosophy, pp. 357–360

Vedanta philosophy has certain peculiarities. In the first place, it is perfectly impersonal; it does not owe its origin to any person or prophet; it does not build itself around one man as a centre. Yet it has nothing today against philosophies which do build themselves around certain persons [...] there is no fight and no antagonism between the Vedanta and any other system in the world [...] One principle it lays down—and that, the Vedanta claims, is to be found in every religion in the world—that man is divine, that all this which we see around us is the outcome of that consciousness of the divine. Everything that is strong, and good, and powerful in human nature is the outcome of that divinity, and though potential in many, there is no difference between man and man essentially, all being alike divine.

The Vedanta claims that there has not been one religious inspiration, one manifestation of the divine man, however great, but it has been the expression of that infinite oneness in human nature; and all that we call ethics and morality, and doing good to others is also but the manifestation of this oneness. There are moments when every man feels that he is one with the universe, and he rushes forth to express it, whether he knows it or not. This expression of oneness is what we call love and sympathy, and it is the basis of all our ethics and morality. This is summed up in the Vedanta philosophy by the celebrated aphorism, Tat Tvam Asi, 'Thou art That.'

Another peculiar idea of the Vedanta is that we must allow this infinite variation in religious thought, and not try to bring everybody to the same opinion, because the goal is the same. As the Vedantist says in his poetical language, 'As so many rivers, having their source in different mountains, roll down, crooked or straight, and at last come into the ocean, so all these various creeds and religions, taking their start from different standpoints and running through crooked or straight courses, at last come unto THEE.'

In India there never was any religious persecution by the Hindus, but only that wonderful reverence, which they have for all the religions of the world. They sheltered a portion of the Hebrews, when they were driven out of their own country; and the Malabar Jews remain as a result. They received at another time the remnant of the Persians, when they were almost annihilated; and they remain to this day, as a part of us and loved by us, as the modern Parsees of Bombay. There were Christians who claimed to have come with St. Thomas, the disciple of Jesus Christ; and they were allowed to settle in India and hold their own opinions; and a colony of them is even now in existence in India. And this spirit of toleration has not died out. It will not and cannot die there.

Vol. 1, Lectures and Discourses, The Spirit and Influence of Vedanta, pp. 387–391

One of the good effects of Vedanta has been freedom of religious thought, which India enjoyed throughout all times of its history. It is something to glory in, that it is the land where there was never a religious persecution, where people are allowed perfect freedom in religion.

Vol. 1. Lectures and Discourses, Vedanta and Privilege, p. 425

The disciples and descendants of Krishna have no name for their religion [although] foreigners call it Hinduism or Brahmanism. There is one religion, and there are many sects. The moment you give it a name, individualise it and separate it from the rest, it is a sect, no more a religion. A sect [proclaims] its own truth and declares that there is no truth anywhere else. Religion believes that there has been, and still is, one religion in the world. There never were two religions. It is the same religion [presenting] different aspects in different places. The task is to conceive the proper understanding of the goal and scope of humanity.

In Krishna we find [...] two ideas [stand] supreme in his message: the first is the harmony of different ideas; the second is non-attachment. A man can attain to perfection, the highest goal, sitting on a throne, commanding armies, working out big plans for nations. In fact, Krishna's great sermon was preached on the battlefield.

Krishna saw plainly through the vanity of all the mummeries, mockeries and ceremonials of the old priests; and yet he saw some good in them [...] why? Because they all lead to the same goal. Ceremonies, books, and forms—all these are links in the chain [...] Get hold of any one of these chains that are stretched out from the common centre [...] Hold on to one of these links, and it will pull you to the centre. Your heart itself will teach the rest. (1.439)

Vol. 1, Lectures and Discourses, Krishna, p. 438

To understand the Gita requires its historical background. The Gita is a commentary on the Upanishads. The Upanishads are the

Bible of India. They occupy the same place as the New Testament does. There are [more than] a hundred books comprising the Upanishads, some very small and some big, each a separate treatise. The Upanishads do not reveal the life of any teacher, but simply teach principles. They are [as it were] shorthand notes taken down of discussion in [learned assemblies], generally in courts of kings. The word Upanishad may mean 'sittings' [or 'sitting near a teacher.'] Those of you who may have studied some of the Upanishads can understand how they are condensed shorthand sketches. After long discussions had been held, they were taken down, possibly from memory. The difficulty is that you get very little of the background. Only the luminous points are mentioned there. The origin of ancient Sanskrit is 5000 B.C.; the Upanishads [are at least] two thousand years before that. Nobody knows [exactly] how old they are. The Gita takes the ideas of the Upanishads and in [some] cases the very words. They are strung together with the idea of bringing out, in a compact, condensed, and systematic form, the whole subject the Upanishads deal with.

The [original] scriptures of the Hindus are called the Vedas. They were so vast—the mass of writings—that if the texts alone were brought here, this room would not contain them. Many of them are lost. They were divided into branches, each branch put into the head of certain priests and kept alive by memory. Such men still exist. They will repeat book after book of the Vedas without missing a single intonation. The larger portion of the Vedas has disappeared. The small portion left makes a whole library by itself. The oldest of these contains the hymns of the Rig-Veda. It is the aim of the modern scholar to restore [the sequence of the Vedic compositions]. The old, orthodox idea is quite different, as your orthodox idea of the Bible is quite different from the modern scholar's. The Vedas are divided into two portions: one the Upanishads, the philosophical portion, the other the work portion.

First of all, the Upanishads believe in God, the creator of the universe, its ruler. [...] Now although we hear the priest, the ideal is much more subtle. Instead of many gods they made one God. The second idea, that you are all bound by the law of Karma, the Upanishads admit, but they declare the way out. The goal of man is to go beyond law. And enjoyment can never be the goal, because enjoyment can only be in nature. In the third place, the Upanishads condemn all the sacrifices and say that is mummery. That may give you all you [want], but it is not desirable, for the more you get, the more you want, and you run round and round in a circle eternally, never getting to the end—enjoying and weeping. Such a thing as eternal happiness is impossible anywhere. It is only a child's dream. The same energy becomes joy and sorrow.

The other point of divergence is: the Upanishads condemn all rituals, especially those that involve the killing of animals. They declare those all nonsense.

Then another great difference between the priests and the Upanishads. The Upanishads say, renounce. That is the test of everything. It is the creative faculty that brings us into all this entanglement [...] Stop creation and you know the truth.

Vol. 1, Lectures and Discourses, The Gita I, pp. 446–453

The Maya of the Vedanta, in its last developed form, is neither Idealism nor Realism, nor is it a theory. It is a simple statement of facts—what we are and what we see around us.

[The Vedantist] has proved beyond all doubt that the mind is limited, that it cannot go beyond certain limits—beyond time, space, and causation. As no man can jump out of his own self, so no man can go beyond the limits that have been put upon him by the laws of time and space. Every attempt to solve the laws of causation, time, and space would be futile, because the very attempt would have to be made by taking for granted the existence of these three. What does the statement of the existence of the world mean, then? 'This world has no existence.' What is meant by that? It means that it has no absolute existence. It exists only in relation to my mind, to your mind, and to the mind of everyone else. We see this world with the five senses but if we had another sense, we would see in it something more. If we had yet another sense, we would see in it something still different. It has, therefore, no real existence; it has no unchangeable, immovable, infinite existence. Nor can it be called non-existence, seeing that it exists, and we have to work in and through it. It is a mixture of existence and non-existence.

Saints die and sinners die, kings die and beggars die. They are all going to death, and yet this tremendous clinging on to life exists. Somehow, we do not know why, we cling to life; we cannot give it up. And this is Maya.

A question was once asked of King Yudhishthira, 'What is the most wonderful thing on this earth?' And the king replied, 'Every day people are dying around us, and yet men think they will never die.' And this is Maya.

The least amount of material prosperity that we enjoy is causing the same amount of misery elsewhere. This is the law. The young, perhaps, do not see it clearly, but those who have lived long enough [...] will understand it. And this is Maya.

Maya is a statement of fact of this universe, of how it is going on. People generally get frightened when these things are told to them. But bold we must be. Hiding facts is not the way to find a remedy.

We often hear that it is one of the features of evolution that it eliminates evil, and this evil being continually eliminated from the world, at last only good will remain. [...] This argument is fallacious from beginning to end. It takes for granted, in the first place, that manifested good and evil in this world are two absolute realities. In the second place, it makes a still worse assumption that the amount of good is an increasing quantity and the amount of evil is a decreasing quantity. [...]

Can it be proved that evil is a lessening quantity? [...] As soon as his [man's] horizon of happiness increases, his horizon of unhappiness increases proportionately. [...] Thus it is that, as we emerge out of the senses, we develop higher powers of enjoyment, and at the same time we have to develop higher powers of suffering too. [...] The more we progress, the more avenues are opened to pain as well as to pleasure. And this is Maya.

Maya is not a theory for the explanation of the world; it is simply a statement of facts as they exist, that the very basis of our being is contradiction. [...] Nor can this state of things be remedied. We may verily imagine that there will be a place where there will be only good and no evil, where we shall only smile and never weep. This is impossible in the very nature of things; for the conditions will remain the same. Wherever there is the power of producing a smile in us, there lurks the power of producing tears. Wherever there is the power of producing happiness, there lurks somewhere the power of making us miserable.

Vol. 2, Jnana-Yoga, Maya and Illusion, pp. 89–97

Unhappiness is the fate of those who are content to live in this world, born as they are. A thousand times greater misery is the fate of those who dare to stand forth for truth and for higher things and who dare to ask for something higher than mere brute existence here. These are facts; but there is no explanation—there cannot be any explanation. But the Vedanta shows the way out.

The whole of human knowledge is a generalisation of this Maya trying to know it as it appears to be. This is the work of Nama-Rupa—name and form. Everything that has form, everything that calls up an idea in your mind, is within Maya; for everything that is bound by the laws of time, space and causation is Maya.

Vol. 2, Jnana-Yoga, Maya and the Evolution of the Conception of God, pp. 111–112

Why should we give him [a man of science] glory? Why should he acquire fame? Does not nature do infinitely more than any human being can do?—and nature is dull, insentient. [...] What glory is there in imitating the insentient? Yet we are all struggling after that. And this is Maya.

Like moths hurling themselves against the flame, we are hurling ourselves again and again into sense-pleasures, hoping to find satisfaction there. We return again and again with freshened energy; thus we go on, till crippled and cheated we die. And this is Maya.

So with our intellect. In our desire to solve the mysteries of the universe, we cannot stop our questioning. We feel we must know and cannot believe that no knowledge is to be gained. A few steps, and there arises the wall of beginningless and endless time which we cannot surmount. A few steps, and there appears a wall of boundless space which cannot be surmounted, and the whole is irrevocably bound in by the walls of cause and effect. We cannot go beyond them. Yet we struggle, and still have to struggle. And this is Maya.

With every breath, with every pulsation of the heart, with every one of our movements, we think we are free, and the very same moment we are shown that we are not. Bound slaves, nature's bond-slaves, in body, in mind, in all our thoughts, in all our feelings. And this is Maya.

It is a most difficult and intricate state of things to understand. It has been preached in every country, taught everywhere, but only believed in by a few, because until we get the experiences ourselves we cannot believe in it. What does it show? Something very terrible. For it is all futile. Time, the avenger of everything, comes, and nothing is left. He swallows up the saint and the sinner, the king and the peasant, the beautiful and the ugly; he leaves nothing. Everything is rushing towards that one goal, destruction. Our knowledge, our arts, our sciences, everything is rushing towards it. None can stem the tide, none can hold it back for a minute. We may try to forget it, in the same way that persons in a plague-stricken city try to create oblivion by drinking, dancing, and other vain attempts, and so becoming paralysed. So we are trying to forget, trying to create oblivion by all sorts of sense-pleasures. And this is Maya.

Two ways have been proposed. One method, which everyone knows, is very common, and that is: 'It may be very true, but do not think of it. 'Make hay while the sun shines,' as the proverb says. It is all true, it is a fact, but do not mind it. Seize the few pleasures you can, do what little you can, do not look at the dark side of the picture, but always towards the hopeful, the positive side.' There is some truth in this, but there is also a danger. The truth is that it is a good motive power. Hope and a positive ideal are very good motive powers for our lives, but there is a certain danger in them. The danger lies in our giving up the struggle in despair.

Is there no hope then? True it is that we are all slaves of Maya, born in Maya, and live in Maya. Is there then no way out, no hope? [...] We find that with all this, with this terrible fact before us, in the midst of sorrow and suffering, even in this world where life and death are synonymous, even here, there is still a small voice that is ringing through all ages, through every country, and in every heart: 'This, My Maya, is divine, made up of qualities, and very difficult to cross. Yet those that come unto Me, cross the river of life.' 'Come unto Me all ye that labour and are heavy laden, and I will give you rest.' This is the voice that is leading us forward. Man has heard it, and is hearing it all through the ages. This voice comes to men when everything seems to be lost and hope has fled, when man's dependence on his own strength has been crushed down and everything seems to melt away between his fingers, and life is a hopeless ruin. Then he hears it. This is called religion.

Vol. 2, Jnana-Yoga, Maya and Freedom, pp. 118–123

What is meant by knowledge in our common-sense idea? It is only something that has become limited by our mind, that we know, and when it is beyond our mind, it is not knowledge. Now if the Absolute becomes limited by the mind, It is no more Absolute; It has become finite. Everything limited by the mind becomes finite. Therefore, to know the Absolute is again a contradiction in terms. That is why this question has never been answered, because if it were answered, there would no more be an Absolute. A God known is no more God; He has become finite like one of us. He cannot be known. He is always the Unknowable One.

Neither known, nor unknown, but something infinitely higher than either. He is your Self. 'Who would live a second, who would breathe a second in this universe, if that Blessed One were not filling it?'

You cannot by any possibility say you know Him; it would be degrading Him. You cannot get out of yourself, so you cannot know Him. Knowledge is objectification. [...] Neither is it unknowable, for what is better known than yourself? It is really the centre of our knowledge. In exactly the same sense, God is neither unknowable nor known, but infinitely higher than both; for He is our real Self.

The Absolute is manifesting Itself as many, through the veil of time, space and causation.

Time, space and causation [...] cannot exist separate from other things. [...] Time depends on two events, just as space has to be related to outside objects. And the idea of causation is inseparable from time and space.

The combination of time, space and causation has neither existence nor non-existence. Secondly, it sometimes vanishes. To give an illustration, there is a wave on the ocean. The wave is the same as the ocean certainly, and yet we know it is a wave, and as such different from the ocean. What makes this difference? The name and the form; that is, the idea in the mind and the form.

Now, can we think of a wave-form as something separate from the ocean? Certainly not. It is always associated with the ocean idea. If the wave subsides, the form vanishes in a moment, and yet the form was not a delusion. So long as the wave existed the form was there, and you were bound to see the form. This is Maya. The whole of this universe, therefore, is, as it were, a peculiar form; the Absolute is that ocean while you and I, and suns and stars, and everything else are various waves of that ocean. And what makes the waves different? Only the form, and that form is time, space and causation, all entirely dependent on the wave. As soon as the individual gives up this Maya, it vanishes for him and he becomes free. The whole struggle is to get rid of this clinging on to time, space and causation, which are always obstacles in our way.

Another peculiarity of the Advaita system is that from its very start it is non-destructive. This is another glory, the boldness to preach, 'Do not disturb the faith of any, even of those who through ignorance have attached themselves to lower forms of worship.' That is what it says, do not disturb, but help everyone to get higher and higher; include all humanity. This philosophy preaches a God who is a sum total. If you seek a universal religion which can apply to everyone, that religion must not be composed of only the parts, but it must always be their sum total and include all degrees of religious development. This idea is not clearly found in any other religious system. They are all parts equally struggling to attain to the whole. The existence of the part is only for this. So, from the very first, Advaita had no antagonism with the various sects existing in India. There are dualists existing today, and their number is by far the largest in India, because dualism naturally appeals to less educated minds. It is a very convenient, natural, common-sense explanation of the universe. But with these dualists, Advaita has no quarrel. The one thinks that God is outside the universe, somewhere in heaven, and the other that He is his own Soul, and that it will be a blasphemy to call Him anything more distant. Any idea of separation would be terrible.

The Advaitist […] has no quarrel with the dualist who is on the right road. […] The Advaitist knows that whatever may be his theories, he is going to the same goal as he himself. There he differs entirely from the dualist who is forced by his point of view to believe that all differing views are wrong. The dualists all the world over naturally believe in a Personal God who is purely anthropomorphic, who like a great potentate in this world is pleased with some and displeased with others. He is arbitrarily pleased with some people or races and showers blessings upon them. Naturally the dualist comes to the conclusion that God has favourites, and he hopes to be one of them. You will find that in almost every religion is the idea: 'We are the favourites of our God, and only by believing as we do, can you be taken into favour with Him.' Some dualists are so narrow as to insist that only the few that have been predestined to the favour of God can be saved; the rest may try ever so hard, but they cannot be accepted. I challenge you to show me one dualistic religion which has not more or less of this exclusiveness. And, therefore, in the nature of things, dualistic religions are bound to fight and quarrel with each other, and this they have ever been doing. Again, these dualists win the popular favour by appealing to the vanity of the uneducated. They like to feel that they enjoy exclusive privileges. The dualist thinks you cannot be moral until you have a God with a rod in His hand, ready to punish you. The unthinking masses are generally dualists, and they, poor fellows, have been persecuted for thousands of years in every country; and their idea of salvation is, therefore, freedom from the fear of punishment. […] But we find that the best and greatest men that have been born in the world have worked with that high impersonal idea. It is the Man who said, 'I and my Father are One,' whose power has descended unto millions. For thousands of years it has worked for good. And we know that the same Man, because he was a non-dualist, was merciful to others. To the masses who could not conceive of anything higher than a Personal God, he said, 'Pray to your Father in heaven.' To others who could grasp a higher idea, he said, 'I am the vine, ye are the branches,' but to his disciples to whom he revealed himself more fully, he proclaimed the highest truth, 'I and my Father are One.'

Vol. 2, Jnana-Yoga, The Absolute and Manifestation, pp. 132–143

The ideal of the Vedanta is that all wisdom and all purity are in the soul already, dimly expressed or better expressed—that is all the difference. The difference between man and man, and all things in the whole creation, is not in kind but only in degree.

Throughout the Vedanta philosophy, there is no such thing as good and bad, they are not two different things; the same thing is good or bad, and the difference is only in degree.

Vol. 2, Jnana-Yoga, Realisation, p. 168

The philosophic teaching of the Upanishads gives up the idea of going to heaven. Happiness is not in this heaven or in that heaven, it is in the soul; places do not signify anything.

The highest heaven, therefore, is in our own souls; the greatest temple of worship is the human soul, grater than all the heavens, says the Vedanta; for in no heaven anywhere can we understand the reality as distinctly and clearly as in this life, in our own soul. Changing places does not help one much. I thought while I was in India that the cave would give me clearer vision. I found it was not so. Then I thought the forest would do so, then, Varanasi. But the same difficulty existed everywhere, because we make our own worlds. If I am evil, the whole world is evil to me. That is what the Upanishad says. And the same thing applies to all worlds. If I die and go to heaven, I should find the same, for until I am pure it is no use going to caves, or forests, or to Varanasi, or to heaven, and if I have polished my mirror, it does not matter where I live, I get the Reality just as It is. So it is useless, running hither and thither, and spending energy in vain, which should be spent only in polishing the mirror. The same idea is expressed again: 'None sees Him, none sees His form with the eyes. It is in the mind, in the pure mind, that He is seen, and thus immortality is gained.'

Vol. 2, Jnana-Yoga, Unity in Diversity, pp. 184–185

The Gita is like a bouquet composed of the beautiful flowers of spiritual truths collected from the Upanishads. But in the Gita you cannot study the rise of the spiritual ideas, you cannot trace them to their source. To do that, as has been pointed out by many, you must study the Vedas.

Vol. 2, Jnana-Yoga, The Freedom of the Soul, p. 189

Of these various sects, in the first place, there can be made two main divisions, the orthodox and the unorthodox. Those that believe in the Hindu scriptures, the Vedas, as eternal revelations of truth, are called orthodox, and those that stand on other authorities, rejecting the Vedas, are the heterodox in India. The chief modern unorthodox Hindu sects are the Jains and the Buddhists. Among the orthodox, some declare that the scriptures are of much higher authority than reason; others again say that only that portion of the scriptures which is rational should be taken and the rest rejected. Of the three orthodox divisions, the Sankhyas, the Naiyayikas, and the Mimamsakas, the former two, although they existed as philosophical schools, failed to form any sect. The one sect that now really covers India is that of the later Mimamsakas or the Vedantists. Their philosophy is called Vedantism.

We find that there are three principal variations among the Vedantists. On one point they all agree, and that is that they all believe in God. All these Vedantists also believe the Vedas to be the revealed word of God, not exactly in the same sense, perhaps, as the Christians or the Mohammedans believe, but in a very peculiar sense. Their idea is that the Vedas are an expression of the knowledge of God, and as God is eternal, His knowledge is eternally with Him, and so are the Vedas eternal. There is another common ground of belief: that of creation in cycles, that the whole of creation appears and disappears; that it is projected and becomes grosser and grosser, and at the end of an incalculable period of time it becomes finer and finer, when it dissolves and subsides, and then comes a period of rest. Again it begins to appear and goes through the same process. They postulate the existence of a material which they call Akasha, which is something like the ether of the scientists, and a power which they call Prana. About this Prana they declare that by its vibration the universe is produced. When a cycle ends, all this manifestation of nature becomes finer and finer and dissolves into that Akasha which cannot be seen or felt, yet out of which everything is manufactured. All the forces that we see in nature, such as gravitation, attraction, and repulsion, or as thought, feeling, and nervous motion—all these various forces resolve into that Prana, and the vibration of the Prana ceases. In that state it remains until the beginning of the next cycle. Prana then begins to vibrate, and that vibration acts upon the Akasha, and all these forms are thrown out in regular succession.

The dualists believe that God, who is the creator of the universe and its ruler, is eternally separate from nature, eternally separate from the human soul. God is eternal; nature is eternal; so are all souls. Nature and the souls become manifested and change, but God remains the same. According to the dualists, again, this God is personal in that He has qualities, not that He has a body. He has human attributes; He is merciful, He is just, he is powerful, He is almighty, He can be approached, He can be prayed to, He can be loved, He loves in return, and so forth. In one word, He is a human God, only infinitely greater than man; He has none of the evil qualities which men have.

The vast mass of Indian people are dualists. Human nature

ordinarily cannot conceive of anything higher. We find that ninety per cent of the population of the earth who believe in any religion are dualists. All the religions of Europe and Western Asia are dualistic [...] This is the religion of the masses all over the world. They believe in a God who is entirely separate from them, a great king, a high, mighty monarch, as it were. At the same time they make Him purer than the monarchs of the earth; they give Him all good qualities and remove the evil qualities from Him. As if it were ever possible for good to exist without evil; as if there could be any conception of light without a conception of darkness!

With all dualistic theories the first difficulty is, how is it possible that under the rule of a just and merciful God, the repository of an infinite number of good qualities, there can be so many evils in this world? This question arose in all dualistic religions, but the Hindus never invented a Satan as an answer to it. The Hindus with one accord laid the blame on man, and it was easy for them to do so. Why? Because, as I have just now told you, they did not believe that souls were created out of nothing.

Another peculiar doctrine of the dualists is that every soul must eventually come to salvation. No one will be left out. Through various vicissitudes, through various sufferings and enjoyments, each one of them will come out in the end. Come out of what? The one common idea of all Hindu sects is that all souls have to get out of this universe. Neither the universe which we see and feel, nor even an imaginary one, can be right, the real one, because both are mixed up with good and evil. According to the dualists, there is beyond this universe a place full of happiness and good only and when that place is reached, there will be no more necessity of being born and reborn, of living and dying; and this idea is very dear to them.

One other idea the dualists preach. They protest against the idea of praying to God, 'Lord, give me this and give me that.' They think that should not be done. If a man must ask some material gift, he should ask inferior beings for it; ask one of these gods, or angels or a perfected being for temporal things. God is only to be loved. It is almost a blasphemy to pray to God, 'Lord, give me this, and give me that.' According to the dualists, therefore, what a man wants, he will get sooner or later, by praying to one of the gods; but if he wants salvation, he must worship God. This is the religion of the masses of India.

The real Vedanta philosophy begins with those known as the qualified non-dualists. They make the statement that the effect is never different from the cause; the effect is but the cause reproduced in another form. If the universe is the effect and God the cause, it must be God Himself—it cannot be anything but that. They start with the assertion that God is both the efficient and the material cause of the universe; that He Himself is the creator, and He Himself is the material out of which the whole of nature is projected. [...] Now, the whole universe, according to this sect, is God Himself.

What do these qualified non-dualists say? Theirs is a very peculiar theory. They say that these three existences, God, nature, and the soul, are one. God is, as it were, the Soul, and nature and souls are the body of God. Just as I have a body and I have a soul, so the whole universe and all souls are the body of God, and God is the Soul of souls. Thus, God is the material cause of the universe. The body may be changed—may be young or old, strong or weak—but that does not affect the soul at all. It is the same eternal existence, manifesting through the body. Bodies come and go, but the soul does not change. Even so, the whole universe is the body of God, and in that sense it is God. But the change in the universe does not affect God. Out of this material He creates the universe, and at the end of a cycle His body becomes finer, it contracts; at the beginning of another cycle it becomes expanded again, and out of it evolve all these different worlds.

Now both the dualists and the qualified non-dualists admit that the soul is by its nature pure, but through its own deeds it becomes impure. The qualified non-dualists express it more beautifully than the dualists, by saying that the soul's purity and perfection become contracted and again become manifest, and what we are now trying to do is to remanifest the intelligence, the purity, the power which is natural to the soul. Souls have a multitude of qualities, but not that of almightiness or all-knowingness. Every wicked deed contracts the nature of the soul, and every good deed expands it, and these souls are all parts of God.

Now we come to Advaitism, the last and, what we may think, the fairest flower of philosophy and religion that any country in any age has produced, where human thought attains its highest expression and even goes beyond the mystery which seems to be impenetrable. This is the non-dualistic Vedantism. It is too abstruse, too elevated to be the religion of the masses. Even in India, its birthplace, where it has been ruling supreme for the last three thousand years, it has not been able to permeate the masses. As we go on we shall find that it is difficult for even the most thoughtful man and woman in any country to understand Advaitism. We have made ourselves so weak; we have made ourselves so low. We may make great claims, but naturally we want to lean on somebody else. We are like little, weak plants, always wanting a support. How many times I have been asked for a 'comfortable religion!' Very few men ask for the truth, fewer still dare to learn the truth, and fewest of all dare to follow it in all its practical bearings.

What does the Advaitist declare? He says, if there is a God, that God must be both the material and the efficient cause of the universe. Not only is He the creator, but He is also the created. He Himself is this universe. How can that be? God, the pure, the spirit, has become the universe? Yes; apparently so. That which all ignorant people see as the universe does not really exist. What are you and I and all these things we see? Mere self-hypnotism; there is but one Existence, the Infinite, the Ever-Blessed One. In that Existence we dream all these various dreams.

It is the name, the form, the body, which are material, and they make all this difference. If you take away these two differences of name and form, the whole universe is one; there are no two, but one everywhere. You and I are one. There is neither nature, nor God, nor the universe, only that one Infinite Existence, out of which, through name and form, all these are manufactured. How to know the Knower? It cannot be known. How can you see your own Self? You can only reflect yourself. So all this universe is the reflection of that One Eternal Being, the Atman, and as the reflection falls upon good or bad reflectors, so good or bad images are cast up. [...] We are looking upon this one Existence in different forms and creating all these images upon It. To the being who has limited himself to the condition of man, It appears as the world of man. To the being who is on a higher plane of existence, It may seem like heaven. There is but one Soul in the universe, not two. It neither comes nor goes. It is neither born, nor dies, nor reincarnates. How can It die? Where can It go? All these heavens, all these earths, and all these places are vain imaginations of the mind. They do not exist, never existed in the past, and never will exist in the future.

Vol. 2, Jnana-Yoga, The Atman, pp. 238–249

According to the Advaita philosophy, there is only one thing real in the universe, which it calls Brahman; everything else is unreal, manifested and manufactured out of Brahman by the power of Maya. To reach back to that Brahman is our goal. We are, each one of us, that Brahman, that Reality, plus this Maya. If we can get rid of this Maya or ignorance, then we become what we really are.

Vol. 2, Jnana-Yoga, The Atman: Its Bondage and Freedom, p. 254

The Vedanta preaches the ideal, and the ideal, as we know, is always far ahead of the real, of the practical, as we may call it. There are two tendencies in human nature: one to harmonise the ideal with the life, and the other to elevate the life to the ideal.

It is a great thing to understand this, for the former tendency is the temptation of our lives [...] Vedanta, though it is intensely practical, is always so in the sense of the ideal. It does not preach an impossible ideal, however high it be, and it is high enough for an ideal. In one word, this ideal is that you are divine, 'Thou art That.'

Vedanta teaches men to have faith in themselves first. As certain religions of the world say that a man who does not believe in a Personal God outside of himself is an atheist, so the Vedanta says, a man who does not believe in himself is an atheist. Not believing in the glory of our own soul is what the Vedanta calls atheism. To many this is, no doubt, a terrible idea; and most of us think that this ideal can never be reached; but the Vedanta insists that it can be realised by every one.

The Vedanta recognises no sin; it only recognises error. And the greatest error, says the Vedanta, is to say that you are weak, that you are a sinner, a miserable creature, and that you have no power and you cannot do this and that. Every time you think in that way, you, as it were, rivet one more link in the chain that binds you down, you add one more layer of hypnotism on to your own soul. Therefore, whosoever thinks he is weak is wrong, whosever thinks he is impure in wrong, and is throwing a bad thought into the world.

Everything is ours already—infinite purity, freedom, love, and power. The Vedanta also says that not only can this be realised in the depths of forests or caves, but by men in all possible conditions of life [...] Most of us here have more time than we think we have, if we really want to use it for good.

The one central ideal of Vedanta is this oneness [...] There is but one life, one world, one existence. Everything is that One, the difference is in degree and not in kind. The difference between our lives is not in kind. The Vedanta entirely denies such ideas as that animals are separate from men, and that they were made and created by God to be used for our food.

So, from the standpoint of the highest ideal, the lowest animal and the highest man are the same. If you believe there is a God, the animals and the highest creatures must be the same. A God who is partial to his children called men, and cruel to his children called brute beasts, is worse than a demon. I would rather die a hundred times than worship such a God. My whole life would be a fight with such a God. But there is no difference, and those who say there is, are irresponsible, heartless people who do not know. Here is a case of the word practical used in a wrong sense. I myself may not be a very strict vegetarian, but I understand the ideal. When I eat meat I know it is wrong. Even if I am bound to eat it under certain circumstances, I know it is cruel. I must not drag my ideal down to the actual and apologise for my weak conduct in this way. The ideal is not to eat flesh, not to injure any being, for all animals are my brothers.

Vol. 2, Practical Vedanta and Other Lectures,
Practical Vedanta: Part I, pp. 293–298

The idea of hell does not occur in the Vedas anywhere. It comes with the Puranas much later. The worst punishment according to the Vedas is coming back to earth, having another chance in this world.

Vol. 2, Practical Vedanta and Other Lectures,
Practical Vedanta: Part II, p. 319

As the universe is without beginning and without end, so is God. We see that it must necessarily be so, because if we say there was a time when there was no creation, either in a gross or a fine form, then there was no God, because God is known to us as Sakshi, the Witness of the universe. When the universe did not exist, neither did He.

We have seen that there is the eternal God, and there is eternal nature. And there is also an infinite number of eternal souls. This is the first stage in religion, it is called dualism, the stage when man sees himself and God eternally separate, when God is a separate entity by Himself, and man is a separate entity by himself and nature is a separate entity by itself.

Then comes another view which I have just shown to you. Man begins to find out that if God is the cause of the universe and the universe the effect, God Himself must have become the universe and the souls, and he is but a particle of which God is the whole. We are but little beings, sparks of that mass of fire, and the whole universe is a manifestation of God Himself. This is the next step. In Sanskrit, it is called Vishishtadvaita [...] In the first view, that of dualism, each one of us is an individual, eternally separate from God and nature. In the second view, we are individuals, but not separate from God. We are like little particles floating in one mass, and that mass is God. We are individuals but one in God. We are all in Him. We are all parts of Him, and therefore we are One. And yet between man and man, man and God, there is a strict individuality, separate and yet not separate.

Then comes a still finer question. The question is: Can infinity have parts? What is meant by parts of infinity? If you reason it out, you will find that it is impossible. Infinity cannot be divided; it always remains infinite. If it could be divided, each part would be infinite. And there cannot be two infinites. Suppose there were, one would limit the other, and both would be finite. Infinity can only be one, undivided. Thus the conclusion will be reached that the infinite is one and not many, and that one Infinite Soul is reflecting itself through thousands and thousands of mirrors, appearing as so many different souls. It is the same Infinite Soul, which is the background of the universe, that we call God. The same Infinite Soul also is the background of the human mind which we call the human soul.

Vol. 2, Practical Vedanta and Other Lectures, Soul, Nature and God, pp. 428–431

This mass of writing called the Vedas is not the utterance of persons. Its date has never been fixed, can never be fixed, and, according to us, the Vedas are eternal. There is one salient point which I want you to remember, that all the other religions of the world claim their authority as being delivered by a Personal God or a number of personal beings, angels, or special messengers of God, unto certain persons; while the claim of the Hindus is that the Vedas do not owe their authority to anybody, they are themselves the authority, being eternal—the knowledge of God. They were never written, never created, they have existed throughout time; just as creation is infinite and eternal, without beginning and without end, so is the knowledge of God without beginning and without end. And this knowledge is what is meant by the Vedas (*Vid* to know). The mass of knowledge called the Vedanta was discovered by personages called Rishis, and the Rishi is defined as a Mantra-drashta, a seer of thought; not that the thought was his own. Whenever you hear that a certain passage of the Vedas came from a certain Rishi, never think that he wrote it or created it out of his mind; he was the seer of the thought which already existed; it existed in the universe eternally. This sage was the discoverer; the Rishis were spiritual discoverers.

This mass of writing, the Vedas, is divided principally into two parts, the Karma Kanda and the Jnana Kanda—the work portion and the knowledge portion, the ceremonial and the spiritual. The work portion consists of various sacrifices; most of them of late have been given up as not practicable under present circumstances, but others remain to the present day in some shape or other. The main ideas of the Karma Kanda, which consists of the duties of man, the duties of the student, of the householder, of the recluse, and the various duties of the different stations of life, are followed more or less down to the present day. But the spiritual portion of our religion is in the second part, the Jnana Kanda, the Vedanta, the end of the Vedas, the gist, the goal of the Vedas. The essence of the knowledge of the Vedas was called by the name of Vedanta, which comprises the Upanishads; and all the sects of India—Dualists, Qualified-Monists, Monists, or the Shaivites, Vaishnavites, Shaktaas, Sauras, Ganapatyas, each one that dares to come within the fold of Hinduism—must acknowledge the Upanishads of the Vedas. They can have their own interpretations and can interpret them in their own way, but they must obey the authority. That is why we want to use the words Vedantist instead of Hindu. All the philosophers of India who are orthodox have to acknowledge the authority of the Vedanta.

Next to the Vedanta come the Smritis. These also are books written by sages, but the authority of the Smritis is subordinate to that of the Vedanta, because they stand in the same relation with us as the scriptures of the other religions stand with regard to them. We admit that the Smritis have been written by particular sages; in that sense they are the same as the scriptures of other religions, but these Smritis are not the final authority. If there is anything in a Smriti which contradicts the Vedanta, the Smriti is to be rejected—its authority is gone. These Smritis, we see again, have varied from time to time. We read that such and such Smriti should have authority in the Satya Yuga, such and such in the Treta Yuga, some in the Dwapara Yuga, and some in the Kali Yuga, and so on. As essential conditions changed, as various circumstances came to have their influence on the race, manners and customs had to be changed, and these Smritis, as mainly regulating the manners and customs of the nation, had also to be changed from time to time. This is a point that I specially ask you to remember. The principles of religion that are in the Vedanta are unchangeable. Why? Because they are all built upon the eternal principles that are in man and nature; they can never change.

Then there are the Puranas [...] the Puranas are of five characteristics—that which treats of history, of cosmology, with various symbological illustration of philosophical principles, and so forth. These were written to popularise the religion of the Vedas. The language in which the Vedas are written in very ancient, and even among scholars very few can trace the date of these books. The Puranas were written in the language of the people of that time, what we call modern Sanskrit. They were then meant not for scholars, but for the ordinary people; and ordinary people cannot understand philosophy. Such things were given unto them in concrete form, by means of the lives of saints and kings and great men and historical events that happened to the race etc. The sages made use of these things to illustrate the eternal principles of religion.

There are still other books, the Tantras. These are very much like Puranas in some respects, and in some of them there is an attempt to revive the old sacrificial ideas of the Karma Kanda.

All these books constitute the scriptures of the Hindus. When there is such a mass of sacred books in a nation and a race which has devoted the greatest part of its energies to the thought of philosophy and spirituality (nobody knows for how any thousands of years), it is quite natural that there should be so many sects; indeed it is a wonder that there are not thousands more. These sects differ very much from each other in certain points. We shall not have time to understand the differences between these sects and all the spiritual details about them; therefore I shall take up the common grounds, the essential principles of all these sects which every Hindu must believe.

The first is the question of creation, that this nature, Prakriti, Maya is infinite, without beginning. It is not that this world was created the other day, not that a God came and created the world and since that time has been sleeping; for that cannot be. The creative energy is still going on. God is eternally creating—is never at rest. If that creative energy which is working all around us, day and night, stops for a second, the whole thing falls to the ground.

What makes this creation? God. What do I mean by the use of the English word God? Certainly not the word as ordinarily used in English—a good deal of difference. There is no other suitable word in English. I would rather confine myself to the Sanskrit word Brahman.

We now come to the second principle on which we all agree, not only all Hindus, but all Buddhists and all Jains. We all agree that life is eternal.

Vol. 3, Vedantism, pp. 118–124

Every Hindu who has tasted the fruits of this world must give up in the latter part of his life, and who does not is not a Hindu. We know that this is the ideal—to give up after seeing and experiencing the vanity of things.

Vol. 3, Lectures from Colombo to Almora, Reply to the Address of Welcome at Ramnad, p. 150

I think it is Vedanta, and Vedanta alone that can become the universal religion of man, and that no other is fitted for the role. Excepting our own almost all the other great religions in the world are inevitably connected with the life or lives of one or more of their founders [...] If there is one blow dealt to the historicity of that life, as has been the case in modern times with the lives of almost all the so-called founders of religion [...] if that rock of historicity as they pretend to call it is shaken and shattered, the whole building tumbles down, broken absolutely, never to regain its lost status.

The second claim of the Vedanta upon the attention of the world is that, of all the scriptures in the world, it is the one scripture the teaching of which is in entire harmony with the results that have been attained by the modern scientific investigations of external nature. Two minds in the dim past of history, cognate to each other in form and kinship and sympathy, started, being placed in different routes. The one was the ancient Hindu mind, and the other the ancient Greek mind. The former started by analysing the internal world. The latter started in search of that goal beyond by analysing the external world [...] It seems clear that the conclusions of modern materialistic science can be acceptable, harmoniously with their religion, only to the Vedantins or Hindus as they are called. It seems clear that modern materialism can hold its own and at the same time approach spirituality by taking up the conclusions of the Vedanta. It seems to us, and to all who care to know that the conclusions of modern science are the very conclusions the Vedanta reached ages ago; only, in modern science they are written in the language of matter.

The modern researches of the West have demonstrated through physical means the oneness and the solidarity of the whole universe; how, physically speaking, you and I, the sun, moon, and stars are but little waves of wavelets in the midst of an infinite ocean of matter; how Indian psychology demonstrated ages ago that similarly both body and mind are but mere names or little wavelets in the ocean of matter, the Samasthi; and how, going one step further, it is also shown in the Vedanta that behind that idea of the unity of the whole show, the real Soul is one. There is but one Soul throughout the universe, all is but One Existence.

Vol. 3, Lectures from Colombo to Almora,
The Mission of the Vedanta, pp. 182–188

The major portion of these books (Vedas) have disappeared, and it is only the minor portion that remains to us. They were all taken charge of by particular families; and either these families died out, or were killed under foreign persecution, or somehow became extinct; and with them that branch of the learning of the Vedas they took charge of became extinct also.

Vol. 3, Lectures from Colombo to Almora, Vedanta in its Application to Indian Life, p. 232

The Vedanta only can be the universal religion, that it is already the existing universal religion in the world, because it teaches principles and not persons. No religion built upon a person can be taken up as a type by all the races of mankind. In our own country we find that there have been so many grand characters; in even a small city many persons are taken up as types by the different minds in that one city.

We find the word Rishi again and again mentioned in the Vedas, and it has become a common word at the present time. The Rishi is the great authority […] the Rishi is the Mantra-drastha, the seer of thought.

How comes, then, the knowledge which the Vedas declare? It comes through being a Rishi. This knowledge is not in the senses, but are the senses the be-all and the end-all of the human being? Who dare say that the senses are the all-in-all of man? […] Men found out ages ago that the soul is not bound or limited by the senses, no, not even by consciousness. We have to understand that this consciousness is only the name of one link in the infinite chain. Being is not identical with consciousness, but consciousness is only one part of Being. Beyond consciousness is where the bold search lies. Consciousness is bound by the senses. Beyond that, beyond the senses, men must go in order to arrive at truths of the spiritual world, and there are even now persons who succeed in going beyond the bounds of the senses. These are called Rishis, because they come face to face with spiritual truths.

This Rishi-state is not limited by time or space, by sex or race. Vatsyayana boldly declares that this Rishihood is the common property of the descendants of the sage, of the Aryan, of the non-Aryan, of even the Mlechchha. This is the sageship of the Vedas, and constantly we ought to remember this ideal of religion in India, which I wish other nations of the world would also remember and learn, so that there may be less fight and less quarrel. Religion is not in books, nor in theories, nor in dogmas, nor in talking, not even in reasoning. It is being and becoming. Ay, my friends, until each one of you has become a Rishi and come face to face with spiritual facts, religious life has not begun for you. Until the superconscious opens for you, religion is mere talk, it is nothing but preparation.

Vol. 3, Lectures from Colombo to Almora,
The Sages of India, p. 250–253

Our scriptures are the best-preserved scriptures in the world. Compared to other books there have been no interpolations, no text-torturing, no destroying of the essence of the thought in them. It is there just at it was first, directing the human mind towards the ideal, the goal.

You find that these texts have been commented upon by different commentators, preached by great teachers, and sects founded upon them; and you find that in these books of the Vedas there are various apparently contradictory ideas. There are certain texts which are entirely dualistic, others are entirely monistic. The dualist commentator, knowing no better, wishes to knock the monistic texts on the head. Preachers and priests want to explain them in the dualistic meaning. The monistic commentator serves the dualistic texts in a similar fashion. Now this is not the fault of the Vedas. It is foolish to attempt to prove that the whole of the Vedas is dualistic. It is equally foolish to attempt to prove that the whole of the Vedas is non-dualistic. They are dualistic and non-dualistic both. We understand them better today in the light of newer ideas. These are but different conceptions leading to the final conclusion that both dualistic and monistic conceptions are necessary for the evolution of the mind, and therefore the Vedas preach them.

Vol. 3, Lectures from Colombo to Almora,
The Work Before Us, pp. 280–281

What is meant by a Rishi? The pure one. Be pure first, and you will have power. Simply saying, 'I am a Rishi' will not do; but when you are a Rishi you will find that others obey you instinctively. Something mysterious emanates from you, which makes them follow you, makes them hear you, makes them unconsciously, even against their will, carry out your plans. That is Rishihood.

Vol. 3, Lectures from Colombo to Almora,
The Future of India, p. 296

Nobody knows when it (the philosophy of the Vedanta) first came to flourish on the soil of India [...] But we Hindus, from the spiritual standpoint, do not admit that they had any origin. This Vedanta, the philosophy of the Upanishads, I would make bold to state, has been the first as well as the final thought on the spiritual plane that has ever been vouchsafed to man.

In spite of all these jarring sects that we see today and all those that have been in the past, the one authority, the basis of all these systems, has yet been the Upanishads, the Vedanta. Whether you are a dualist, or a qualified monist, an Advaitist, or a Vishishtadvaitist, a Shuddhadvaitist, or any other Advaitist, or Dvaitist, or whatever you may call yourself, there stand behind you an authority, your Shastras, your scriptures, the Upanishads. Whatever system in India does not obey the Upanishads cannot be called orthodox, and even the systems of the Jains and the Buddhists have been rejected from the soil of India only because they did not bear allegiance to the Upanishads. Thus the Vedanta, whether we know it or not, has penetrated all the sects in India, and what we call Hinduism this might banyan with its immense, almost infinite ramifications, has been throughout interpenetrated by the influence of the Vedanta. Whether we are conscious of it or not, we think the Vedanta, we live in the Vedanta, we breathe the Vedanta, and we die in the Vedanta, and every Hindu does that.

Many times the great sages of yore themselves could not understand the underlying harmony of the Upanishads [...] This is my attempt, my mission in life, to show that the Vedantic schools are not contradictory, that they all necessitate each other, all fulfil each other, and one, as it were, is the stepping-stone to the other, until the goal, the Advaita, the Tat Tvam Asi, is reached.

Vol. 3, Lectures from Colombo to Almora,
The Vedanta in All its Phases, pp. 322–324

There are certain great principles in which, I think, we [...] are all one, and whoever calls himself a Hindu believes in these principles [...] Perhaps all who are here will agree on the first point that we believe the Vedas to be the eternal teachings of the secrets of religion [...] The second point we all believe in is God [...] We may differ as to our conception of God [...] Preach whatever conception you have to give, but preach God; that is all we want. One idea may be better than another but, mind you, not one of them is bad [...] The third idea [...] is that, unlike all other races of the world, we do not believe that this world was created only so many thousand years ago and is going to be destroyed eternally on a certain day. Nor do we believe that the human soul has been created along with this universe just out of nothing. Here is another point I think we are all able to agree upon. We believe in nature being without beginning and without end; only at psychological periods this gross material of the outer universe goes back to its finer state, thus to remain for a certain period, again to be projected outside to manifest all this infinite panorama we call nature. This wavelike motion was going on even before time began, through eternity, and will remain for an infinite period of time. Next, all Hindus believe that man is not only a gross material body; not only that within this there is the finer body, the mind, but there is something yet greater—for the body changes and so does the mind—something beyond, the Atman [...] this Atman inhabits body after body until there is no more interest for it to continue to do so, and it becomes free, not to be born again. I refer to the theory of Samsara and the theory of eternal souls taught by our Shastras.

Vol. 3, Lectures from Colombo to Almora,
The Common Bases of Hinduism, pp. 372–374

The Indian mind got all that could be had from the external world, but it did not feel satisfied with that; it wanted to search further, to dive into its own soul, and the final answer came. The Upanishads, or the Vedanta, or the Aranyakas, or Rahasya is the name of this portion of the Vedas. Here we find at once that religion has got rid of all external formalities. Here we find at once that spiritual things are told not in the language of matter, but in the language of the spirit; the superfine in the language of the superfine [...] Even the Jnana Kanda of the Vedas is a vast ocean; many lives are necessary to understand even a little of it.

Unfortunately there is the mistaken notion in modern India that the word Vedanta has reference only to the Advaita system; but you must always remember that in modern India the three Prasthanas are considered equally important in the study of all the systems of religion. First of there are the Revelations, the Shrutis, by which I mean the Upanishads. Secondly, among our philosophies, the Sutras of Vyasa have the greatest prominence on account of their being the consummation of all the preceding systems of philosophy. These systems are not contradictory to one another, but one is based on another, and there is a gradual unfolding of the theme which culminates in the Sutras of Vyasa. Then, between the Upanishads and the Sutra, which are the systematising of the marvellous truths of the Vedanta, comes in the Gita, the divine commentary of the Vedanta.

The Upanishads, the Vyasa-Sutras, and the Gita, therefore, have been taken up by every sect in India that wants to claim orthodoxy, whether dualist, of Vishishtadvaitist, or Advaitist; the authorities of each are the three Prasthanas. We find that a Shankaracharya, or a Ramanuja, or a Madhvacharya, or a Vallabhacharya, or a Chaitanya—any one who wanted to propound a new sect—had to take up these three systems and write only a new commentary on them. Therefore, it would be wrong to confine the word Vedanta only to one system which has arisen out of the Upanishads. All these are covered by the word Vedanta. The Vishishtadvaitist has as much right to be called a Vedantist as the Advaitist; in fact I will go a little further and say that what we really mean by the word Hindu is really the same as Vedantist.

Vol. 3, Lectures from Colombo to Almora, The Vedanta, pp. 394–396

We must always remember that our backbone is spirituality, and to do that we must have a guide who will show the path to us, that path about which I am talking just now. If any of you do not believe it, if there be a Hindu boy amongst us who is not ready to believe that his religion is pure spirituality, I do not call him a Hindu.

Vol. 3, Lectures from Colombo to Almora, The Influence of Indian Spiritual Thought in England. p. 444

Why should you feel ashamed to take the name of Hindu, which is your greatest and most glorious possession?

Vol. 3, Lectures from Colombo to Almora, The Religion We Are Born In, p. 461

The Hindu idea, you know, is not to join anybody. Wherever you are, that is a point from which you can start to the centre. All right. It—Hinduismhas this advantage. Its secret is that doctrines and dogmas do not mean anything: what you are is what matters. If you talk all the best philosophies the world ever produced [but] if you are a fool in your behaviour, they do not count; and if in your behaviour you are good, you have more chances. This being so, the Vedantist can wait for everybody. Vedantism teaches that there is but one existence and one thing real, and that is God.

It is beyond all time and space and causation and everything. We can never define Him. We can never say what He is except [that] he is Absolute Existence, Absolute Knowledge, Absolute Blissfulness. He is the only reality. Of everything He is the reality; of you and me, of the wall and of [everything] everywhere. It is His knowledge upon which all our knowledge depends; it is His blissfulness upon which depends our pleasure; and He is the only reality. And when man realises this, he knows that 'I am the only reality, because I am He—what is real in me is He also.' So that, when a man is perfectly pure and good and beyond all grossness, he finds, as Jesus found: 'I and my Father are one.' The Vedantist has patience to wait for everybody. Wherever you are, this is the highest: 'I and my Father are one.' Realise it. If an image helps, you are welcome. If worshipping a great man helps you, you are welcome. If worshipping Mohammed helps you, go on. Only be sincere; and if you are sincere, says Vedantism, you are sure to be brought to the goal. None will be left. Your heart, which contains all truth, will unfold itself chapter after chapter, till you know the last truth, that 'I and my Father are one.' And what is salvation? To live with God. Where? Anywhere. Here this moment. One moment in infinite time is quite as good as any other moment. This is the old doctrine of the Vedas, you see. This was revived. Buddhism died out of India. It left its mark on their charity, its animals etc. in India; and Vedantism is reconquering India from one end to the other.

Vol. 3, Buddhistic India, pp. 536–537

The book known as the Gita forms a part of the Mahabharata. To understand the Gita properly, several things are very important to know. First, whether it formed a part of the Mahabharata, i.e. whether the authorship attributed to Veda-Vyasa was true, or it was merely interpolated within the great epic; secondly, whether there was any historical personality of the name of Krishna; thirdly, whether the great war of Kurukshetra as mentioned in the Gita actually took place; and fourthly, whether Arjuna and others were real historical persons.

According to some, this Kurukshetra War is only an allegory. When we sum up its esoteric significance it means the war which is constantly going on within man between the tendencies of good and evil. This meaning, too, may not be irrational.

There is enough ground of doubt as regards the historicity of Arjuna and others [...] Even if the historicity of the whole thing is proved to be absolutely false today, it will not in the least be any loss to us. (4.105)

Now it is for us to see what there is in the Gita. If we study the Upanishads we notice, in wandering through the mazes of many irrelevant subjects, the sudden introduction of the discussion of a great truth, just as in the midst of a huge wilderness a traveller unexpectedly comes across here and there an exquisitely beautiful rose, with its leaves, thorns, roots, all entangled. Compared with that, the Gita is like these truths beautifully arranged together in their proper places—like a fine garland or a bouquet of the choicest flowers. The Upanishads deal elaborately with Shraddha in many places, but hardly mention Bhakti. In the Gita, on the other hand, the subject of Bhakti is not only again and again dealt with, but in in it, the innate spirit of Bhakti has attained its culmination.

Now let us see some of the main points discussed in the Gita. Wherein lies the originality of the Gita which distinguishes it from all preceding scriptures? It is this: though before its advent, Yoga, Jnana, Bhakti etc. had each its strong adherents, they all quarrelled among themselves, each claiming superiority for his own chosen path; no one ever tried to seek for reconciliation among these different paths. It was the author of the Gita who for the first time tried to harmonise these. But even where Krishna failed to show a complete reconciliation (Samanvaya) among these warring sects, it was fully accomplished by Ramakrishna Paramahansa in this nineteenth century.

The next is, Nishkama Karma, or work without desire. People nowadays understand what is meant by this in various ways [...] The true Nishkama Karmi (performer of work without desire) is neither to be like a brute, nor to be inert, nor heartless. He is not Tamasika but of pure Sattva. His heart is so full of love and sympathy that he can embrace the whole world with his love. The world at large cannot generally comprehend his all-embracing love and sympathy.

The reconciliation of the different paths of Dharma, and work without desire or attachment—these are the two special characteristics of the Gita.

Vol. 4, Thoughts on the Gita, pp. 102–107

The one idea the Hindu religions differ in from every other in the world, the one idea to express which the sages almost exhaust the vocabulary of the Sanskrit language, is that man must realise God even in this life. And the Advaita texts very logically add, 'To know God is to become God.'

Vol. 4, Writings: Prose and Poems, Reply to the Madras Address, p. 342

All of religion is contained in the Vedanta, that is, in the three stages of the Vedanta philosophy, the Dvaita, Vishishtadvaita and Advaita; one comes after the other. These are the three stages of spiritual growth in man. Each one is necessary. This is the essential of religion: the Vedanta, applied to the various ethnic customs and creeds of India, is Hinduism. The first stage i.e. Dvaita, applied to the ideas of the ethnic groups of Europe, is Christianity; as applied to the Semitic groups, Mohammedanism. The Advaita, as applied in its Yoga-perception form, is Buddhism etc. Now by religion is meant the Vedanta; the applications must vary according to the different needs, surroundings, and other circumstances of different nations. You will find that although the philosophy is the same, the Shaktas, Shaivas etc. apply it each to their own special cult and *forms*.

Vol. 5, Epistles, (First Series), XXXIX, pp. 81–82

The correct meaning of the statement 'The Vedas are beginningless and eternal' is that the law or truth revealed by them to man is permanent and changeless. Logic, Geometry, Chemistry etc. reveal also a law or truth which is permanent and changeless, and in that sense they are also beginningless and eternal. But no truth or law is absent from the Vedas, and I ask any one of you to point out to me any truth which is not treated of in them.

Our philosophy does not depend upon any personality for its truth. Thus Krishna did not teach anything new or original to the world, nor does Ramayana profess anything which is not contained in the Scriptures. It is to be noted that Christianity cannot stand without Christ, Mohammedanism without Mohammed, and Buddhism without Buddha, but Hinduism stands independent of any man, and for the purpose of estimating the philosophical truth contained in any Purana, we need not consider the question whether the personages treated of therein were really material men or were fictitious characters. The object of the Puranas was the education of mankind, and the sages who constructed them contrived to find some historical personages and to superimpose upon them all the best or worst qualities just as they wanted to, and laid down the rules of morals for the conduct of mankind.

Vol. 5, Interviews, With the Swami Vivekananda at Madura, pp. 205–208

With all my respects for the Rishis of yore, I cannot but denounce their method in instructing the people. They always enjoined upon them to do certain things but took care never to explain to them the reason for it. This method was pernicious to the very core; and instead of enabling men to attain the end it laid upon their shoulders a mass of meaningless nonsense. Their excuse for keeping the end hidden from view was that the people could not have understood their real meaning even if they had presented it to them, not being worthy recipients. The

Adhikarivada is the outcome of pure selfishness. They knew that by this enlightenment on their special subject they would lose their superior position of instructors to the people. Hence their endeavour to support this theory. If you consider a man too weak to receive these lessons, you should try the more to teach and educate him; you should give him the advantage of more teaching, instead of less, to train up his intellect, so as to enable him to comprehend the more subtle problems. These advocates of Adhikarivada ignored the tremendous fact of the infinite possibilities of the human soul. Every man is capable of receiving knowledge if it is imparted in his own language. A teacher who cannot convince others should weep on account of his own inability to teach the people in their own language, instead of cursing them and dooming them to live in ignorance and superstition, setting up the pleas that the higher knowledge is not for them. Speak out the truth boldly, without any fear that it will puzzle the weak. Men are selfish; they do not want others to come up to the same level of their knowledge, for fear of losing their own privilege and prestige over others. Their contention is that the knowledge of the highest spiritual truths will bring about confusion in the understanding of the weak-minded men.

I cannot believe in the self-contradictory statement that light brings greater darkness. It is like losing life in the ocean of Sachchidananda, in the ocean of Absolute Existence and Immortality [...] How absurd! Knowledge paving the way to error! Enlightenment leading to confusion! Is it possible? Men are not bold enough to speak out broad truths, for fear of losing the respect of the people. They try to make a compromise between the real, eternal truths and the nonsensical prejudices of the people, and thus set up the doctrine that Lokacharas (customs of the people) and Deshacharas (customs of the country) must be adhered to.

The result of this sort of compromise is that the grand truths are soon buried under heaps of rubbish, and the latter are eagerly held as real truths. Even the grand truths of the Gita, so boldly preached by Shri Krishna, received the gloss of compromise in the hands of future generations of disciples, and the result is that the grandest scripture of the world is now made to yield many things which lead men astray.

This attempt at compromise proceeds from arrant downright cowardice.

Vol. 5, Notes from Lectures and Discourses, The Evils of Adhikarivada, pp. 262–264

The Vedas teach three things: this Self is first to be heard, then to be reasoned, and then to be meditated upon. When a man first hears it, he must reason on it, so that he does not believe it ignorantly, but knowingly; and after reasoning what it is, he must meditate upon it, and then realise it. And that is religion. Belief is no part of religion. We say religion is a superconscious state.

Vol. 5, Questions and Answers, I, Discussion at the Graduate Philosophical Society of Harvard University, p. 302

One peculiarity of the Vedas is that they are the only scriptures that again and again declare that you must go beyond them. The Vedas say that they were written just for the child mind; and when you have grown, you must go beyond them.

Vol. 5, Questions and Answers, II, At the Twentieth Century Club of Boston, p. 311

No such question as 'Whence has Maya come?' can be asked. Time-space causation is what is called Maya. You, I and everyone else are within this Maya; and you are asking about what is beyond Maya? How can you do so while living within Maya?

Vol. 5, Conversations and Dialogues, III, p. 339

Of all the scriptures of the world it is the Vedas alone that declare that even the study of the Vedas is secondary. The real study is 'that by which we *realise* the Unchangeable'. And that is neither reading, nor believing, nor reasoning, but superconscious perception, or Samadhi.

Vol. 5, Sayings and Utterances, 36, p. 411

With us, the prominent idea is Mukti; with the Westerners, it is Dharma. What we desire is Mukti; what they want is Dharma. Here the world 'Dharma' is used in the sense of the Mimamsakas. What is Dharma? Dharma is that which makes man seek for happiness in this world or the next. Dharma is established on work; Dharma is impelling man day and night to run after and work for happiness.

What is Mukti? That which teaches that even the happiness of this life is slavery, and the same is the happiness of the life to come, because neither this world nor the next is beyond the laws of nature; only, the slavery of this world is to that of the next as an iron chain is to a golden one. Again, happiness, wherever it may be, being within the laws of nature, is subject to death and will not last *ad infinitum*. Therefore man must aspire to become Mukta, he must go beyond the bondage of the body; slavery will not do. This Moksha-path is only in India and nowhere else. Hence is true the oft-repeated saying that Mukta souls are only in India and in no other country. But it is equally true that in future they will be in other countries as well; that is well and good, and a thing of great pleasure to us. There was a time in India when Dharma was compatible with Mukti. There were worshippers of Dharma, such as Yudhishthira, Arjuna, Duryodhana, Bhishma, and Karna, side by side with the aspirants of Mukti, such as Vyasa, Shuka, and Janaka. On the advent of Buddhism, Dharma was entirely neglected and the path of Moksha alone became predominant.

Vol. 5, Writings: Prose and Poems, The East and the West, Introduction, pp. 446–447

In every religion, you find there are the three stages: philosophy, mythology and ceremonial. There is one advantage which can be pleaded for the Vedanta, that in India fortunately, these three stages have been sharply defined. In other religions the principles are so interwoven with the mythology that it is very hard to distinguish one from the other. The mythology stands supreme, swallowing up the principles, and in course of centuries the principles are lost sight of.

The Vedas, as the Hindus say, are eternal. We now understand what they mean by their being eternal, i.e. that the laws have neither beginning nor end, just as nature has neither beginning nor end. Earth after earth, system after system, will evolve, run for a certain time, and then dissolve back into chaos; but the universe remains the same. Millions and millions of systems are being born, while millions are being destroyed. The universe remains the same. The beginning and the end of time can be told as regards a certain planet; but as regards the universe, time has no meaning at all. So are the laws of nature, the physical laws, the mental laws, the spiritual laws. Without beginning and without end are they; and it is within a few years, comparatively speaking, a few thousand years at best, that man has tried to reveal them. The infinite mass remains before us. Therefore the one great lesson that we learn from the Vedas, at the start, is that religion has just begun. The infinite ocean of spiritual truth lies before us to be worked on, to be discovered, to be brought into our lives. The world has seen thousands of prophets, and the world has yet to see millions.

The plan of Vedanta, therefore, is: first, to lay down the principles, map out for us the goal, and then to teach us the method by which to arrive at the goal, to understand and realise religion. Again, these methods must be various. Seeing that we are various in our natures, the same method can scarcely be applied to any two of us in the same manner.

Vedanta understands that and wants to lay before the world

different methods through which we can work. Take up any one you like; and if one does not suit you, another may. From this standpoint we see how glorious it is that there are so many religions in the world, how good it is that there are so many religions in the world, how good it is that there are so many teachers and prophets, instead of there being only one, as many persons would like to have it.

It is a most glorious dispensation of the Lord that there are so many religions in the world; and would to God that these would increase every day, until every man had a religion unto himself!

Vedanta understands that and therefore preaches the one principle and admits various methods. It has nothing to say against anyone—whether you are a Christian, or a Buddhist, or a Jew, or a Hindu, whatever mythology you believe, whether you owe allegiance to the prophet of Nazareth, or of Mecca, or of India, or of anywhere else, whether you yourself are a prophet—it has nothing to say. It only preaches the principle which is the background of every religion and of which all the prophets and saints and seers are but illustrations and manifestations. Multiply your prophets if you like; it has no objection. It only preaches the principle, and the method it leaves to you. Take any path you like; follow any prophet you like; but have only that method which suits your own nature, so that you will be sure to progress.

Vol. 6, Lectures and Discourses,
The Methods and Purpose of Religion, pp. 6–17

The three essentials of Hinduism are belief in God, in the Vedas as revelation, in the doctrine of Karma and transmigration. If one studies the Vedas between the lines, one sees a religion of harmony. One point of difference between Hinduism and other religions is that in Hinduism we pass from truth to truth—from a lower truth to a higher truth—and never from error to truth. The Vedas should be studied through the eye-glass of evolution. They contain the whole history of the progress of religious consciousness, until religion has reached perfection in unity. The Vedas are Anadi, eternal. The meaning of the statement is not, as is erroneously supposed by some, that the words of the Vedas are Anadi, but that the spiritual laws inculcated by the Vedas are such. These laws which are immutable and eternal have been discovered at various times by great men or Rishis, though some of them are forgotten now, while others are preserved.

Vol. 6, Notes of Class Talks and Lectures, Notes Taken Down in Madras 1892–93, p. 103

The fault with all religions like Christianity is that they have one set of rules for all. But Hindu religion is suited to all grades of religious aspirations and progress. It contains all the ideals in their perfect form. For example, the ideal of Shanta or blessedness is to be found in Vashishtha; that of love in Krishna; that of duty in Rama and Sita; and that of intellect in Shukadeva. Study the characters of these and of other ideal men. Adopt one which suits you best.

Vol. 6, Notes of Class Talks and Lectures, Notes Taken Down in Madras 1892–93, pp. 120–121

The authority of the Vedas extends to all ages, climes and persons; that is to say, their application is not confined to any particular place, time and persons. The Vedas are the only exponent of the universal religion. Although the supersensuous vision of truths is to be met with in some measure in our Puranas and Itihasas and in the religious scriptures of other races, still the fourfold scripture known among the Aryan race as the Vedas being the first, the most complete, and the most undistorted collection of spiritual truths, deserve to occupy the highest place among all scriptures, command the respect of all nations of the earth, and furnish the rationale of all their respective scriptures.

With regard to the whole Vedic collection of truths discovered by the Aryan race, this also has to be understood that those portions alone which do not refer to purely secular matters and which do not merely record tradition or history, or merely provide incentives to duty, form the Vedas in the real sense.

The Vedas are divided into two portions, the Jnana-kanda (knowledge-portion) and the Karma-kanda (ritual-portion). The ceremonies and the fruits of the Karma-kanda are confined within the limits of the world of Maya, and therefore they have been undergoing and will undergo transformation according to the law of change which operates through time, space, and personality.

It is the Jnana-kanda or the Vedanta only that has for all time commanded recognition for leading men across Maya and bestowing salvation on them through the practice of Yoga, Bhakti, Jnana, or selfless work; and as its validity and authority remain unaffected by any limitations of time, place or persons, it is the only exponent of the universal and eternal religion for all mankind.

Vol. 6, Writings: Prose and Poems, Hinduism and Shri Ramakrishna, pp. 181–183

Good and evil are not two things but one, the difference being only in manifestation—one of degree, not kind. Our very lives depend upon the death of others—plants or animals or bacilli! The other great mistake we often make is that good is taken as an ever-increasing item, whilst evil is a fixed quantity. From this it is argued that evil being diminished every day, there will come a time when good alone will remain. The fallacy lies in the assumption of a false premise. If good is increasing, so is evil [...] The progress of the world means more enjoyment and more misery too. This mixture of life and death, good and evil, knowledge and ignorance is what is called Maya—or the universal phenomenon. You may go on for eternity inside this net, seeking happiness—you find much, and much evil too. To have good and no evil is childish nonsense. Two ways are left open—one by giving up all hope to take up the world as it is and bear the pangs and pains in the hope of a crumb of happiness now and then. The other, to give up the search for pleasure, knowing it to be pain in another form, and seek for *truth*—and those that dare try for truth succeed in finding that truth as ever present—present in themselves.

Vol. 6, Epistles (Second Series), CXII, pp. 379–380

Whether we call it Vedantism or any *ism*, the truth is that Advaitism is the last word of religion and thought and the only position from which one can look upon all religions and sects with love. I believe it is the religion of the future enlightened humanity. The Hindus may get the credit of arriving at it earlier than other races., they being an older race than either the Hebrew or the Arab; yet practical Advaitism, which looks upon and behaves to all mankind as one's own soul, was never developed among the Hindus universally.

Vol. 6, Epistles (Second Series), CXLII, p. 415

The Hindus have been criticised so many years by their conquerors that they (the Hindus) dare to criticise their religion themselves, and this makes them free. Their foreign rulers struck off their fetters without knowing it. The most religious people on earth, the Hindus have actually no sense of blasphemy; to speak of holy things in any way is to them in itself sanctification. Nor have they any artificial respect for prophets or books, or for hypocritical piety.

Vol. 7, Inspired Talks, 3 July 1895, p. 30

The four Vedas, sciences, languages, philosophy, and all other learnings are only ornamental. The real learning, the true knowledge is that which enables us to reach Him who is unchangeable in His love.

Vol. 7, Epistles (Third Series), X, p. 455

The greatest teacher of the Vedanta philosophy was Shankaracharya. By solid reasoning he extracted from the Vedas the truth of Vedanta, and on them built up the wonderful system of Jnana that is taught in his commentaries. He unified all the conflicting descriptions of Brahman and showed that there is only one Infinite Reality. He showed too that as man can only travel slowly on the upward road, all the varied presentations are needed to suit his varying capacity.

Shankara taught that three things were the great gifts of God: (1) human body, (2) thirst after God, and (3) a teacher who can show us the light. When these three great gifts are ours, we may know that our redemption is at hand. Only knowledge can free and save us, but with knowledge must go virtue.

The essence of Vedanta is that there is but one Being and that every soul is that Being in full, not a part of that Being.

Vol. 8, Lectures and Discourses, Discourses on Jnana-Yoga, II, p. 6

Philosophy in Sanskrit means 'clear vision,' and religion is practical philosophy. Mere theoretic, speculative philosophy is not much regarded in India. There is no church, no creed, no dogma. The two great divisions are the 'Dvaitists' and the 'Advaitists.' The former say, 'The way to salvation is through the mercy of God; the law of causation, once set in motion, can never be broken; only God, who is not bound by this law, by His mercy helps us to break it.' The latter say, 'Behind all this nature is something that is free; and finding that which is beyond all law gets us freedom; and freedom is salvation.' Dualism is only one phase; Advaitism goes to the ultimate. To become pure is the shortest path to freedom. Only that is ours which we earn. No authority can save us, no beliefs. If there is a God, *all* can find Him.

Vol. 8, Lectures and Discourses, Discourses on Jnana-Yoga, IV, p. 15

The great Aryans, Buddha among the rest, have always put woman in an equal position with man. For them sex in religion did not exist. In the Vedas and Upanishads, women taught the highest truths and received the same veneration as men.

Vol. 8, Lectures and Discourses, Discourses on Jnana-Yoga, VII, p. 28

Vedanta is not antagonistic to anything, though it does not compromise or give up the truths which it considers fundamental.

Vedanta does not believe in a book—that is the difficulty to start with. It denies the authority of any book over any other book. It denies emphatically that any one book can contain all the truths about God, soul, the ultimate reality. Those of you who have read the Upanishads remember that they say again and again, 'Not by the reading of books can we realise the Self.' Second, it finds veneration for some particular person still more difficult to uphold. Those of you who are students of Vedanta—by Vedanta is always meant the Upanishads—know that this is the only religion that does not cling to any person. Not one man or woman has ever become the object of worship among the Vedantins. It cannot be. A man is no more worthy of worship than any bird, any worm. We are all brothers. The difference is only in degree [...] A still greater difficulty is about God. You want to be democratic in this country (USA). It is the democratic God that Vedanta teaches.

Its God is not the monarch sitting on a throne, entirely apart [...] You are all Gods. One God is not sufficient. You are all Gods, says the Vedanta. This makes Vedanta very difficult. It does not teach the old idea of God at all. In place of that God who sat above the clouds and managed the affairs of the world without asking our permission, who created us out of nothing just because He liked it and made us undergo all this misery just because He liked it, Vedanta teaches the God that is in everyone, has become everyone and everything.

What is the idea of God in heaven? Materialism. The Vedantic idea is the infinite principle of God embodied in every one of us. God sitting up on a cloud! Think of the utter blasphemy of it! It is materialism—downright materialism. When babies think this way, it may be all right, but when grown-up men try to teach such things, it is downright disgusting.

Vedanta knows no sin. There are mistakes, but no sin; and in the long run everything is going to be all right. No Satan—none of this nonsense. Vedanta believes in only one sin, only one in the world, and it is this: the moment you think you are a sinner or anybody is a sinner, that is sin. From that follows every other mistake or what is usually called sin. There have been many mistakes in our lives. But we are going on. Glory be unto us that we have made mistakes! Take a long look at your past life. If your present condition is good, it has been caused by all the past mistakes as well as successes.

What does Vedanta teach us? In the first place, it teaches that you need not even go out of yourself to know the truth. Al the past and all the future are here in the present. No man ever saw the past. Did any of you see the past? When you think you are knowing the past, you only imagine the past in the present moment. To see the future, you would have to bring it down to the present, which is the only reality—the rest is imagination.

Vedanta formulates, not universal brotherhood, but universal oneness. I am the same as any other man, as any animal—good, bad, anything. It is one body, one mind, one soul throughout. Spirit never dies. There is no death anywhere, not even for the body. Not even the mind dies. How can even the body die? One leaf may fall—does the tree die? The universe is my body. See how it continues.

Worship everything as God—every form in His temple. All else is delusion. Always look within, never without. Such is the God that Vedanta preaches, and such is His worship. Naturally there is no sect, no creed, no caste in Vedanta. How can this religion be the national religion of India?

The meaning of the word 'Veda,' from which the word

'Vedanta' comes, is knowledge. All knowledge is Veda, infinite as God is infinite. Nobody ever creates knowledge. It is only discovered—what was covered is uncovered. It is always here, because it is God Himself. Past, present, and future knowledge, all exist in all of us. We discover it; that is all. All this knowledge is God Himself. The Vedas are a great Sanskrit book. In our country we go down on our knees before the man who reads the Vedas, and we do not care for the man who is studying physics. That is superstition; it is not Vedanta at all. It is utter materialism. With God every knowledge is sacred. Knowledge is God. Infinite knowledge abides within every one in the fullest measure. You are not really ignorant, though you may appear to be so. You are incarnations of God, all of you. You are the incarnations of the Almighty, Omnipresent, Divine Principle. You may laugh at me now, but the time will come when you will understand. You must. Nobody will be left behind.

What is the goal? This that I have spoken of—Vedanta—is not a new religion. So old—as old as God Himself. It is not confined to any time and place; it is everywhere.

This Vedanta is everywhere, only you must become conscious of it. These masses of foolish beliefs and superstitions hinder us in our progress. If we can, let us throw them off and understand that God is spirit to be worshipped in spirit and in truth. Try to be materialists no more! Throw away all matter! The conception of God must be truly spiritual. All the different ideas of God, which are more or less materialistic, must go. As man becomes more and more spiritual, he has to throw off all these ideas and leave them behind. As a matter of fact, in every country there have always been a few who have been strong enough to throw away all matter and stand out in the shining light, worshipping the spirit by the spirit.

If Vedanta—this conscious knowledge that all is one spirit—spreads, the whole of humanity will become spiritual. But is it possible? I do not know. Not within thousands of years. The old superstitions must run out. You are all interested in how to perpetuate all your superstitions. Then there are the ideas of the family brother, the caste brother, the national brother. All these are barriers to the realisation of Vedanta. Religion has been religion to very few.

I am the servant of the man who has passed away. I am only the messenger. I want to make the experiment. The teachings of the Vedanta I have told you about were never really experimented with before. Although Vedanta is the oldest philosophy in the world, it has always become mixed up with superstitions and everything else.

Christ said, 'I and my Father are one,' and you repeat it. Yet it has not helped mankind. For nineteen hundred years men have not understood that saying. They make Christ the saviour of men. He is God and we are worms! Similarly in India. In every country, this sort of belief is the backbone of every sect. For thousands or years millions and millions all over the world have been taught to worship the Lord of the world, the Incarnations, the saviours, the prophets. They have been taught to consider themselves helpless, miserable creatures and to depend upon the mercy of some person or persons for salvation. There are no doubt many marvellous things in such beliefs. But even at their best, they are but kindergartens of religion, and they have helped but little. Men are still hypnotised into abject degradation. However, there are some strong souls who get over that illusion. The hour comes when great men shall arise and cast off these kindergartens of religion and shall make vivid and powerful the true religion, the worship of the spirit by the spirit.

Vol. 8, Lectures and Discourses, Is Vedanta the Future Religion?, pp. 122–141

I preach only the Upanishads [...] I have never quoted anything but the Upanishads. And of the Upanishads, it is only that one idea—strength. The quintessence of the Vedas and Vedanta and all lies in that one word.

Vol. 8, Sayings and Utterances, 23, p. 267

The Puranas the Swami considered to be the effort of Hinduism to bring lofty ideas to the door of the masses. There had been only one mind in India that had foreseen this need, that of Krishna, probably the greatest man who ever lived.

Vol. 8, Sayings and Utterances, 24, p. 268

”

Chapter 6

THE SOUL AND REINCARNATION

The human soul (Atman) is divine, eternal and immortal, perfect and infinite. It is indivisible, indestructible and without beginning or end. The Atman is never born, nor does it ever die. The soul was not created, for creation implies that it must die. The soul will go on evolving up or reverting back from birth to birth and death to death. This round of birth and death is called Samsara. Sooner or later, everyone will become free. But all must struggle. Some do so consciously, others unconsciously.

Every soul is a circle whose circumference is nowhere, but whose centre is located in the body, and death means a change of this centre from body to body. The soul is formless, and takes the form of the vessel it fills. The soul is held in the bondage of matter. Perfection will be reached when this bond bursts. Mukti, or freedom from the bonds of imperfection, from death and misery, comes only to the pure through the mercy of God.

The Atman is separate from the mind as well as the body. It is immaterial. Because it is immaterial, it cannot be a compound, and because it is not a compound, it does not obey the law of cause and effect, and so is immortal, without beginning and without end. It also follows that it must be formless, because everything that has form must have a beginning and an end. It is nature that is moving before the Atman, and the reflection of this motion is on the Atman. The Atman ignorantly thinks that it is in bondage (called Jiva), but when it finds that it never moves, and is omnipresent, freedom comes. If purity is not the nature of the soul, it can never attain purity. The Atman cannot be attained by the study of the Veda, by the intellect or by learning. Doing good deeds, having a calm mind and meditation enable us to understand and realize the Atman.

Although there is a soul in every person, there is still a unity of idea among the souls that enables one soul to act upon another. Thus, there is a metaphysical necessity of admitting another soul that covers all the infinite number of souls in the world. This universal Soul is Paramatman, the Lord, God, the universe.

There are many arguments in favour of reincarnation. Everything that we do or think creates an impression (Samskara) upon the mind, and the sum total of these impressions creates a person's character. The character of a man is what he has created for himself as a result of the mental and physical actions that he has done in this life. The sum total of the Samskaras is the force that gives a man the next direction after death. Reincarnation explains life's inequalities. Some people are born happy, physically healthy and mentally fit, and have the means to live a fulfilling life, whereas others may be born physically and mentally challenged and live a miserable existence. If souls are all created, why should a just and merciful God be so partial? Logically, this means that a soul's past actions are responsible for its present state. Every theory of the soul's creation from nothing leads to fatalism and preordination. Instead of a Merciful Father, it places before us a hideous, cruel and ever-angry God to worship, and to the horrible idea among some Christians and Muslims that heathens ought to be killed.

Secondly, if one is going to exist in eternity hereafter, it implies that you must have existed through eternity in the past. Our existence does not depend on our remembering our past. None of us remembers our early childhood, but that does not prove that we did not exist as babies! At the same time, there are instances where this memory does come back to some people in that life in which they will become free. According to thinkers in India, the fact that in this life we feel a deep love at first sight towards a particular person who may not be endowed with extraordinary qualities is explained as arising out of associations of a past incarnation. Apart from that, in every country and every age, there have been instances of people who have astonishing powers of reading the past and the future of a person's life.

Thirdly, without any existing experience, any new experience would be impossible, for there would be nothing to which to refer the new experience. Our actions (Karma) remain still unperceived (Adrishta) and reappear again in their effect as tendencies (Pravrittis). If we have not experienced it in this life, we must have experienced it in other lives. The fear of death, and all involuntary actions that have become instinctive, are the results of past experiences. This experience does not belong to the body, which disintegrates upon death, but to the soul. Christians and Muslims bury the dead body, thereby implying that the body is all. Hindus, on the other hand, cremate the dead body because they believe that the soul is not in the body and that it lives on.

If a person is born without the experience of a former life, it means his path is charted by others' experiences. Therefore, because he does not make his own fortune, he is not free. If freedom is not in your nature, you cannot become free. Supposing you were free and in some way you lost that freedom, this would show that you were not free to begin with. Had you been free, what could have made you lose it? One cannot establish the immortality of the soul unless one grants that it is by its nature free, and that it cannot be acted upon by anything outside.

Reincarnation is the nearest to a logical explanation for many of the things we are confronted with in the realm of religion. Admittedly, it is not a doctrine, but at best, only a theory, whose proof is only personal experience. Is there something better and more satisfactory to replace this theory?

"

The soul was not created, for creation means a combination which means a certain future dissolution. If then the soul was created, it must die. Some are born happy, enjoy perfect health, with beautiful body, mental vigour and all wants supplied. Others are born miserable, some are without hands or feet, others again are idiots and only drag on a wretched existence. Why, if they are all created, why does a just and merciful God create one happy and another unhappy, why is He so partial? Nor would it mend matters in the least to hold that those who are miserable in this life will be happy in a future one. Why should a man be miserable even here in the reign of a just and merciful God?

In the second place, the idea of a creator God does not explain the anomaly, but simply expresses the cruel fiat of an all-powerful being. There must have been causes then, before his birth, to make a man miserable or happy and those were his past actions.

We cannot deny that bodies acquire certain tendencies from heredity, but those tendencies only mean the physical configuration, through which a peculiar mind alone can act in a peculiar way. There are other tendencies peculiar to a soul caused by its past actions. And a soul with a certain tendency would by the laws of affinity take birth in a body which is the fittest instrument for the display of that tendency. This is in accord with science, for science wants repetitions. So repetitions are necessary to explain the natural habits of a new-born soul. And since they were not obtained in this present life, they must have come down from past lives.

The Hindu believes that every soul is a circle whose circumference is nowhere, but whose centre is located in the body, and that death means the change of this centre from body to body. Nor is the soul bound by the conditions of matter. In its very essence it is free, unbounded, holy, pure, and perfect. But somehow or other it finds itself tied down to matter, and thinks of itself as matter.

Why should the free, perfect, and pure being be thus under the thraldom of matter, is the next question. How can the perfect soul be deluded into the belief that it is imperfect? We have been told that the Hindus shirk the question and say that no such question can be there.

The human soul is eternal and immortal, perfect and infinite, and death means only a change of centre from one body to another. The present is determined by our past actions, and the future by the present. The soul will go on evolving up or reverting back from birth to birth and death to death.

The Vedas teach that the soul is divine, only held in the bondage of matter; perfection will be reached when this bond will burst, and the word they use for it is therefore, Mukti—freedom, freedom from the bonds of imperfection, freedom from death and misery. And this bondage can only fall off through the mercy of God, and this mercy comes on the pure. So purity is the condition of His mercy.

Vol. 1, Addresses at the Parliament of Religions, Why We Disagree, pp. 8–12

But why should the soul take to itself a body? For the same reason that I take a looking-glass—to see myself. Thus, in the body, the soul is reflected. The soul is God, and every human being has a perfect divinity within himself, and each one must show his divinity sooner or later.

Every religion has it that man's present and future are modified by the past, and that the present is but the effect of the past. How is it, then, that every child is born with an experience that cannot be accounted for by hereditary transmission? How is it that one is born of good parents, receives a good education and becomes a good man, while another comes from besotted parents and ends on the gallows? How do you explain this inequality without implicating God? Why should a merciful Father set His child in such conditions which must bring forth misery? It is no explanation to say God will make amends later on—God has no blood-money. Then, too, what becomes of my liberty, if this be my first birth? Coming into this world without the experience of a former life, my independence would be gone, for my path would be marked out by the experience of others. If I cannot be the maker of my own fortune, then I am not free. I take upon myself the blame for the misery of this existence, and say I will unmake the evil I have done in another existence. This, then, is the philosophy of the migration of the soul. We come into this life with the experience of another, and the fortune or misfortune of this existence is the result of our acts in a former existence, always becoming better, till at last perfection is reached.

We believe in a God, the Father of the universe, infinite and omnipotent. But if our soul at last becomes perfect, it also must become infinite. But there is no room for two infinite unconditional beings, and hence we believe in a Personal God, and we ourselves are He. These are the three stages which every religion has taken. First we see God in the far beyond, then we come nearer to Him and give Him omnipresence so that we live in Him; and at last we recognize that we are He.

Vol. 1, Lectures and Discourses, The Hindu Religion, pp. 330–331

In this country [America], there are millions who believe that God is [has?] a body [...] Whole sects say it. [They believe that] He rules the world, but there is a place where He has a body. He sits upon a throne. They light candles and sing songs just as they do in our temples.

But in India they are sensible enough never to make [their God a physical being]. You never see in India a temple of Brahma. Why? Because the idea of the soul always existed.

The Indian people have no regard for the dead body at all. [Their attitude is:] 'Let us take it and burn it.' The son has to set fire to his father's body.

The Indian idea is that the soul is formless. Whatever is form must break some time or other.

If thoughts were the real man, as soon as thought ceases, he ought to die. Thought ceases in meditation; even the mind's elements are quite quiet. Blood circulation stops. His breath stops, but he is not dead. If thought were he, the whole thing ought to go, but they find it does not go. That is practical [proof]. They came to the conclusion that even mind and thought were not the real man. Then speculation showed that it could not be.

Now, therefore, the real man does not belong to nature. It is the person whose mind and body belong to nature […] In nature alone are forms. That which is not of nature cannot have any forms, fine or gross. It must be formless. It must be omnipresent […] The soul is nameless because it is formless […] It takes the form of the vessel it fills.

Vol. 1, Lectures and Discourses, The Soul and God, pp. 493–495

The word used for the Soul is very significant: it is He who has gone inward, the innermost reality of our being, the heart centre, the core, from which, as it were, everything comes out […] The Infinite must be sought in that alone which is infinite, and the only thing infinite about us is that which is within us, our own soul.

Vol. 2, Jnana-Yoga, Unity in Diversity, p. 175

Why should you go to seek for what you never lost? You are pure already, you are free already. If you think you are free, free you are this moment, and if you think you are bound, bound you will be.

For, supposing that freedom is not your nature, by no manner of means can you become free. Supposing you were free and in some way you lost that freedom, that shows that you were not free to begin with. Had you been free, what could have made you lose it? The independent can never be made dependent; if it is really dependent, its independence was a hallucination.

You cannot establish the immortality of the soul, unless you grant that it is by its nature free or, in other words, that it cannot be acted upon by anything outside.

Vol. 2, Jnana-Yoga, The Freedom of the Soul, pp. 195–196

Neither you nor I nor anyone present has come out of zero, nor will go back to zero. We have been existing eternally, and will exist, and there is no power under the sun or above the sun which can undo your or my existence or send us back to zero. Now this idea of reincarnation is not only not a frightening idea, but is most essential for the moral well-being of the human race. It is the only logical conclusion that thoughtful men can arrive at. If you are going to exist in eternity hereafter, it must be that you have existed through eternity in the past: it cannot be otherwise.

The first objection is why do we not remember our past? Do we remember all our past in this life? How many of you remember what you did when you were babies? None of you remember early childhood, and if upon memory depends your existence, then this argument proves that you did not exist as babies, because you do not remember your babyhood. It is simply unmitigated nonsense to say that our existence depends on our remembering it.

Although we have seen that it is not necessary for the theory that there shall be the memory of past lives, yet at the same time we are in a position to assert that there are instances which show that this memory does come, and that each one of us will get back this memory in that life in which he will become free. Then alone you will find that this world is but a dream; then alone you will realise in the soul of your soul that you are but actors and the world is a stage; then alone will the idea of non-attachment come to you with the power of thunder; then all this thirst for enjoyment, this clinging on to life and this world will vanish for ever; then the mind will see clearly as daylight how many times all these existed for you, how many millions of times you had fathers and mothers, sons and daughters, husbands and wives, relatives and friends, wealth and power. They came and went. How many times you were on the topmost crest of the wave, and how many times you were down at the bottom of despair!

Are there any arguments, any rational proofs for this reincarnation of the soul? So far we have been giving the negative side, showing that the opposite arguments to disprove it are not valid. Are there any positive proofs? There are; and most valid ones, too. No other theory except that of reincarnation accounts for the wide divergence that we find between man and man in their powers to acquire knowledge.

Without a fund of already existing experience, any new experience would be impossible, for there would be nothing to which to refer the new impression. [...] We see that the power of acquiring knowledge varies in each individual, and this shows that each one of us has come with his own fund of knowledge. Knowledge can only be got in one way, the way of experience; there is no other way to know. If we have not experienced it in this life, we must have experienced it in other lives.

The fear of death [...] and all involuntary actions in the human being which have become instinctive, are the results of past experiences. So far we have proceeded very clearly, and so far the latest science is with us. But here comes one more difficulty. The latest scientific men are coming back to the ancient sages, and as far as they have done so, there is perfect agreement. They admit that each man and each animal is born with a fund of experience, and that all these actions in the mind are the result of past experience. 'But what,' they ask, 'is the use of saying that

that experience belongs to the soul? Why not say it belongs to the body, and the body alone? Why not say it is hereditary transmission?'

The simple hereditary theory takes for granted the most astonishing proposition without any proof, that mental experience can be recorded in matters, that mental experience can be involved in matter. [...] But what proof is there for assuming that the mental impression can remain in the body, since the body goes to pieces?

The soul migrates and manufactures body after body, and each thought we think, and each deed we do, is stored in it in fine forms, ready to spring up again and take a new shape. [...] So, what directs the soul when the body dies? The resultant, the sum total of all the works it has done, of the thoughts it has thought. If the resultant is such that it has to manufacture a new body for further experience, it will go to those parents who are ready to supply it with suitable material for that body. Thus, from body to body it will go, sometimes to a heaven, and back again to earth, becoming man, or some lower animal. This way it will go on until it has finished its experience, and completed the circle. It then knows its own nature, knows what it is, and ignorance vanishes, its powers become manifest, it becomes perfect; no more is there any necessity for the soul to work through physical bodies, nor is there any necessity for it to work through finer, or mental bodies. It shines in its own light, and is free, no more to be born, no more to die.

Vol. 2, Jnana-Yoga, The Cosmos, The Microcosm, pp. 217–224

How is it possible for anyone to see what the future will be, unless there is a regulated future? Effects of the past will recur in the future, and we see that it is so. [...] Nature is like the chain of the Ferris Wheel, endless and infinite, and these little carriages are the bodies or forms in which fresh batches of souls are riding, going up higher and higher until they become perfect and come out of the wheel. But the wheel goes on. And so long as the bodies are in the wheel, it can be absolutely and mathematically foretold where they will go, but not so of the souls. Thus it is possible to read the past and the future of nature with precision.

No force can die, no matter can be annihilated. What becomes of it? It goes on changing, backwards and forwards, until it returns to the source from which it came. There is no motion in a straight line. Everything moves in a circle; a straight line, infinitely produced, becomes a circle. If that is the case, there cannot be eternal degeneration for any soul.

The body cannot be the soul. Why not? Because it is not intelligent.

You are everywhere in the universe. How is it then that I am born and I am going to die, and all that? That is the talk of ignorance, hallucination of the brain. You were neither born, nor will you die. You have had neither birth, nor will have rebirth, nor life, nor incarnation, nor anything. What do you mean by coming and going? All shallow nonsense. You are everywhere. Then what is this coming and going? It is the hallucination produced by the change of this fine body which you call the mind. […] How could there be mortality when there was no birth?

You are the omniscient, omnipresent being of the universe. But of such beings can there be many? Can there be a hundred thousand millions of omnipresent beings? Certainly not. Then, what becomes of us all? You are only one; there is only one such Self, and that One Self is you. Standing behind this little nature is what we call the Soul. There is only One Being, One Existence, the ever-blessed, the omnipresent, the omniscient, the birthless, the deathless.

Therefore know that thou art He; thou art the God of this universe, 'Tat Tvam Asi' (That thou art). All these various ideas that I am a man or a woman, or sick or healthy, or strong or weak, or that I hate or I love, or have a little power, are but hallucinations.

Vol. 2, Jnana-Yoga, Immortality, pp. 230–236

The Atman is the only existence in the human body which is immaterial. Because it is immaterial, it cannot be a compound, and because it is not a compound, it does not obey the law of cause and effect, and so it is immortal. That which is immortal can have no beginning because everything with a beginning must have an end. It also follows that it must be formless; there cannot be any form without matter. Everything that has form must have a beginning and an end.

Each work we do, each thought we think, produces an impression, called in Sanskrit Samskara, upon the mind and the sum total of these impressions becomes the tremendous force which is called 'character.' The character of a man is what he has created for himself; it is the result of the mental and physical actions that he has done in his life. The sum total of the Samskaras is the force which gives a man the next direction after death.

All our lives, past, present and future, form, as it were, an infinite chain, without beginning and without end, each link of which is one life, with two ends, birth and death. What we are and do here is being repeated again and again, with but little variation. So if we know these two links, we shall know all the passages we shall have to pass through in this world. We see, therefore, that our passage into this world has been exactly determined by our previous passages. Similarly we are in this world by our own actions.

The Atman never comes nor goes, is never born nor dies. It is nature moving before the Atman, and the reflection of this motion is on the Atman; and the Atman ignorantly thinks that it is in bondage; but when it comes to find it never moves, that it is omnipresent, then freedom comes. The Atman in bondage is called Jiva. Thus you see that when it is said that the Atman comes and goes, it is said only for facility of understanding, just as for convenience in studying astronomy you are asked to suppose that the sun moves round the earth, though such is not the case. So the Jiva, the soul, comes to higher or lower states. This is the well-known law of reincarnation; and this law binds all creation.

People in this country [USA] think it is too horrible that man should come up from an animal. Why? What will be the end of these millions of animals? Are they nothing? If we have a soul, so have they, and if they have none, neither have we. It is absurd to say that man alone has a soul, and the animals none. I have seen men worse than animals.

The human soul has sojourned in lower and higher forms, migrating from one to another, according to the Samskaras or impressions, but it is only in the highest form as man that it attains to freedom. The man form is higher than even the angel form, and of all forms it is the highest; man is the highest being in creation, because he attains to freedom.

The going from birth to death, this travelling, is what is called Samsara in Sanskrit, the round of birth and death literally. All creation, passing through this round, will sooner or later become free. The question may be raised that if we all shall come to freedom, why should we *struggle* to attain it? If every one is going to be free, we will sit down and wait. It is true that every being will become free, sooner or later; no one can be lost. Nothing can come to destruction; everything must come up. If that is so, what is the use of our struggling? In the first place, the struggle is the only means that will bring us to the centre, and in the second place, we do not know why we struggle. We have to. 'Of thousands of men some are awakened to the idea that they will become free.' The vast masses of mankind are content with material things, but there are some who awake, and want to get back, who have had enough of this playing, down here. These struggle consciously, while the rest do it unconsciously.

Suppose we have all come from God, but we find this world is pleasurable and nice; then why should we not rather try to get more and more of this world? Why should we try to get out of it? They say, look at the wonderful improvements going on in the world every day, how much luxury is being manufactured for it. This is very enjoyable. Why should we go away, and strive for something which is not this? The answer is that the world is certain to die, to be broken into pieces and that many times we have had the same enjoyments. All the forms which we are seeing now have been manifested again and again, and the world in which we live has been here many times before.

Astonishing powers of reading the past and the future of a man's life have been known in every country and every age. The explanation is that so long as the Atman is within the realm of causation—though its inherent freedom is not entirely lost and can assert itself, even to the extent of taking the soul out of the causal chain, as it does in the case of men who become free—its actions are greatly influenced by the causal law and thus make it possible for men, possessed with the insight to trace the sequence of effects, to tell the past and the future.

Vol. 2, Jnana-Yoga, The Atman: Its Bondage and Freedom, pp. 254–261

All the knowledge that we have in this world, where did it come from? It was within us. What knowledge is outside? None. Knowledge was not in matter; it was in man all the time. Nobody ever created knowledge; man brings it from within. It is lying there. The whole of that big banyan tree which covers acres of ground, was in the little seed which was, perhaps, no bigger than one eighth of a mustard seed; all that mass of energy was there confined. The gigantic intellect, we know, lies coiled up in the protoplasmic cell, and why should not the infinite energy? We know that it is so. It may seem like a paradox, but is true. Each one of us has come out of one protoplasmic cell, and all the powers we possess were coiled up there. You cannot say they came from food; for if you heap up food mountains high, what power comes out of it? The energy was there, potentially no doubt, but still there. So is infinite power in the soul of man, whether he knows it or not. Its manifestation is only a question of being conscious of it.

Vol. 2, Practical Vedanta and Other Lectures, Practical Vedanta: Part III, pp. 339–340

This Atman is not to be attained by the study of the Vedas, nor by the highest intellect, nor by much learning. Whom the Atman seeks, he gets the Atman; unto him He discloses His glory. He who is continuously doing evil deeds, he whose mind is not calm, he who cannot meditate, he who is always disturbed and fickle—he cannot understand and realise this Atman who has entered the cave of the heart. This body, O Nachiketas, is the chariot, the organs of the senses are the horses, the mind is the reins, the intellect is the charioteer, and the soul is the rider in the chariot. When the soul joins himself with the charioteer, Buddhi or intellect, and then through it with the mind, the reins, and through it again with the organs, the horses, he is said to be the enjoyer; he perceives, he works, he acts.

Vol. 2, Practical Vedanta and Other Lectures, The Way to Blessedness, pp. 409–410

The soul is not composed of any materials. It is unity indivisible. Therefore it must be indestructible. For the same reasons it must also be without any beginning. So the soul is without any beginning and end.

Vol. 2, Practical Vedanta and Other Lectures, Soul, Nature and God, p. 428

After the meeting, to a Post reporter Mr. Kananda said: 'I claim no affiliation with any religious sect, but occupy the position of an observer, and so far as I may, of a teacher to mankind.

All religion to me is good. About the higher mysteries of life and existence I can do no more than speculate, as others do. Reincarnation seems to me to be the nearest to a logical explanation for many things with which we are confronted in the realm of religion. But I do not advance it as a doctrine. It is no more than a theory at best, and is not susceptible of proof except by personal experience, and that proof is good only for the man who has it. Your experience is nothing to me, nor mine to you. I am not a believer in miracles—they are repugnant to me in matters of religion. You might bring the world tumbling down about my ears, but that would be no proof to me that there was a God, or that you worked by his agency, if there was one.

I must, however, believe in a past and a hereafter as necessary to the existence of the present. And if we go on from here, we must go in other forms, and so comes my belief in reincarnation. But I can prove nothing, and anyone is welcome to deprive me of the theory of reincarnation provided they will show me something better to replace it. Only up to the present I have found nothing that offers so satisfactory an explanation to me.'

Vol. 2, Reports in American Newspapers,
All Religions are Good, pp. 497–498

What is the soul? We cannot understand God in our scriptures without knowing the soul. There have been attempts in India, and outside of India too, to catch a glimpse of the beyond by studying external nature and we all know what an awful failure has been the result. Instead of giving us a glimpse of the beyond, the more we study the material world, the more we tend to become materialised. The more we handle the material world, even the little spirituality which we possessed before vanishes. Therefore that is not the way to spirituality, to knowledge of the Highest; but it must come through the heart, the human soul. The external workings do not teach us anything about the beyond, about the Infinite, it is only the internal that can do so. Through soul, therefore, the analysis of the human soul alone can we understand God. There are differences of opinion as to the nature of the human soul among the various sects in India, but there are certain points of agreement. We all agree that souls are without beginning and without end, and immortal by their very nature; also that all powers, blessing, purity, omnipresence, omniscience are buried in each soul. That is a grand idea we ought to remember. In every man and in every animal, however weak or wicked, great or small, resides the same omnipresent, omniscient soul. The difference is not in the soul, but in the manifestation. Between me and the smallest animal, the difference is only in manifestation, but as a principle he is the same as I am, he is my brother, he has the same soul as I have. This is the greatest principle that India has preached. The talk of the brotherhood of man becomes in India the brotherhood of universal life, of animals, and of all life down to the little ants—all these are our bodies. Even as our scripture says, 'Thus the sage, knowing that the same Lord inhabits all bodies, will worship every body as such.' That is why in India there have been such merciful ideas about the poor, about animals, about everybody, and everything else. This is one of the common grounds about our ideas of the soul.

Naturally, we come to the idea of God. One thing more about the soul. Those who study the English language are often deluded by the words, soul and mind. Our Atman and soul are entirely different things. What we call Manas, the mind, the Western people call soul. The West never had the idea of soul until they got it through Sanskrit philosophy, some twenty years ago. The body is here, beyond that is the mind, yet the mind is not the Atman; it is the fine body, the Sukshma Sharira, made of fine particles, which goes from birth to death, and so on; but behind the mind is the Atman, the soul, the Self of man. It cannot be translated by the word soul or mind, so we have to use the word Atman, the soul, the Self of man. It cannot be translated by the word soul, so we have to use the word Atman, or, as Western philosophers have designated it, by the word Self. Whatever word you use, you must keep it clear in your mind that the Atman is separate from the mind, as well as from the body, and this Atman goes through birth and death, accompanied by the mind, the Sukshma Sharira.

Vol. 3, Lectures from Colombo to Almora, Vedantism, pp. 125–126

And then this peculiar idea, different from that of all other races of men, that this Atman inhabits body after body until there is no more interest for it to continue to do so, and it becomes free, not to be born again. I refer to the theory of Samsara and the theory of eternal souls taught by our Shastras. This is another point where we all agree, whatever sect we may belong to. There may be differences as to the relation between soul and God. According to one sect the soul may be eternally different from God, according to another it may be a spark of that infinite fire, yet again according to others it may be one with that Infinite. It does not matter what our interpretation is, so long as we hold on to the one basic belief that the soul is infinite, that this soul was never created, and therefore will never die, that it had to pass and evolve into various bodies, till it attained perfection in the human one—in that we are all agreed. And then comes the most differentiated, the grandest, and the most wonderful discovery in the realms of spirituality that has ever been made. Some of you, perhaps, who have been studying Western thought, may have observed already that there is another radical difference severing at one stroke all that is Western from all that is Eastern. It is this that we hold, whether we are Shaktas, Sauras, or Vaishnavas, even whether we are Bauddhas or Jainas, we all hold in India that the soul is by its nature pure and perfect, infinite in power and blessed. Only, according to the dualist, this natural blissfulness of the soul has become contracted by past bad work, and through the grace of God it is again going to open out and show its perfection; while according to the monist, even this idea of contraction is a partial mistake, it is the veil of Maya that causes us to think the soul has lost its powers, but the powers are there fully manifest.

As says our great philosopher Kapila, if purity has not been the nature of the soul, it can never attain purity afterwards, for anything that was not perfect by nature, even if it attained to perfection, that perfection would go away again. If impurity is the nature of man, then man will have to remain impure, even though he may be pure for five minutes. The time will come when this purity will wash out, pass away, and the old natural impurity will have its sway once more. Therefore, say all our philosophers, good is our nature, perfection is our nature, not imperfection, not impurity—and we should remember that [...] Follies there are, weaknesses there must be, but remember your real nature always—that is the only way to cure the weakness, that is the only way to cure the follies.

Vol. 3, Lectures from Colombo to Almora, The Common Bases of Hinduism, pp. 374–377

If there is an external world, it is always unknown and unknowable. What we know of it is as it is moulded, formed, fashioned by our own mind. So with the internal world. The same applies to our own soul, the Atman. In order to know the Atman, we shall have to know It through the mind and, therefore, what little we know of this Atman is simply the Atman plus the mind. That is to say, the Atman covered over, fashioned and moulded by the mind, and nothing more.

In spite of people's curious notions about Advaitism, people's fright about Advaitism, it is the salvation of the world, because therein alone is to be found the reason of things. Dualism and other *isms* are very good as means of worship, very satisfying to the mind, and maybe they have helped the mind onward; but if man wants to be rational and religious at the same time, Advaita is the one system in the world for him.

The idea is this, that in spite of the continuous change in the body, and in spite of this continuous change in the mind, there is in us something that is unchangeable, which makes our ideas of things appear unchangeable [...] Therefore there must be something which is neither the body nor the mind, something which changes not, something permanent, upon which all our ideas, our sensations fall to form a unity and a complete whole; and this is the real soul, the Atman of man.

Taking for granted that there is a soul, unchangeable, in each man, which is neither the mind nor the body, there is still a unity of idea among the souls, a unity of feeling, of sympathy. How is it possible that my soul can act upon your soul, where is the medium through which it can work, where is the medium through which it can act? How is it I can feel anything about your souls? What is it that is in touch both with your soul and my soul? Therefore there is a metaphysical necessity of admitting another soul, for it must be a soul which acts in contact with all the different souls, and in and through matter—one soul which covers and interpenetrates all the infinite number of souls in the world, in and through which they live, in and through which they sympathise, and love, and work for one another. And this universal Soul is Paramatman, the Lord God of the universe. Again, it follows that because the soul is not made of matter, it cannot be judged by the laws of matter. It is, therefore, unconquerable, birthless, deathless, and changeless.

Vol. 3, Lectures from Colombo to Almora, The Vedanta, pp. 403–406

The Vedas teach us that the soul of man is immortal. The body is subject to the law of growth and decay; what grows must of necessity decay. But the indwelling spirit is related to the infinite and eternal life; it never had a beginning and it never will have an end. One of the chief distinctions between the Hindu and the Christian religions is that the Christian religion teaches that each human soul had its beginning at its birth into this world, whereas the Hindu religion asserts that the spirit of man is an emanation of the Eternal Being, and had no more a beginning than God Himself. Innumerable have been and will be its manifestations in its passage from one personality to another, subject to the great law of spiritual evolution, until it reaches perfection, when there is no more change.

Vol. 4, Lectures and Discourses, Indian Religious Thought, pp. 188–189

This soul is without birth and without death; it is not a compound or combination but an independent individual, and as such it cannot be created or destroyed. It is only travelling through different states.

Naturally, the question arises: Where was it all this time? The Hindu philosophers say, 'It was passing through different bodies in the physical sense, or, really and metaphysically speaking, passing through different mental planes.

Are there any proofs apart from the teachings of the Vedas upon which the doctrine of reincarnation has been founded by the Hindu philosophers? There are, and we hope to show later on that there are grounds as valid for it as for any other universally accepted doctrine.

The premises from which the inference is drawn of a previous existence, and that too on the plane of conscious action, as adduced by the Hindu philosophers, are chiefly these:

First, how else to explain this world of inequalities? [...] There is no other way to vindicate the glory and the liberty of the human soul and reconcile the inequalities and the horrors of this world than by placing the whole burden upon our legitimate cause—our own independent actions or Karma. Not only so, but every theory of the creation of the soul from nothing inevitably leads to fatalism and preordination, and instead of a Merciful Father, places before us a hideous, cruel and an ever-angry God to worship. And so far as the power of religion for good or evil is concerned, this theory of a created soul, leading to its corollaries of fatalism and predestination, is responsible for the horrible idea prevailing among some Christians and Mohammedans that the heathens are the lawful victims of their swords, and all the horrors that have followed and are following it still.

But an argument which the philosophers of the Nyaya school have always advanced in favour of reincarnation, and which to us seems conclusive, is this: Our experiences cannot be annihilated. Our actions (Karma) though apparently disappearing, remain still unperceived (Adrishta), and reappear again in their effect as tendencies (Pravrittis). Even little babies come with certain tendencies—fear of death, for example.

Now if a tendency is the result of repeated actions, the tendencies with which we are born must be explained on that ground too. Evidently we could not have got them in this life; therefore we must have to seek for their genesis in the past. Now it is also evident that some of our tendencies are the effects of the self-conscious efforts peculiar to man; and if it is true that we are born with such tendencies, it rigorously follows that their causes were conscious efforts in the past—that is, we must have been on the same mental plane which we call the human plane, before this present life.

So far as explaining the tendencies of the present life by past conscious efforts goes, the reincarnationists of India and the latest school of evolutionists are at once; the only different is that the Hindus, as spiritualists, explain it by the conscious efforts of individual souls, and the materialistic school of evolutionists, by a hereditary physical transmission. The schools which hold to the theory of creating out of nothing are entirely out of court.

The issue has to be fought between the reincarnationists who hold that all experiences are stored up as tendencies in the subject of those experiences, the individual soul, and are transmitted by reincarnation of that unbroken individuality—and the materialists who hold that the brain is the subject of all actions and the theory of the transmission through cells.

It is thus that the doctrine of reincarnation assumes an infinite importance to our mind, for the fight between reincarnation and mere cellular transmission is, in reality, the fight between spiritualism and materialism. If cellular transmission is the all-sufficient explanation, materialism is inevitable, and there is no necessity for the theory of a soul. If it is not a sufficient explanation, the theory of an individual soul bringing into this life the experiences of the past is as absolutely true. There is no escape from the alternative, reincarnation or materialism. Which shall we accept?

Vol. 4, Writings: Prose and Poems, Reincarnation, pp. 265–271

That in this life we feel a deep love at first sight towards a particular person who may not be endowed with extraordinary qualities, is explained by the thinkers of our country as due to the associations of a past incarnation.

Vol. 5, Epistles (First Series), LXXXIX, p. 147

When you (British) say a man dies, your phrase is, 'He gave up the ghost,' whereas we say, 'He gave up the body.' Similarly, you more than imply that the body is the chief part of man by saying it possesses a soul. Whereas we say a man is a soul and possesses a body.

Vol. 5, Interviews, India and England, p. 195

It is possible for those that have uncovered the hidden powers of their nature to remember the incidents connected with their past incarnations, for their present brain had its Bija (seed) in the Sukshma man after death.

Vol. 5, Interviews, With the Swami Vivekananda at Madura, p. 208

Hinduism indicates one duty, only one, for the human soul. It is to seek to realise the permanent amidst the evanescent. No one presumes to point out any one way in which this may be done. Marriage or non-marriage, good or evil, learning or ignorance, any of these is justified, if it leads to the goal.

Vol. 5, Interviews, On Indian Women—Their Past, Present and Future, p.232

The Soul is beyond life and death. You were never born, and you will never die. Birth and death belong to the body only.

Vol. 5, Notes from Lectures and Discourses, The Cosmos and the Self, p. 257

The soul is a circle whose circumference is nowhere (limitless) but whose centre is in some body. Death is but a change of centre. God is a circle whose circumference is nowhere, and whose centre is everywhere. When we can get out of the limited centre of body, we shall realise God, our true Self.

Vol. 5, Notes from Lectures and Discourses, On Jnana-Yoga), p. 271

The Vedantist says that a man is neither born nor dies nor goes to heaven, and that reincarnation is really a myth with regard to the soul. The example is give of a book being turned over. It is the book that evolves, not the man. Every soul is omnipresent, so where can it come or go? These births and deaths are changes in nature which we are mistaking for changes in us.

Reincarnation is the evolution of nature and the manifestation of the God within.

The Vedanta says that each life is built upon the past, and that when we can look back over the whole past we are free. The desire to be free will take the form of a religious disposition from childhood. A few years will, as it were, make all truth clear to one. After leaving this life, and while waiting for the next, a man is still in the phenomenal.

We would describe the soul in these words: This soul the sword cannot cut, nor the spear pierce; the fire cannot burn nor water melt it; indestructible, omnipresent is this soul. Therefore weep not for it.

Vol. 5, Notes from Lectures and Discourses,
On the Vedanta Philosophy, p. 281

Man's free agency is not of the mind, for that is bound. There is no freedom there. Man is not mind; he is soul. The soul is ever free, boundless and eternal. Herein is man's freedom, in the soul. The soul is always free, but the mind identifying itself with its own ephemeral waves, loses sight of the soul and becomes lost in the maze of time, space, and causation—Maya. This is the cause of our bondage. We are always identifying ourselves with the mind, and the mind's phenomenal changes.

Vol. 6, Lectures and Discourses, Nature and Man, p. 35

After every happiness comes misery; they may be far apart or near. The more advanced the soul, the more quickly does one follow the other. *What we want is neither happiness nor misery.* Both make us forget our true nature; both are chains—one iron, one gold; behind both is the Atman, who knows neither happiness nor misery. These are *states* and states must ever change; but the nature of the Soul is bliss, peace, unchanging. We have not to get it, we have it; only wash away the dross and see it.

Vol. 7, Inspired Talks, 25 June 1895, p. 11

Two people have given all the religion to the world—the Hindus and the Jews. But it is only with the Hindus that the idea of soul comes at first, and that was shared by the Aryan races. The peculiarity you find is that the Semitic races and the Egyptians try to preserve the dead bodies, while the Aryans try to destroy them. The Greeks, the Germans, the Romans—your ancestors before they became Christians—used to burn the dead. It was only when Charlemagne made you Christians with the sword—and when you refused, [he] cut off a few hundred heads, and the rest jumped into the water—that burying came here. You see at once the metaphysical significance of burning the dead. The burying of the dead can only remain when there is no idea of the soul, and the body is all. At best there came the idea later on that this very body will come out and begin to walk the streets again. But with the Aryans the idea was from the first that the soul is not the body, but would live on.

Vol. 9, Lectures and Discourses, History of the Aryan Race, p. 261

”

Chapter 7

BUDDHA AND BUDDHISM

Buddha was God incarnate on earth. He did not believe in any God or soul. He was a perfect agnostic. Buddha was not interested in knowing about or discussing various theories about God and the soul. He put forward no claims that he was an Incarnation of God. Yet all his teachings came when he was in a supersensuous state of mind, not through intellectual cogitations.

He was the perfect Karma-Yogi. He had no personal motives, and did not want anything. He gave up his throne. The life of Buddha shows that even a man who does not believe in God, has no metaphysics, belongs to no sect, does not go to any church or temple, and is a confessed materialist, can attain to the highest. He tried to break down castes, destroy privilege, preach equality and eschew superstition. He was the greatest teacher of morality, who taught everyone that a person should do good deeds and be good, which will lead to freedom and to whatever truth there is. Most noteworthy is Buddha's sympathy for everybody, especially the ignorant and the poor, which is why he spoke in the language of the people of that time. Buddha was good for good's sake. He loved for love's sake. Above all, he never claimed worship. He said, 'Buddha is not a man, but a state. I have found the door. Enter, all of you!'

The relation between Hinduism and Buddhism is comparable to that between Judaism and Christianity. Buddha came to preach nothing new. He came to fulfil, not to destroy. Every one of Buddha's teachings is founded in the Vedanta. In fact, he was the living embodiment of the Vedanta. Buddha brought out the truths hidden in the Vedas, gave it to the people, and thereby, saved India. He was the logical development, the fulfilment, of the religion of the Hindus. Before Buddha came, crude materialism was widespread. Buddha was disgusted at the prevalent eternal metaphysical discussions, the iron grip that the priests exercised over spiritual knowledge, the cumbersome rituals, and the caste system. Buddha had the brain, the power and the heart to change the prevalent situation. The Buddhistic reformation represented a gigantic social movement that sought, on the religious side, freedom from ceremonials and, on the political side, the overthrow of the priesthood by the Kshatriyas.

Buddha was agnostic about metaphysics and theories about God, whereas Vedantism is a much more thoughtful and grander philosophy of life. Buddhism said, 'Realize all this as illusion,' while Hinduism said, 'Realize that within the illusion is the Real.' Buddhism prescribed monasticism, whereas Hinduism did not enunciate any rigid law and averred that one could realize God through any state of life. However, no one can ignore the awesome moral force of his teachings. There is need for both the brain and the philosophy of the Hindus, as well as for the heart, the reforming zeal, the sympathy and the charity of the Buddhists. The reality is that Hinduism cannot live without Buddhism and vice-versa. This separation is what has led to the impoverishment and enslavement of its people and the resultant downfall of India.

Unfortunately, Buddha's disciples did not properly understand him. The original Buddhism could not hold the mind of the masses, because most people were very ignorant. A thousand years after his death, Buddha's teachings degenerated. Under the influence of the Tibetans and the

Tartars, Buddhism in India became a hotchpotch of beliefs in the hands of mobs and uncivilized, uncultured races that had converted to Buddhism. They were enthusiastic, but lacked thought and intellect. They degraded Buddhism by introducing all kinds of superstitions, obscene books, hideous forms of worship and bestial customs. They led the way, perhaps unconsciously, to some of the hideous Vamacharas. They tried to destroy and disown the Vedas, but their efforts did not succeed. Buddhism spread not only across India. For many centuries, the majority of the people in India followed Buddhism. However, it ultimately failed to retain its hold on the people. Buddhism laid excessive emphasis on the negative elements of Hinduism. It took away from the people that eternal God to which everyone fondly clings, with the result that Buddhism did not survive in India. The exclusiveness of the old form of Vedic religions debarred it from taking ready help from outside. At the same time, this exclusiveness kept it pure and free from many debasing elements that Buddhism in its propagandist zeal was forced to assimilate.

It was Shankaracharya who revived the philosophy of the Vedanta. If Buddha stressed the moral dimension of philosophy, Shankaracharya focused on its intellectual content. He worked out, rationalised, and placed before people the coherent system of Advaita. He showed that the real essence of Buddhism and that of the Vedanta are not very different. Philosophically, the Vedanta has no quarrel with the Mahayana school of Buddhism. But the Theravada school of Buddhism prevalent in Southeast Asia and Sri Lanka insists that there is only a phenomenal world, and rejects the idea of a noumenal world. It also rejects the notion of God and the soul. Hinduism has become so great only by absorbing all the ideas of Buddha. Over the succeeding centuries, thanks to the efforts of reformers like

Shankaracharya, Ramanuja and Madhva in southern India, the purity of the Vedantic religion has been slowly brought back to the people of India. The mother that gave it birth absorbed this gigantic child, with the result that Buddhism almost completely disappeared from India.

However, Buddhism spread widely all over the whole civilised world as known at that time. It was the first missionary religion. It is noteworthy that it spread peacefully, not with the sword. It spread less because of the doctrines and personality of Buddha than because of the huge temples that were built, the idols that were erected and the gorgeous ceremonials that were instituted under the banner of Buddhism.

Even as all the Buddhists have flocked back to the old religions, Buddhism has left its mark on India. The emphasis on charity, vegetarianism and stoppage of animal sacrifices etc. are the results of the influence of Buddhism. The introduction of idols into India was the result of Buddha's constantly inveighing against a Personal God. Hinduism retained the forms to which the people had become accustomed in the name of Buddhism, such as temples, idols, symbols and bones of saints. Idolatry started with Buddhism. The use of images was unknown before Buddha. The institution of Sannyas also originated with Buddhism. Interestingly, it was the fear that people might become Buddhists that led to the prohibition on people undertaking sea voyages.

For all its strengths, Buddhism suffered from many weaknesses. One is the emphasis on monasticism. It is all right for the few, but if all able-bodied people with strong and vigorous minds became monks living in monasteries, only the weaklings would be left to procreate and to continue the race. This would inevitably lead to national decay. There is nothing in Buddhism for the person who neither wants Moksha nor is fit to receive it. The attempt to make everyone in India a monk or a nun was an impossible ideal that inevitably led to the dubious and immoral practices of Tantric Buddhism. In introducing the community life of religious houses, Buddhism necessarily made women inferior to men, since the great abbesses could take no important step without the advice of certain abbots. Another problematic concept is that of practicing non-resistance, which is all right as an idea, but there is no practical way to attain it.

“

I am not a Buddhist, as you have heard, and yet I am. If China, or Japan, or Ceylon follow the teachings of the Great Master, India worships him as God incarnate on earth. You have just now heard that I am going to criticise Buddhism, but by that I wish you to understand only this. Far be it from me to criticise him whom I worship as God incarnate on earth. But our views about Buddha are that he was not understood properly by his disciples. The relation between Hinduism (by Hinduism, I mean the religion of the Vedas) and what is called Buddhism at the present day is nearly the same as between Judaism and Christianity. Jesus Christ was a Jew, and Shakya Muni was a Hindu. The Jews rejected Jesus Christ, nay, crucified him, and the Hindus have accepted Shakya Muni as God and worship him. But the real difference that we Hindus want to show between modern Buddhism and what we should understand as the teachings of Lord Buddha lies principally in this: Shakya Muni came to preach nothing new. He also, like Jesus, came to fulfil and not to destroy. Only, in the case of Jesus, it was the old people, the Jews, who did not understand him, while in the case of the Buddha, it was his own followers who did not realise the import of his teachings. As the Jew did not understand the fulfilment of the Old Testament, so the Buddhist did not understand the fulfilment of the truths of the Hindu religion. Again, I repeat, Shakya Muni came not to destroy, but he was the fulfilment, the logical conclusion, the logical development of the religion of the Hindus.

In religion there is no caste; caste is simply a social institution. Shakya Muni himself was a monk, and it was his glory that he had the large-heartedness to bring out the truths from the hidden Vedas and throw them broadcast them all over the world. He was the first being in the world who brought missionarising into practice—nay, he was the first to conceive the idea of proselytising.

The great glory of the Master lay in his wonderful sympathy for everybody, especially for the ignorant and the poor. Some of his disciples were Brahmins. When Buddha was teaching, Sanskrit was no more the spoken language in India. It was then only in the books of the learned. Some of Buddha's Brahmin disciples wanted to translate his teachings into Sanskrit, but he distinctly told them, 'I am for the poor, for the people; let me speak in the tongue of the people.' And so this day the great bulk of his teachings are in the vernacular of that day in India.

On the philosophic side the disciples of the Great Master dashed themselves against the eternal rocks of the Vedas and could not crush them, and on the other side they took away from the nation that eternal God to which every one, man or woman, clings so fondly. And the result was that Buddhism had to die a natural death in India. At the present day there is not one who calls oneself a Buddhist in India, the land of its birth.

But at the same time, Brahminism lost something—that reforming zeal, that wonderful sympathy and charity for everybody, that wonderful leaven which Buddhism had brought to the masses and which had rendered Indian society so great that a Greek historian who wrote about India of that time was led to say that no Hindu was known to tell an untruth and no Hindu woman was known to be unchaste.

Hinduism cannot live without Buddhism, nor Buddhism without Hinduism. Then realise what the separation has shown to us, that the Buddhists cannot stand without the brain and philosophy of the Brahmins, nor the Brahmin without the heart of the Buddhist. This separation between the Buddhists and the Brahmins is the cause of the downfall of India. That is why India is populated by three hundred million of beggars, and that is why India has been the slave of conquerors for the last thousand years. Let us then join the wonderful intellect of the Brahmins with the heart, the noble soul, the wonderful humanising power of the Great Master.

Vol. 1, At the Parliament of Religions, Buddhism, The Fulfilment of Hinduism, pp. 21–23

Let me tell you in conclusion a few words about one man who actually carried this teaching of Karma-Yoga into practice. That man is Buddha. He is the one man who ever carried this into perfect practice. All the prophets of the world, except Buddha, had external motives to move them to unselfish action. The prophets of the world, with this single exception, may be divided into two sets, one set holding that they are incarnations of God come down to earth, and the other holding that they are only messengers from God; and both draw their impetus for work from outside, expect reward from outside, however highly spiritual may be the language they use. But Buddha is the only prophet who said, 'I do not care to know your various theories about God. What is the use of discussing all the subtle doctrines about the soul? Do good and be good. And this will take you to freedom and to whatever truth there is.' He was, in the conduct of his life, absolutely without personal motives; and what man worked more than he? Show me in history one character who has soared so high above all. The whole human race has produced but one such character, such high philosophy, such wide sympathy. This great philosopher, preaching the highest philosophy, yet had the deepest sympathy for the lowest of animals, and never put forth any claims for himself. He is the ideal Karma-Yogi, acting entirely without motive, and the history of humanity shows him to have been the greatest man ever born; beyond compare the greatest combination of heart and brain that ever existed, the greatest soul-power that has ever been manifested. He is the first great reformer the world has seen [...] This man represents the very highest ideal of Karma-Yoga.'

Vol. 1, Karma-Yoga, Chapter VIII, The Ideal of karma-Yoga, pp. 116–118

Buddhism is a great religion in some respects, but to confuse Buddhism with Vedanta is without meaning; anyone may mark just the difference that exists between Christianity and the Salvation Army. There are great and good points in Buddhism, but these great points fell into hands which were not able to keep them safe. The jewels which came from philosophers fell into the hands of mobs, and the mobs took up their ideas. They had a great deal of enthusiasm, some marvellous ideas, great and humanitarian ideas, but, after all, there is something else that is necessary—thought and intellect—to keep everything safe. Now this Buddhism went as the first missionary religion to the world, penetrated the whole of the civilised world as it existed at that time, and never was a drop of blood shed for that religion. We read how in China the Buddhist missionaries were persecuted, and thousands were massacred by two or three successive emperors, but after that, fortune favoured the Buddhists, and one of the emperors offered to take vengeance on the persecutors, but the missionaries refused. All that we own to this one verse. That is why I want you to remember it: 'Whom they call Indra, Mitra, Varuna—That which exists is One; sages call It by various names.'

Vol. 1, Lectures and Discourses, Vedic Religious Ideals, p. 349

Once a gigantic attempt was made to preach Vedantic ethics, which succeeded to a certain extent for several hundred years, and we know historically that those years were the best times of that nation. I mean the Buddhistic attempt to break down privilege. Some of the most beautiful epithets addressed to Buddha that I remember are, 'Thou the breaker of castes, destroyer of privileges, preacher of equality to all beings.' So, he preached this one idea of equality. Its power has been misunderstood to a certain extent in the brotherhood of Shramanas, where we find that hundreds of attempts have been made to make them into a church, with superiors and inferiors. You cannot make much of a church when you tell people they are all gods.

Vol. 1, Lectures and Discourses, Vedanta and Privilege, pp. 424–425

It may be asked—if the Buddhists do not believe in any God or soul, how can their religion be derived from the supersensuous state of existence? The answer to this is that even the Buddhists find an eternal moral law, and that moral law was not reasoned out in our sense of the word. But Buddha [...] discovered it, in a supersensuous state. Those of you who have studied the life of Buddha, even as briefly given in that beautiful poem, *The Light of Asia,* may remember that Buddha is represented as sitting under the Bo-tree until he reached that supersensuous state of mind. All his teachings came through this, and not through intellectual cogitations.'

Vol. 2, Jnana-Yoga, The Necessity of Religion, pp. 60–61

Before the Buddha came, materialism had spread to a fearful extent, and it was of a most hideous kind, not like that of the present day, but of a far worse nature [...] the materialism that prevailed before Buddha was that crude sort of materialism which taught, 'Eat, drink, and be merry; there is no God, soul, or heaven; religion is a concoction of wicked priests.' It taught the morality that so long as you live, you must try to live happily; eat, though you have to borrow money for the food, and never mind about repaying it. That was the old materialism, and that kind of philosophy spread so much that even today it has got the name of 'popular philosophy.' Buddha brought the Vedanta to light, gave it to the people, and saved India. A thousand years after his death a similar state of things again prevailed. The mobs, the masses, and various races had been converted to Buddhism; naturally the teachings of the Buddha became in time degenerated, because most of the people were very ignorant. Buddhism taught no God, no Ruler of the universe, so gradually the masses brought their gods, and devils, and hobgoblins out again, and a tremendous hotchpotch was made of Buddhism in India. Again materialism came to the fore, taking the form of licence with the higher classes and superstition with the lower. Then Shankaracharya arose and once more revivified the Vedanta philosophy. He made it a rationalistic philosophy. In the Upanishads the arguments are often very obscure. By Buddha the moral side of the philosophy was laid stress upon, and by Shankaracharya the intellectual side. He worked out, rationalised, and place before men the wonderful coherent system of Advaita.

In Buddha we had the great, universal heart and infinite patience, making religion practical and bringing it to everyone's door. In Shankaracharya we saw tremendous intellectual power, throwing the scorching light of reason upon everything. We want today that bright sun of intellectuality joined with the heart of Buddha, the wonderful infinite heart of love and mercy. This union will give us the highest philosophy. Science and religion will meet and shake hands. Poetry and philosophy will become friends. This will be the religion of the future, and if we can work it out we may be sure that it will be for all times and peoples. This is the one way that will prove acceptable to modern science, for it has almost come to it.

Vol. 2, Jnana-Yoga, The Absolute and Manifestation, pp. 138–140

I would like to see moral men like Gautama Buddha, who did not believe in a Personal God or a personal soul, never asked about them, but was a perfect agnostic, and yet was ready to lay down his life for anyone, and worked all his life for the good of all, and thought only of the good of all. Well has it been said by his biographer, in describing his birth, that he was born for the good of many, as a blessing to the many. He did not go to the forest to meditate for his own salvation; he felt that the world was burning, and that he must find a way out. 'Why is there so much misery in the world?' was the one question that dominated his whole life. Do you think we are so moral as the Buddha?

Vol. 2, Practical Vedanta and Other Lectures, Practical Vedanta: Part IV, p. 352

The Buddhists, the first missionary religion, have double the number of converts of any other religion and they did not use the sword.

Vol. 2, Reports in American Newspapers, Religious Harmony, p. 482

In order to understand Buddhism fully we must go back to the mother religion from which it came. The books of Veda have two parts; the first, Cura makand [Karma Kanda], contains the sacrificial portion, while the second part, the Vedanta, denounces sacrifices, teaching charity and love, but not death. Each sect took up what portion it liked. The charvaka, or materialist, basing his doctrine on the first part, believed that all was matter and that there is neither a heaven nor a hell, neither a soul nor a God. The second sect, the Gains [Jains], were very moral atheists, who, while rejecting the idea of a God, believed that there is a soul, striving for more perfect development. These two sects were called the heretics. A third sect was called orthodox, because it accepted the Vedas, although it denied the existence of a personal God, believing that everything sprang from the atom or nature.

Thus the intellectual world was divided before Buddha came. But for a correct understanding of his religion, it is also necessary to speak of the caste then existing. The Vedas teach that he who knows God is a Brahma [Brahmin]; he who protects his fellows is a Chocta [Kshatriya], while he who gains his livelihood in trade is a Visha [Vaishya]. These different social diversions [divisions] developed or degenerated into iron-bound casts [castes], and an organized and crystallized priestcraft stood upon the neck of the nation. At this time Buddha was born, and his religion is therefore the culmination of an attempt at a religious and a social reformation.

Buddha never fought true castes, for they are nothing but the congregation of those of a particular tendency, and they are always valuable. But Buddha fought the degenerated castes with their hereditary privileges, and spoke to the Brahmins: 'True Brahmins are not greedy, nor criminal nor angry—are you such? If not, do not mimic the genuine, real men. Caste is a state, not an iron-bound class, and everyone who knows and loves God is a true Brahmin.' And with regard to the sacrifices, he said: 'Where do the Vedas say that sacrifices make us pure? They may please, perhaps, the angels, but they make us no better. Hence, let off the mummeries—love God and strive to be perfect.'

In later years these doctrines were forgotten. Going to lands yet unprepared for the reception of these noble truths, they came back tainted with the foibles of these nations. Thus the Nihilists arose—a sect whose doctrine it was that the whole universe, God and soul, had no basis, but that everything is continually changing. They believed in nothing but the enjoyment of the moment, which eventually resulted in the most revolting orgies. That, however, is not the doctrine of Buddha, but a horrible degradation of it, and honor to the Hindoo nation, who stood up and drove it out.

Every one of Buddha's teachings is founded in the Vedanta. He was one of those monks who wanted to bring out the truths, hidden in those books and in the forest monasteries. I do not believe that the world is ready for them even now; it still wants those lower religions, which teach of a personal God. Because of this, the original Buddhism could not hold the popular mind, until it took up the modifications, which were reflected back from Thibet and the Tartars. Original Buddhism was not at all nihilistic. It was but an attempt to combat caste and priestcraft; it was the first in the world to stand as champion of the dumb animals, the first to break down the caste, standing between man and man.

Vol. 2, Reports in American Newspapers, True Buddhism, pp. 507–509

Today it is the fashion to talk of Buddhism and Buddhistic agnosticism, especially in the South. Little do they dream that this degradation which is with us today has been left by Buddhism. This is the legacy which Buddhism has left to us. You read in books written by men who had never studied the rise and fall of Buddhism that the spread of Buddhism was owing to the wonderful ethics and the wonderful personality of Gautama Buddha. I have every respect and veneration for Lord Buddha, but mark my words, the spread of Buddhism was less owing to the doctrines and the personality of the great preacher, than to the temples that were built, the idols that were erected, and the gorgeous ceremonials that were put before the nation. Thus Buddhism progressed. The little fire-places in the houses in which the people poured their libations were not strong enough to hold their own against these gorgeous temples and ceremonies; but later on the whole thing degenerated. It became a mass of corruption of which I cannot speak before this audience; but those who want to know about it may see a little of it in those big temples, full of sculptures, in Southern India; and this is all the inheritance we have from the Buddhists.

Then arose the great reformer Shankaracharya and his followers, and during these hundreds of years, since his time to the present day, there has been the slow bringing back of the Indian masses to the pristine purity of the Vedantic religion.

Vol. 3, Lectures from Colombo to Almora,
My Plan of Campaign, pp. 216–217

This is what I mean by the word Vedanta, that it covers the ground of dualism, of qualified monism, and Advaitism in India. Perhaps we may even take in parts of Buddhism, and of Jainism too, if they would come in—for our hearts are sufficiently large. But it is they that will not come in, we are ready for upon severe analysis you will always find that the essence of Buddhism was all borrowed from the same Upanishads; even the ethics, the so-called great and wonderful ethics of Buddhism, were there word for word in some one or other of the Upanishads; and so all the good doctrines of the Jains were there, minus the vagaries.

Vol. 3, Lectures from Colombo to Almora, Vedanta in its Application to Indian Life, p. 230

And from the topmost crest of the wave that deluged India for nearly a thousand years, we see another glorious figure and that was our Gautama Shakyamuni. You all know about his teachings and preachings. We worship him as God incarnate, the greatest, the boldest preacher of morality that the world ever saw, the greatest Karma-Yogi; as disciple of himself, as it were, the same Krishna came to show how to make his theories practical [...] As it were to give a living example of this preaching, as it were to make at least one part of it practical, the preacher himself came in another form, and this was Shakyamuni, the preacher to the poor and the miserable, he who rejected even the language of the gods to speak in the language of the people, so that he might reach the hearts of the people, he who gave up a throne to live with beggars, and the poor, and the downcast, he who pressed the Pariah to his breast like a second Rama.

You all know about his great work, his grand character. But the work had one great defect, and for that we are suffering even today. No blame attaches to the Lord. He is pure and glorious, but unfortunately such high ideals could not be well assimilated by the different uncivilised and uncultured races of mankind who flocked within the fold of the Aryans. These races, with varieties of superstition and hideous worship, rushed within the fold of the Aryans and for a time appeared as they had become civilised, but before a century had passed they brought out their snakes, their ghosts, and all the other things their ancestors used to worship, and thus the whole of India became one degraded mass of superstition. The earlier Buddhists in their rage against the killing of animals had denounced the sacrifices of the Vedas; and these sacrifices used to be held in every house. There was a fire burning and that was all the paraphernalia of worship. These sacrifices were obliterated, and in their place came gorgeous temples, gorgeous ceremonies, and gorgeous priests, and all that you see in India in modern times. I smile when I read books written by some modern people who ought to have known better, that the Buddha was the destroyer of Brahminical idolatry. Little do they know that Buddhism created Brahminism and idolatry in India.

Thus, in spite of the preaching of mercy to animals, in spite of the sublime ethical religion, in spite of the hair-splitting discussions about the existence or non-existence of a permanent soul, the whole building of Buddhism tumbled down piecemeal, and the ruin was simply hideous. The most hideous ceremonies, the most horrible, the most obscene books that human hands ever wrote or the human brain ever conceived, the most bestial forms that ever passed under the name of religion, have all been the creation of degraded Buddhism.

But India has to live, and the spirit of the Lord descended again. He who declared, 'I will come whenever virtue subsides,' came again, and this time the manifestation was in the South, and up rose that young Brahmin of whom it has been declared that at the age of sixteen he had completed all his writings; the marvellous boy Shankaracharya arose. The writings of this boy of sixteen are the wonders of the modern world, and so was the boy. He wanted to bring back the Indian world to its pristine purity, but think of the amount of the task before him. I have told you a few points about the state of things that existed in India.

All these horrors that you are trying to reform are the outcome of that reign of degradation. The Tartars and the Baluchis and all the hideous races of mankind came to India and became Buddhists, and assimilated with us, and brought their national customs, and the whole of our national life became a huge page of the most horrible and the most bestial customs. That was the inheritance which that boy got from the Buddhists, and from that time to this, the whole work in India is a reconquest of this Buddhistic degradation by the Vedanta. It is still going on, it is not yet finished. Shankara came, a great philosopher, and showed that the real essence of Buddhism and that of the Vedanta are not very different, but that the disciples did not understand the Master and have degraded themselves, denied the existence of the soul and of God, and have become atheists. That was what Shankara showed, and all the Buddhists began to come back to the old religion. But then they had become accustomed to all these forms; what could be done?

Vol. 3, Lectures from Colombo to Almora,
The Sages of India, pp. 262–265

Buddhistic India is our subject tonight. Almost all of you, perhaps, have read Edwin Arnold's poem on the life of Buddha, and some of you, perhaps, have gone into the subject with more scholarly interest, as in English, French and German, there is quite a lot of Buddhistic literature. Buddhism itself is the most interesting of subjects, for it is the first historical outburst of a world religion. There have been great religions before Buddhism arose, in India and elsewhere, but, more or less, they are confined within their own races. The ancient Hindus or ancient Jews or ancient Persians, every one of them had a great religion, but these religions were more or less racial. With Buddhism first begins that peculiar phenomenon of religion boldly starting out to conquer the world. Apart from its doctrines and the truths it taught and the message it had to give, we stand face to face with one of the tremendous cataclysms of the world. Within a few centuries of its birth, the barefooted, shaven-headed missionaries of Buddha had spread over all the then known civilised world, and they penetrated even further—from Lapland on the one side to the Philippine Islands on the other. They had spread widely within a few centuries of Buddha's birth; and in India itself, the religion of Buddha had at one time nearly swallowed up two-thirds of the population.

The whole of India was never Buddhistic. It stood outside. Buddhism had the same fate as Christianity had with the Jews; the majority of the Jews stood aloof. So the old Indian religion lived on. But the comparison stops here. Christianity, though it could not get within its fold all the Jewish race, itself took the country. Where the old religion existed—the religion of the Jews—that was conquered by Christianity in a very short time and the old religion was dispersed, and so the religion of the Jews lives a sporadic life in different parts of the world. But in India this gigantic child was absorbed, in the long run, by the mother that gave it birth, and today the very name of Buddha is almost unknown all over India.

It is his doctrines that appeal to many modern thinkers whom you call agnostics. He was a great preacher of the brotherhood of mankind [...] But as to other things, he was very agnostic.

Non-killing of animals and charity towards animals was an already existing doctrine when he was born; but it was new with him—the breaking down of caste, that tremendous movement. And the other thing that was new: he took forty of his disciples and sent them all over the world.

I do not believe many of his doctrines; of course, I do not. I believe that the Vedantism of the old Hindus is much more thoughtful, is a grander philosophy of life. I like his method of work, but what I like [most] in that man is that, among all the prophets of mankind, here was a man who never had any cobwebs in his brain, and who was sane and strong. When kingdoms were at his feet, he was still the same man, maintaining 'I am a man amongst men.' [...] He died always declaring that he was but man. None of his adulators could draw from him one remark that he was anything different from any other man.

The sanest philosopher the world ever saw. Its best and its sanest teacher. And never the man bent before the power of the tyrannical Brahmins.

I do not sympathise with his metaphysics at all; but my mind is jealous when I think of the moral force.

Buddhism was and did become a great political power in India. Gradually it also fell to pieces—after all, this tremendous missionary enterprise. But to their credit it must be said they never took up the sword to preach religion. Excepting the Buddhistic religion, there is not one religion in the world which could make one step without bloodshed—not one which could get a hundred thousand converts just by brain power alone.

There have been three things in Buddhism: the Buddha himself, his law, his church. At first it was so simple. when the Master died, before his death, they said: 'What shall we do with you?' 'Nothing.' 'What monument shall we make over you?' He said: 'Just make a little heap if you want, or just do not do anything.' By and by, there arose huge temples and all the paraphernalia. The use of images was unknown before then. There are images of Buddha and all the saints, sitting about and praying. All this paraphernalia went on multiplying with this organisation. Then these monasteries became rich. The real cause of the downfall is here. Monasticism is all very good for a few; but when you preach it in such a fashion that every man or woman who has a mind immediately gives up social life, when you find over the whole of India monasteries, some containing a hundred thousand monks, sometimes twenty thousand monks in one building—huge, gigantic buildings, these monasteries, scattered all over India and, of course, centres of learning, and all that—who were left to procreate progeny, to continue the race?

Only the weaklings. All the strong and vigorous minds went out. And then came national decay by the sheer loss of vigour.

I will tell you of this marvellous brotherhood. It is great. But theory and idea is one thing and actual working is another thing. The idea is very great: practising non-resistance and all that, but if all of us go out in the street and practise non-resistance, there would be very little left in this city. That is to say, the idea is all right, but nobody has yet found a practical solution [as to] how to attain it.

When Buddhism broke down everything by introducing all sorts of foreign barbarians into India—their manners and customs and things—there was a reaction, and that reaction was led by a young monk [Shankaracharya]. And [instead of] preaching new doctrines and always thinking new thoughts and making sects, he brought back the Vedas to life; and modern Hinduism has thus an admixture of ancient Hinduism, over which the Vedantists predominate. But, you see, what once dies never comes back to life, and those ceremonials [of Hinduism] never came back to life.

Buddhism was the first sect in India. They were the first to say: 'Ours is the only path. Until you join our church, you cannot be saved.' That was what they said: 'It is the correct path.' But, being of Hindu blood, they could not be such stony-hearted sectarians as in other countries. There will be salvation for you: nobody will go wrong for ever. No, No. [There was] too much of Hindu blood in them for that. The heart was not so stony as that. But you have to join them.

Buddhism died out of India. It left its mark on their charity, its animals etc. in India; and Vedantism is reconquering India from one end to the other.

Vol. 3, Buddhistic India, pp. 511–537

Buddhism is one of our sects. It was founded by a great man called Gautama who became disgusted at the eternal metaphysical discussions of his day, and the cumbrous rituals, and more especially with the caste system. He was also against the tremendous priestcraft. He preached a religion in which there was no motive power, and was perfectly agnostic about metaphysics or theories about God. He was often asked if there was a God, and he answered he did not know. When asked about right conduct, he would reply, 'Do good and be good.'

He was the only man who was bereft of all motive power. There were other great men who all said they were the Incarnations of God Himself and that those who would believe in them would go to heaven. But what did Buddha say with his dying breath? 'None can help you; help yourself; work out your own salvation.' He said about himself, 'Buddha is the name of infinite knowledge, infinite as the sky; I, Gautama, have reached that state; you will all reach that too if you struggle for it.' Bereft of all motive power, he did not want to go to heaven, did not want money; he gave up his throne and everything else and went about begging his bread through the streets of India, preaching for the good of men and animals with a heart as wide as the ocean.

He was the only man who was ever ready to give up his life for animals to stop a sacrifice. He once said to a king, 'If the sacrifice of a lamb helps you to go to heaven, sacrificing a man will help you better; so sacrifice me.' The king was astonished. And yet this man was without any motive power. He stands as the perfection of the active type, and the very height to which he attained shows that through the power of work we can also attain to the highest spirituality.

To many the path becomes easier if they believe in God. But the life of Buddha shows that even a man who does not believe in God, has no metaphysics, belongs to no sect, and does not go to any church, or temple, and is a confessed materialist, even he can attain to the highest. We have no right to judge him. I wish I had one infinitesimal part of Buddha's heart. Buddha may or may not have believed in God; that does not matter to me. He reached the same state of perfection to which others come by Bhakti, Yoga, or Jnana. Perfection does not come from belief or faith. Talk does not count for anything. Parrots can do that. Perfection comes through the disinterested performance of action.

Vol. 4, Lectures and Discourses, On Lord Buddha, pp. 135–137

Ancient India had for centuries been the battlefield for the ambitious projects of two of her foremost classes—the Brahmins and the Kshatriyas.

On the one hand, the priesthood stood between the lawless social tyranny of the princes over the masses, who the Kshatriyas declared to be their legal food. On the other hand, the Kshatriya power was the one potent force which struggled with any success against the spiritual tyranny of the priesthood and the ever-increasing chain of ceremonials which they were forging to bind down the people with.

The tug of war began in the earliest periods of the history of our race and throughout the Shrutis it can be distinctly traced. A momentary lull came when Shri Krishna, leading the faction of Kshatriya power and of Jnana, showed the way to reconciliation. The result was the teachings of the Gita—the essence of philosophy, of liberality, of religion. Yet the causes were there, and the effect must follow.

The ambition of these two classes to be the masters of the poor and ignorant was there, and the strife once more became fierce. The meagre literature that has come down to us from that period brings to us but faint echoes of that mighty past strife, but at last it broke out as a victory for the Kshatriyas, a victory for Jnana, for liberty—and ceremonials had to go down, much of it for ever. This upheaval was what is known as the Buddhistic reformation. On the religious side, it represented freedom from ceremonials; on the political side, overthrow of the priesthood by the Kshatriyas.

It is a significant fact that the two greatest men ancient India produced were both Kshatriyas—Krishna and Buddha—and still more significant is the fact that both of these God-men threw open the door of knowledge to everyone, irrespective of birth or sex. (4.325–326)

In spite of its wonderful moral strength, Buddhism was extremely iconoclastic; and much of its force being spent in merely negative attempts, it had to die out in the land of its birth, and what remained of it became full of superstitions and ceremonials, a hundred times cruder than those it was intended to suppress. Although it partially succeeded in putting down the animal sacrifices of the Vedas, it filled the land with temples, images, symbols, and bones of saints.

Above all, in the medley of Aryans, Mongols, and aborigines which it created, it unconsciously led the way to some of the hideous Vamacharas. This was especially the reason why this travesty of the teaching of the great Master had to be driven out of India by Shri Shankara and his band of Sannyasins.

Thus even the current of life, set in motion by the greatest soul that ever wore a human form, the Bhagavan Buddha himself, became a miasmatic pool, and India had to wait for centuries until Shankara arose, followed in quick succession by Ramanuja and Madhva.

By this time, an entirely new section had opened in the history of India. The ancient Kshatriyas and Brahmins had disappeared. The land between the Himalayas and the Vindhyas, the home of the Aryas, the land which gave birth to Krishna and Buddha, the cradle of great Rajarshis and Brahmarshis, became silent, and from the very farther end of the Indian Peninsula, from races alien in speech and form, from families claiming descent from the ancient Brahmins, came the reaction against the corrupted Buddhism.

What had become of the Brahmins and Kshatriyas of Aryavarta? They had entirely disappeared, except here and there a few mongrel clans claiming to be Brahmins and Kshatriyas, and in spite of their inflated, self-laudatory assertions [...] they had to sit in sackcloth and ashes, in all humility, to learn at the feet of the Southerners. The result was the bringing back of the Vedas to India—a revival of Vedanta, such as India never before had seen; even the householders began to study the Aranyakas.

In the Buddhistic movement, the Kshatriyas were the real leaders, and whole masses of them became Buddhists. In the zeal of reform and conversion, the popular dialects had been almost exclusively cultivated to the neglect of Sanskrit, and the larger portion of Kshatriyas had become disjointed from the Vedic literature and Sanskrit learning. Thus this wave of reform, which came from the South, benefited to a certain extent the priesthood, and the priests only. For the rest of India's millions, it forged more chains than they had ever known before.

The Kshatriyas had always been the backbone of India, so also they had been the supporters of science and liberty, and their voices had run out again and again to clear the land from superstitions; and throughout the history of India they ever formed the invulnerable barrier to aggressive priestly tyranny.

When the greater part of their number sank into ignorance, and another portion mixed their blood with savages from Central Asia and lent their swords to establish the rules of priests in India, her cup became full to the bring, and down sank the land of Bharata, not to rise again, until the Kshatriya rouses himself, and making himself free, strikes the chains from the feet of the rest. Priestcraft is the bane of India. Can man degrade his brother, and himself escape degradation?

Vol. 4, Writings: Prose and Poems, Reply to Address of Maharaja of Khetri, pp. 325–327

(Q: In what way do you see this importance of Buddhism in India today?)

It is obvious and overwhelming. You see India never loses anything; only she takes time to turn everything into bone and muscle. Buddha dealt a blow to animal sacrifice from which India has never recovered; and Buddha said, 'Kill no cows,' and cow killing is an impossibility with us.

Vol. 5, Interviews, Reawakening of Hinduism on a National Basis, p. 226

(Q: How do you account for the evil influence which you attribute to Buddhism?)

It came only with the decay of the faith. Every movement triumphs by dint of some unusual characteristic, and when it fails, that point of pride becomes its chief element of weakness. The Lord Buddha—greatest of men—was a marvellous organiser and carried the world by this means. But his religion was the religion of a monastic order. It had, therefore, the evil effect of making the very robe of the monk honoured. He also introduced for the first time the community life of religious houses and thereby necessarily made women inferior to men, since the great abesses could take no important step without the advice of certain abbots. It ensured its immediate object, the solidarity of the faith, you see, only its far-reaching effects are to be deplored.

Vol. 5, Interviews, On Indian Women—Their Past, Present and Future, p. 230

The Vedanta philosophy is the foundation of Buddhism and everything else in India; but what we call the Advaita philosophy of the modern school has a great many conclusions of the Buddhists. Of course, the Hindus will not admit it—that is the orthodox Hindus, because to them the Buddhists are heretics. But there is a conscious attempt to stretch out the whole doctrine to include the heretics also.

The Vedanta has no quarrel with Buddhism. The idea of the Vedanta is to harmonise all. With the northern Buddhists we have no quarrel at all. But the Burmese and Siamese and all the Southern Buddhists say that there is a phenomenal world, and ask what right we have to create a noumenal world behind this. The answer of the Vedanta is that this is a false statement. The Vedanta never contended that there was a noumenal and a phenomenal world. There is one. Seen through the senses it is phenomenal, but it is really the noumenal all the time [...] So the Buddhistic statement of our position, that we believe there are two worlds, is entirely false. They have the right to say it is the phenomenal if they like, but no right to contend that other men have not the right to say it is the noumenal.

Vol. 5, Notes from Lectures and Discourses,
Buddhism and Vedanta, pp. 279–280

The Buddhists never had much caste, and there are very few Buddhists in India. Buddha was a social reformer. Yet in Buddhistic countries I find that there have been strong attempts to manufacture caste, only they have failed. The Buddhists' caste is practically nothing, but they take pride in it in their own minds.

Buddha was one of the Sannyasins of the Vedanta. He started a new sect, just as others are started even today. The ideas, which now are called Buddhism, were not his. They were much more ancient. He was a great man who gave the ideas power. The unique element in Buddhism was its social element.

Vol. 5, Questions and Answers, I, pp. 308–309

Buddhism did not really decline in India; it was only a gigantic social movement. Before Buddha great numbers of animals were killed for sacrifice and other reasons, and people drank wine and ate meat in large quantities. Since Buddha's teaching drunkenness has almost disappeared, and the killing of animals has almost gone.

Vol. 5, Questions and Answers, II, p. 311

The Bauddhas tried to make everyone in India a monk or a nun. We cannot expect that from everyone. This led to gradual relaxation among monks and nuns. It was also caused by their imitating Tibetan and other barbarous customs in the name of religion. They went to preach in those places and assimilated their corruptions, and then introduced them to India.

Vol. 5, Questions and Answers, IV, p. 317

Buddhism and Vaishnavism are not two different things. During the decline of Buddhism in India, Hinduism took from her a few cardinal tenets of conduct and made them her own, and these have now come to be known as Vaishnavism. The Buddhist tenet, 'Non-killing is supreme virtue,' is very good but in trying to enforce it upon all by legislation without paying any heed to the capacities of the people at large, Buddhism has brought ruin upon India.

Vol. 5, Conversations and Dialogues (Recorded by Disciples), XV, p. 401

What does Buddha or Christ prescribe for the man who neither wants Moksha nor is fit to receive it?—Nothing! Either you must have Moksha or you are doomed to destruction—these are the only two ways held forth by them, and there is no middle course.

The aims of the Buddhistic and the Vedic religions are the same, but the means adopted by the Buddhistic are not right. If the Buddhistic means were correct, then why have we been thus hopelessly lost and ruined? It will not do to say that the efflux of time has naturally wrought this. Can time work, transgressing the laws of cause and effect?

Therefore, though the aims are the same, the Bauddhas for want of right means have degraded India. Perhaps my Bauddha brothers will be offended at this remark, and fret and fume; but there's no help for it; the truth ought to be told, and I do not care for the result.

Vol. 5, Writings: Prose and Poems, The East and the West, I, Introduction, pp. 454–455

Is man a soul, an unchanging substance, or is he a constantly changing quantity? All religions, except primitive Buddhism, believe that man is a soul, an identity, a unit that never dies but is immortal.

The primitive Buddhists believe that man is a constantly changing quantity, and that his consciousness consists in an almost infinite succession of incalculably rapid changes, each change, as it were, being unconnected with the others, standing alone, thus precluding the theory of the law of sequence or causation.

If there is a unit, there is a substance. A unit is always simple. A simple is not a compound of anything. It does not depend on anything else. It stands alone and is immortal.

Primitive Buddhists contend that everything is unconnected; nothing is a unit; and that the theory of man being a unit is a mere belief and cannot be proved.

All religions believe in God and the soul except the primitive Buddhist. The modern Buddhists believe in God and the soul. Among the primitive Buddhists are the Burmese, Siamese, Chinese etc.

Arnold's book, *The Light of Asia,* represents more of Vedantism than Buddhism.

Vol. 6, Notes of Class Talks and Lectures, On Proof of Religion, pp. 95–97

Sea voyage was prohibited later on, partly because there came the fear that people might thereby become Buddhists.

Buddhism was the rebellion of newly-formed Kshatriyas against Vedic priestcraft.

Hinduism threw away Buddhism after taking its sap. The attempt of all the Southern Acharyas was to effect a reconciliation between the two. Shankaracharya's teaching shows the influence of Buddhism. His disciples perverted his teaching and carried it to such an extreme point that some of the later reformers were right in calling the Acharya's followers 'crypto-Buddhists.'

Ramanuja's important work is the conversion of Jains and Buddhists to Hinduism. He is a great advocate of image-worship. He introduced love and faith as potent means of salvation.

Hindus believe Buddha to be an Avatar.

Hindus believe in God positively. Buddhism does not try to know whether He is or not.

Buddha came to whip us into practice. Be good, destroy the passions. Then you will know for yourself whether Dvaita or Advaita philosophy is true—whether there is one or there are more than one.

Buddha was a reformer of Hinduism.

Buddhism proves nothing about the Absolute Entity. In a stream the water is changing; we have no right to call the stream *one*. Buddhists deny the *one* and say it is *many*. We say it is *one* and deny the *many*. What they call Karma is what we call the soul. According to Buddhism, man is a series of waves. Every wave dies, but somehow the first wave causes the second. That the second wave is identical to the first is illusion. To get rid of illusion good Karma is necessary. Buddhists do not postulate anything beyond the world. We say, beyond the relative there is the Absolute. Buddhism accepts that there is misery, and sufficient it is that we can get rid of this Dukkha (misery); whether we get Sukha (happiness) or not, we do not know. Buddha preached not the soul preached by others. According to the Hindus, soul is an entity or substance, and God is absolute. Both agree in this, that they destroy the relative. But Buddhists do not give what is the effect of that destruction of the relative.

Present-day Hinduism and Buddhism were growths from the same branch. Buddhism degenerated, and Shankara lopped it off!

Buddha is said to have denied the Vedas because there is so much Himsa (killing) and other things. Every page of Buddhism is a fight with the Vedas (the ritualistic aspect). But he had no authority to do so.

Buddha is expressly agnostic about God; but God is everywhere preached in our religion.

Buddha, we may say now, ought to have understood the harmony of religions. He introduced sectarianism.

Modern Hinduism, modern Jainism, and Buddhism branched off at the same time. For some period, each seemed to have wanted to outdo the others in grotesqueness and humbuggism.

Vol. 6, Notes of Class Talks and Lectures, Notes Taken Down in Madras 1892–93, pp. 104–120

In their reaction against the privileged priesthood, Buddhists swept off almost every bit of the old ritual of the Vedas, subordinated the gods of the Vedas to the position of servants to their own human saints, and declared the 'Creator and Supreme Ruler' as an invention of priestcraft and superstition.

But the aim of Buddhism was reform of the Vedic religion by standing against ceremonials requiring offerings of animals, against hereditary caste and exclusive priesthood, and against belief in permanent souls. It never attempted to destroy that religion, or overturn the social order. It introduced a vigorous method by organising a class of Sannyasins into a strong monastic brotherhood, and the Brahmavidinis into a body of nuns—by introducing images of saints in the place of altar-fires. It is probable that the reformers had for centuries the majority of the Indian people with them. The older forces were never entirely pacified, but they underwent a good deal of modification during the centuries of Buddhist supremacy.

The Buddhist reformation and its chief field of activity were also in the same eastern region; and when the Maurya kings, forced possibly by the bar sinister on their escutcheon, patronised and led the new movement, the new priest power joined hands with the political power of the empire of Pataliputra. The popularity of Buddhism and its fresh vigour made the Maurya kings the greatest emperors that India ever had. The power of the Maurya sovereign made Buddhism that world-wide religion that we see even today.

The exclusiveness of the old form of Vedic religions debarred it from taking ready help from outside. At the same time, it kept it pure and free from many debasing elements which Buddhism in its propagandist zeal was forced to assimilate.

This extreme adaptability in the long run made Indian Buddhism lose almost all its individuality, and extreme desire to be of the people made it unfit to cope with the intellectual forces of the mother religion in a few centuries. The Vedic party in the meanwhile got rid of a good deal of its most objectionable features, as animal sacrifice, and took lessons from the rival daughter in the judicious use of images, temple processions and other impressive performances, and stood ready to take within her fold the whole empire of Indian Buddhism, already tottering to its fall.

And the crash came with the Scythian invasions and the total destruction of the empire of Pataliputra.

The invaders, already incensed at the invasion of their central Asiatic home by the preachers of Buddhism, found in the sun-worship of the Brahmins a great sympathy with their own solar religion—and when the Brahmins partly were ready to adapt and spiritualise many of the customs of the newcomers, the invaders threw themselves heart and soul into the Brahminic cause.

Then there is a veil of darkness and shifting shadows; there are tumults of war, rumours of massacres; and the next scene rises upon a new phase of things.

The empire of Magadha was gone. Most of northern India was under the rule of petty chiefs always at war with one another. Buddhism was almost extinct except in some eastern and Himalayan provinces and in the extreme south and the nation after centuries of struggle against the power of a hereditary priesthood awoke to find itself in the clutches of a double priesthood of hereditary Brahmins and exclusive monks of the new regime, with all the powers of the Buddhistic organisation and without their sympathy for the people.

A renascent India, bought by the valour and blood of the heroic Rajputs, defined by the merciless intellect of a Brahmin from the same historical though-centre of Mithila, led by a new philosophical impulse organised by Shankara and his bands of Sannyasins, and beautified by the arts and literature of the courts of Malava—arose on the ruins of the old.

The task before it was profound, problems vaster than any their ancestors had ever faced. A comparatively small and compact race of the same blood and speech and the same social and religious aspiration, trying to save its unity by unscalable walls around itself, grew huge by multiplication and addition during the Buddhistic supremacy and (it) was divided by race, colour, speech, spiritual instinct, and social ambitions into hopelessly jarring factions. And this had to be unified and welded into one gigantic nation. This task Buddhism had also come to solve, and had taken it up when the proportions were not so vast.

So long as it was a question of Aryanising the other types that were pressing for admission and thus, out of different elements, making a huge Aryan body. In spite of concessions and compromises, Buddhism was eminently successful and remained the national religion of India. But the time came when the allurements of sensual forms of worship, indiscriminately taken in along with various low races, were too dangerous for the central Aryan core, and a longer contact would certainly have destroyed the civilisation of the Aryans. Then came a natural reaction for self-preservation, and Buddhism as a separate sect ceased to live in most parts of its land of birth.

The reaction-movement, led in close succession by Kumarila in the north, and Shankara and Ramanuja in the south, has become the last embodiment of that vast accumulation of sects and doctrines and rituals called Hinduism. For the last thousand years or more, its great task has been assimilation, with now and then an outburst of reformation. This reaction first wanted to revive the rituals of the Vedas—failing which, it made the Upanishads or the philosophic portions of the Vedas its basis. It brought Vyasa's system of Mimamsa philosophy and Krishna's sermon, the Gita, to the forefront; and all succeeding movements have followed the same. The movement of Shankara forced its way through its high intellectuality; but it could be of little service to the masses, because of its adherence to strict caste laws, very small scope for ordinary emotion, and making Sanskrit the only vehicle of communication. Ramanuja, on the other hand, with a most practical philosophy, a great appeal to the emotions, an entire denial of birth rights before spiritual attainments, and appeals through the popular tongue completely succeeded in bringing the masses back to the Vedic religion.

Vol. 6, Writings: Prose and Poems, Historical Evolution of India, pp. 161–165

The Tantrika rites among the Tibetans that you have spoken of arose in India itself, during the decline of Buddhism. It is my belief that the Tantras, in vogue amongst us, were the creation of the Buddhists themselves. Those Tantrika rites are even more dreadful than our own doctrine of Vamachara; for in them adultery got a free rein, and it was only when the Buddhists became demoralised through immorality that they were driven away by Kumarila Bhatta. As some Sannyasins speak of Shankara, or the Bauls of Shri Chaitanya, that he was in secret an epicure, a drunkard, and one addicted to all sorts of abominable practices—so the modern Tantrika Buddhists speak of the Lord Buddha as a dire Vamachari and give an obscene interpretation to the many beautiful precepts of the *Prajnaparamita*, such as the *Tattvagatha* and the like. The result of all this has been that the Buddhists are divided into two sects nowadays; the Burmese and the Sinhalese have generally set the Tantras at naught, have likewise banished the Hindu gods and goddesses, and at the same time have thrown overboard the Amitabha Buddha held in regard among the Northern School of Buddhists. The long and short of it is that the Amitabha Buddha and the other gods whom the Northern School worship are not mentioned in books like the *Prajnaparamita,* but a lot of gods and goddesses are recommended for worship. And the Southern people have wilfully transgressed the Shastras and eschewed the gods and goddesses. The phase of Buddhism which declares 'Everything for others,' and which you find spread throughout Tibet, has greatly struck modern Europe. Concerning that phase, however, I have a good deal to say—which it is impossible to do in this letter. What Buddha did was to break wide open the gates of that very religion which was confined in the Upanishads to a particular caste. His greatness lies in his unrivalled sympathy. The high orders of Samadhi etc. that lend gravity to his religion are almost all there in the Vedas; what are absent there are his intellect and heart, which have never since been paralleled throughout the history of the world.

The Vedic doctrine of Karma is the same as in Judaism and all other religions, that is to say, the purification of the mind through sacrifices and such other external means—and Buddha was the first man who stood against it. But the inner essence of the ideas remained as of old—look at that doctrine of mental exercises which he preached, and that mandate of his to believe in the Suttas instead of the Vedas. Caste also remained as of old (caste was not wholly obsolete at the time of Buddha), but it was now determined by personal qualifications; and those that were not believers in his religion were declared as heretics, all in the old style. 'Heretic,' was a very ancient word with the Buddhists, but then they never had recourse to the sword (good souls!) and had great toleration. Argument blew up the Vedas. But what is the proof of your religion? Well, put faith in it!—the same procedure as in all religions. It was however an imperative necessity of the times; and that was the reason of his having incarnated himself. His doctrine is like that of Kapila. But that of Shankara, how far more grand and rational! Buddha and Kapila are always saying the world is full of grief and nothing but that—flee from it—ay, for your life, do! Is happiness altogether absent here? It is a statement of the nature of what the Brahmos say—the world is full of happiness! There is grief, forsooth, but what can be done? Perchance some will suggest that grief itself will appear as happiness when you become used to it by constant suffering. Shankara does not take this line of argument. He says: This world *is* and *is not—manifold yet one*; I shall unravel its mystery—I shall know whether grief be there, or anything else; I do not flee from it as from a bugbear. I will know all about it—as to the infinite pain that attends its search, well, I am embracing it in its fullest measure. Am I a beast that you frighten me with happiness and misery, decay and death, which are but the outcome of the senses? I will know about it—will give up my life for it. There is nothing to know about in this world—therefore, if there be anything beyond this relative existence—what the Lord Buddha has designated as *Prajnapara*—the transcendental—if such there be, I want that alone. Whether happiness attends it or grief, I do not care. What a lofty idea! How grand! The religion of Buddha has reared itself on the Upanishads, and upon that also the philosophy of Shankara. Only, Shankara had not the slightest bid of Buddha's wonderful heart, dry intellect merely! For fear of the Tantras, for fear of the mob, in his attempt to cure the boil, he amputated the very arm itself One has to write a big volume if one has to write about them at all—but I have neither the learning not the leisure for it.

The Lord Buddha is my Ishta—my God. He preached no theory about Godhead—he was himself God, I fully believe it. But no one has the power to put a limit to God's infinite glory. No, not even God Himself has the power to make Himself limited.

Vol. 6, Epistles (Second Series), XXIII, pp. 224–227

The many monasteries that you now see in India occupied by monks were once in the possession of Buddhism. The Hindus have only made them their own now by modifying them in their own fashion. Really speaking, the institution of Sannyasa originated with Buddha; it was he who breathed life into the dead bones of this institution [...]

Please read history, and you will find that Hinduism has become so great only by absorbing all the ideas of Buddha.

(Q: It seems to me that Buddha has only left revivified the great Hindu ideas, by thoroughly practising in his life such principles as renunciation, non-attachment, and so on.)

But this position can't be proved. For we don't get any history before Buddha was born. If we accept history only as authority, we have to admit that in the midst of the profound darkness of the ancient times, Buddha only shines forth as a figure radiant with the light of knowledge.

Vol. 6, Conversations and Dialogues, X, pp. 508–509

The result of Buddha's constant inveighing against a personal God was the introduction of idols into India. In the Vedas they knew them not, because they saw God everywhere, but the reaction against the loss of God as Creator and Friend was to make idols, and Buddha became an idol—so too with Jesus. The range of idols is from wood and stone to Jesus and Buddha, but we must have idols.

Vol. 7, Inspired Talks, 1 July 1895, pp. 21–22

Buddhism, one of the most philosophical religions in the world, spread all through the populace, the common people of India. What a wonderful culture there must have been among the Aryans twenty-five hundred years ago, to be able to grasp ideas!

Buddha was the only great Indian philosopher who would not recognise caste, and not one of his followers remains in India. All the other philosophers pandered more or less to social prejudices; no matter how high they soared, still a bit of the vulture remained in them.

Vol. 7, Inspired Talks, 9 July 1895, p. 39

Buddha was more brave and sincere than any teacher. He said: 'Believe no book; the Vedas are all humbug. If they agree with me, so much the better for the books. I am the greatest book; sacrifice and prayer are useless.' Buddha was the first human being to give to the world a complete system of morality. He was good for good's sake, he loved for love's sake.

Vol. 7, Inspired Talks, 10 July 1895, pp. 40–41

The Buddhists were the most logical agnostics. You can really stop nowhere between nihilism and absolutism. The Buddhists were intellectually all-destroyers, carrying their theory to its ultimate logical issue.

Vol. 7, Inspired Talks, 11 July 1895, p. 43

> Buddha was a great Vedantist (for Buddhism was really only an offshoot of Vedanta), and Shankara is often called a 'hidden Buddhist.' Buddha made the analysis, Shankara made the synthesis out of it. Buddha never bowed down to anything—neither Veda, nor caste, nor priest, nor custom. He fearlessly reasoned so far as reason could take him. Such a fearless search for truth and such love for every living thing the world has never seen. Buddha was the Washington of the religious world; he conquered a throne only to give it to the world, as Washington did to the American people. He sought nothing for himself.

Vol. 7, Inspired Talks, 19 July 1895, p. 59

Buddha [...] was not fully perfect. Buddha, however, recognised woman's right to an equal place in religion, and his first and one of his greatest disciples was his own wife, who became the head of the whole Buddhistic movement among the women of India. But we ought not to criticise these great ones, we should only look upon them as far above ourselves. Nevertheless we must not pin our faith to any man, however great; we too must become Buddhas and Christs.

Vol. 7, Inspired Talks, 29 July 1895, pp. 77–78

What was there in this country before Buddha's advent? Only a number of religious principles recorded on bundles of palm leaves—and those too known only to a few. It was Lord Buddha who brought them down to the practical field and showed how to apply them in the everyday life of the people. In a sense, *he* was the living embodiment of true Vedanta.

It was not through his teachings that Buddhism came to such degradation, it was the fault of his followers. By becoming too philosophic they lost much of their breadth of heart. Then gradually the corruption known as Vamachara (unrestrained mixing with women in the name of religion) crept in and ruined Buddhism. Such diabolical rites are not to be met with in any modern Tantra! One of the principal centres of Buddhism was Jagannatha or Puri, and you have simply to go there and look at the abominable figures carved on the temple walls to be convinced of this. Puri has come under the sway of the Vaishnavas since the time of Ramanuja and Shri Chaitanya. Through the influence of great personages like these the place now wears an altogether different aspect.

Vol. 7, Conversations and Dialogues, II, pp. 118–119

I am perfectly convinced that what they call modern Hinduism with all its ugliness is only stranded Buddhism. Let the Hindus understand this clearly, and then it would easier for them to reject it without murmur. As for the ancient form which the Buddha preached, I have the greatest respect for it, as well as for His person. And you well know that we Hindus worship

Him as an Incarnation. Neither is the Buddhism of Ceylon any good. My visit to Ceylon has entirely disillusioned me, and the only living people there are the Hindus. The Buddhists are all much Europeanised—even Mr. Dharmapala and his father had European names, which they have since changed. The only respect the Buddhists pay to their great tenet of non-killing is by opening 'butcher-stalls' in every place! And the priests encourage this. The real Buddhism, I once thought, would yet do *much good.* But I have given up the idea entirely, and I clearly see the reason why Buddhism was driven out of India, and we will only be too glad if the Ceylonese carry off the remnant of this religion with its hideous idols and licentious rites.

Vol. 7, Epistles (Third Series), XXXIX, pp. 505–506

The introduction of idols into India was the result of Buddha's constantly inveighing against a Personal God. The Vedas knew them not, but the reaction against the loss of God as Creator and Friend led to making idols of the great teachers, and Buddha himself became an idol and is worshipped as such by millions of people. Violent attempts at reform always end in retarding true reform. To worship is inherent in every man's nature; only the highest philosophy can rise to pure abstraction. So man will ever personify his God in order to worship Him.

Vol. 8, Discourses on Jnana-Yoga, IX, p. 33

Buddhism is historically the most important religion—historically, not philosophically—because it was the most tremendous religious movement that the world ever saw, the most gigantic spiritual wave ever to burst upon human society. There is no civilisation on which its effect has not been felt in some way or other.

The followers of Buddha were most enthusiastic and very missionary in spirit. They were the first among the adherents of various religions not to remain content with the limited sphere of their Mother Church. They spread far and wide. They travelled east and west, north and south. They reached into darkest Tibet; they went into Persia, Asia Minor; they went into Russia, Poland, and many other countries of the Western world. They went into China, Korea, Japan; they went into Burma, Siam, the East Indies, and beyond. When Alexander the Great, through his military conquests, brought the Mediterranean world in contact with India, the wisdom of India at once found a channel through which to spread over vast portions of Asia and Europe. Buddhist priests went out teaching among the different nations; and as they taught, superstition and priestcraft began to vanish like mist before the sun.

To understand this movement properly you should know what conditions prevailed in India at the time Buddha came [...] When you study the civilisation of India, you find that it has died and revived several times; this is its peculiarity. Most races rise once and then decline for ever. There are two kinds of people; those who grow continually and those whose growth comes to an end. The peaceful nations, India and China, fall down, yet rise again; but the others, once they go down, do not come up—they die. Blessed are the peacemakers, for they shall enjoy the earth.

At the time Buddha was born, India was in need of a great spiritual leader, a prophet. There was already a most powerful body of priests.

The priests in India, the Brahmins, possessed great intellectual and psychic powers. It was they who began the spiritual development of India, and they accomplished wonderful things. But the time came when the free spirit of development that had at first actuated the Brahmins disappeared. They began to arrogate powers and privileges to themselves [...] But while the priests were flourishing, there existed also the poet-prophets called Sannyasins [...] So these poet-prophets of ancient India repudiated the ways of the priest and declared the pure truth. They tried to break the power of the priests, and they succeeded a little. But in two generations their disciples went back to the superstitious, roundabout ways of the priests—became priests themselves: 'You can get truth only through us!' Truth became crystallised again, and again prophets came to break the encrustations and free the truth, and so it went on.

India was full of it in Buddha's day. There were the masses of people, and they were debarred from all knowledge. If just a word of the Vedas entered the ears of a man, terrible punishment was visited upon him. The priests had made a secret of the Vedas—the Vedas that contained the spiritual truths discovered by the ancient Hindus.

At last one man could bear it nor more. He had the brain, the power, and the heart—a heart as infinite as the broad sky. He felt how the masses were being led by the priests and how the priests were glorying in their power, and he wanted to do something about it. He did not want any power over any one, and he wanted to break the mental and spiritual bonds of men. His heart was large. The heart, many around us may have, and we also want to help others. But we do not have the brain; we do not know the ways and means by which help can be given. But this man had the brain to discover the means of breaking the bondages of souls. He learnt why men suffer, and he found the way out of suffering. He was a man of accomplishment, he worked everything out; he taught one and all without distinction and made them realise the peace of enlightenment. This was the man Buddha.

Buddha was the triumph in the struggle that had been going on between the priests and the prophets in India. One thing can be said for these Indian priests—they were not and never are intolerant of religion; they never have persecuted religion. Any man was allowed to preach against them. Theirs is such a religion; they never molested any one for his religious views. But they suffered from the peculiar weaknesses of all priests; they also sought power, they also promulgated rules and regulations and made religion unnecessarily complicated, and thereby undermined the strength of those who followed their religion.

Buddha cut through all these excrescences. He preached the most tremendous truths. He taught the very gist of the philosophy of the Vedas to one and all without distinction, he taught it to the world at large, because one of his great messages was the equality of man. Men are all equal. No concession there to anybody! Buddha was the great preacher of equality.

His doctrine was this: Why is there misery in our life? Because we are selfish. We desire things for ourselves—that is why there is misery. What is the way out? The giving up of the self. The self does not exist; the phenomenal world, all this that we perceive, is all that exists. There is nothing called soul underlying the cycle of life and death. There is the stream of thought, one thought following another in succession, each thought coming into existence and becoming non-existent at the same moment, that is all; there is no thinker of the thought, no soul. The body is changing all the time; so is mind, consciousness. The self therefore is a delusion. All selfishness comes of holding on to the self, to this illusory self. If we know the truth that there is no self, then we will be happy and make others happy.

This was what Buddha taught. And he did not merely talk; he was ready to give up his own life for the world. He said, 'If sacrificing an animal is good, sacrificing a man is better,' and he offered himself as a sacrifice. He said, 'This animal sacrifice is another superstition. God and soul are the two big superstitions. God is only a superstition invented by the priests. If there is a God, as these Brahmins preach, why is there so much misery in the world? He is just like me, a slave to the law of causation. If he is not bound by the law of causation, then why does he create? Such a God is not at all satisfactory. There is the ruler in heaven that rules the universe according to his sweet will and leaves us all here to die in misery—he never has the goodness to look at us for a moment. Our whole life is continuous suffering; but this is not sufficient punishment—after death we must go to places where we have other punishments. Yet we continually perform all kinds of rites and ceremonies to please this creator of the world.'

Buddha said, 'These ceremonials are all wrong. There is but one ideal in the world. Destroy all delusions; what is true will remain. As soon as the clouds are gone, the sun will shine.' How to kill the self? Become perfectly unselfish, read to give up your life even for an ant. Work not for any superstition, not to please any God, not to get any reward, but because you are seeking your own release by killing your self. Worship and prayer and all that, these are nonsense. You all say, 'I thank God,'—but where does He live? You do not know, and yet you are all going crazy about God.

Hindus can give up everything except their God. To deny God is to cut off the very ground from under the feet of devotion. Devotion and God the Hindus must cling to. They can never relinquish these. And here, in the teaching of Buddha, are no God and no soul—simply work. What for? Not for the self, for the self is a delusion. We shall be ourselves when this delusion has vanished. Very few are there in the world that can rise to that height and work for work's sake.

Yet the religion of Buddha spread fast. It was because of the marvellous love which, for the first time in the history of humanity, overflowed a large heart and devoted itself to the service not only of all men but of all living things—a love which did not care for anything except to find a release from suffering for all beings.

This teacher wanted to make truth shine as truth. No softening, no compromise, no pandering to the priests, the powerful, the kings. No bowing before superstitious traditions, however hoary; no respect for forms and books just because they came down from the distant past. He rejected all scriptures, all forms of religious practice. Even the very language, Sanskrit, in which religion had been traditionally taught in India, he rejected, so that his followers would not have any chance to imbibe the superstitions which were associated with it.

Buddha's idea is that there is no God, only man himself. He repudiated the mentality which underlies the prevalent ideas of God. He found it made men weak and superstitious. If you pray to God to give you everything, who is it, then, that goes out and works? God comes to those who work hard. God helps them that help themselves. An opposite idea of God weakens our nerves, softens our muscles, makes us dependent. Everything independent is happy; everything dependent is miserable. Man has infinite power within himself, and he can realise it—he can realise himself as the one infinite Self. It can be done; but you do not believe it. You pray to God and keep your powder dry all the time. Buddha taught the opposite. Do not let men weep. Let them have none of this praying and all that. God is not keeping shop.

Buddhism apparently has passed away from India; but really it has not. There was an element of danger in the teaching of Buddha—it was a reforming religion. In order to bring about the tremendous spiritual change he did, he had to give many negative teachings. But if a religion emphasises the negative side too much, it is in danger of eventual destruction. Never can a reforming sect survive if it is only reforming; the formative elements alone—the real impulse, that is the principles—live on and on. After a reform has been brought about, it is the positive side that should be emphasised; after the building is finished the scaffolding must be taken away.

It so happened in India that as time went on, the followers of Buddha emphasised the negative aspect of his teaching too much and thereby caused the eventual downfall of their religion. The positive aspects of truth were suffocated by the forces of negation; and thus India repudiated the destructive tendencies that flourished in the name of Buddhism. That was the decree of the Indian national thought.

The negative elements of Buddhism—there is no God and no soul—died out. I can say that God is the only being that exists; it is a very positive statement. He is the one reality. When Buddha says there is no soul, I say, 'Man, thou art one with the universe; thou art all things.' How positive! The reformative element died out; but the formative element has lived through all time. Buddha taught kindness towards lower beings; and since then there has not been a sect in India that has not taught charity to all beings, even to animals. This kindness, this mercy, this charity—greater than any doctrine—are what Buddhism left to us.

The life of Buddha has an especial appeal. All my life I have been very fond of Buddha, but not of his doctrine. I have more veneration for that character than for any other—that boldness, that fearlessness, and that tremendous love! He was born for the good of men. Others may seek God, others may seek truth for themselves; he did not even care to know truth for himself. He taught truth because people were in misery. How to help them, that was his only concern. Throughout his life he never had a thought for himself. How can we ignorant, selfish, narrow-minded human beings ever understand the greatness of this man?

And consider his marvellous brain! No emotionalism. The giant brain never was superstitious. Believe not because an old manuscript has been produced, because it has been handed down to you from your forefathers, because your friends want you to—but think for yourself; search truth for yourself; realise it yourself. Then if you find it beneficial to one and many, give it to people. Soft-brained men, weak-minded, chicken-hearted, cannot find the truth. One has to be free, and as broad as the sky. One has to have a mind that is crystal clear; only then can truth shine in it.

Of all the teachers of the world, he was the one who taught us most to be self-reliant, who freed us not only from the bondages of our false selves but from dependence on the invisible being or beings called God or gods. He invited everyone to enter into that state of freedom which he called Nirvana. All must attain to it one day; and that attainment is the complete fulfilment of man.

Vol. 8, Lectures and Discourses, Buddha's Message to the World, pp. 93–105

The three cycles of Buddhism were five hundred years of the Law, five hundred years of images, and five hundred years of Tantras. You must not imagine that there was ever a religion in India called Buddhism with temples and priests of its own order! Nothing of the sort. It was always within Hinduism. Only at one time the influence of Buddha was paramount, and this made the nation monastic.

Vol. 8, Sayings and Utterances, 19, p. 265

Jainism represents [...] the slow destruction of the body by self-torture. Hence Buddhism, you see, is reformed Jainism; and this is the real meaning of Buddha's leaving the company of the five ascetics.

Vol. 8, Sayings and Utterances, 24, p. 268

Buddha made the fatal mistake of thinking that the whole world could be lifted to the height of the Upanishads. And self-interest spoilt all. Krishna was wiser, because He was more politic. But Buddha would have no compromise. The world before now has seen even the Avatara ruined by compromise, tortured to death for want of recognition, and lost. But Buddha would have been worshipped as God in his own lifetime, all over Asia, for a moment's compromise. And his reply was only: 'Buddhahood is an achievement, not a person!' Verily was He the only man in the world who was ever quite sane, the only one man ever born!

Vol. 8, Sayings and Utterances, 32, pp. 271–272

The great point of contrast between Buddhism and Hinduism lies in the fact that Buddhism said, 'Realise all this as illusion,' while Hinduism said, 'Realise that within the illusion is the Real.' Of *how* this was to be done, Hinduism never presumed to enunciate any rigid law. The Buddhist command could only be carried out through monasticism; the Hindu might be fulfilled through any state of life. All alike were roads to the One Real [...] Thus Buddhism became the religion of a monastic order, but Hinduism, in spite of its exaltation of monasticism, remains ever the religion of faithfulness to daily duty, whatever it be, as the path by which man may attain God.

Vol. 8, Sayings and Utterances, 34, pp. 273–274

I am the servant of the servants of Buddha. Who was there ever like him?—the Lord—who never performed one action for himself—with a heart that embraced the whole world! So full of pity that he—prince and monk—would give his life to save a little goat! So loving that he sacrificed himself to the hunger of a tigress!—to the hospitality of a pariah and blessed him! And he came into my room when I was a boy and I fell at his feet! For I knew it was the Lord Himself!

Vol. 8, Sayings and Utterances, 44, p. 278

Buddha! Buddha! Surely he was the greatest man who ever lived. He never drew a breath for himself. Above all, he never claimed worship. He said, 'Buddha is not a man, but a state. I have found the door. Enter, all of you!'

Vol. 9, Excerpts from Sister Nivedita's Book, Notes of Some Wanderings with Swami Vivekananda, Chapter VIII, The Temple of Pandrenthan, p. 379

”

Part III

MAKING INDIA GREAT AGAIN

Chapter 8

LEVERAGING INDIA'S STRENGTHS

Superficial observations can lead to the erroneous conclusion that Indians are only a conquered and suffering people, a race of dreamers and philosophers. However, in the realm of spirituality, India is a conquering nation with global influence. The national idea of Hindus is spirituality, which is what has enabled India to survive. Whereas for other nations religion is only one among the many occupations of life, in India, religion is the only occupation. Every race has its own raison d'être, its special mission. India's mission is to conserve, to preserve and to accumulate all the spiritual energy of the race, and to share it with the world when the circumstances are right. India is the treasure house of religion and spirituality. India's gift to the world is in the realm of spirituality–be it philosophy, religion, wisdom, ethics, sweetness, gentleness or love. Religion is the keynote, the backbone and the bedrock upon which India's life has been based, and which is a pre-requisite for India's growth and well-being. If a Hindu is not spiritual, he cannot be called a Hindu. Whether it is a good thing or not is beside the point; the reality is that you cannot change it. Social and political reform in India will succeed only if it is seen to improve spirituality. The common man in India has a far better and more sophisticated understanding of spirituality than many so-called philosophers in other countries. In India, the poorer a man is, the more moral he is.

India's contributions to the world have been plentiful and diverse–in the realms of science, mathematics, philosophy, philology, literature, craftsmanship, etc. India was a flourishing civilization, predating the Greeks and the Romans, at a time when the forefathers of modern Europeans lived in forests. It was a prosperous country, which had ancient and extensive trading ties with Africa and elsewhere. This is why India attracted the attention of—in fact, fascinated—other parts of the world. Our ancestors did bring out the secrets of external nature, but they gave it up to focus on spirituality.

The possession of India by a foreign power has always been a turning point in the history of that power, bringing to it wealth, prosperity, territory and spiritual ideas. India's role has been akin to that of the morning dew, that slowly and silently brings about tremendous results. Today, a West weary of worldly enjoyments and luxuries is once again turning to India to satisfy its spiritual needs. While the West is focused on the problem of how much a man can possess, India is focused on how little a man needs to live. India finds itself in a very critical and responsible position, and is morally obliged to help.

The British Empire's vast global reach provides the conditions for the spread of India's message, but this has to be a message of lofty principle, not superstitions. England is the karma of India, which will give rise to a new national hope for India and lead to its salvation. It is the English who have unlocked the literature and religion of India. Preaching the truths of the Shastras to the world must be India's eternal foreign policy. India must conquer the world or die.

For centuries, outsiders have invaded India, massacred its people, and impoverished the country. The world has vilified India and been contemptuous of it. But India has survived. It is not afraid and does not beg for mercy. It is not in India's nature to fight to conquer; Indians have trust in the eternity of truth. India's attitude is to return good for evil in the quiet belief that calmness, goodness and patience will eventually triumph. The patient and mild Hindu has always been the blessed child of God. India can teach lessons of mildness, gentleness, forbearance, tolerance, sympathy and brotherhood to all. The fact that Indians have never been a conquering race is a blessing that has enabled us to survive, despite prolonged foreign persecution and oppression. India, too, has had its 'conquerors', like Asoka, but these conquests were in the realm of religion and spirituality. Compare this with what has happened to other civilizations and great empires like those of the Greeks, Romans, Arabs and Spaniards, who conquered and imposed their will by force of arms and extensive bloodshed.

All civilizations whose greatness was based on materialism have disappeared. All this Western pomp is only vanity. There is talk of 'survival of the fittest.' Physical strength is not a criterion to form a judgment, otherwise how is it that the Hindu race and civilization have survived for so many millennia, whereas other nations and civilizations have come and gone? No one could destroy the core of our religion. India has survived despite the multiple assaults on it over many centuries. It retains its strength and life because it still has much to contribute to the world's civilizations. Our Europeanised elite should stop praying to the Europeans to save them. With all its faults, India is the only place where the soul finds its freedom.

It was India's fate to be conquered, but in its turn, India also conquered the conquerors, seen in the emergence of the Sufi tradition among Muslims, and in the approach of the Mughal king Akbar. Some European philosophers have said that the influence of Indian thought on Europe would be as momentous as the revival of Greek and Latin culture after the Dark Ages.

The important thing is that Indians should have faith in themselves. If we are conscious that we are great, we will become great. However degraded and degenerated we may have become, Indians can become great only if we begin to work in earnest on behalf of our religion. We should be proud of our ancestors. It is a matter of pride that whereas many other countries trace their descent to some plunderer or robber baron, Indians take pride in being the descendants of Rishis and sages. The name 'Hindu' should stand for everything that is glorious and spiritual; it is not a name of opprobrium, designating the downtrodden and the worthless.

India should be patient, for the future is ours. Western people, proud of their prosperity and achievements, are like prattling babies. They are proud of their wealth and look down upon Indians. The Hindu's attitude is to be patient and quiet. True, India has made many mistakes, but it has learnt its lessons. The tinplate Western institutions are evanescent and won't survive for long, whereas India's institutions have stood the test of time. If the West's ideal is matter and mortal, Western society will also be mortal. But India's ideal is the Spirit, and therefore it will live forever. With all their faults, Hindus are head and shoulders above all other nations in morality and spirituality. We should strive to combine these virtues with some of the commendable attributes of the West. India needs to send to the West good and credible men of religion and spirituality to change the West's flawed perceptions about India and to gain respect for India.

“

People who are capable of seeing only the gross external aspect of things can perceive in the Indian nation only a conquered and suffering people, a race of dreamers and philosophers. They seem to be incapable of perceiving that in the spiritual realm India conquers the world [...] What may be that force which causes this afflicted and suffering people, the Hindu, and the Jewish too (the two races from which have originated all the great religions of the world) to survive, when other nations perish? The cause can only be their spiritual force [...] The philosophy of India percolates throughout the whole civilised world, modifying and permeating as it goes. So also in ancient times, her trade reached the shores of Africa before Europe was known, and opened communication with the rest of the world, thus disproving the belief that Indians never went outside of their own country. It is remarkable also that the possession of India by a foreign power has always been a turning point in the history of that power, bringing to it wealth, prosperity, dominion, and spiritual ideas.

Vol. 1, Lectures and Discourses, Vedanta as a Factor in Civilisation, p. 383

The ideal of faith in ourselves is of the greatest help to us. If faith in ourselves had been more extensively taught and practised, I am sure a very large portion of the evils and miseries that we have would have vanished. Throughout the history of mankind, if any motive power has been more potent than another in the lives of all great men and women, it is that of faith in themselves. Born with the consciousness that they were to be great, they became great [...] Faith in ourselves will do everything. I have experienced it in my own life, and am still doing so; and as I grow older that faith is becoming stronger and stronger. He is an atheist who does not believe in himself. The old religions said that he was an atheist who did not believe in God. The new religion says that he is the atheist who does not believe in himself. But it is not selfish faith, because the Vedanta, again, is the doctrine of oneness. It means faith in all, because you are all. Millions of years have passed since man first came here, and yet but one infinitesimal part of his powers has been manifested. Therefore, you must not say that you are weak. How do you know what possibilities lie behind that degradation on the surface? You know but little of that which is within you. For behind you is the ocean of infinite power and blessedness.

Vol. 2, Practical Vedanta and Other Lectures,
Practical Vedanta: Part I, pp. 301–302

What we are to understand is this, that what we call mistakes or evil, we commit because we are weak, and we are weak because we are ignorant. I prefer to call them mistakes. The word sin, although originally a very good word, has got a certain flavour about it that frightens me. Who makes us ignorant? We ourselves. We put our hands over our eyes and weep that it is dark.

Vol. 2, Practical Vedanta and Other Lectures,
Practical Vedanta: Part IV, p. 356

With the Hindus you will find one national idea—spirituality. In no other religion, in no other sacred books of the world, will you find so much energy spent in defining the idea of God. They tried to define the ideal of soul so that no earthly touch might mar it. The spirit must be divine; and spirit understood as spirit must not be made into a man [...] Renunciation and spirituality are the two great ideas of India, and it is because India clings to these ideas that all her mistakes count for so little.

Vol. 2, Practical Vedanta and Other Lectures,
The Way to the Realisation of a Universal Religion, p. 372

Swami Vivekananda, the Hindoo monk, delivered a lecture Monday night [...] His subject was 'India's Gift to the World.'

He spoke of the wondrous beauties of his native land, 'where stood the earliest cradle of ethics, arts, sciences, and literature, and the integrity of whose sons and the virtue of whose daughters have been sung by all travellers.' Then the lecturer showed in rapid details, what India has given to the world.

'India has given to antiquity the earliest scientific physicians and, according to Sir William Hunter, she has even contributed to modern medical science by the discovery of various chemicals and by teaching you how to reform misshapen ears and noses. Even more it has done in mathematics, for algebra, geometry, astronomy, and the triumph of modern science—mixed mathematics—were all invented in India, just so much as the ten numerals, the very cornerstone of all present civilisation, were discovered in India and are in reality Sanskrit words.

In philosophy we are even now head and shoulders above any other nation, as Schopenhauer, the great German philosopher has confessed. In music, India gave to the world her system of notation, with the seven cardinal notes and the diatonic scale, all of which we enjoyed as early as 350 B.C., while it came to Europe only in the eleventh century. In philology, our Sanskrit language is now universally acknowledged to be the foundation of all European languages, which in fact are nothing but jargonized Sanskrit.

In literature, our epics and poems and dramas rank as high as those of any language; our *Shakuntala* was summarised by Germany's greatest poet, as 'heaven and earth united.' India has given to the world the fables of Aesop, which were copied by Aesop from an old Sanskrit book; it has given the Arabian Nights, yes, even the story of Cinderella and the Beanstalks. In manufacture, India was the first to make cotton and purple [dye], it was proficient in all works of jewellery, and the very word 'sugar', as well as the article itself, is the product of India. Lastly she has invented the game of chess and the cards and the dice. So great, in fact, was the superiority of India in every respect that it drew to her borders the hungry cohorts of Europe, and thereby indirectly brought about the discovery of America.

And now, what has the world given India in return for all that? Nothing by nullification [vilification] and curse and contempt. The world waded in her children's life blood, it reduced India to poverty and her sons and daughters to slavery, and now it adds insult to injury by preaching to her a religion which can only thrive on the destruction of every other religion. But India is not afraid. It does not beg for mercy at the hands of any nation. Our only fault is that we cannot fight to conquer; but we trust in the eternity of truth. India's message to the world is, first of all, her blessing; she is returning good for the evil which is done her, and thus she puts into execution this noble idea, which had its origin in India. Lastly, India's message is that calm, goodness, patience and gentleness will ultimately triumph. For where are the Greeks, the one-time masters of the earth? They are gone. Where are the Romans, at the tramp of whose cohorts the world trembled? Passed away. Where are the Arabs, who in fifty years had carried their banners from the Atlantic to the Pacific? And where are the Spaniards, the cruel murderers of millions of men? Both races are nearly extinct. But thanks to the morality of her children, the kinder race will never perish, and she will yet see the hour of her triumph.

Vol. 2, Reports in American Newspapers, India's Gift to the World, pp. 510–513

If there is any land on this earth that can lay claim to be the blessed Punya Bhumi, to be the land to which all souls on this earth must come to account for Karma, the land to which every soul that is wending its way Godward must come to attain its last home, the land where humanity has attained its highest towards gentleness, towards purity, towards calmness, above all, the land of introspection and of spirituality—it is India. Hence have started the founders of religions from the most ancient times, deluging the earth again and again with the pure and perennial waters of spiritual truth. Hence have proceeded the tidal waves of philosophy that have covered the earth, East or West, North or South, and hence again must start the wave which is going to spiritualise the material civilisation of the world. Herem is the life-giving water with which must be quenched the burning fire of materialism which is burning the core of the hearts of millions in other lands. Believe me, my friends, this is going to be.

The debt which the world owes to our Motherland is immense. Taking country with country, there is not one race on this earth to which the world owes so much as to the patient Hindu, the mild Hindu. 'The mild Hindu' sometimes is used as an expression of reproach; but if ever a reproach concealed a wonderful truth, it is in the term 'the mild Hindu,' who has always been the blessed child of God. Civilisations have arisen in other parts of the world. In ancient times and in modern times, great ideas have emanated from strong and great races. In ancient and in modern times, wonderful ideas have been carried forward from one race to another. In ancient and in modern times, seeds of great truth and power have been cast abroad by the advancing tides of national life, but mark you, my friends, it has been always with the blast of war trumpets and with the march of embattled cohorts. Each idea had to be soaked in a deluge of blood. Each idea had to wade through the blood of millions of our fellow-beings. Each word of power had to be followed by the groans of millions, by the wails of orphans, by the tears of widows. This, in the main, other nations have taught; but India has for thousands of years peacefully existed. Here activity prevailed when even Greece did not exist, when Rome was not thought of, when the very fathers of the modern Europeans lived in the forests and painted themselves blue. Even earlier, when history has no record, and tradition dares not peer into the gloom of that intense past, even from then until now, ideas after ideas have marched out from her, but every word has been spoken with a blessing behind it and peace before it. We, of all nations of the world, have never been a conquering race, and that blessing is on our head, and therefore we live.

To the other nations of the world, religion is one among the many occupations of life. There is politics, there are the enjoyments of social life, there is all that wealth can buy or power can bring, there is all that the senses can enjoy; and among all these various occupations of life and all this searching after something which can give et a little more whetting to the cloyed senses—among all these, there is perhaps a little bit of religion. But here in India religion is the one and the only occupation of life.

Everyone born into this world has a bent, a direction towards which he must go, through which he must live, and what is true of the individual is equally true of the race. Each race, similarly, has a peculiar bent, each race has a peculiar *raison d'être*, each race has a peculiar mission to fulfil in the life of the world. Each race has to make its own result, to fulfil its own mission. Political greatness or military power is never the mission of our race; it never was and, mark my words, it never will be. But there has been the other mission given to us, which is to conserve, to preserve, to accumulate, as it were, into a dynamo, all the spiritual energy of the race, and that concentrated energy is to pour forth in a deluge on the world whenever circumstances are propitious. Let the Persian or the Greek, the Roman, the Arab, or the Englishman march his battalions, conquer the world, and link the different nations together, and the philosophy and spirituality of India is ever ready to flow along the new-made channels into the veins of the nations of the world. The Hindu's calm brain must pour out its own quota to give to the sum total of human progress. India's gift to the world is the light spiritual.

But there is another peculiarity, as I have already hinted to you. We never preached our thoughts with fire and sword. If there is one word in the English language to represent the gift of India to the world, if there is one word in the English language to express the effect which the literature of India produces upon mankind, it is this one word, 'fascination.' It is the opposite of anything that takes you suddenly; it throws on you, as it were, a charm imperceptibly. To many, Indian thought, Indian manners, Indian customs, Indian philosophy, Indian literature are repulsive at first sight; but let them persevere, let them read, let them become familiar with the great principles underlying these ideas, and it is ninety-nine to one that the charm will come over them, and fascination will be the result. Slow and silent, as the gentle dew that falls in the morning, unseen and unheard yet producing a most tremendous result, has been the work of the calm, patient, all-suffering spiritual race upon the world of thought.

The little toleration that is in the world, the little sympathy that is yet in the world for religious thought, is practically here in the land of the Aryas, and nowhere else. It is here that Indians build temples for Mohammedans and Christians; nowhere else. If you go to other countries and ask Mohammedans or people of other religions to build a temple for your, see how they will help. They will instead try to breakdown your temple and you too if they can. The one great lesson, therefore, that the world wants most, that the world has yet to learn from India, is the idea not only of toleration, but of sympathy.

We have again to learn the one central truth that was preached only here in our Motherland, and that has to be preached once more from India. Why? Because not only is it in our books, but it runs through every phase of our national literature and is in the national life. Here and here alone is it practised every day, and any man whose eyes are open can see that it is practised here and here alone. Thus we have to teach religion. There are other and higher lessons that India can teach, but they are only for the learned. The lessons of mildness, gentleness, forbearance, toleration, sympathy and brotherhood everyone may learn, whether man, woman or child, learned or unlearned, without respect of race, case or creed.

Vol. 3, Lectures from Colombo to Almora, First Public Lecture in the East, pp. 105–115

I discard the idea that India was ever passive. Nowhere has activity been more pronounced than in this blessed land of ours, and the great proof of this activity is that our most ancient and magnanimous race still lives, and at every decade in its glorious career seems to take on fresh youth—undying and imperishable. This activity manifests itself here in religion.

The eyes of the whole world are now turned towards this land of India for spiritual food; and India has to provide it for all the races. Here alone is the best ideal for mankind; and Western scholars are now striving to understand this ideal which is enshrined in our Sanskrit literature and philosophy, and which has been the characteristic of India all through the ages.

Since the dawn of history, no missionary went out of India to propagate the Hindu doctrines and dogmas; but now a wonderful change is coming over us. Shri Bhagavan Krishna says, 'Whenever virtue subsides and immorality prevails, then I come again and again to help the world.' Religious researches disclose to us the fact that there is not a country possessing a good ethical code but has borrowed something of it from us, and there is not one religion possessing good ideas of the immortality of the soul but has derived it directly or indirectly from us.

There never was a time in the world's history when there was so much robbery, and high-handedness, and tyranny of the strong over the weak, as at this latter end of the nineteenth century. Everybody should know that there is no salvation except through the conquering of desires, and that no man is free who is subject to the bondage of matter. This great truth all nations are slowly coming to understand and appreciate. As soon as the disciple is in a position to grasp this truth, the words of the Guru come to his help. The Lord sends help to His own children in His infinite mercy which never ceaseth and is ever flowing in all creeds. Our Lord is the Lord of all religions. This idea belongs to India alone; and I challenge any one of you to find it in any other scripture of the world.

We Hindus have now been placed, under God's providence, in a very critical and responsible position. The nations of the

West are coming to us for spiritual help. A great moral obligation rests on the sons of India to fully equip themselves for the work of enlightening the world on the problems of human existence. One thing we may note that wherever you will find that good and great men of other countries take pride in tracing back their descent to some robber baron who lived in a mountain fortress and emerged from time to time to plunder passing wayfarers, we Hindus, on the other hand, take pride in being the descendants of Rishis and sages who lived on roots and fruits in mountains and caves, meditating on the future. We may be degraded and degenerated now; but however degraded and degenerated we may be, we can become great if only we begin to work in right earnest on behalf of our religion.

Vol. 3, Lectures from Colombo to Almora, Reply to the Address of Welcome at Pamban, pp. 137–139

Religion and religion alone is the life of India, and when that goes India will die, in spite of politics, in spite of social reforms, in spite of Kubera's wealth poured on the head of every one of her children.

This is the motherland of philosophy, of spirituality, and of ethics, of sweetness, gentleness and love. These still exist, and my experience of the world leads me to stand on firm ground and make the bold statement that India is still the first and foremost of all the nations of the world in this respect.

Let others talk of politics, of the glory of acquisition of immense wealth poured in by trade, of the power and spread of commercialism, of the glorious fountain of physical liberty; but these the Hindu mind does not understand and does not want to understand. Touch him on spirituality, on God, on the soul, on the infinite, on spiritual freedom, and I assure you, the lowest peasant in India is better informed on these subjects than many a so-called philosopher in other lands. I have said, gentlemen, that we have yet something to teach to the world. This is the very reason, the raison d'être that this nation has lived on, in spite of hundreds of years of persecution, in spite of nearly a thousand years of foreign rule and foreign oppression. This nation still lives; the *raison d'être* is it still holds to God, to the treasure house of religion and spirituality.

Vol. 3, Lectures from Colombo to Almora, Reply to the Address of Welcome at Ramnad, pp. 146–148

I have seen a little of the world, travelling among the races of the East and the West; and everywhere I find among nations one great ideal, which forms the backbone, so to speak, of that race. With some it is politics, with others it is social culture; others again may have intellectual culture and so on for their national background. But this, our motherland, has religion and religion alone for its basis, for its backbone, for the bedrock upon which the whole building of its life has been based.

I am not just now discussing whether it is good to have the vitality of the race in religious ideals or in political ideals, but so far it is clear to us that, for good or for evil, our vitality is concentrated in our religion. You cannot change it. You cannot destroy it and put in its place another. You cannot transplant a large growing tree from one soil to another and make it immediately take root there. For good or evil, the religious ideal has been flowing into India for thousands of years; for good or for evil, the Indian atmosphere has been filled with ideals of religion for shining scores of centuries; for good or for evil, we have been born and brought up in the very midst of these ideas of religion, till it has entered into our very blood and tingled with every drop in our veins, and has become one with our constitution, become the very vitality of our lives. Can you give such religion up without the rousing of the same energy in reaction, without filling the channel which that mighty river has cut out for itself in the course of thousands of years? Do you want that the Ganga should go back to its icy bed and begin a new course? Even if that were possible, it would be impossible for this country to give up her characteristic course of religious life and take up for herself a new career of politics or something else. You can work only under the law of least resistance, and this religious line is the line of least resistance in India. This is the line of life, this is the line of growth, and this is the line of well being in India—to follow the track of religion.

Do you not know how for the last hundred or two hundred years you have been hearing again and again out of the lips of men who ought to have known better, from the mouths of those who pretend at least to know better, that all the arguments they produce against the Indian religion is this—that our religion does not conduce to well-being in this world, that it does not bring gold to us, that it does not make us robbers of nations, that it does not make the strong stand upon the bodies of the weak and feed themselves with the life-blood of the weak. Certainly our religion does not do that. It cannot send cohorts, under whose feet the earth trembles, for the purpose of destruction and pillage and the ruination of races. Therefore they say—what is there in this religion? It does not bring any grist to the grinding mill, any strength to the muscles; what is there in such a religion?

They little dream that that is the very argument with which we prove our religion, because it does not make for this world. Ours is the only true religion because, according to it, this little sense-world of three days' duration is not to be made the end and aim of all, is not to be our great goal.

Ay, it is a curious fact that while nations after nations have come upon the stage of the world, played their parts vigorously for a few moments, and died almost without leaving a mark or a ripple on the ocean of time, here we are living, as it were, an eternal life. They talk a great deal of the new theories about the survival of the fittest, and they think that it is the strength of the muscles which is the fittest to survive. If that were true, any one of the aggressively known old world nations would have lived a life of glory today, and we, the weak Hindus, who never conquered even one other race or nation, ought to have died out; yet we live here three hundred million strong! (A young English lady once told me: What have the Hindus done? They never even conquered a single race!) And it is not at all true that all its energies are spent, that atrophy has overtaken its body; that is not true. There is vitality enough, and it comes out in torrents and deluges the world when the time is ripe and requires it.

We have, as it were, thrown a challenge to the whole world from the most ancient times. In the West, they are trying to solve the problem how much a man can possess, and we are trying here to solve the problem on how little a man can live. This struggle and this difference will still go on for some centuries. But if history has any truth in it and if prognostications ever prove true, it must be that those who train themselves to live on the least and control themselves well will in the end gain the battle, and that those who run after enjoyment and luxury, however vigorous they may seem for the moment, will have to die and become annihilated. There are times in the history of a man's life, nay, in the history of the lives of nations, when a sort of world-weariness becomes painfully predominant. It seems that such a time of world-weariness has come upon the Western world.

Vol. 3, Lectures from Colombo to Almora, The Mission of the Vedanta, pp. 177–181

Did India ever stand in want of reformers? Do you read the history of India? Who was Ramanuja? Who was Shankara? Who was Nanak? Who was Chaitanya? Who was Kabir? Who was Dadu? Who were all these great preachers, one following the other, a galaxy of stars of the first magnitude? Did not Ramanuja feel for the lower classes? Did he not try all his life to admit even the Pariah to his community? Did he not try to admit even Mohammedans to his own fold? Did not Nanak confer with Hindus and Mohammedans, and try to bring about a new state of things? They all tried, and their work is still going on. The difference is this. They had not the fanfaronade of the reformers of today; they had no curses on their lips as modern reformers have; their lips pronounced only blessings. They never condemned. They said to the people that the race must always grow. They looked back and they said, 'O Hindus, what you have done is good but, my brothers, let us do better.' They did not say, 'You have been wicked, now let us be good.' They said, 'You have been good, but now let us be better.' That makes a whole world of difference. We must grow according to our nature. Vain is it to attempt the lines of action that foreign societies have engrafted upon us; it is impossible. Glory unto God, that it is impossible, that we cannot be twisted and tortured into the shape of other nations. I do not condemn the institutions of other races; they are good for them, but not for us. This is the first lesson to learn. With other sciences, other institutions, and other traditions behind them, they have got their present system. We, with our traditions, with thousands of years of Karma behind us, naturally can only follow our own bent, run in our own grooves; and that we shall have to do.

I see that each nation, like each individual, has one theme in this life, which is its centre, the principal note round which every other note comes to form the harmony. In one nation political power is its vitality, as in England, artistic life in another, and so on. In India, religious life forms the centre, the keynote of the whole music of national life; and if any nation attempts to throw off its national vitality—the direction which has become its own through the transmission of centuries—that nation dies if it succeeds in the attempt. And, therefore, if you succeed in the attempt to throw off your religion and take up either politics, or society, or any other things as your centre, as the vitality of your national life, the result will be that you will become extinct. To prevent this you must make all and everything work through that vitality of your religion. I have seen that I cannot preach even religion to Americans without showing them its practical effect on social life. I could not preach religion in England without showing the wonderful political changes the Vedanta would bring. So, in India, social reform has to be preached by showing how much it will improve the one thing that the nation wants—its spirituality. Every man has to make his own choice; so has every nation. We made our choice ages ago, and we must abide by it. And, after all, it is not such a bad choice. Is it such a bad choice in this world to think not of matter but of spirit, not of man but of God?

So every improvement in India requires first of all an upheaval in religion. Before flooding India with socialistic or political ideas, first deluge the land with spiritual ideas. The first work that demands our attention is that the most wonderful truths confined in our Upanishads, in our scriptures, in our Puranas must be brought out from the books, brought out from the monasteries, brought out from the forests, brought out from the possession of selected bodies of people, and scattered broadcast all over the land, so that these truths may run like fire all over the country from north to south and east to west, from the Himalayas to Comorin, from Sindh to the Brahmaputra.

Vol. 3, Lectures from Colombo to Almora,
My Plan of Campaign, pp. 219–221

Those of you who think that the Hindus have been always confined within the four walls of their country through all ages, are entirely mistaken; you have not studied the old books, you have not studied the history of the race aright if you think so. Each nation must give in order to live. When you give life, you will have life; when you receive, you must pay for it by giving to all others; and that we have been living for so many thousands of years is a fact that stares us in the face, and the solution that remains is that we have been always giving to the outside world, whatever the ignorant may think. But the gift of India is the gift of religion and philosophy, and wisdom and spirituality. And religion does not want cohorts to march before its path and clear its way. Wisdom and philosophy do not want to be carried on floods of blood. Wisdom and philosophy do not march upon bleeding human bodies, do not march with violence but come on the wings of peace and love, and that has always been so.

If I ask myself what has been the cause of India's greatness, I answer, because we have never conquered. That is our glory. You are hearing every day, and sometimes, I am sorry to say, from men who ought to know better, denunciations of our religion, because it is not at all a conquering religion. To my mind that is the argument why our religion is truer than any other religion, because it never conquered, because it never shed blood, because its mouth always shed on all, words of blessing, of peace, words of love and sympathy. It is here and here alone that the ideals of toleration were first preached. And it is here and here alone that toleration and sympathy have become practical; it is theoretical in every other country. It is here and here alone, that the Hindu builds mosques for the Mohammedans and churches for the Christians.

So you see, our message has gone out to the world many a time, but slowly, silently, unperceived. It is on a par with everything in India. The one characteristic of Indian thought is its silence, its calmness. At the same time the tremendous power that is behind it is never expressed by violence. It is always the silent mesmerism of Indian thought.

Like the gentle dew that falls unseen and unheard, and yet brings into blossom the fairest of roses, has been the contribution of India to the thought of the world. Silent, unperceived, yet omnipotent in its effect, it has revolutionised the thought of the world, yet nobody knows when it did so.

Those great masterminds producing momentous results in the hearts of mankind were content to write their books without even putting their names, and to die quietly, leaving the books to posterity. Who knows the writers of our Puranas? They all pass under the generic name of Vyasa, and Kapila, and so on. They have been true children of Shri Krishna. They have been true followers of the Gita; they practically carried out the great mandate, 'To work you have the right, but to the fruits thereof.'

Before even the Buddhists were born, there are evidences accumulating every day that Indian thought penetrated the world. Before Buddhism, Vedanta had penetrated into China, into Persia, and the Island of the Eastern Archipelago. Again when the mighty mind of the Greek had linked the different parts of the Eastern world together there came Indian thought; and Christianity with all its boasted civilisation is but a collection of little bits of Indian thought. Ours is the religion of which Buddhism with all its greatness is a rebel child, and of which Christianity is a very patchy imitation.

One of these cycles has again arrived. There is the tremendous power of England which has linked the different parts of the world together. English roads no more are content like roman roads to run over lands, but they have also ploughed the deep in all directions. From ocean to ocean run the roads of England. Every part of the world has been linked to every other part, and electricity plays a most marvellous part as the new messenger. Under all these circumstances we find again India reviving and ready to give her own quota to the progress and civilisation of the world. And that I have been forced, as it were, by nature, to go over and preach to America and England is the result. Every one of us ought to have seen that the time had arrived. Everything looks propitious, and Indian thought, philosophical and spiritual, must once more go over and conquer the world. The problem before us, therefore, is assuming larger proportions every day. It is not only that we must revive our own country—that is a small matter; I am an imaginative man—and my idea is the conquest of the whole world by the Hindu race.

There have been great conquering races in the world. We also have been great conquerors. The story of our conquest has been described by that noble Emperor of India, Asoka, as the conquest of religion and spirituality. Once more the world must be conquered by India. This is the dream of my life, and I wish that each one of you who hear me today will have the same dream in your minds, and stop not till you have realised the dream. They will tell you every day that we had better look to our own homes first and then go to work outside. But I will tell you in plain language that you work best when you work for others. The best work that you ever did for yourselves was when you worked for others, trying to disseminate your ideas in foreign languages beyond the seas, and this very meeting is proof how the attempt to enlighten other countries with your thoughts is helping your own country. One-fourth of the effect that has been produced in this country by my going to England and America would not have been brought about, had I confined my ideas only to India.

Spirituality must conquer the West. Slowly they are finding out that what they want is spirituality to preserve them as nations. They are waiting for it, they are eager for it. Where is the supply to come from? [...] We must go out, we must conquer the world through our spirituality and philosophy. There is no other alternative, we must do it or die. The only condition of national life, of awakened and vigorous national life, is the conquest of the world by Indian thought.

At the same time we must not forget that what I mean by the conquest of the world by spiritual thought is the sending out of the life-giving principles, not the hundreds of superstitions that we have been hugging to our breasts for centuries. These have to be weeded out even on this soil, and thrown aside, so that they may die forever. These are the causes of the degradation of the race and will lead to softening of the brain. That brain which cannot think high and noble thoughts, which has lost all power of originality, which has lost all vigour, that brain which is always poisoning itself with all sorts of little superstitions passing under the name of religion, we must beware of.

I would rather see every one of you rank atheists than superstitious fools, for the atheist is alive and you can make something out of him. But if superstition enters, the brain is gone, the brain is softening, degradation has seized upon the life. Avoid these two. Brave, bold men, these are what we want. What we want is vigour in the blood, strength in the nerves, iron muscles and nerves of steel, not softening namby-pamby ideas. Avoid all these. Avoid all mystery. There is no mystery in religion. Is there any mystery in the Vedanta, or in the Vedas, or in the Samhitas, or in the Puranas? What secret societies did the sages of yore establish to preach their religion? What sleight-of-hand tricks are there recorded as used by them to bring their grand truths to humanity? Mystery mongering and superstitions are always signs of weakness. These are always signs of degradation and of death. Therefore beware of them; be strong, and stand on your own feet.

Vol. 3, Lectures from Colombo to Almora,
The Work Before Us, pp. 273–279

In Europe, owing to the inclemency of the climate and many other circumstances, poverty and sin go together, but not so in India. In India, on the other hand, my experience is that the poorer the man the better he is in point of morality. Now this takes time to understand, and how many foreign people are there who will stop to understand this, the very secret of national existence in India. Few are there who will have the patience to study the nation and understand. Here, and here alone, is the only race where poverty does not mean crime, poverty does not mean sin; and here is the only race where not only poverty does not mean crime, but poverty has been deified, and the beggar's garb is the garb of the highest in the land.

India must conquer the world, and nothing less than that is my ideal. It may be very big, it may astonish many of you, but it is so. We must conquer the world or die. There is no other alternative. The sign of life is expansion; we must go out, expand, show life, or degrade, fester, and die. There is no other alternative. Take either of these, either live or die. Now, we all know about the petty jealousies and quarrels that we have in our country. Take my word, it is the same everywhere. The other nations with their political lives have foreign policies. When they find too much quarrelling at home, they look for somebody abroad to quarrel with, and the quarrel at home stops. We have these quarrels at home without any foreign policy to stop them. This must be our eternal foreign policy, preaching the truths of our Shastras to the nations of the world. I ask you who are politically minded, do you require an other roof that this will unite us as a race?

Vol. 3, Lectures from Colombo to Almora,
Address of Welcome Presented at Calcutta and Reply, pp. 311–316

We are Hindus. I do not use the word Hindu in any bad sense at all, nor do I agree with those that think there is any bad meaning in it. In old times, it simply meant people who lived on the other side of the Indus; today a good many among those who hate us may have put a bad interpretation upon it, but names are nothing. Upon us depends whether the name Hindu will stand for everything that is glorious, everything that is spiritual, or whether it will remain a name of opprobrium, one designating the downtrodden, the worthless, the heathen. If at present the word Hindu means anything bad, never mind; by our action let us be ready to show that this is the highest word that any language can invent. It has been one of the principles of my life not to be ashamed of my own ancestors. I am one of the proudest men ever born, but let me tell you frankly, it is not for myself, but on account of my ancestry. The more I have studied the past, the more I have looked back, more and more has this pride come to me, and it has given me the strength and courage of conviction, raised me up from the dust of the earth, and set me working out that great plan laid out by those great ancestors of ours.

Wave after wave of barbarian conquest has rolled over this devoted land of ours. 'Allah Ho Akbar!' has rent the skies for hundreds of years, and no Hindu knew what moment would be his last. This is the most suffering and the most subjugated of all the historic lands of the world. Yet we still stand practically the same race, ready to face difficulties again and again if necessary; and not only so, of late there have been signs that we are not only strong but ready to go out, for the sign of life is expansion.

We find today that our ideas and thoughts are no more cooped up within the bounds of India, but whether we will it or not, they are marching outside, filtering into the literature of nations, taking their place among nations, and in some, even getting a commanding dictatorial position. Behind this we find the explanation that the great contribution to the sum total of the world's progress from India is the greatest, the noblest, the sublimest theme that can occupy the mind of man—it is philosophy and spirituality. Our ancestors tried many other things; they, like other nations, first went to bring out the secrets of external nature as we all know, and with their gigantic brains that marvellous race could have done miracles in that line of which the world could have been proud forever. But they gave it up for something higher; something better rings out from the pages of the Vedas: ' That science is the greatest which makes us know Him who never changes!'

This is the national characteristic, and this cannot be touched. Barbarians with sword and fire, barbarians bringing barbarous religions, not one of them could touch the core, not one could touch the 'jewel,' not one had the power to kill the 'bird' which the soul of the race inhabited. This, therefore, is the vitality of the race, and so long as that remains there is no power under the sun that can kill the race. All the tortures and miseries of the world will pass over without hurting us, and we shall come out of the flames like Prahlada so long as we hold on to this grandest of all our inheritances, spirituality. If a Hindu is not spiritual, I do not call him Hindu.

The mightiest buildings, if built upon the loose sand foundations of materialism, must come to grief one day, must totter to their destruction some day. The history of the world is our witness. Nation after nation has arisen and based its greatness upon materialism, declaring man was all matter. Ay, in Western language, a man gives up the ghost, but in our language a man gives up his body. The Western man is a body first, and then he has a soul; with us a man is a soul and spirit, and he has a body. Therein lies a world of difference. All such civilisations, as have been based upon such sand foundations as material comfort and all that, have disappeared one after another, after short lives, from the face of the world; but the civilisation of India and the other nations that have stood at India's feet to listen and learn, namely Japan and China, live even to the present day, and there are signs even of revival among them. Their lives are like that of the Phoenix, a thousand times destroyed, but ready to spring up again more glorious. But a materialistic civilisation once dashed down, never came up again; that building once thrown down is broken into pieces once for all. Therefore have patience and wait, the future is in store for us.

Vol. 3, Lectures from Colombo to Almora, The Common Bases of Hinduism, pp. 368–380

In the remote past, our country made gigantic advances in spiritual ideas. Let us, today, bring before our mind's eye that ancient history. But the one great danger in meditating over long-past greatness is that we cease to exert ourselves for new things, and content ourselves with vegetating upon that bygone ancestral glory and priding ourselves upon it. We should guard against that. In ancient times there were, no doubt, many Rishis and Maharshis who came face to face with Truth. But if this recalling of our ancient greatness is to be of real benefit, we too must become Rishis like them.

Vol. 3, Lectures from Colombo to Almora,
The Religion We Are Born In, p. 454

We all hear so much about the degradation of India. There was a time when I also believed in it. But today, standing on the vantage-ground of experience, with eyes cleared of obstructive predispositions and above all of the highly-coloured pictures of other countries toned down to their proper shade and light by actual contact, I confess in all humility that I was wrong. Thou blessed land of the Aryas, thou wast never degraded.

Race after race has taken the challenge up and tried their utmost to solve the world-riddle on the plane of desires. They have all failed in the past—the old ones have become extinct under the weight of wickedness and misery, which lust for power and gold bring in its train, and the new ones are tottering to their fall. The question has yet to be decided whether peace will survive or war; whether patience will survive or wickedness; whether muscle will survive or brain; whether worldliness will survive or spirituality. We have solved our problem ages ago, and held on to it through good or evil fortune, and mean to hold on to it till the end of time. Our solution is unworldliness—renunciation.

This is the theme of Indian life-work, the burden of her eternal songs, the backbone of her existence, the foundation of her being, the *raison d'être* of her very existence—the spirtualisation of the human race. In this her life-course she has never deviated, whether the Tartar ruled or the Turk, whether the Mogul ruled or the English.

And I challenge anybody to show one single period of her national life when India was lacking in spiritual giants capable of moving the world. But her work is spiritual, and cannot be done with blasts of war-trumpets or the march of cohorts. Her influence has always fallen upon the world like that of the gentle dew, unheard and scarcely marked, yet bringing into bloom the fairest flowers of the earth. This influence, being in its nature gentle, would have to wait for a fortunate combination of circumstances, to go out of the country into other lands, though it never ceased to work within the limits of its native land. As such, every educated person knows that whenever the empire-building Tartar or Persian or Greek or Arab brought this land in contact with the outside world, a mass of spiritual influence immediately flooded the world from here. The very same circumstances have presented themselves once more before us. The English high roads over land and sea and the wonderful power manifested by the inhabitants of that little island have once more brought India in contact with the rest of the world, and the same work has already begun. Mark my words, this is but the small beginning, big things are to follow; what the result of the present work outside India will be I cannot exactly state, but this I know for certain that millions, I say deliberately, millions in every civilised land are waiting for the message that will save them from the hideous abyss of materialism into which modern money-worship is driving them headlong, and many of the leaders of the new social movements have already discovered that Vedanta in its highest form can alone spiritualise their social aspirations.

Vol. 4, Writings: Prose and Poems, India's Message to the World, pp. 314–316

The majority of mankind can only understand power when it is presented to them in a concrete form, fitted to their perceptions. To them, the rush and excitement of war, with its power and spell, is something very tangible, and any manifestation of life that does not come like a whirlwind, bearing down everything before it, is to them as death. And India, for centuries at the feet of foreign conquerors, without any idea or hope of resistance, without the least solidarity among its masses, without the least idea of patriotism, must needs appear to such, as a land of rotten bones, a lifeless putrescent mass. It is said, the fittest alone survive. How is it then that this most unfitted of all races, according to commonly accepted ideas, could bear the most awful misfortunes that ever befall a race, and yet not show the least signs of decay? How is it that, while the multiplying powers of the so-called vigorous and active races are dwindling every day, the immoral (?) Hindu shows a power of increase beyond them all? Great laurels are due, no doubt, to those who can deluge the world with blood at a moment's notice; great indeed is the glory of those who, to keep up a population of a few millions in plenty, have to starve half the population of the earth, but is no credit due to those who can keep hundreds of millions in peace and plenty, without snatching the bread from the mouth of anyone else? Is there no power displayed in bringing up and guiding the destinies of countless millions of human beings, through hundreds of centuries, without the least violence to others?

In religion lies the vitality of India, and so long as the Hindu race do not forget the great inheritance of their forefathers, there is no power on earth to destroy them.

Vol. 4, Writings: Prose and Poems, Reply to Address of Maharaja of Khetri, pp. 323–324

It was India's Karma, her fate, to be conquered, and in her turn to conquer her conqueror. She has already done so with her Mohammedan victors: educated Mohammedans are Sufis, scarcely to be distinguished from Hindus. Hindu thought has permeated their civilisation; they assumed the position of learners. The great Akbar, the Mogul Emperor, was practically a Hindu. And England will be conquered in her turn. Today she has the sword, but it is worse than useless in the world of ideas. You know what Schopenhauer said of Indian thought. He foretold that its influence would be as momentous in Europe, when it became well known, as the revival of Greek and Latin culture after the Dark Ages.

Vol. 5, Interviews, India's Mission, pp. 190–191

The reason we Indians are still living, in spite of so much misery, distress, poverty, and oppression from within and without is that we have a national idea, which is yet necessary for the preservation of the world.

Why did not this Hindu race die out, in the face of so many troubles and tumults of a thousand years? If our customs and manners are so very bad how is it that we have not been effaced from the face of the earth by this time? Have the various foreign conquerors spared any pains to crush us out? Why then, were not the Hindus blotted out of existence, as happened with men in other countries which are uncivilised? Why was not India depopulated and turned into a wilderness? Why, then foreigners would have lost no time to come and settle in India, and till her fertile lands in the same way as they did and are still doing in America, Australia, and Africa! Well, then, my foreigner, you are not so strong as you think yourself to be; it is a vain imagination. First understand that India has strength as well, has a substantial reality of her own yet. Furthermore, understand that India is still living, because she has her own quota yet to give to the general store of the world's civilisation. And you too understand this full well, I mean those of our countrymen who have become thoroughly Europeanised both in external habits and in ways of thought and ideas, and who are continually crying their eyes out and praying to the European to save them.

Vol. 5, Writings: Prose and Poems, The East and the West, Introduction, pp. 443–444

There have been two lines of progress in this world—political and religious. In the former, the Greeks are everything, the modern political institutions being only the development of the Grecian; in the latter the Hindus are everything.

There is no new religious idea preached anywhere which is not found in the Vedas.

In everything, there are two kinds of development—analytical and synthetical. In the former the Hindus excel other nations. In the latter they are nil.[1]

Vol. 6, Notes of Class Talks and Lectures, Notes Taken Down in Madras 1892–93, p. 105

India is the only place where, with all its faults, the soul finds its freedom, its God. All this Western pomp is only vanity, only bondage of the soul. Never more in my life I realised more forcefully the vanity of the world.

Vol. 6, Epistles (Second Series), XCIII, p. 359

The British Empire with all its drawbacks is the greatest machine that ever existed for the dissemination of ideas. I mean to put my ideas in the centre of this machine, and they will spread all over the world. Of course, all great work is slow, and the difficulties are too many, especially as we Hindus are the conquered race. Yet, that is the very reason why it is bound to work, for spiritual ideals have always come from the downtrodden.

Vol. 6, Epistles (Second Series), CII, pp. 365–366

Do you know what my idea is? By preaching the profound secrets of the Vedanta religion in the Western world, we shall attract the sympathy and regard of these mighty nations, maintaining forever the position of their teacher in spiritual matters, and they will remain our teachers in all material concerns. The

---

[1]Here by the term 'synthesis' is meant a scientific generalization, and by the term 'analysis' an ontological reduction of facts and objects to their immanent principles.

day when, surrendering the spiritual into their hands, our countrymen would sit at the feet of the West to learn religion, that day indeed the nationality of this fallen nation will be dead and gone for good. Nothing will come of crying day and night before them, 'Give me this or give me that.' When there will grow a link of sympathy and regard between two nations by this give-and-take intercourse, there will be then no need for these noisy cries. I believe that by this cultivation of religion and the wider diffusion of Vedanta, both this country and the West will gain enormously. To me the pursuit of politics is a secondary means in comparison with this. I will lay down my life to carry out this belief practically. If you believe in any other way of accomplishing the good of India, well, you may go on working your own way.

Vol. 6, Conversations and Dialogues, I, pp. 448–449

We know, you Western people have the youthful blood coursing through your veins. We know that nations, like men, have their day. Where is Greece? Where is Rome? Where is that mighty Spaniard of the other day? Who knows through it all what becomes of India? Thus they are born, and thus they die; they rise and fall. The Hindu as a child knows of the Mogul invader whose cohorts no power on earth could stop, who has left in your language the terrible word 'Tartar.' The Hindu has learnt his lesson. He does not want to prattle, like the babes of today. Western people, say what you have to say. This is your day. Onward, go on, babes; have your prattle out. This is the day of the babies, to prattle. We have learnt our lesson and are quiet. You have a little wealth today, and you look down upon us. Well, this is your day. Prattle, babes, prattle—this is the Hindu's attitude.

The Lord of Lords is not to be attained by much frothy speech. The Lord of Lords is not to be attained by the powers of the intellect. He is not gained by much power of conquest. That man who knows the secret source of things and that everything else is evanescent, unto him He, the Lord, comes; unto none else.

India has learnt her lesson through ages and ages of experience. She has turned her face towards Him. She has made many mistakes; loads and loads of rubbish are heaped upon the race. Never mind; what of that? What is the clearing of rubbish, the cleaning of cities, and all that? Does that give life? Those that have fine institutions, they die. And what of institutions, those tinplate Western institutions, made in five days and broken on the sixth? One of these little handful nations cannot keep alive for two centuries together. And our institutions have stood the test of ages. Says the Hindu, 'Yes, we have buried all the old nations of the earth and stand here to bury all the new races also, because our ideal is not this world, but the other. Just as your ideal is, so shall you be. If your ideal is mortal, if your ideal is of this earth, so shalt thou be. If your ideal is matter, matter shalt thou be. Behold! Our ideal is the Spirit. That alone exists, nothing else matters; and like Him, we live forever.'

Vol. 8, Lectures and Discourses, Women of India, pp. 71–72

I have come to this conclusion that there is only one country in the world which understands religion—it is India; that with all their faults the Hindus are head and shoulders above all other nations in morality and spirituality; and that with proper care and attempt and struggle of all her disinterested sons, by combining some of the active and heroic elements of the West with calm virtues of the Hindus, there will come a type of men far superior to any that have ever been in this world.

Vol. 8, Epistles (Fourth Series), XXIX, p. 322

America is a grand country. It is a paradise of the poor and women. There is almost no poor in the country, and nowhere else in the world women are so free, so educated, so cultured. They are everything in society.

This is a great lesson. The Sannyasin has not lost a bit of his Sannyasinship, even his mode of living. And in this most hospitable country, every home is open to me. The Lord who guides me in India, would He not guide me here? And He has.

You may not understand why a Sannyasin should be in America, but it was necessary. Because the only claim you have to be recognised by the world is your religion, and good specimens of our religious men are required to be sent abroad to give other nations an idea that India is not dead.

Some representative men must come out of India and go to all nations of the earth to show at least that you are not savages. You may not feel the necessity of it from your Indian home, but, believe me, much depends upon that for your nation. And a Sannyasin who has no idea of doing good to his fellows is a brute, not a Sannyasin.

I spoke at the Parliament of Religions, and with what effect I may quote to you from a few newspapers and magazines ready at hand. I need not be self-conceited, but to you in confidence I am bound to say, because of your love, that no Hindu made such an impression in America, and if my coming has done nothing, it has done this that the Americans have come to know that India even today produces men at whose feet even the most civilized nations may learn lessons of religion and morality. Don't you think that is enough to say for the Hindu nation sending over here their Sannyasin?

Vol. 8, Epistles (Fourth Series), XXXIII, pp. 325–326

'But for English rule I could not be here now,' said the monk, 'though your lowest free-born American Negro holds higher position in India politically than is mine. Brahmin and coolie, we are all 'natives.' But it is all right, in spite of the misunderstanding and oppression. England is the Tharma [Karma?] of India, attracted inevitably by some inherent weaknesses, past mistakes, but from her blood and fibre will come the new national hope for my countrymen. I am a loyal subject of the Empress of India! And here the Swami salaamed before an imaginary potentate, bowing very low, perhaps too low for reverence.

'But such an apostle of freedom—', I murmured.

'She is the widow for many years, and such we hold in high worth in India,' said the philosopher seriously. 'As to freedom, yes, I believe the goal of all development is freedom, law and order. There is more law and order in the grave than anywhere else—try it.'

'I must go,' I said. 'I have to catch a train.'

'That is like all Americans,' smiled the Swami, and I had a glimpse of all eternity in his utter restfulness. 'You must catch this car or that train always. Is there not another, later?'

But I did not attempt to explain the Occidental conception of the value of time to this child of the Orient, realizing its utter hopeless and my own renegade sympathy. It must be delightful beyond measure to live in the land of 'time enough.' In the Orient there seems time to breathe, time to think, time to live; as the Swami says, what have we in exchange? We live in time; they in eternity.

Vol. 9, Conversations and Interviews, A Dusky Philosopher from India, pp. 326–327

'Tell you about the English in India? But I do not wish to talk of politics. But from the higher standpoint, it is true that but for the English rule I could not be here. We natives know that it is through the intermixture of English blood and ideas that the salvation of India will come. Fifty years ago, all the literature and religion of the race were locked up in the Sanskrit language; today the drama and the novel are written in the vernacular, and the literature of religion is being translated. That is the work of the English, and it is unnecessary, in America, to descant upon the value of the education of the masses.'

Vol. 9, Conversations and Interviews, "We are Hypnotized into Weakness by our Surroundings", pp. 327–328

"

Chapter 9

OVERCOMING INDIA'S WEAKNESSES

Religion

While the ideal of a Hindu is to become a Sannyasin, this can be realized only after a certain amount of experience. Presently, Hindu society is organised only for spiritual men. Where should those who want to enjoy the world go? It is a mistake to try to bind down everyone by the same laws by which the Sannyasin is bound, and to try to force the highest truths upon those large numbers of Indians who are not yet ready to imbibe spiritual knowledge. Monastic systems have both great merits and defects. In India, the monks enjoy more power than the rulers. While the monastics have been the bulwark of the people, they stand between priestcraft and knowledge. So much power is not good. What is needed is to somehow transform this tremendous power in the hands of the Sannyasins to uplift the masses.

Spirituality has no meaning for the poor and starving masses who are drowning in disease and sorrow. They first need bread, and then the opportunity to enjoy themselves a bit. Renunciation will come to the poor man in due course. Let us not delude ourselves by believing that we are at present in a state of Sattva. We are, in fact, very far away from Sattva. India is drowned in a state of Tamas or dark ignorance. Dyspeptic Babajis living only on vegetables; pusillanimous, effeminate people who never protest or are moved even if kicked by anybody—those are all signs of deep Tamas, not of Sattva. For now, India badly needs Rajas. We will have to pass through the stage of Rajas, be active and fulfil our thirst for Bhoga or enjoyment before we reach the stage of Sattva or absolute purity. There is a difference between idleness and renunciation. How can renunciation come when there is no Vairagya or dispassion for all the charms of enjoyment? A person's cravings will go away when Sattva is highly developed. The great fault of our religion in India is that it focuses only on renunciation and Mukti—there is nothing for the householder!

We have to arise, awake and work to protect our spirituality. But first, we must be physically strong and fit. It is better for young people to focus on playing football than on studying the Gita. Focus first on giving bread to the people; religion will come afterwards. How can one believe in a God who cannot give bread here but will give eternal bliss in heaven? We will understand our scriptures better if we are strong in body.

India's problems are more complicated and graver than those of any other country. There is such a great diversity of race, religion, language, government, manners and customs in India. But our only common ground, the only unifying factor, is religion. Our vigour, our strength, indeed our national life, is in our religion. Whether this is good or right or beneficial is not the point. It is there. It is the life of our race and it must be strengthened. Our forefathers sacrificed a lot to preserve our religion. Visiting the old temples of South India, and temples like Somnath, which have been repeatedly attacked and destroyed but have been rebuilt, rejuvenated and are strong as ever, will teach us wisdom and give us a keener insight into the history of our race. Of course, things other than religion are necessary, but they are secondary; religion is primary. Recognition of our unity in religion is absolutely necessary as the first condition of the future of India. The highest and most urgent priority has to be attached to strengthening this unity, and to giving up our little sectarian quarrels and differences. Our life-blood is spirituality. We must cleanse the blood of all impurities. If it is clear and strong, pure and vigorous, all our political, social and any other material defects and problems, even our poverty, will be overcome. Three things are needed to make every man and every nation great, viz. conviction in the power of goodness; absence of jealousy and suspicion; and the urge to help all who are trying to do good.

How is this to be done? Religion should be made dynamic and be freely accessible to all. It should enter the lives of everyone. Thus, in the first instance, there is a need to bring out the gems of spirituality that are stored up in our books and are in the possession of only a few people, hidden, as it were, in monasteries and forests. These texts, which are in Sanskrit, should be widely disseminated and popularized in the languages of the ordinary people. At the same time, Sanskrit should also be taught to the masses. The fact that Ramanuja, Kabir and Chaitanya did not preach in Sanskrit and did nothing to spread knowledge of Sanskrit among the people was a shortcoming that resulted in their teachings fizzling out after a while. Buddha's failure can be similarly explained. For it is culture, not a simple mass of knowledge, that can withstand shocks.

Caste

The overwhelming majority of people do not properly understand caste. It is a mistake to consider caste a religious institution when it is only a crystallized social institution. Religion should be kept within its proper limits and society should have the freedom to grow. India has always had religious freedom, but there have been restrictions in social matters. That is why there is tremendous spiritual power in religious thought in India, whereas the society is rigid and cramped.

Caste is a natural order. Every country has a system of castes. It is natural and inevitable that men form themselves into groups. Castes serve a very important function. In Europe, for example, all the learning was preserved by a small group of scholars, without whom Islam would have destroyed Europe's heritage and culture. In India, too, had it not been for caste, there would have been no Sanskrit books to study. Caste made walls around which all sorts of invasions rolled and surged but could not penetrate. Of course, caste is an imperfect institution, and the caste we have now is not that of seven hundred years ago. Yet, the caste system in India is better than that of other countries. If caste is unavoidable, it is preferable to have a caste of purity, culture and self-sacrifice than a caste of the rich, as in America.

Creativity comes only when there is variety and diversity. The qualities that make a man a Brahmin, a Kshatriya, a Vaishya or a Shudra are inherent in every person. At times, one quality is dominant; at other times, another, depending on what a person is doing. The original idea of jati was to give freedom to an individual to express his Prakriti, his jati or his caste. There was no prohibition on inter-dining or inter-marriage. People became members of a particular caste because of their strengths in a particular field. Those with the power of the sword became Kshatriyas; of learning, the Brahmins; and of wealth, the Vaishyas. A person can also change his caste. Thus, Vishwamitra became a Brahmin and Parshurama, a Kshatriya. Freedom is the only condition of growth. Caste disappears when there is competition. As one can see nowadays, it is remarkable how many Brahmins today are engaged in commercial activity. Thousands of people are seeking and finding the highest level that they were born for, instead of vegetating at the bottom.

There cannot be inequality or special privilege or pretensions to superiority and excellence based on birth. The Brahmins, because of their superior intellect, but tempered by spirituality, placed themselves at the top of the social order. The ideal man of our ancestors was the Brahmin of spiritual culture, renunciation, absence of worldliness, unselfishness and true wisdom. Thus, the highest honour in India belongs to the Brahmin who traces his descent to a Rishi. In the Satya Yuga, there was only one caste, that of the Brahmins. Holding no property, the Brahmins were poor, but they were good and noble persons. However, over time, they began to degenerate. Their weakness was their arrogance, their ego, and their hunger for power. Believing themselves to be 'twice-born' or sons of God, they considered themselves to be above the law and any punishment. Their social tyranny created tensions between Brahmins and non-Brahmins, especially in South India. The Brahmins monopolized the Vedas and never let the non-Brahmin classes read them. One must reject the myth that Brahmins supposedly have more aptitude for learning than the poor. If that is so, money should be spent on educating the poor, not on the Brahmin. Brahmins have been selfish, immoral and oppressive, teaching all kinds of mummeries and tomfoolery, and willing to write out any kind of sanction or prohibition, provided they are paid enough money. It is not the job of the Brahmins to make money. Brahmins should recognize that the days of privileges and exclusive claims have gone. It is the duty of every aristocracy to dig its own grave, and the sooner it does so, the better. Brahmins, as the trustees of the accumulated culture of ages, should actively share their knowledge with the people. They should have taken the lead in sharing with the non-Brahmins the knowledge and culture accumulated over centuries and, thereby, in working for the salvation of the rest of society.

There is no need to abolish caste, but it should evolve and be readjusted. The solution of the caste problem in India lies not in degrading or crushing out the Brahmin. What is needed is to raise the lower castes to the level of the higher ones, and not to bring down the higher castes. With all the defects in the Brahmin caste now, we should acknowledge that from the Brahmins have come more men with real Brahminness in them than from all the other castes. Besides, the non-Brahmins themselves have been indifferent and lazy, neglecting spirituality and Sanskrit learning instead of appropriating the culture and education that is the strength of the higher castes. Non-Brahmins have also been fuelling caste hatred. Live in any caste you like, but that is no reason to hate another man or another caste. Cursing, vilifying and abusing do not and cannot produce anything good. There is need to stop these futile inter-caste quarrels and fighting that have only weakened and divided us and retarded growth.

Every caste has to play a role in nation building. The Brahmins and Kshatriyas promote learning and advance civilisation. The Vaishya spreads wealth, uses his money to curb royal power, and trades with countries across the world, disseminating new ideas, knowledge, art and culture. But the Shudras, who constitute the majority and the real body of society, are oppressed. Historically, they have been kept down and denied opportunities for making money or acquiring education. Their lot in society is wretched. It is not as if the Shudras do not have their faults. They are either completely servile or brute beasts. Unfortunately, even when talented Shudras have risen to high positions, the benefits have remained confined to people belonging to the Shudra caste. It is important that the upper classes sympathize with and bring up the lower classes, imparting learning and culture to them. They are the source of power for the ruling classes. A time will come when they will gain absolute supremacy in society, not only in India but also all over the world. The rise of socialism, anarchism and nihilism are the vanguard of the coming social revolution. Once the masses rise, they will come to understand the oppression of the upper classes and will blow them away. At the same time, they will also remember and remain indebted for the good services that the upper classes have rendered to them.

Education

There is an urgent need for educational reforms. The country cannot progress without the spread of education. Education cannot be monopolized by a small section of society; it has to be spread among the masses. While the education currently being imparted has some good points, it is entirely a negative education. Education lacks Shraddha—of the kind that emboldened Nachiketa to face Yama and question him. Education is not cramming undigested information in your brain. First, it is important to teach how to control the mind. Education should build character. It is essential to impart both spiritual and secular education along national lines through national methods as far as practicable. Most of it will have to be given orally. Education should involve personal contact with the teacher. Nobody can teach anybody. The teacher only awakens the knowledge that is within man. Teachers should be trained so that they can impart both religious and secular education. First of all, there is need for self-knowledge. This does not imply matted hair, a staff, a Kamandalu and mountain caves! It is necessary for people to be taught the commonalities across all sects of Hinduism. Let every sect teach its doctrine without quarrelling with other sects. There is need for Tyagis (men of renunciation) to impart knowledge. The methodology for spreading education should be such that teachers go from village to village, disseminating practical knowledge orally, using teaching aids, to the poor, who are too caught up in working in the fields to earn a living to spare time to attend schools.

One must remember that living by Shastric injunctions does not lead to excellence. Strictly following the rules and blind, meaningless customs handed down through generations is not tantamount to virtue. Education is not book-learning or diversity of knowledge. Education should stimulate a person's mind, evoke feelings, give rise to fresh and independent thinking, give a different perspective, and bring out dormant creative genius. The Hindu mind has been deductive, not inductive. There are a couple of reasons for this. India's hot climate drives people towards rest and contemplation rather than towards activity. Secondly, the Brahmins never travelled to distant lands. It was only the traders who did so, and their focus was on making money, not on intellectual development. Thus, we have not developed sciences that are the result of observation and generalization. Unfortunately, parents and relatives often sacrifice the best interests of their children for their own selfish ends. It is young people who must courageously and selflessly take the lead and spread education among the masses, even if it is only with small beginnings. This can be done only gradually, over time. It is traitorous and cowardly for people who have been educated at the expense of the poor, downtrodden, marginalized and tyrannized masses not to pay heed to their upliftment and education. India will rise only when the privileged start working for the welfare of the poor.

Unfortunately, we have had a negative education all along. We are being taught nothing positive, nothing about the great men of our country, only how we are nobodies. We don't need an educational system that teaches us that our customs and religion are bad, and that what the Westerners have is good. Students like to master every detail concerning things and nations outside of India, but have no knowledge about their own forefathers. This is not unimportant. If a person feels that he is of noble descent, it engenders self-belief and pride and improves his character and behaviour. A nation that has no history of its own has nothing in this world. But that history has to be rewritten and restated. It should be suited to the understanding and ways of thinking which our people have acquired at present through Western education.

The education system as it exists today does not produce any original thoughts. Schools and colleges as they exist today are only making us a race of dyspeptics, who work like mere machines and live a jellyfish existence. Universities are merely an examination body to turn out clerks, postmasters, telegraph operators, and the like. Real education is not imbibing the thoughts of others in a foreign language, passing an examination and delivering good lectures. While we must study the various branches of knowledge, both indigenous and foreign, including the English language and Western science, higher education is not merely the study of material sciences. The goal of education is not to become a clerk, a lawyer or a low-level magistrate. It is to find out how to equip yourself for the struggle for life. It should enable us to stand on our own feet, bring out strength of character, courage, and a spirit of philanthropy. We must produce great men in much larger numbers. We need to learn history, geography, science, literature and, of course, the profound truths of religion. Vocational training and technical education are important so that instead of seeking service, people are able to earn enough to live a decent life. Our education system must be independent of foreign control. There is much that we can learn from the Japanese, who have taken everything from the Europeans but have remained Japanese. By contrast, in India, there is a terrible mania to become Westernised. People, alas, look upon their own gold as brass, while the foreigner's brass looks like gold to them.

Education is essential for women too. They should not feel helpless or be totally dependent on others. Women should acquire the spirit of valour and heroism, and learn how to defend themselves. Sita, Savitri, Damayanti, Lilavati, Khana and Mira could serve as ideals to inspire them to develop the qualities of affection, compassion, contentment, reverence and a spirit of service. Religion has to be central to the education of girls. Apart from the Puranas and rites of worship, some of the subjects that should be taught to women are history, housekeeping, cooking, sewing, hygiene, the arts, ethics and spirituality. Great men are born only in the homes of educated and pious mothers.

Character

Weakness is the cause of all misery. We have been hypnotized into thinking that we are weak and powerless. Weakness and fear are evils that ought to be shunned. There has been much talk of reforms and ideals for the past hundred years, but there are no concrete outcomes. The selfishness that afflicts India is not real selfishness but despair, which is the outcome of centuries of failure, repression and slavery. We have weak minds and bodies, and no faith in ourselves. We need strength. In order to succeed, we must restore our faith in ourselves. If you constantly think you are miserable nobodies, no good will come out of you. Believe in yourselves! Don't be weak! Have strong nerves! Be physically strong! Stand on your feet! Don't weep! Reject anything that makes you weak physically, intellectually or spiritually. That is the secret of greatness. Feel that you are great and you become great. In India, the masses have been hypnotized into a state of slavery and weakness. This does not create the foundations to build a great nation. We have to come out of this age-long sleep to take our true place in the hierarchy of nations. The people of a nation must have self-belief and self-reliance if a nation is to become great and strong in all respects, be it material wealth, intellectual brilliance or spiritual insights. It is because we have become weak that we have given in to occultism and mysticism. Therefore, it is important to go back to the Upanishads and preach the Advaita aspect of the Vedanta, so that people are roused from their stupor and the glory of their souls is revealed to them. The Advaita has to be brought down into the material world. Indians are the most moral and godly people in the world. What is needed is not reformation but growth, expansion and development on national lines. The holes in the leaking ship of the nation have to be plugged.

Despite our thousand years of slavery, we should be aware that infinite power, knowledge and power reside in us. Don't forget that the brains of Indians have produced marvellous results in the past and are incomparable even today. We should not be ashamed of our ancestors; rather, be proud of them, for we are the inheritors of a great civilization and the descendants of sages and Rishis. We have to retain our historically acquired character as a people. It is important to be patriotic. We have done great things in the past, and we can and will do greater things in future. India must study and not forget the past, because the past teaches us lessons. Just as a beautiful ripe fruit falls to the ground, decays and rots, and out of that decay springs the root and the future tree, perhaps mightier than the first one, so the past will mould our glorious future. Our past should inspire us, but let us not meditate over it and be merely proud of our past glory and greatness.

Unfortunately, our national vigour went out a century or two before the Muslim conquest of India. There was a degradation of everything–in religion, art, music, sciences, etc. India became an insular country, and developed a frog-in-the-well mentality. We foolishly thought we could do without the outside world, and hence we paid the penalty. It was the Hindus' ignorance of material civilization that led to the conquest of India by Muslims. Material civilization, even luxury, is necessary to create work for the poor. India's isolation from the rest of the world has been one of the main reasons for India's misery and downfall. One lesson to be learnt is that you must expand if you want to live.

Our national character has many flaws–physical weakness, laziness, meanness, hypocrisy, selfishness, jealousy, insincerity, cheating, infighting, childish dependence, and a propensity for squabbling and for focusing on frivolities. People lack the qualities of appreciation and gratitude. In scathing remarks, Swami Vivekananda says: 'A cloud of impenetrable darkness has at present equally enveloped us all. Now there is neither firmness of purpose nor boldness of enterprise, neither courage of heart nor strength of mind, neither aversion to maltreatment by others nor dislike for slavery, neither love in the heart nor hope nor manliness; but what we have in India are only deep-rooted envy and strong antipathy against one another, a morbid desire to ruin by hook or by crook the weak, and to lick dog-like the feet of the strong. Now the highest satisfaction consists in the display of wealth and power, devotion in self-gratification, wisdom in the accumulation of transitory objects, Yoga in hideous diabolical practices, work in the slavery of others, civilisation in base imitation of foreign nations, eloquence in the use of abusive language, the merit of literature in extravagant flatteries of the rich or in the diffusion of ghastly obscenities!'[2]

One other thing is absolutely essential: be not jealous

---

[2]*Vol. 4, Translations of Writings: Prose and Poems, Modern India*, p. 467

and try to pull down other Indians who are doing well, and do not meekly accept the kicks that foreigners give us. These are the traits of slaves! We want more power from the English, but those who get power as a result will only use it to keep the people down. If you are not ready to give liberty, you do not deserve liberty. Slaves want power to make slaves. Hindus have to give up nothing. All they have to do is to shake off the inertia that is the result of centuries of servitude. We could not advance during the period of Islamic tyranny, for then it was not a question of progress but of life and death. Now that there is no such pressure, we must move ahead.

Indians must learn to be patriotic. It is deeply troubling that so many people in India are ready to kill their own fathers and brothers for the sake of money. Too many Indians are cowards, physically, morally and spiritually. It is shameful that when Indians go to the West, they praise the virtues of the West and criticise their own faith and country. They ingratiate themselves so that they can get praise or money. Those who go whimpering before foreigners how very low, mean, and degraded we are need to be told that the whole nation cannot and must not be included in that 'We!' In any case, good qualities are not the privileged monopoly of one nation only.

One has to acknowledge that the Muslim, and later, the British, conquest of India taught us some good things, including in matters of eating and dressing. Islam came as a salvation to the downtrodden and poor masses. All conversions to Islam and Christianity were not forced. It was not merely the fear of getting killed that led people to convert to Islam. The inequities and tyrannies of the prevalent caste system played an important role too. People converted to Islam to escape from the tyranny of the zamindars and the priests. If large numbers of the population have converted to Islam, Christianity and Buddhism, the fault is essentially ours. We have to ask ourselves what we did for those people who gave up their religion. Our aristocratic ancestors brutalized and tormented the masses, destroyed their spirits and crushed their dignity. The last six or seven centuries have been a period of degradation, where we have been arguing over bizarre, meaningless—indeed insane—rituals and obsessed with 'don't touchism,' which has become a kind of mental disease! We have lost all originality, all mental strength and activity, and have been just going round and round over inconsequential matters of detail.

Role of the West

We can learn many things from foreign nations such as material knowledge, the arts and physical sciences. In fact, India cannot rise without the help of the West. Seeing how difficult it is to raise money in India, money will have to come from the West. In India, there is no appreciation of merit, no financial strength and not the slightest bit of practicality. We must learn how to be more organized, including being more methodical and strict in keeping accounts. Indians are also totally lacking in the faculty of organization. We must organize ourselves better (for which the first requisite is obedience), accumulate power and coordinate our wills if we are to build a great future for India. There is need for strict integrity.

One of the benefits of British rule is that it has brought India into contact with the outside world. However, this was not done for the welfare of our people, but to exploit them. There is a reign of terror and the people's voices are suppressed. If, today, European materialism has swamped India, much of the fault lies with us. We must introspect, and only then will we realize that it is we alone who are responsible for our misery and degradation.

Should India revert to the old orthodoxy, or follow the path of modern European civilization? It is preferable to follow our own path. We must learn everything that is good from others, but must always remember that when we take anything from others, we should mould it as it suits us. We must add to our stock of knowledge what others have to teach, but be always careful to keep intact what is essentially our own. Thus, it is not necessary to dress, behave and eat like another race. Do not imitate others! Do not be slaves and follow what Europeans do. Take as true everything that comes from India unless there are cogent reasons for disbelieving it. On the other hand, take everything that comes from Europe as false unless there are cogent reasons for believing it.

We have to build upon our splendid heritage. The Europeanized, half-educated, denationalized man in India has no backbone but only unassimilated, undigested, unharmonized and heterogeneous ideas picked up from random sources. There is no need to be patronized by the English people over our so-called evil customs. Certainly, India must learn from others and assimilate new ideas, but we should never jettison our splendid heritage of spirituality. Indians should not fall under the spell of imitating the West and adopt Western ideas, language, food, dress and manners. If we were to simply ape the West, the nation's backbone would be broken, the foundation upon which the national edifice has been built would be undermined and, eventually, our race would become extinct.

The secret of life is to give and take. Therefore, while learning from others, we can, and must, at the same time, teach them our religion and spirituality, on which they themselves are very keen. Western dogmatic religions are crumbling under the blows and pressures of modern science, but Veda-based religions like Hinduism and Buddhism are reviving. The tables have been turned. We need not be always students; we must be teachers too. There can be no friendship without equality. Go to the West not as beggars but as teachers of religion, and work for the good of humanity.

Social Reform

When northern India was under the rule of Central Asian conquerors, South India was the refuge of Indian religion and civilization. The reform movements in northern India during the period of Islamic rule attempted to hold back people from converting to Islam. Thus, the orders founded by Ramananda, Kabir, Dadu, Chaitanya and Nanak preached the equality of man. Though they did succeed in keeping the masses within the fold of the Hindu religion, there was little energy for new thoughts. One could say that they were mere apologists struggling to get permission to live. On the other hand, Guru Gobind Singh, who founded the political organisation of the Sikhs, was a creative genius, a great ruler and a worshipper of Shakti. Unfortunately, both the Maratha and Sikh empires had no intellectual efflorescence or spiritual aspirations, and lost all their motive power once they had defeated the Muslims.

The 19th century reform movements under British rule were the feeble pleas of a terrorized people seeking the approval of the British authorities for permission to live, only too eager to adjust their spiritual views and social norms to suit the rulers. Of course, these well-meaning reform movements did have some good points and in many respects their aims are laudable. They did help to preserve the Hindu religion. Their great work was in the realm of social reform, to tackle the social evils prevalent in India. But the objective has to be to find solutions, not merely criticize, condemn and abuse. The reformatory zeal of these reform movements was necessary to rouse the sleeping leviathan. Unfortunately, they did not have much popular resonance, and have not produced any permanent or valuable results because their approach was entirely destructive, not constructive. The principal reason for their failure is their denunciation of the Hindu race and its civilization. They laid all the evils of India at the door of religion. They lacked a proper understanding of their own religion. Hinduism cannot be reformed with new-fangled reform movements. The 'booby' religion that they preached could not hold its own against the old 'Vedanta'. The state of our society is not bad because of religion, but because religion has not been applied to society as it should have been. Most of the modern reform movements have been imitations of Western means and methods of work, and the reformers simply play into the hands of Europeans and pander to their vanity. That cannot work in India. India can never be Europe. It can assimilate the surrounding elements, but a tree grows only according to its own nature. That is why all reforming sects that rejected the Vedantic ideal have been failures.

Let us learn from the experience of these reform movements. Unquestionably, there is need for social reform. We must accept that serious weaknesses have developed in our society, our institutions and our character. It is not that our society is bad or that we have done badly, but society should be better still. Of course, we must make people aware of our shortcomings, and find ways and work to overcome them. But let us refrain from cursing, abusing or condemning our institutions. There can be no social reform without spiritual reform first. Moreover, it takes time to overcome problems that have existed for centuries. Nor are the solutions easy. Historically, at times, great men would evolve new ideas of progress, and kings would give them the sanction of law. Now that kings are no longer there, power is with the people. There is need to have a healthy and strong public opinion that favours reforms. One has to wait till the people become educated, understand their needs and are able to solve their problems. A few men who think that certain things are evil cannot move a nation. The tyranny of the minority is the worst possible tyranny in the world.

We have to work for the salvation of India—indeed, of the whole world. One should not expect anything from the rich people. It is the youth who must play a critical role in the task of national rejuvenation. They must be intelligent, physically strong and masculine, fond of martial rather than effeminate forms of music, celibate, large-hearted, ready to give up their desire to enjoy life's luxuries and be willing to exert themselves to the utmost for the well-being of their countrymen. The qualities that are needed are good motives, sincerity and infinite love, as well as muscles of iron and nerves of steel. They must heed the call, 'Awake, arise, and stop not till the goal is reached!'

What should we do? First, feel from the heart. Love and empathy for the poor and oppressed will open the most impossible gates. Let us get rid of our hatred and our dried-up hearts. Second, don't just talk but find practical solutions. Three, be steadfast and have the will to surmount the formidable obstacles we will encounter. We must always remember that every nation must save itself, and not look to others for help.

"

The Vedanta was (and is) the boldest system of religion. It stopped nowhere, and it had one advantage. There was no body of priests who sought to suppress every man who tried to tell the truth. There was always absolute religious freedom. In India the bondage of superstition is a social one; here in the West society is very free. Social matters in India are very strict, but religious opinion is free.

We, in India, allowed liberty in spiritual matters, and we have a tremendous spiritual power in religious thought even today. You grant the same liberty in social matters, and so have a splendid social organisation. We have not given any freedom to the expansion of social matters, and ours is a cramped society. You have never given any freedom in religious matters but with fire and sword have enforced your beliefs, and the result is that religion is a stunted, degenerated growth in the European mind. In India, we have to take off the shackles from society; in Europe, the chains must be taken from the feet of spiritual progress.

Vol. 2, Jnana-Yoga, Maya and the Evolution of the Conception of God, pp. 113–115

It is weakness, says the Vedanta, which is the cause of all misery in this world. Weakness is the one cause of suffering. We become miserable because we are weak. We lie, steal, kill, and commit other crimes, because we are weak. We suffer because we are weak. We die because we are weak. Where there is nothing to weaken us, there is no death nor sorrow. We are miserable through delusion. Give up the delusion, and the whole thing vanishes. It is plain and simple indeed. Through all these philosophical discussions and tremendous mental gymnastics we come to this one religious idea, the simplest in the whole world.

If the whole responsibility is thrown upon our own shoulders, we shall be at our highest and best; when we have nobody to grope towards, no devil to lay our blame upon, no Personal God to carry our burdens, when we are alone responsible, then we shall rise to our highest and best. I am responsible for my fate, I am the bringer of good unto myself, I am the bringer of evil. I am the Pure and Blessed One. We must reject all thoughts that assert the contrary.

Vol. 2, Jnana-Yoga, The Freedom of the Soul, pp. 198–202

All these various ideas that I am a man or a woman, or sick or healthy, or strong or weak, or that I hate or I love, or have a little power, are but hallucinations. Away with them! What makes you weak? What makes you fear? You are the One Being in the universe. What frightens you? Stand up then and be free. Know that every thought and word that weakens you in this world is the only evil that exists. Whatever makes men weak and fear is the only evil that should be shunned.

Vol. 2, Jnana-Yoga, Immortality, p. 236

Have we to learn anything from the world? We have, perhaps, to gain a little in material knowledge, in the power of organisation, in the ability to handle powers, organising powers in bringing the best results out of the smallest of causes. This perhaps to a certain extent we may learn from the West.

Yet, perhaps some sort of materialism, toned down to our own requirements, would be a blessing to many of our brothers who are not yet ripe for the highest truth. This is the mistake made in every country and in every society, and it is a greatly regrettable thing that in India, where it was always understood, the same mistake of forcing the highest truths on people who are not ready for them has been made of late. The Sannyasin, as you all know, is the ideal of the Hindu's life, and every one by our Shastras is compelled to give up in the latter part of his life, and he who does not is not a Hindu and has no more right to call himself a Hindu. We know that this is the ideal—to give up after seeing and experiencing the vanity of things. Having found out that the heart of the material world is a mere hollow, containing only ashes, give it up and go back. The mind is circling forward, as it were, towards the senses, and that mind has to circle backwards; the Pravritti has to stop and the Nivritti has to begin. That is the ideal. But that ideal can only be realised after a certain amount of experience.

But unfortunately, in later times, there has been a tendency to bind everyone down by the same laws as those by which the Sannyasin is bound, and that is a great mistake. But for that, a good deal of the poverty and the misery that you see in India need not have been. A poor man's life is hemmed in and bound down by tremendous spiritual and ethical laws for which he has no use. Hands off! Let the poor fellow enjoy himself a little, and then he will raise himself up, and renunciation will come to him of itself. Perhaps in this line, we can be taught something by the Western people; but we must be very cautious in learning these things. I am sorry to say that most of the examples one meets nowadays of men who have imbibed the Western ideas are more or less failures.

There are two great obstacles on our path in India, the Scylla of old orthodoxy and the Charybdis of modern European civilisation. Of these two, I vote for the old orthodoxy, and not for the Europeanised system; for the old orthodox man may be ignorant, he may be crude, but he is man, he has a faith, he has strength, he stands on his own feet; while the Europeanised man has no backbone, he is a mass of heterogeneous ideas picked up at random from every source—and these ideas are unassimilated, undigested, unharmonised. He does not stand on his own feet, and his head is turning round and round. Where is the motive power of his work?—in a few patronising pats from the English people. His schemes of reforms, his vehement vituperations against the evils of certain social customs, have, as the mainspring, some European patronage. Why are some of our customs called evil? Because the Europeans say so. That is about the reason he gives. I would not submit to that. Stand and die in your own strength, if there is any sin in the world, it is weakness; avoid all weakness, for weakness is sin, weakness is death. These unbalanced creatures are not yet formed into distinct personalities; what are we to call them—men, women, or animals? While those old orthodox people were staunch and were men.

Stand on your own feet, and assimilate what you can; learn from every nation, take what is of use to you. But remember that as Hindus everything else must be subordinated to our own national ideals. Each man has a mission in life, which is the result of all his infinite past Karma. Each of you was born with a splendid heritage, which is the whole of the infinite past life of your glorious nation. Millions of your ancestors are watching, as it were, every action of yours, so be alert.

The secret of a true Hindu's character lies in the subordination of his knowledge of European sciences and learning, of his wealth, position and name to that one principal theme which is inborn in every Hindu child—the spirituality and purity of the race. Therefore between these two, the case of the orthodox man who has the whole of that life-spring of the race, spirituality, and the other man whose hands are full of Western imitation-jewels but has no hold on the life-giving principle, spirituality—of these, I do not doubt that every one here will agree that we should choose the first, the orthodox, because there is some hope in him—he has the national theme, something to hold to so he will live, but the other will die.

If you give up that spirituality, leaving it aside to go after the materialising civilisation of the West, the result will be that in three generations you will be an extinct race, because the backbone of the nation will be broken, the foundation upon which the national edifice has been built will be undermined, and the result will be annihilation all round.

Vol. 3, Lectures from Colombo to Almora, Reply to the Address of Welcome at Ramnad, pp. 149–153

But now I have to say a few harsh words, which I hope you will not take unkindly. For the complaint has just been made that European materialism has well nigh swamped us. It is not all the fault of the Europeans, but a good deal our own. We, as Vedantists, must always look at things from an introspective viewpoint, from its subjective relations. We, as Vedantists, know for certain that there is no power in the universe to injure us unless we first injure ourselves. One-fifth of the population of India have become Mohammedans. Just as before that, going further back, two-thirds of the population in ancient times had become Buddhists, one-fifth are now Mohammedans. Christians are already more than a million. Whose fault is it? […] The question is: what did we do for these people who forsook their own religion? Why should they have become Mohammedans? […] We are weeping for these renegades now, but what did we do for them before? Let every one of us ask ourselves, what have we learnt? Have we taken hold of the torch of truth, and if so how far did we carry it? We did not help them then. This is the question we should ask ourselves. That we did not do so was our own fault, our own Karma. Let us blame none, let us blame our own Karma.

Think of the last six hundred or seven hundred years of degradation when grown-up men by hundreds have been discussing for years whether we should drink a glass of water with the right hand or the left, whether the hand should be washed three times or four times, whether we should gargle five or six times. What can you expect from men who pass their lives in discussing such momentous questions as these and writing most learned philosophies on them! There is a danger of our religion getting into the kitchen. We are neither Vedantists, most of us now, nor Pauranics, nor Tantrics. We are just 'Don't-touchists.' Our religion is in the kitchen. Our God is the cooking pot, and our religion is, 'Don't touch me, I am holy.' If this goes on for another century, every one of us will be in a lunatic asylum. It is a sure sign of softening of the brain when the mind cannot grasp the highest problems of life; all originality is lost, the mind has lost all its strength, its activity, and in power of thought, and just tries to go round and round the smallest curve it can find. This state of things first has to be thrown overboard, and then we must stand up, be active and strong, and then we shall recognise our heritage to that infinite treasure that the whole world requires today. The world will die if this treasure is not distributed. Bring it out, distribute it broadcast.

Vol. 3, Lectures from Colombo to Almora, Reply to the Address of Welcome at Shivaganga and Manamadura, pp. 166–167

Faith, faith, faith in ourselves—this is the secret of greatness. If you have faith in all the three hundred and thirty millions of your mythological gods, and in all the gods which foreigners have now and again introduced into your midst, and still have no faith in yourselves, there is no salvation for you. Have faith in yourselves, and stand up on that faith and be strong; that is what we need. Why is it that we three hundred and thirty millions of people have been ruled for the last one thousand years by any and every handful of foreigners who chose to walk over our prostrate bodies? Because they had faith in themselves and we had not.

We have lost faith in ourselves. Therefore to preach the Advaita aspect of the Vedanta is necessary to rouse up the hearts of men, to show them the glory of their souls. It is therefore, that I preach this Advaita; and I do so not as a sectarian, but upon universal and widely acceptable grounds.

I read in the newspaper how, when one of our fellows is murdered or ill-treated by an Englishman, howls go up all over the country; I read and I weep, and the next moment comes to my mind the question: Who is responsible for it all? As a Vedantist I cannot but put that question to myself. The Hindu is a man of introspection; he wants to see things in and through himself, through the subjective vision. I, therefore, ask myself: Who is responsible? And the answer comes every time: Not the English; no, they are not responsible; it is we who are responsible for all our misery and all our degradation, and we alone are responsible. Our aristocratic ancestors went on treading the common masses of our country underfoot, till they became helpless, till under this torment the poor, poor people nearly forgot that they were human beings. They have been compelled to be merely hewers of wood and drawers of water. With all our boasted education of modern times, if anybody says a kind word for them, I often find our men shrink at once from the duty of lifting them up, these poor downtrodden people. Not only so, but I also find that all sorts of most demoniacal and brutal arguments, culled from the crude ideas of hereditary transmission and other such gibberish from the Western world, are brought forward in order to brutalise and tyrannise over the poor all the more.

Ay, Brahmins, if the Brahmin has more aptitude for learning on the ground of heredity than the Pariah, spend no more money on the Brahmin's education, but spend all on the Pariah. Give to the weak, for there all the gift is needed. If the Brahmin is born clever, he can educate himself without help. If the others are not born clever, let them have all the teaching and the teachers they want. This is justice and reason, as I understand it. Our poor people, these downtrodden masses of India, therefore, require to hear and to know what they really are.

Here naturally comes the difficult and the vexed question of caste and of social reformation, which has been uppermost for centuries in the minds of our people. I must frankly tell you that I am neither a caste-breaker nor a mere social reformer. I have nothing to do directly with your castes or with your social reformation. Live in any caste you like, but that is no reason why you should hate another man or another caste. It is love and love alone that I preach, and I base my teaching on the great Vedantic truth of the sameness and omnipresence of the Soul of the Universe. For nearly the past one hundred years, our country has been flooded with social reformers and various social reform proposals. Personally, I have no fault to find with these reformers. Most of them are good, well-meaning men, and their aims too are very laudable on certain points but it is quite a patent fact that this one hundred years of social reform has produced no permanent and valuable result appreciable throughout the country. Platform speeches have been made by the thousand, denunciations in volumes after volumes have been hurled upon the devoted head of the Hindu race and its civilisation, and yet no good practical result has been achieved; and where is the reason for that? The reason is not hard to find. It is in the denunciation itself. As I told you before, in the first place, we must try to keep our historically acquired character as a people. I grant that we have to take a great many things from other nations, that we have to learn many lessons from outside; but I am sorry to say that most of our modern reform movements have been inconsiderate imitations of Western means and methods of work; and that surely will not do for India; therefore, it is that all our recent reform movements have had no result.

In the second place, denunciation is not at all the way to do good. That there are evils in our society even a child can see; and in what society are there no evils? And let me take this opportunity, my countrymen, of telling you that in comparing the different races and nations of the world I have been among, I have come to the conclusion that our people are on the whole the most moral and the most godly, and our institutions are, in their plan and purpose, best suited to make mankind happy. I do not, therefore, want any reformation. My ideal is growth, expansion, development on national lines. As I look back upon the history of my country, I do not find in the whole world another country which has done quite so much for the improvement of the human mind. Therefore I have no words of condemnation for my nation. I tell them, 'You have done well; only try to do better.' Great things have been done in the past in this land, and there is both time and room for greater things to be done. I am sure you know that we cannot stand still. If we stand still, we die. We have either to go forward or to go backward. We have either to progress or to degenerate. Our ancestors did great things in the past, but we have to grow into a fuller life and march beyond their great achievements. How can we now go back and degenerate ourselves? That cannot be; that must not be; going back will lead to national decay and death. Therefore let us go forward and do yet greater things; that is what I have to tell you.

I am no preacher of any momentary social reform. I am not trying to remedy evils. I only ask you to go forward and to complete the practical realisation of the scheme of human progress that has been laid out in the most perfect order by our ancestors. I only ask you to work to realise more and more the Vedantic ideal of the solidarity of man and his inborn divine nature. Had I the time, I would gladly show you how everything we have now to do was laid out years ago by our ancient law-givers, and how they actually anticipated all the different changes that have taken place and are still to take place in our national institutions. They also were breakers of caste, but they were not like our modern men. They did not mean by the breaking down of caste that all the people in a city should sit down together to a dinner of beef-steak and champagne, nor that all fools and lunatics in the country should marry when, where, and whom they chose and reduce the country to a lunatic asylum, nor did they believe that the prosperity of a nation is to be gauged by the number of husbands its widows get. I have yet to see such a prosperous nation.

The ideal man of our ancestors was the Brahmin. In all our books stands out prominently this ideal of the Brahmin. In Europe there is my Lord the Cardinal, who is struggling hard and sending thousands of pounds to prove the nobility of his ancestors, and he will not be satisfied until he has traced his ancestry to some dreadful tyrant who lived on a hill and watched the people passing by, and whenever he had the opportunity, sprang out on them and robbed them. That was the business of these nobility-bestowing ancestors, and my Lord Cardinal is not satisfied until he can trace his ancestry to one of these. In India, on the other hand, the greatest princes seek to trace their descent to some ancient sage who dressed in a bit of loincloth, lived in a forest, eating roots and studying the Vedas. It is there that the Indian prince goes to trace his ancestry. You are of the high caste when you can trace your ancestry to a Rishi, and not otherwise.

Our ideal of high birth, therefore, is different from that of others. Our ideal is the Brahmin of spiritual culture and renunciation. By the Brahmin ideal what do I mean? I mean the ideal Brahmin-ness in which worldliness is altogether absent and true wisdom is abundantly present. That is the ideal of the Hindu race. Have you not heard how it is declared that he, the Brahmin, is not amenable to law, that he has no law, that he is not governed by kings, and that his body cannot be hurt? That is perfectly true. Do not understand it in the light thrown upon it by interested and ignorant fools, but understand it in the light of the true and original Vedantic conception. If the Brahmin is he who has killed all selfishness and who lives and works to acquire and propagate wisdom and the power of love—if a country is altogether inhabited by such Brahmins, by men and women who are spiritual and moral and good, is it strange to think of that country as being above and beyond all law? Why should anyone govern them at all? Why should they live under a government? They are good and noble, and they are the men of God; these are our ideal Brahmins, and we read that in the Satya Yuga there was only one caste, and that was the Brahmin. We read in the Mahabharata that the whole world was in the beginning peopled with Brahmins, and that as they began to degenerate, they became divided into different castes, and that when the cycle turns round, they will all go back to that Brahminical origin.

This cycle is turning round now, and I draw your attention to this fact. Therefore our solution of the caste question is not degrading those who are already high up, is not running amuck through food and drink, is not jumping out of our own limits in order to have more enjoyment, but it comes by every one of us, fulfilling the dictates of our Vedantic religion, by our attaining spirituality, and by our becoming the ideal Brahmin. There is a law laid on each one of you in this land by your ancestors, whether you are Aryans or non-Aryans, Rishis or Brahmins, or the very lowest outcaste. The command is the same to you all, that you must make progress without stopping, and that from the highest man to the lowest Pariah, everyone in this country has to try and become the ideal Brahmin. This Vedantic idea is applicable not only here but over the whole world. Such is our ideal of caste as meant for raising all humanity slowly and gently towards the realisation of that great ideal of the spiritual man who is non-resisting, calm, steady, worshipful, pure, and meditative. In that ideal there is God.

How are these things to be brought about? I must again draw your attention to the fact that cursing and vilifying and abusing do not and cannot produce anything good. They have been tried for years and years, and no valuable result has been obtained. Good results can be produced only through love, through sympathy. It is a great subject, and it requires several lectures to elucidate all the plans that I have in view, and all the ideas that are, in this connection, coming to my mind day after day.

I must, therefore, conclude, only reminding you of this fact that this ship of our nation, O Hindus, has been usefully plying here for ages. Today, perhaps, it has sprung a leak; today, perhaps, it has become a little worn out. And if such is the case, it behoves you and me to try our best to stop the leak and holes. Let us tell our countrymen of the danger, let them awake and help us. I will cry at the top of my voice from one part of this country to the other, to awaken the people to the situation and their duty. Suppose they do not hear me, still I shall have one word of abuse for them, not one word of cursing. Great has been our nation's work in the past; and if we cannot do greater things in the future, let us have this consolation that we can sink and die together in peace. Be patriots, love the race which has done such great things for us in the past. Ay, the more I compare notes, the more I love you, my fellow-countrymen; you are good and pure and gentle. You have been always tyrannised over, and such is the irony of this material world of Maya. Never mind that; the Spirit will triumph in the long run. In the meanwhile let us work and let us not abuse our country, let us not curse and abuse the weather-beaten and work-worn institutions of our thrice-holy motherland. Have no word of condemnation even for the most superstitious and the most irrational of its institutions, for they also must have served some good in the past. Remember always that there is not in the world any other country whose institutions are really better in their aims and objects than the institutions of this land. I have seen castes in almost every country in the world, but nowhere is their plan and purpose so glorious as here. If caste is thus unavoidable, I would rather have a caste of purity and culture and self-sacrifice, than a caste of dollars. Therefore utter no words of condemnation. Close your lips and let your hearts open. Work out the salvation of this land and of the whole world, each of you thinking that the entire burden is on your shoulders. Carry the light and the life of the Vedanta to every door, and rouse up the divinity that is hidden within every soul. Then, whatever may be the measure of your success, you will have this satisfaction that you have lived, worked, and died for a great cause. In the success of this cause, howsoever brought about, is centred the salvation of humanity here and hereafter.

Vol. 3, Lectures from Colombo to Almora,
The Mission of the Vedanta, pp. 190–199

Evils are plentiful in our society, but so are there evils in every other society. Here the earth is soaked sometimes with widows' tears; there in the West, the air is rent with the sighs of the unmarried. Here poverty is the great bane of life; there the life-weariness of luxury is the great bane that is upon the race. Here men want to commit suicide because they have nothing to eat; there they commit suicide because they have so much to eat.

We admit that there are evils. Everybody can show what evil is, but he is the friend of mankind who finds a way out of the difficulty. Like the drowning boy and the philosopher—when the philosopher was lecturing him, the boy cried, 'Take me out of the water first'—so our people cry: We have had lectures enough, societies enough, papers enough; where is the man who will lend us a hand to drag us out? Where is the man who really loves us? Where is the man who has sympathy for us?' Ay, that man is wanted. That is where I differ entirely from these reform movements. For a hundred years they have been here. What good has been done except the creation of a most vituperative, a most condemnatory literature? Would to God it was not here! They have criticised, condemned, abused the orthodox, until the orthodox have caught their tone and paid them back in their own coin; and the result is the creation of a literature in every vernacular which is the shame of the race, the shame of the country. Is this reform? Is this leading the nation to glory? Whose fault is this?

There is, then, another great consideration. Here in India, we have always been governed by kings; kings have made all our laws. Now the kings are gone, and there is no one left to make a move. The government dare not; it has to fashion its ways according to the growth of public opinion. It takes time, quite a long time, to make a healthy, strong, public opinion which will solve its own problems; and in the interim we shall have to wait. The whole problem of social reform, therefore, resolves itself into this: where are those who want reform? Make them first. Where are the people? The tyranny of a minority is the worst tyranny that the world ever sees. A few men who think that certain things are evil will not make a nation move. Why does not the nation move? First educate the nation, create your legislative body, and then the law will be forthcoming. First create the power, the sanction from which the law will spring. The kings are gone; where is the new sanction, the new power of the people? Bring it up. Therefore, even for social reform, the first duty is to educate the people, and you will have to wait till that time comes. Most of the reforms that have been agitated for during the past century have been ornamental. Every one of these reforms only touches the first two castes, and no other. The question of widow remarriage would not touch seventy per cent of the Indian women, and all such questions only reach the higher castes of Indian people who are educated, mark you, at the expense of the masses. Every effort has been spent in cleaning their own houses. But that is no reformation. You must go down to the basis of the thing, to the very root of the matter. That is what I call radical reform. Put the fire there and let it burn upwards and make an Indian nation. And the solution of the problem is not so easy, as it is a big and a vast one. Be not in a hurry, this problem has been known several hundred years.

Vol. 3, Lectures from Colombo to Almora, My Plan of Campaign, pp. 213–216

The masses have been told all over the world that they are not human beings. They have been so frightened for centuries, till they have nearly become animals. Never were they allowed to hear of the Atman—that even the lowest of the low have the Atman within, which never dies and never is born [...] Let them have faith in themselves, for what makes the difference between the Englishman and you? Let them talk their religion and duty and so forth. I have found the difference. The difference is here, that the Englishman believes in himself and you do not. He believes in his being an Englishman, and he can do anything he likes. That brings out the God within him, and he can do anything he likes. You have been told and taught that you can do nothing, and nonentities you are becoming every day. What we want is strength, so believe in yourselves. We have become weak, and that is why occultism and mysticism come to us—these creepy things; there may be great truths in them, but they have nearly destroyed us. Make your nerves strong. What we want is muscles of iron and nerves of steel. We have wept long enough. No more weeping, but stand on your feet and be men. It is a man-making religion that we want. It is man-making theories that we want. It is man-making education all round that we want.

And here is the test of truth—anything that makes you weak physically, intellectually, and spiritually, reject as poison; there is no life in it, it cannot be true. Truth is strengthening. Truth is purity, truth is all-knowledge; truth must be strengthening, must be enlightening, must be invigorating. These mysticisms, in spite of some grains of truth in them, are generally weakening.

Go back to your Upanishads—the shining, the strengthening, the bright philosophy—and part from all these mysterious things, all these weakening things. Take up this philosophy; the greatest truths are the simplest things in the world, simple as your own existence. The truths of the Upanishads are before you. Take them up, live up to them, and the salvation of India will be at hand.

I believe in patriotism, and I also have my own ideal of patriotism. Three things are necessary for great achievements. First, feel from the heart. What is in the intellect or reason? It goes a few steps and there it stops. But through the heart comes inspiration. Love opens the most impossible gates; love is the gate to all the secrets of the universe. Feel, therefore, my would-be reformers, my would-be patriots! Do you feel? Do you feel that millions and millions of the descendants of gods and of sages have become next-door neighbours to brutes? Do you feel that millions are starving today, and millions have been starving for ages? Do you feel that ignorance has come over the land as a dark cloud? Does it make you restless? Does it make you sleepless? Has it gone into your blood, coursing through your veins, becoming consonant with your heartbeats? Has it made you almost mad? Are you seized with that one idea of the misery of ruin, and have you forgotten all about your name, your fame, your wives, your children, your property, even your own bodies? Have you done that? That is the first step to become a patriot, the very first step.

You may feel, then; but instead of spending your energies in frothy talk, have you found any way out, any practical solution, some help instead of condemnation, some sweet words to soothe their miseries, to bring them out of this living death?

Yet that is not all. Have you got the will to surmount mountain-high obstructions? If the whole world stands against you sword in hand, would you still dare to do what you think is right? If your wives and children are against you, if all your money vanishes, would you still stick to it? Would you still pursue it and go on steadily towards your own goal? [...] Have you got that steadfastness? If you have these three things, each one of you will work miracles. You need not write in the newspapers, you need not go about lecturing; your very face will shine. If you live in a cave, your thoughts will permeate even through the rock walls, will go on vibrating all over the world for hundreds of years, maybe, until they will fasten on to some brain and work out there. Such is the power of thought, of sincerity, and of purity of purpose.

Vol. 3, Lectures from Colombo to Almora, My Plan of Campaign, pp. 224–227

What do we want in India? If foreigners want these things, we want them twenty times more. Because, in spite of the greatness of the Upanishads, in spite of our boasted ancestry of sages, compared to many other races, I must tell you that we are weak, very weak. First of all is our physical weakness. That physical weakness is the cause of at least one-third of our miseries. We are lazy, we cannot work; we cannot combine, we do not love each other; we are intensely selfish, not three of us can come together without hating each other, without being jealous of each other. That is the state in which we are—hopelessly disorganised mobs, immensely, selfish, fighting each other for centuries as to whether a certain mark is to be put on our forehead this way or that way, writing volumes and volumes upon such momentous questions as to whether the look of a man spoils my food or not! This we have been doing for the past few centuries. We cannot expect anything high from a race whose whole brain energy has been occupied in such wonderfully beautiful problems and researches! And we are not ashamed of ourselves? Ay, sometimes we are; but though we think these things frivolous, we cannot give them up. We speak of many things parrot-like, but never do them; speaking and not doing has become a habit with us. What is the cause of that? Physical weakness. This sort of weak brain is not able to do anything; we must strengthen it. First of all, our young men must be strong. Religion will come afterwards. Be strong, my young friends, that is my advice to you. You will be nearer to Heaven through football than through the study of the Gita. These are bold words; but I have to say them, for I love you. I know where the shoe pinches. I have gained a little experience. You will understand the Gita better with your biceps, your muscles a little stronger. You will understand the mighty genius and the mighty strength of Krishna better with a little of strong blood in you. You will understand the Upanishads better and the glory of the Atman when your body stands firm upon your feet, and you feel yourselves as men. Thus, we have to apply these to our needs.

Feel that you are great and you become great. What did I get as my experience all over the world, is the question. They may talk about sinners—and if all Englishmen really believed that they were sinners, Englishmen would be no better than the negroes in Central Africa. God bless them that they do not believe it! On the other hand, the Englishman believes he is born the lord of the world. He believes he is great and can do anything in the world; if he wants to go to the sun or the moon, he believes he can; and that makes him great. If he had believed his priests that he was a poor miserable sinner, going to be barbecued through all eternity, he would not be the same Englishman that he is today. So I find in every nation that, in spite of priests and superstition, the divine within lives and asserts itself. We have lost faith. Would you believe me, we have less faith than the Englishman and woman—a thousand times less faith! These are plain words; but I say these, I cannot help it. Don't you see how Englishmen and women, when they catch our ideals, become made as it were; and although they are the ruling class, they come to India to preach our own religion notwithstanding the jeers and ridicule of their own countrymen? How many of you could do that? Do you not know it? You know more than they do; you are more wise than is good for you, that is your difficulty! Simply because your blood is only like water, your brain is sloughing, your body is weak! You must change the body. Physical weakness is the cause and nothing else. You have talked of reforms, of ideals, and all these things for the past hundred years; but when it comes to practice, you are not to be found anywhere—till you have disgusted the whole world, and the very name of reform is a thing of ridicule! And what is the cause? Do you not know? You know too well. The only cause is that you are weak, weak, weak; your body is weak, your mind is weak, you have no faith in yourselves! Centuries and centuries, a thousand years of crushing tyranny of castes and kings and foreigners and your own people have taken out all your strength, my brethren. Your backbone is broken. You are like downtrodden worms. Who will give you strength? Let me tell you, strength, strength is what we want. And the first step in getting strength is to uphold the Upanishads, and believe—'I am the Soul,' 'Me the sword cannot cut; nor weapons pierce; me the fire cannot burn; me the air cannot dry; I am the Omnipotent, I am the Omniscient.' So repeat these blessed, saving words. Do not say we are weak; we can do anything and everything. What can we not do? Everything can be done by us; we all have the same glorious soul, let us believe in it. Have faith, as Nachiketa. At the time of his father's sacrifice, faith came unto Nachiketa; ay, I wish that faith would come to each of you; and everyone of you would stand up a giant, a world-mover with a gigantic intellect—an infinite God in every respect. That is what I want you to become. This is the strength that you get from the Upanishads, this is the faith that you get from there.

Caste is a natural order; I can perform one duty in social life, and you another; you can govern a country, and I can mend a pair of old shoes, but that is no reason why you are greater that I, for can you mend my shoes? Can I govern the country? I am clever in mending shoes, you are clever in reading Vedas, but that I no reason why you should trample on my head. Why if one commits murder should he be praised, and if another steals an apple why should he be hanged? This will have to go. Caste is good. That is the only natural way of solving life. Men must form themselves into groups, and you cannot get rid of that. Wherever you go, there will be caste. But that does not mean that there should be these privileges. They should be knocked on the head. If you teach Vedanta to the fisherman, he will say, I am as good a man as you; I am a fisherman, you are a philosopher, but I have the same God in me and you have in you. And that is what we want, no privilege for any one, equal chances for all; let every one be taught that the divine is within, and everyone will work out his own salvation.

Vol. 3, Lectures from Colombo to Almora, Vedanta in its Application to Indian Life, pp. 241–246

Two curious nations there have been—sprung of the same race, but placed in different circumstances and environments, working out the problems of life each in its own particular way. I mean the ancient Hindu and the ancient Greek. The Indian Aryan—bounded on the north by the snow-caps of the Himalayas, with fresh-water rivers like rolling oceans surrounding him in the plains, with eternal forests which, to him, seemed to be the end of the world—turned his vision inward; and given the natural instinct, the superfine brain of the Aryan, with this sublime scenery surrounding him, the natural result was that he became introspective. The analysis of his own mind was the great theme of the Indo-Aryan. With the Greek, on the other hand, who arrived at a part of the earth which was more beautiful than sublime, the beautiful islands of the Grecian Archipelago, nature all around him generous yet simple—his mind naturally went outside. It wanted to analyse the external world. And as a result we find that from India have sprung all the analytical sciences, and from Greece all the sciences of generalisation. The Hindu mind went on in its own direction and produced the most marvellous results. Even at the present day, the logical capacity of the Hindus, and the tremendous power which the Indian brain still possesses, is beyond compare. We all know that our boys pitched against the boys of any other country triumph always.

At the same time, when the national vigour went, perhaps one or two centuries before the Mohammedan conquest of India, this national faculty became so much exaggerated that it degraded itself, and we find some of this degradation in everything in India, in art, in music, in sciences, in everything. In art, no more was there a broad conception, no more the symmetry of form and sublimit of conception, but the tremendous attempt at the ornate and florid style had arisen. The originality of the race seemed to have been lost. In music no more were there the soul-stirring ideas of the ancient Sanskrit music, no more did each note stand, as it were, on its own feet, and produce the marvellous harmony, but each not had lost its individuality. The whole of modern music is a jumble of notes, a confused mass of curves. That is a sign of degradation in music. So, if you analyse your idealistic conceptions, you will find the same attempt at ornate figures, and loss of originality.

And even in religion, your special field, there came the most horrible degradations. What can you expect of a race which for hundreds of years has been busy in discussing such momentous problems as whether we should drink a glass of water with the right hand or the left? What more degradation can there be than that the greatest minds of a country have been discussing about the kitchen for several hundreds of years, discussing whether I may touch you or you touch me, and what is the penance for this touching! The themes of the Vedanta, the sublimest and the most glorious conceptions of God and soul ever preached on earth, were half-lost, buried in the forests, preserved by a few Sannyasins, while the rest of the nation discussed the momentous questions of touching each other, and dress, and food.

The Mohammedan conquest gave us many good things, no doubt; even the lowest man in the world can teach something to the highest; at the same time it could not bring vigour into the race. Then for good or evil, the English conquest of India took place. Of course, every conquest is bad, for conquest is an evil, foreign government is an evil, no doubt; but even through evil comes good sometimes, and the great good of the English conquest is this: England, nay the whole of Europe, has to thank Greece for its civilisation. It is Greece that speaks through everything in Europe. Every building, every piece of furniture has the impress of Greece upon it; European science and art are nothing but Grecian. Today the ancient Greek is meeting the ancient Hindu on the soil of India. Thus slowly and silently the leaven has come; the broadening, the life-giving and the revivalist movement that we see all around us has been worked out by these forces together.

We cannot do without the world outside India; it was our foolishness that we thought we could, and we have paid the penalty by about a thousand years of slavery. That we did not go out to compare things with other nations, did not mark the working that have been all around us, has been the one great cause of this degradation of the Indian mind. We have paid the penalty; let us do it no more. All such foolish ideas that Indians must not go out of India are childish. They must be knocked on the head; the more you go out and travel among the nations of the world, the better for you and for your country. If you had done that for hundreds of years past, you would not be here today at the feet of every nation that wants to rule India. The first manifest effect of life is expansion. You must expand if you want to live. The moment you have ceased to expand, death is upon you, danger is ahead.

Vol. 3, Lectures from Colombo to Almora,
The Work Before Us, pp. 269–272

Many times have I been told that looking into the past only degenerates and leads to nothing, and that we should look to the future. That is true. But out of the past is built the future. Look back, therefore, as far as you can, drink deep of the eternal fountains that are behind, and after that, look forward, march forward and make India brighter, greater, much higher than she ever was. Our ancestors were great. We must first recall that. We must learn the elements of our being, the blood that courses in our veins; we must have faith in that blood and what it did in the past; and out of that faith and consciousness of past greatness, we must build an India yet greater than what she has been. There have been periods of decay and degradation. I do not attach much importance to them; we all know that. Such periods have been necessary. A mighty tree produces a beautiful ripe fruit. That fruit falls on the ground, it decays and rots, and out of that decay springs the root and the future tree, perhaps mightier than the first one. This period of decay through which we have passed was all the more necessary. Out of this decay is coming the India of the future; it is sprouting, its first leaves are already out, and a mighty, gigantic tree, the Urdhvamuda, is here, already beginning to appear.

The problems in India are more complicated, more momentous, than the problems in any other country. Race, religion, language, government—all these together make a nation. The elements which compose the nations of the world are indeed very few, taking race after race, compared to this country. Here have been the Aryan, the Dravidian, the Tartar, the Turk, the Mogul, the European—all the nations of the world, as it were, pouring their blood into this land. Of languages the most wonderful conglomeration is here; of manners and customs there is more difference between two Indian races than between the European and the Eastern races.

The one common ground that we have is our sacred tradition, our religion. That is the only common ground, and upon that we shall have to build. In Europe, political ideas form the national unity. In Asia, religious ideals form the national unity. The unity in religion, therefore, is absolutely necessary as the first condition of the future of India. There must be the recognition of one religion throughout the length and breadth of this land.

What do I mean by one religion? Not in the sense of one religion as held among the Christians, or the Mohammedans, or the Buddhists. We know that our religion has certain common grounds, common to all sects, however varying their conclusions may be, however different their claims may be.

We see how in Asia, and especially in India, race difficulties, linguistic difficulties, social difficulties, national difficulties, all melt away before this unifying power of religion. We know that to the Indian mind there is nothing higher than religious ideals, that this is the keynote of Indian life, and we can only work in the line of least resistance. It is not only true that the ideal of religion is the highest ideal; in the case of India it is the only possible means of work; work in any other line, without first strengthening this, would be disastrous. Therefore the first plank in the making of a future India, the first step that is to be hewn out of that rock of ages, is this unification of religion. All of us have to be taught that we Hindus—dualists, qualified monists, or monists, Shaivas, Vaishnavas, or Pashupatas—to whatever denomination we may belong, have certain common ideas behind us, and that the time has come when for the well-being of ourselves, for the well-being of our race, we must give up all our little quarrels and differences.

With the giving up of quarrels all other improvements will come. When the life-blood is strong and pure, no disease germ can live in that body. Our life-blood is spirituality. If it flows clear, if it flows strong and pure and vigorous, everything is right; political, social, any other material defects, even the poverty of the land, will all be cured if that blood is pure. For if the disease germ be thrown out, nothing will be able to enter into the blood.

It is when the national body is weak that all sorts of disease germs, in the political state of the race or in its social state, in its educational or intellectual state, crowd into the system and produce disease. To remedy it, therefore, we must go to the root of this disease and cleanse the blood of all impurities.

We have seen that our vigour, our strength, nay, our national life is in our religion. I am not going to discuss now whether it is right or not, whether it is correct or not, whether it is beneficial or not in the long run, to have this vitality in religion, but for good or evil it is there; you cannot get out of it, you have it now and for ever, and you have to stand by it, even if you have not the same faith that I have in our religion. You are bound by it, and if you give it up, you are smashed to pieces. That is the life of our race and must be strengthened. You have withstood the shocks of centuries simply because you took great care of it, you sacrificed everything else for it. Your forefathers underwent everything boldly, even death itself, but preserved their religion. Temple after temple was broken down by the foreign conqueror, but no sooner had the wave passed than the spire of the temple rose up again. Some of these old temples of Southern India and those like Somnath of Gujarat will teach you volumes of wisdom, will give you a keener insight into the history of the race than any amount of books. Mark how these temples bear the marks of a hundred attacks and a hundred regenerations, continually destroyed and continually springing up out of the ruins, rejuvenated and strong as ever! That is the national mind, that is the national life-current. Follow it and it leads to glory. Give it up and you die; death will be the only result, annihilation the only effect, the moment you step beyond that life-current. I do not mean to say that other things are not necessary. I do not mean to say that political or social improvements are not necessary, but what I mean is this, and I want you to bear it in mind, that they are secondary here and that religion is primary. The Indian mind is first religious, then anything else. So this is to be strengthened, and how to do it? I will lay before you my ideas. They have been in my mind for a long time, even years before I left the shores of Madras for America, and that I went to America and England was simply for propagating those ideas. I did not care at all for the Parliament of Religions or anything else; it was simply an opportunity; for it was really those ideas of mine that took me all over the world.

My idea is first of all to bring out the gems of spirituality that are stored up in our books and in the possession of a few only, hidden, as it were, in monasteries and forests—to bring them out; to bring the knowledge out of them, not only from the hands where it is hidden, but from the still more inaccessible chest, the language in which it is preserved, the incrustation of centuries of Sanskrit words. In one word, I want to make them popular.

Therefore the ideas must be taught in the language of the people; at the same time, Sanskrit education must go on along with it, because the very sound of Sanskrit words gives a prestige and a power and strength to the race.

The attempts of the great Ramanuja and of Chaitanya and of Kabir to raise the lower classes of India show that marvellous results were attained during the lifetime of those great prophets; yet the later failures have to be explained, and cause shown why the effect of their teachings stopped almost within a century of the passing away of these great Masters. The secret is here. They raised the lower classes; they had all the wish that these should come up, but they did not apply their energies to the spreading of the Sanskrit language among the masses. Even the great Buddha made one false step when he stopped the Sanskrit language from being studied by the masses. He wanted rapid and immediate results, and translated and preached in the language of the day,

Pali. That was grand; he spoke in the language of the people, and the people understood him. That was great; it spread the ideas quickly and made them reach far and wide. But along with that, Sanskrit ought to have spread. Knowledge came, but the prestige was not there, culture was not there.

It is culture that withstands shocks, not a simple mass of knowledge. You can put a mass of knowledge into the world, but that will not do it much good. There must come culture into the blood. We all know in modern times of nations that have masses of knowledge, but what of them? They are like tigers, they are like savages, because culture is not there. Knowledge is only skin-deep, as civilisation is, and a little scratch brings out the old savage. Such things happen; this is the danger. Teach the masses in the vernaculars, give them ideas; they will get information, but something more is necessary; give them culture. Until you give them that, there can be no permanence in the raised condition of the masses. There will be another caste created, having the advantage of the Sanskrit language, which will quickly get above the rest and rule them all the same. The only safety, I tell you men who belong to the lower castes, the only way to raise your condition is to study Sanskrit, and this fighting and writing and frothing against the higher castes is in vain, it does no good, and it creates fight and quarrel, and this race, unfortunately already divided, is going to be divided more and more. The only way to bring about the levelling of caste is to appropriate the culture, the education which is the strength of the higher castes. That done, you have what you want.

In connection with this, I want to discuss one question which has a particular bearing with regard to Madras. There is a theory that there was a race of mankind in Southern India called Dravidians, entirely differing from another race in Northern India called the Aryans, and that the Southern Indian Brahmins are the only Aryans that came from the North, the other men of Southern India belong to an entirely different case and race to those of the Southern India Brahmins. Now I beg your pardon, Mr. Philologist, this is entirely unfounded. The only proof of it is that there is a difference of language between the North and the South. I do not see any other difference. We are so many Northern men here, and I ask my European friends to pick out the Northern and Southern men from this assembly. Where is the difference? A little difference of language. But the Brahmins are a race that came here speaking the Sanskrit language! Well then, they took up the Dravidian language and forgot their Sanskrit. Why should not the other castes have done the same? Why should not all the other castes have come one after the other from Northern India, taken up the Dravidian language, and so forgotten their own? That is an argument working both ways. Do not believe in such silly things. There may have been a Dravidian people who vanished from here, and the few who remained lived in forests and other places. It is quite possible that the language may have been taken up, but all these are Aryans who came from the North. The whole of India is Aryan, nothing else.

Then there is the other idea that the Shudra caste are surely the aborigines [...] There is not one word in our scriptures, not one, to prove that the Aryan ever came from anywhere outside of India, and in ancient India was included Afghanistan. There it ends. And the theory that the Shudra caste were all non-Aryans and they were a multitude, is equally illogical and equally irrational. It could not have been possible in those days that a few Aryans settled and lived there with a hundred thousand slaves at their command. These slaves would have eaten them up, made 'chutney' of them in five minutes. The only explanation is to be found in the Mahabharata, which says that in the beginning of the Satya Yuga there was one caste, the Brahmins, and then by difference of occupations they went on dividing themselves into different castes, and that is the only true and rational explanation that has been given. And in the coming Satya Yuga all the other castes will have to go back to the same condition.

The solution of the caste problem in India, therefore, assumes this form, not to degrade the higher castes, nor to crush out the Brahmin. The Brahminhood is the ideal of humanity in India, as wonderfully put forward by Shankaracharya at the beginning of his commentary on the Gita, where he speaks about the reason for Krishna's coming as a preacher for the preservation of Brahminhood, of Brahminness. That was the great end. This Brahmin, the man of God, he who has known Brahman, the ideal man, the perfect man, must remain; he must not go. And with all the defects of the caste now, we know that we must all be ready to give to the Brahmins this credit, that from them have come more men with real Brahminness in them than from all the other castes. We must be bold enough, must be brave enough to speak of their defects, but at the same time we must give the credit that is due to them. Therefore, my friends, it is no use fighting among the castes. What good will it do? It will divide us all the more, weaken us all the more, degrade us all the more. The days of exclusive privileges and exclusive claims are gone, gone for ever from the soil of India, and it is one of the great blessings of the British Rule in India. Even to the Mohammedan Rule we owe that great blessing, the destruction of exclusive privilege. That Rule was, after all, not all bad; nothing is all bad, and nothing is all good. The Mohammedan conquest of India came as a salvation to the downtrodden, to the poor. That is why one-fifth of our people have become Mohammedans. It was not the sword that did it all. It would be the height of madness to think it was all the work of sword and fire. And one-fifth—one half—of your Madras people will become Christians if you do not take care. Was there ever a sillier thing before in the world than what I saw in Malabar country? The poor Pariah is not allowed to pass through the same street as the high-caste man, but if he changes his name to a hodge-podge English name, it is all right; or to a Mohammedan name, it is all right. What inference would you draw except that these Malabaris are all lunatics, their homes so many lunatic asylums, and that they are to be treated with derision by every race in India until they mend their manners and know better. Shame upon them that such wicked and diabolical customs are allowed; their own children are allowed to die of starvation, but as soon as they take up some other religion they are well fed. There ought to be no more fight between the castes.

The solution is not by bringing down the higher, but by raising the lower up to the level of the higher. And that is the line of work that is found in all our books, in spite of what you ay hear from some people whose knowledge of their own scriptures and whose capacity to understand the mighty plans of the ancients are only zero. They do not understand, but those do that have brains, that have the intellect to grasp the whole scope of the work. They stand aside and follow the wonderful procession of national life through the ages. They can trace it step by step through all the books, ancient and modern. What is the plan? The ideal at one end is the Brahmin, and the ideal at the other end is the Chandala, and the whole work is to raise the Chandala up to the Brahmin. Slowly and slowly you find more and more privileges granted to them.

We find that all the castes are to rise slowly and slowly. There are thousands of castes, and some are even getting admission into Brahminhood, for what prevents any caste from declaring that they are Brahmins? Thus caste, with all its rigour, has been created in that manner. Let us suppose that there are castes here with ten thousand people in each. If these put their heads together and say, we will call ourselves Brahmins, nothing can stop them; I have seen it in my own life. Some castes become strong, and as soon as they all agree, who is to say nay? Because whatever it was, each caste was exclusive of the other. It did not meddle with others' affairs; even the several divisions of one caste did not meddle with the other divisions, and those powerful epoch-makers, Shankaracharya and others, were the great caste-makers. I cannot tell you all the wonderful things they fabricated, and some of you may resent what I have to say. But in my travels and experiences I have traced them out, and have arrived at the most wonderful results. They would sometimes get hordes of Baluchis and at once make them Kshatriyas, also get hold of hordes of fishermen and make them Brahmins forthwith. They were all Rishis and sages, and we have to bow down to their memory.

Especially do I regret that in modern times there should be so much dissension between the castes. This must stop. It is useless on both sides, especially on the side of the higher caste, the Brahmin, because the day for these privileges and exclusive claims is gone. The duty of every aristocracy is to dig its own grave, and the sooner it does so, the better. The more it delays, the more it will fester and the worse death it will die. It is the duty of the Brahmin, therefore, to work for the salvation of the rest of mankind in India. If he does that, and so long as he does that, he is a Brahmin, but he is no Brahmin when he goes about making money. You on the other hand should give help only to the real Brahmin who deserves it; that leads to heaven. But sometimes a gift to another person who does not deserve it leads to the other place, says our scripture. You must be on you guard about that. He only is the Brahmin who has no secular employment. Secular employment is not for the Brahmin but for the other castes. To the Brahmins I appeal, that they must work hard to raise the Indian people by teaching them what they know, by giving out the culture that they have accumulated for centuries. It is clearly the duty of the Brahmins of India to remember what real Brahminhood is. As Manu says, all these privileges and honours are given to the Brahmin, because 'with him is the treasury of virtue.' He must open that treasury and distribute its valuables to the world. It is true that he was the earliest preacher to the Indian races, he was the first to renounce everything in order to attain to the higher realisation of life before others could reach to the idea. It was not his fault that he marched ahead of the other castes. Why did not the other castes so understand and do as he did? Why did they sit down and be lazy, and let the Brahmins win the race?

But it is one thing to gain an advantage, and another thing to preserve it for evil use. Whenever power is used for evil, it becomes diabolical; it must be used for good only. So this accumulated culture of ages of which the Brahmin has been the trustee, he must now give to the people at large, and it was because he did not give it to the people that the Mohammedan invasion was possible. It was because he did not open this treasury to the people from the beginning, that for a thousand years we have been trodden under the heels of every one who chose to come to India. It was through that we have become degraded, and the first task must be to break open the cells that hide the wonderful treasures which our common ancestors accumulated; bring them out and give them to everybody and the Brahmin must be the first to do it. There is an old superstition in Bengal that if the cobra that bites sucks out his own poison from the patient, the man must survive. Well then, the Brahmin must suck out his own poison.

To the non-Brahmin castes I say, wait, be not in a hurry. Do not seize every opportunity of fighting the Brahmin, because, as I have shown, you are suffering from your own fault. Who told you to neglect spirituality and Sanskrit learning? What have you been doing all this time? Why have you been indifferent? Why do you now fret and fume because somebody else had more brains, more energy, more pluck and go, than you? Instead of wasting your energies in vain discussions and quarrels in the newspapers, instead of fighting and quarrelling in your own homes—which is sinful—use all your energies in acquiring the culture which the Brahmin has, and the thing is done. Why do you not become Sanskrit scholars? Why do you not spend millions to bring Sanskrit education to all the castes of India? That is the question. The moment you do these things, you are equal to the Brahmin. That is the secret of power in India.

Sanskrit and prestige go together in India. As soon as you have that, none dares say anything against you. That is the one secret; take that up.

Why is it that organisations are so powerful? Do not say organisation is material. Why is it, to take a case in point, that forty millions of Englishmen rule three hundred millions of people here? What is the psychological explanation? These forty millions put their will together and that means infinite power, and you three hundred millions have a will each separate from the other. Therefore to make a great future India, the whole secret lies in organisation, accumulation of power, coordination of wills.

Being of one mind is the secret of society. And the more you go on fighting and quarrelling about all trivialities such as 'Dravidian' and 'Aryan,' and the question of Brahmins and non-Brahmins and all that, the further you are off from that accumulation of energy and power which is going to make the future India. For mark you, the future India depends entirely upon that. That is the secret—accumulation of will-power, coordination, bringing them all, as it were, in one focus.

There is yet another defect in us. Ladies, excuse me, but through centuries of slavery, we have become like a nation of women. You scarcely can get three women together for five minutes in this country or any other country but they quarrel. Women make big societies in European countries, and make tremendous declarations of women's power and so on; then they quarrel, and some man comes and rules them all. All over the world they still require some man to rule them. We are like them. Women we are. If a woman comes to lead women, they all begin immediately to criticise her, tear her to pieces, and make her sit down. If a man comes and gives them a little harsh treatment, scolds them now and then, it is all right, they have been used to that sort of mesmerism. The whole world is full of such mesmerists and hypnotists. In the same say, if one of our countrymen stands up and tries to become great, we all try to hold him down, but if a foreigner comes and tries to kick us, it is all right. We have been used to it, have we not? And slaves must become great masters! So give up being a slave.

We must have a hold on the spiritual and secular education of the nation. Do you understand that? You must dream it, you must talk it, you must think it, and you must work it out. Till then there is no salvation for the race. The education that you are getting now has some good points, but it has a tremendous disadvantage, which is so great that the good things are all weighed down. In the first place it is not a man-making education, it is merely and entirely a negative education. A negative education or any training that is based on negation is worse than death. The child is taken to school, and the first thing he learns is that his father is a fool, the second thing that his grandfather is a lunatic, the third thing that all his teachers are hypocrites, the fourth that all the sacred books are lies! By the time he is sixteen, he is a mass of negation, lifeless and boneless. And the result is that fifty years of such education has not produced one original man in the three Presidencies. Every man of originality that has been produced has been educated elsewhere, and not in this country, or they have gone to the old universities once more to cleanse themselves of superstitions.

Education is not the amount of information that is put into your brain and runs riot there, undigested, all your life. We must have life-building, man-making, character-making assimilation of ideas. If you have assimilated five ideas and made them your life and character, you have more education than any man who has got by heart a whole library. 'The ass carrying its load of sandalwood knows only the weight and not the value of the sandalwood.' If education is identical with information, the libraries are the greatest sages in the world, and encyclopaedias are the Rishis. The ideal, therefore, is that we must have the whole education of our country, spiritual and secular, in our own hands, and it must be on national lines, through national methods as far as practical.

Of course, this is a very big scheme, a very big plan. I do not know whether it will every work out. But we must begin this work. But how? Take Madras, for instance. We must have a temple, for with Hindus religion must come first. Then, you may say, all sects will quarrel about it. But we will make it a non-sectarian temple, having only 'Om' as the symbol, the greatest symbol of any sect. If there is any sect here which believes that 'Om' ought not to be the symbol, it has no right to call itself Hindu. All will have the right to interpret Hinduism, each one according to his own sect ideas, but we must have a common temple. You can have your own images and symbols in other places, but do not quarrel here with those who differ from you. Here should be taught the common grounds of our different sects, and at the same time the different sects should have perfect liberty to come and teach their doctrines, with only one restriction, that is, not to quarrel with other sects. Say what you have to say, the world wants it; but the world has no time to hear what you think about other people; you can keep that to yourselves.

Secondly, in connection with this temple there should be an institution to train teachers who must go about preaching religion and giving secular education to our people; they must carry both. As we have been already carrying religion from door to door, let us along with it carry secular education also. That can be easily done. Then the work will extend through these bands of teachers and preachers, and gradually we shall have similar temples in other places, until we have covered the whole of India. That is my plan. It may appear gigantic, but it is much needed. Money is not needed. Money is nothing. For the last twelve years of my life, I did not know where the next meal would come from; but money and everything else I want must come, because they are my slaves, not I theirs; money and everything else must come.

Must—that is the word. Where are the men? That is the question.

Young men of Madras, my hope is in you. Will you respond to the call of your nation? Each one of you has a glorious future if you dare believe me. Have a tremendous faith in yourselves, like the faith I had when I was a child, and which I am working out now. Have that faith, each one of you, in yourself—that eternal power is lodged in every soul—and you will revive the whole of India. Ay, we will then go to every country under the sun, and our ideas will before long be a component of the many forces that are working to make up every nation in the world. We must enter into the life of every race in India and abroad; we shall have to work to bring this about. Now for that, I want young men. 'It is the young, the strong, and healthy, of sharp intellect that will reach the Lord,' say the Vedas. This is the time to decide your future—while you possess the energy of youth, not when you are worn out and jaded, but in the freshness and vigour of youth. Work—this is the time; for the freshest, the untouched, and unsmelled flowers alone are to be laid at the feet of the Lord, and such He receives. Rouse yourselves, therefore, for life is short. There are greater works to be done than aspiring to become lawyers and picking quarrels and such things. A far greater work is this sacrifice of yourselves for the benefit of your race, for the welfare of humanity. What is in this life? You are Hindus, and there is the instinctive belief in you that life is eternal. Sometimes I have young men come and talk to me about atheism; I do not believe a Hindu can become an atheist. He may read European books, and persuade himself he is a materialist, but it is only for a time. It is not in your blood. You cannot believe what is not in your constitution; it would be a hopeless task for you. Do not attempt that sort of thing. I once attempted it when I was a boy, but it could not be. Life is short, but the soul is immortal and eternal, and one thing being certain, death, let us therefore take up a great ideal and give up our whole life to it. Let this be our determination, and may He, the Lord, who 'comes again and again for the salvation of His own people,' to quote from our scriptures—may the great Krishna bless us and lead us all to the fulfilment of our aims!

Vol. 3, Lectures from Colombo to Almora,
The Future of India, pp. 285–304

All the culture, practically, which the nation possessed, was among the Brahmins, and they also had been the thinkers of the nation. Take away the means of living which enabled them to be thinkers, and the nation as a whole would suffer.

Vol. 3, Lectures from Colombo to Almora, On Charity, p. 305

One of the great causes of India's misery and downfall has been that she narrowed herself, went into her shell as the oyster does, and refused to give her jewels and treasures to the other races of mankind, refused to give the life-giving truths to thirsting nations outside the Aryan fold. That has been the one great cause; that we did not go out, that we did not compare notes with other nations—that has been the one great cause of our downfall, and every one of you know that that little stir, the little life that you see in India, begins from the day when Raja Rammohan Roy broke through the walls of that exclusiveness. Since that day, history in India has taken another turn, and now it is growing with accelerated motion. If we have had little rivulets in the past, deluges are coming, and none can resist them. Therefore we must go out, and the secret of life is to give and take. Are we to take always, to sit at the feet of the Westerners to learn everything, even religion? We can learn mechanism from them. We can learn many other things. But we have to teach them something, and that is our religion, that is our spirituality. For a complete civilisation the world is waiting, waiting for the treasures to come out of India, waiting for the marvellous spiritual inheritance of the race, which, through decades of degradation and misery, the nation has still clutched to her breast. The world is waiting for that treasure; little do you know how much of hunger and of thirst there is outside of India for these wonderful treasures of our forefathers. We talk here, we quarrel with each other, we laugh at and we ridicule everything sacred, till it has become almost a national vice to ridicule everything holy. Little do we understand the heart-pangs of millions waiting outside the walls, stretching forth their hands for a little sip of that nectar which our forefathers have preserved in this land of India. Therefore we must go out, exchange our spirituality for anything they have to give us; for marvels of the region of spirit we will exchange the marvels of the region of matter. We will not be students always, but teachers also. There cannot be friendship without equality, and there cannot be equality when one party is always the teacher and the other party sits always at his feet. If you want to become equal with the Englishman or the American, you will have to teach as well as to learn, and you have plenty yet to teach to the world for centuries to come. This has to be done. Fire and enthusiasm must be in our blood.

I have faith in my country, and especially in the youth of my country. The youth of Bengal have the greatest of all tasks that has ever been placed on the shoulders of young men. I have travelled for the last ten years or so over the whole of India, and my conviction is that from the youth of Bengal will come the power which will raise India once more to her proper spiritual place. Ay, from the youth of Bengal, with this immense amount of feeling and enthusiasm in the blood, will come those heroes who will march from one corner of the earth to the other, preaching and teaching the eternal spiritual truths of our forefathers. And this is the great work before you. Therefore, let me conclude by reminding you once more, 'Arise, awake and stop not till the desired end is reached.' Be not afraid, for all great power, throughout the history of humanity, has been with the people. From out of their ranks have come all the greatest geniuses of the world, and history can only repeat itself. Be not afraid of anything. You will do marvellous work. The moment you fear, you are nobody. It is fear that is the great cause of misery in the world. It is fear that is the greatest of all superstitions. It is fear that is the cause of our woes, and it is fearlessness that brings heaven even in a moment.

Vol. 3, Lectures from Colombo to Almora, Address of Welcome Presented at Calcutta and Reply, pp. 317–321

This is one great point to understand, and, my friends, my brethren, let me tell you, this is the one point we shall have to insist upon in the future. For I am firmly convinced, and I beg you to understand this one fact—no good comes out of the man who day and night thinks he is nobody. If a man, day and night, thinks he is miserable, low and nothing, nothing he becomes [...] That is the great fact which you ought to remember. We are the children of the Almighty, we are sparks of the infinite, divine fire. How can we be nothings? We are everything, ready to do everything, we can do everything, and man must do everything. This faith in themselves was in the hearts of our ancestors, this faith in themselves was the motive power that pushed them forward and forward in the march of civilisation; and if there has been degeneration, if there has been defect, mark my works, you will find that degradation to have started on the day our people lost this faith in themselves. Losing faith in one's self means losing faith in God. Do you believe in that infinite, good Providence working in and through you? [...] Therefore, my brethren, teach this life-saving, great, ennobling grand doctrine to your children, even from their very birth [...] Follies there are, weakness there must be, but remember your real nature always—that is the only way to cure the weakness, that is the only way to cure the follies.

Do not be in a hurry, do not go out to imitate anybody else. This is another great lesson we have to remember: imitation is not civilisation. I may deck myself out in a Raja's dress, but will that make me a Raja? An ass in a lion's skin never makes a lion. Imitation, cowardly imitation, never makes for progress. It is verily the sign of awful degradation in a man. Ay, when a man has begun to hate himself, then the last blow has come. When a man has begun to be ashamed of his ancestors, the end has come. Here am I, one of the least of the Hindu race, yet proud of my race, proud of my ancestors. I am proud to call myself a Hindu, I am proud that I am a countryman of yours, you the descendants of the sages, you the descendants of the most glorious Rishis the world ever saw. Therefore have faith in yourselves, be proud of your ancestors, instead of being ashamed of them. And do not imitate, do not imitate! Whenever you are under the thumb of others, you lose your own independence. If you are working, even in spiritual things, at the dictation of others, slowly you lose all faculty, even of thought. Bring out through your own exertions what you have, but do not imitate, yet take what is good from others [...] We have indeed many things to learn from others, yea, that man who refuses to learn is already dead [...] Learn everything that is good from others, but bring it in, and in your own way absorb it; do not become others. Do not be dragged away out of this Indian life; do not for a moment think that it would be better for India if all the Indians dressed, ate and behaved like another race.

Religion for a long time has come to be static in India. What we want is to make it dynamic. I want it to be brought into the life of everybody. Religion, as it always has been in the past, must enter the palaces of kings as well as the homes of the poorest peasants in the land. Religion, the common inheritance, the universal birth right of the race, must be brought free to the door of everybody. Religion in India must be made as free and as easy of access as is God's air. And this is the kind of work we have to bring about in India, but not by getting up little sects and fighting on points of difference. Let us preach where we all agree and leave the differences to remedy themselves. As I have said to the

Indian people again and again, if there is darkness of centuries in a room and we go into the room and begin to cry, 'Oh, it is dark, it is dark!', will the darkness go? Bring in the light and the darkness will vanish at once. This is the secret of reforming men. Suggest to them higher things; believe in man first. Why start with the belief that man is degraded and degenerated?

Vol. 3, Lectures from Colombo to Almora, The Common Bases of Hinduism, pp. 375–383

The secret of Advaita is: Believe in yourselves first, and then believe in anything else. In the history of the world, you will find that only those nations that have believed in themselves have become great and strong. In the history of each nation, you will always find that only those individuals who have believed in themselves have become great and strong. Here, to India, came an Englishman who was only a clerk, and for want of funds and other reasons he twice tried to blow his brains out; and when he failed, he believed in himself, he believed that he was born to do great things; and that man became Lord Clive, the founder of the Empire. If he had believed the Padres and gone crawling all his life—'O Lord, I am weak, and I am low'—where would he have been? In a lunatic asylum. You also are made lunatics by these evil teachings. I have seen, all the world over, the bad effects of these weak teachings of humility destroying the human race. Our children are brought up in this way, and is it a wonder that they become semi-lunatics?

This is teaching on the practical side. Believe, therefore, in yourselves, and if you want material wealth, work it out; it will come to you. If you want to be intellectual, work it out on the intellectual plane, and intellectual giants you shall be. And if you want to attain to freedom, work it out on the spiritual plane, and free you shall be and shall enter into Nirvana, the Eternal Bliss. But one defect which lay in the Advaita was its being worked out so long on the spiritual plane only, and nowhere else; now the time has come when you have to make it practical. It shall no more be a Rahasya, a secret, it shall no more live with monks in caves and forests, and in the Himalayas; it must come down to the daily, everyday life of the people; it shall be worked out in the palace of the king, in the cave of the recluse; it shall be worked out in the cottage of the poor, by the beggar in the street, everywhere; anywhere it can be worked out. Therefore, do not fear whether you are a woman or a Shudra, for this religion is so great, says Lord Krishna, that even a little of it brings a great amount of good.

Therefore, children of the Aryans, do not sit idle; awake, arise, and stop not till the goal is reached. The time has come when this Advaita is to be worked out practically. Let us bring it down from heaven unto the earth; this is the present dispensation. Ay, the voices of our forefathers of old are telling us to bring it down from heaven to the earth. Let your teachings permeate the world, till they have entered into every pore of society, till they have become the common property of everybody, till they have become part and parcel of our lives, till they have entered into our veins and tingle with every drop of blood there.

Ay, in this country of ours, the very birthplace of the Vedanta, our masses have been hypnotised for ages into that state (of slavery and weakness). To touch them is pollution, to sit with them is pollution! Hopeless they were born; hopeless they must remain! And the result is that they have been sinking, sinking, sinking, and have come to the last stage to which a human being can come. For what country is there in the world where man has to sleep with the cattle? And for this, blame nobody else, do not commit the mistake of the ignorant. The effect is here and the cause is here too. We are to blame. Stand up, be bold, and take the blame on your own shoulders. Do not go about throwing mud at others; for all the faults you suffer from, you are the sole and only cause. Young men of Lahore, understand this, therefore, this great sin, hereditary and national, is on our shoulders.

Where is the heart here to build upon? No sooner do we start a little joint-stock company than we try to cheat each other, and the whole thing comes down with a crash. You talk of imitating the English and building up as big a nation as they are. But where are the foundations? Ours are only sand, and therefore the building comes down with a crash in no time.

Therefore, young men of Lahore, raise once more that mighty banner of Advaita, for on no other ground can you have that wonderful love until you see that the same Lord is present everywhere. Unfurl that banner of love! 'Arise, awake, and stop not till the goal is reached.' Arise, arise once more, for nothing can be done without renunciation.

'Arise and awake.' What matters it if this little life goes? Everyone has to die, the saint or the sinner, the rich or the poor. Arise and awake and be perfectly sincere. Our insincerity in India is awful; what we want is character, that steadiness and character that make a man cling on to a thing like grim death.

Arise and awake, for the time is passing and all our energies will be frittered away in vain talking. Arise and awake, let minor things, and quarrels over little details and fights over little doctrines be thrown aside, for here is the greatest of all works, here are the sinking millions. When the Mohammedans first came into India, what a great number of Hindus were here; but mark, how today they have dwindled down! Every day they will become less and less till they wholly disappear. Let them disappear, but with them will disappear the marvellous ideas, of which, with all their defects and all their misrepresentations, they still stand as representatives. And with them will disappear this marvellous Advaita, the crest-jewel of all spiritual thought. Therefore, arise, awake, with your hands stretched out to protect the spirituality of the world. And first of all, work it out for your own country. What we want is not so much spirituality as a little of the bringing down of the Advaita into the material world. First bread and then religion. We stuff them too much with religion, when the poor fellows have been starving. No dogmas will satisfy the cravings of hunger. There are two curses here: first our weakness; secondly, our hatred, our dried-up hearts.

Vol. 3, Lectures from Colombo to Almora, The Vedanta, pp. 426–432

Everybody knows now how much the world owes to India's spirituality, and what a potent factor in the present and the past of humanity have been the spiritual powers of India. These are things of the past. I find another most remarkable phenomenon, and that is that the most stupendous powers of civilisation, and progress towards humanity and social progress, have been effected by that wonderful race—I mean the Anglo-Saxon. I may go further and tell you that had it not been for the power of the Anglo-Saxons we should not have met here to discuss, as we are doing, the influence of our Indian spiritual thought. And coming back to our own country, coming from the West to the East, I see the same Anglo-Saxon powers working here with all their defects, but retaining their peculiarly characteristic good features, and I believe that at last the grand result is achieved. The British idea of expansion and progress is forcing us up, and let us remember that the civilisation of the West has been drawn from the fountain of the Greeks, and that the great idea of Greek civilisation is that of *expression.* In India we *think*—but unfortunately sometimes we think so deeply that there is no power left for expression. Gradually, therefore, it came to pass that our force of expression did not manifest itself before the world, and what is the result of that? The result is this—we worked to hide everything we had. It began first with individuals as a faculty of hiding, and it ended by becoming a national habit of hiding—there is such a lack of power of expression with us that we are now considered a dead nation. Without expression, how can we live? The backbone of Western civilisation is—expansion and expression. This side of the work of the Anglo-Saxon race in India, to which I draw your attention, is calculated to rouse our nation once more to express itself, and it is inciting it to bring out its hidden treasures before the world by using the means of communication provided by the same mighty race. The Anglo-Saxons have created a future for India, and the space through which our ancestral ideas are now ranging is simply phenomenal.

Remember your great mission in life. We Indians, and especially those of Bengal, have been invaded by a vast amount of foreign ideas that are eating into the very vitals of our national religion. Why are we so backward nowadays? Why are ninety-nine per cent of us made up of entirely foreign ideas and elements? This has to be thrown out if we want to rise in the scale of nations. If we want to rise, we must also remember that we have many things to learn from the West. We should learn from the West her arts and her sciences. From the West we have to learn the sciences of physical nature, while on the other hand the West has to come to us to learn and assimilate religion and spiritual knowledge. We Hindus must believe that we are the teachers of the world. We have been clamouring here for getting political rights and many other such things. Very well. Rights and privileges and other things can only be expected between two equals. When one of the parties is a beggar, what friendship can there be? It is all very well to speak so, but I say that without mutual cooperation we can never make ourselves strong men. So, I must call upon you to go out to England and America, not as beggars but as teachers of religion. The law of exchange must be applied to the best of our power. If we have to learn from them the ways and methods of making ourselves happy in this life, why, in return, should we not give them the methods and ways that would make them happy for all eternity? Above all, work for the good of humanity. Give up the so-called boast of your narrow orthodox life. Death is waiting for every one, and mark you this—the most marvellous historical fact—that all the nations of the world have to sit down patiently at the feet of

India to learn the eternal truths embodied in her literature.

Today we are far behindhand in spiritual insight and spiritual thoughts. India had plenty of spirituality, so much so that her spiritual greatness made India the greatest nation of the then existing races of the world; and if traditions and hopes are to be believed, those days will come back once more to us, and that depends on you. You, young men of Bengal, do not look up to the rich and great men who have money. The poor did all that great and gigantic work of the world. You, poor men of Bengal, come up, you can do everything, and you must do everything. Many will follow your example, poor though you are. Be steady, and above all be pure and sincere to the backbone. Have faith in your destiny. You, young men of Bengal, are to work out the salvation of India. Mark that, whether you believe it or not, do not think that it will be done today or tomorrow. I believe in it as I believe in my own body and my own soul. Therefore my heart goes to you—young men of Bengal. It depends upon you who have no money; because you are poor, therefore you will work. Because you have nothing, therefore you will be sincere. Because you are sincere, you will be ready to renounce all.

Vol. 3, Lectures from Colombo to Almora, The Influence of Indian Spiritual Thought in England, pp. 440–445

A veritable ethnological museum! Possibly, the half-ape skeleton of the recently discovered Sumatra link will be found on search here, too. The Dolmens are not wanting. Flint implements can be dug out almost anywhere. The lake-dwellers—at least the river-dwellers—must have been abundant at one time. The cave-men and leaf-wearers still persist. The primitive hunters living in forests are in evidence in various parts of the country. Then there are the more historical varieties—the Negrito-Kolarian, the Dravidian, and the Aryan. To these have been added from time to time dashes of nearly all the known races, and a great many yet unknown—various breeds of Mongoloids, Mongols, Tartars, and the so-called Aryans of the philologists. Well, here are the Persian, the Greek, the Yunchi, the Hun, the Chin, the Scythian, and many more, melted and fused, the Jews, Parsees, Arabs, Mongols, down to the descendants of the Vikings and the lords of the German forests, yet undigested—an ocean of humanity, composed of these race-waves seething, boiling, struggling, constantly changing form, rising to the surface, and spreading, and swallowing little ones, again subsiding—this is the history of India.

In the midst of this madness of nature, one of the contending factions discovered a method and, through the force of its superior culture, succeeded in bringing the largest number of Indian humanity under its sway. The superior race styled themselves the Aryas or nobles, and their method was the Varnashramachara—the so-called caste. Of course, the men of the Aryan race reserved for themselves, consciously or unconsciously, a good many privileges; yet the institution of caste has always been very flexible, sometimes too flexible, to ensure a healthy uprise of the races very low in the scale of culture. It put, theoretically at least, the whole of India under the guidance—not of wealth, nor of the sword—but of intellect—intellect chastened and controlled by spirituality. The leading caste in India is the highest of the Aryans—Brahmins.

Though apparently different from the social methods of other nations, on close inspection, the Aryan method of caste will not be found so very different except on two points:

The first is, in every other country the highest honour belongs to the Kshatriya—the man of the sword. The Pope of Rome will be glad to trace his descent to some robber baron on the banks of the Rhine. In India, the highest honour belongs to the man of peace—the Sharman, the Brahmin, the man of God.

The greatest Indian king would be gratified to trace his descent to some ancient sage who lived in the forest, probably a recluse, possessing nothing, and all his life trying to solve the problems of this life and the life hereafter.

The second point is the difference of *unit*. The law of caste in every other country takes the individual man or woman as the sufficient unit. Here, the unit is all the members of a caste community. Wealth, power, intellect, or beauty suffices for the individual to leave the status of birth and scramble up to anywhere he can.

Here, the unit is all the members of a caste community.

Here, too, one has every chance of rising from a low caste to a higher or the highest; only, in this birth-land of altruism, one is compelled to take his whole caste along with him.

In India, you cannot, on account of your wealth, power, or any other merit, leave your fellows behind and make common cause with your superiors; you cannot deprive those who helped you in your acquiring the excellence of any benefit therefrom and give them in return only contempt. If you want to rise to a higher caste in India, you have to elevate all your caste first, and then there is nothing in your onward path to hold you back.

This is the Indian method of fusion, and this has been going on from time immemorial. For in India, more than elsewhere, such words as Aryan and Dravidians are only of philological import, the so-called craniological differentiation finding no solid ground to work upon. Even so are the names Brahmin, Kshatriya etc. They simply represent the status of a community in itself continuously fluctuating, even when it has reached the summit and all further endeavours are towards fixity of the type by non-marriage, by being forced to admit fresh groups, from lower castes or foreign lands, within its pale.

Whatever caste has the power of the sword becomes Kshatriya; whatever learning, Brahmin; whatever wealth, Vaishya.

The groups that have already reached the coveted goal, indeed, try to keep themselves aloof from the newcomers by making sub-divisions in the same caste, but the fact remains that they coalesce in the long run. This is going on before our own eyes, all over India.

Naturally, a group having raised itself would try to preserve the privileges to itself. Hence, whenever it was possible to get the help of a king, the higher castes, especially the Brahmins, have tried to put down similar aspirations in lower castes, by the sword if practicable. But the question is: Did they succeed? Look closely into your Puranas and Upa-puranas, look especially into the local Khandas of the big Puranas, look around and see what is happening before your eyes, and you will find the answer.

We are, in spite of our various castes, and in spite of the modern custom of marriage restricted within the sub-divisions of a caste (though this is not universal), a mixed race in every sense of the word. Whatever may be the import of the philological terms 'Aryan' and 'Tamilian,' even taking for granted that both these grand sub-divisions of Indian humanity came from outside the Western frontier, the dividing line had been, from the most ancient times, one of language and not of blood. Not one of the epithets expressive of contempt for the ugly physical features of the Dasyus of the Vedas would apply to the great Tamilian race; in fact if there be a toss for good looks between the Aryans and Tamilians, no sensible man would dare prognosticate the result.

The super-arrogated excellence of birth of any caste in India is only pure myth, and in no part of India has it, we are sorry to say, found such congenial soil, owing to linguistic differences, as in the South.

We purposely refrain from going into the details of the social tyranny in the South, just as we have stopped ourselves from scrutinising the genesis of the various modern Brahmins and other castes. Sufficient for us to note the extreme tension of feeling that is evident between the Brahmins and non-Brahmins of the Madras Presidency.

We believe in Indian caste as one of the greatest social institutions that the Lord gave to man. We also believe that though the unavoidable defects, foreign persecutions, and, above all, the monumental ignorance and pride of many Brahmins who do not deserve the name, have thwarted, in many ways, the legitimate fructification of this most glorious Indian institution, it has already worked wonders for the land of Bharata and is destined to lead Indian humanity to its goal.

We earnestly entreat the Brahmins of the South not to forget the ideal of India—the production of a universe of Brahmins, pure as purity, good as God Himself: this was at the beginning, says the Mahabharata, and so will it be in the end.

Then anyone who claims to be a Brahmin should prove his pretension, first by manifesting that spirituality, and next by raising others to the same status. On the face of it, it seems that most of them are only nursing a false pride of birth; and any schemer, native or foreign, who can pander to this vanity and inherent laziness by fulsome sophistry, appears to satisfy most.

Beware, Brahmins, this is the sign of death! Arise and show your manhood, your Brahminhood, by raising the non-Brahmins around you—not in the spirit of a master—not with the rotten canker of egotism crawling with superstitions and charlatanry of East and West—but in the spirit of a servant. For verily he who knows how to serve knows how to rule.

The non-Brahmins also have been spending their energy in kindling the fire of caste hatred—vain and useless to solve the problem—to which every non-Hindu is only too glad to thrown on a load of fuel.

Not a step forward can be made by these inter-caste quarrels, not one difficulty removed; only the beneficent onward march of events would be thrown back, possibly for centuries, if the fire bursts out into flames.

It would be a repetition of Buddhistic political blunders.

A gentle yet clear brushing off of the cobwebs of the so-called Aryan theory and all its vicious corollaries is therefore absolutely necessary, especially for the South, and a proper self-respect created by a knowledge of the past grandeur of one of the great ancestors of the Aryan race—the great Tamilians.

We stick, in spite of Western theories, to that definition of the word 'Arya' which we find in our sacred books, and which includes only the multitude we now call Hindus. This Aryan race, itself a mixture of two great races, Sanskrit-speaking and Tamil-speaking, applies to all Hindus alike. That the Shudras have in some Smritis been excluded from this epithet meaning nothing, for the Shudra were and still are only the waiting Aryas—Aryas in novitiate.

Vol. 4, Writings: Prose and Poems, Aryans and Tamilians, pp. 296–301

Nowadays, everybody blames those who constant look back to their past. It is said that so much looking back to the past is the cause of all India's woes. To me, on the contrary, the opposite is true. So long as they forgot the past, the Hindu nation remained in a state of stupor; and as soon as they have begun to look into their past, there is on every side a fresh manifestation of life. It is out of this past that the future has to be moulded; the past will become the future. The more, therefore, the Hindus study the past, the more glorious will be their future, and whoever tries to bring the past to the door of everyone, is a great benefactor to his nation. The degeneration of India came not because the laws and customs of the ancients were bad, but because they were not allowed to be carried to their legitimate conclusion.

Vol. 4, Writings: Prose and Poems, Reply to Address of Maharaja of Khetri, pp. 324

In India religion was never shackled. No man was ever challenged in the selection of his Ishta Devati, or his sect, or his preceptor, and religion grew, as it grew nowhere else. On the other hand, a fixed point was necessary to allow this infinite variation to religion, and society was chosen as that point in India. As a result, society became rigid and almost immovable. For liberty is the only condition of growth.

On the other hand, in the West the field of variation was society, and the constant point was religion. Conformity was the watchword, and even now is the watchword of European religion, and each new departure had to gain the least advantage only by wading through a river of blood. The result is a splendid social organisation, with a religion that never rose beyond the grossest materialistic conceptions.

In India, new circumstances at the same time are persistently demanding a new adjustment of social organisations. For the last three-quarters of a century, India has been bubbling over with reform societies and reformers. But, alas, every one of them has proved a failure. They did not know the secret. They had not learnt the great lesson to be learnt. In their haste, they laid all the evils in our society at the door of religion; and like the man in the story, wanting to kill the mosquito that sat on a friend's forehead, they were trying to deal such heavy blows as would have killed man and mosquito together. But in this case, fortunately, they only dashed themselves against immovable rocks and were crushed out of existence in the shock of recoil. Glory unto those noble and unselfish souls who have struggled and failed in their misdirected attempts. Those galvanic shocks of reformatory zeal were necessary to rouse the sleeping leviathan. But they were entirely destructive, and not constructive, and as such they were mortal and therefore died.

Let us bless them and profit by their experience. They had not learnt the lesson that all is a growth from inside out, that all evolution is only a manifestation of a preceding involution. They did not know that the seed can only assimilate the surrounding elements, but grows a tree in its own nature. Until all the Hindu race becomes extinct, and a new race takes possession of the land, such a thing can never be—try East or West. India can never be Europe until she dies.

Shall India die? Then from the world all spirituality will be extinct, all moral perfection will be extinct, all sweet-souled sympathy for religion will be extinct, all idealism will be extinct; and in its place will reign the duality of lust and luxury as the male and female deities; with money as its priest; fraud, force and competition its ceremonies; and the human soul its sacrifice. Such a thing can never be. The power of suffering is infinitely greater than the power of doing; the power of love is infinitely greater than the power of hatred. Those that think that the present revival of Hinduism is only a manifestation of patriotic impulse are deluded.

Is it not curious that, whilst under the terrific onset of modern scientific research, all the old forts of Western dogmatic religions are crumbling into dust; whilst the sledge-hammer blows of modern science are pulverising the porcelain mass of systems whose foundation is either in faith or in belief or in the majority of votes of church synods; whilst Western theology is at its wit's end to accommodate itself to the ever-rising tide of aggressive modern thought; whilst in all other sacred books the texts have been stretched to their utmost tension under the ever-increasing pressure of modern thought, and the majority of them are broken and have been stored away in lumber rooms; whilst the vast majority of thoughtful Western humanity have broken asunder all their ties with the church and are drifting about in a sea of unrest, the religions which have drunk the water of life at that fountain of light, the Vedas—Hinduism and Buddhism—alone are reviving?

The restless Western atheist or agnostic finds in the Gita or the *Dhammapada* the only place where his soul can anchor.

The tables have been turned, and the Hindu, who saw through tears of despair his ancient homestead covered with incendiary fire, ignited by unfriendly hands, now sees, when the searchlight of modern thought has dispersed the smoke, that his home is the one that is standing in all its strength, and all the rest have either vanished or are building their houses anew after the Hindu plan. He has wiped away his tears, and has found that the axe that tried to cut down to the roots [...] has proved the merciful knife of the surgeon.

He has found that he has neither to torture texts nor commit any other form of intellectual dishonesty to save his religion.

He has not therefore to give up anything, nor go about seeking for anything anywhere, but it will be enough for him if he can utilise only a little from the infinite store he has inherited and apply it to his needs. And that he has begun to do and will do more and more. Is this not the real cause of this revival?

Let us wipe off first that mark which nature always puts on the forehead of a slave—the stain of jealousy. Be jealous of none. Be ready to lend a hand to every worker of good. Send a good thought for every being in the three worlds.

First, let us be Gods, and then help others to be Gods. 'Be and make.' Let this be our motto. Say not man is a sinner. Tell him that he is a God. Even if there were a devil, it would be our duty to remember God always, and not the devil. If the room is dark, the constant feeling and repeating of darkness will not take it away, but bring in the light. Let us know that all that is negative, all that is destructive, all that is mere criticism, is bound to pass away; it is the positive, the affirmative, the constructive that is immortal, that will remain forever.

Manifest the divinity within you, and everything will be harmoniously arranged around it.

India will be raised, not with the power of the flesh, but the power of the spirit; not with the flag of destruction, but with the flag of peace and love, the garb of the Sannyasin; not by the power of wealth, but by the power of the begging bowl. Say not that you are weak. The spirit is omnipotent.

Vol. 4, Writings: Prose and Poems, Reply to the Madras Address, pp. 346–352

Jealousy is the bane of our national character, natural to slaves. Even the Lord with all His power could do nothing on account of this jealousy.

Vol. 4, Writings: Prose and Poems, What We Believe In, pp. 360–361

The one thing that is at the root of all evils in India is the condition of the poor. The poor in the West are devils; compared to them ours are angels, and it is therefore so much the easier to raise our poor. The only service to be done for our lower classes is to give them education, *to develop their lost individuality.* That is the great task between our people and princes. Up to now nothing has been done in that direction. Priest-power and foreign conquest have trodden them down for centuries, and at last the poor of India have forgotten that they are human beings. They are to be given ideas; their eyes are to be opened to what is going on in the world around them; and then they will work out their own salvation.

Vol. 4, Writings: Prose and Poems, Our Duty to the Masses, p. 362

To my mind, the one great cause of the downfall and the degeneration of India was the building of a wall of custom—whose foundation was hatred of others—round the nation, and the real aim of which in ancient times was to prevent the Hindus from coming into contact with the surrounding Buddhistic nations.

Whatever cloak ancient or modern sophistry may try to throw over it, the inevitable result—the vindication of the moral law, that none can hate others without degenerating himself—is that the race that was foremost amongst the ancient races is now a byword, and a scorn among nations. We are object-lessons of the violation of that law which our ancestors were the first to discover and disseminate.

Give and take is the law; and if India wants to raise herself once more, it is absolutely necessary that she brings out her treasures and throws them broadcast among the nations of the earth, and in return be ready to receive what others have to give her. Expansion is life, contraction is death. Love is life, and hatred is death. We commenced to die the day we began to hate other races; and nothing can prevent our death unless we come back to expansion, which is life.

We must mix, therefore, with all the races of the earth. And every Hindu that goes out to travel in foreign parts renders more benefit to his country than hundreds of men who are bundles of superstitions and selfishness, and whose one aim in life seems to be like that of the dog in the manger. The wonderful structures of national life which the Western nations have raised, are supported by the strong pillars of character, and until we can produce numbers of such, it is useless to fret and fume against this or that power.

Do any deserve liberty who are not ready to give it to others? Let us calmly and in a manly fashion go to work, instead of dissipating our energy in unnecessary frettings and fumings. I, for one, thoroughly believe that no power in the universe can withhold from anyone anything he really deserves. The past was great no doubt, but I sincerely believe that the future will be more glorious still.

Vol. 4, Writings: Prose and Poems,
Reply to the Calcutta Address, pp. 365–366

We talk foolishly against material civilisation. The grapes are sour. Even taking all that foolishness for granted, in all India there are, say, a hundred thousand really spiritual men and women. Now, for the spiritualisation of these, must three hundred millions be sunk in savagery and starvation? Why should any starve? How was it possible for the Hindus to have been conquered by the Mohammedans? It was due to the Hindus' ignorance of material civilisation. Even the Mohammedans taught them to wear tailor-made clothes. Would the Hindus have learnt from the Mohammedans how to eat in a cleanly way without mixing their food with the dust of the streets! Material civilisation, nay, even luxury, is necessary to create r. Bread! Bread! I do not believe in a God, who cannot give me bread here, giving me eternal bliss in heaven! Pooh! India is to be raised, the poor are to be fed, education is to be spread, and the evil of priestcraft is to be removed. No priestcraft, no social tyranny! More bread, more opportunity for everybody! Our young fools organise meetings to get more power from the English. They only laugh. None deserves liberty who is not ready to give liberty. Suppose the English give over to you all the power. Why, the powers that be then, will hold the people down, and let them not have it. Slaves want power to make slaves. Now this is to be brought about slowly, and by only insisting on our religion and giving liberty to society. Root up priestcraft from the old religion, and you get the best religion in the world. Do you understand me? Can you make a European society with India's religion? I believe it is possible, and must be.

Vol. 4, Writings: Prose and Poems, To My Brave Boys, p. 368

I fully agree with the educated classes in India that a thorough overhauling of society is necessary. But how to do it? The destructive plans of reformers have failed. My plan is this. We have not done *badly* in the past, certainly not. Our society is not *bad* but good, only I want it to be better still. Not from error to truth, nor from bad to good, but from truth to higher truth, from good to better, best. I tell my countrymen that so far they have done well—now is the time to do better.

Now, take the case of caste—in Sanskrit, Jati i.e. species. Now, this is the first idea of creation. Variation (Vichitrata), that is to say Jati, means creation. 'I am One, I become many' (various Vedas). Unity is before creation, diversity is creation. Now if this diversity stops, creation will be destroyed. So long as any species is vigorous and active, it must throw out varieties. When it ceases or is stopped from breeding varieties, it dies. Now the original idea of Jati was this freedom of the individual to express his nature, his Prakriti, his Jati, his caste; and so it remained for thousands of years. Not even in the latest books is inter-dining prohibited, not in any of the older books is inter-marriage forbidden. Then what was the cause of India's downfall?—the giving up of this idea of caste. As Gita says, with the extinction of caste the world will be destroyed. Now does it seem true that with the stoppage of these variations the world will be destroyed? It really has prevented the free action of Jati, i.e. caste or variation. Any crystallised custom or privilege or hereditary class in any shape really prevents case (Jati) from having its full sway; and whenever any nation ceases to produce this immense variety, it must die. Therefore what I have to tell you, my countrymen is this, that India fell because you prevented and abolished caste. Every frozen aristocracy or privileged class is a blow to caste and is not-caste. Let Jati have its sway; break down every barrier in the way of caste, and we shall rise. Now look at Europe when it succeeded in giving free scope to caste and took away most of the barriers that stood in the way of individuals, each developing his caste—Europe rose. In America there is the best scope for caste (real Jati) to develop, and so the people are great. Every Hindu knows that astrologers try to fix the caste of every boy or girl as soon as he or she is born. That is the real caste—the individuality, and Jyotisha (astrology) recognises that. And we can only rise by giving it full sway again. This variety does not mean inequality, nor any special privilege.

This is my method—to show the Hindus that they have to give up nothing, but only to move on in the line laid down by the sages and shake off their inertia, the result of centuries of servitude. Of course, we had to stop advancing during the Mohammedan tyranny, for then it was not a question of progress but of life and death. Now that that pressure has gone, we must move forward, not on the lines of destruction directed by renegades and missionaries, but along our own line, our own road. We had to stop building during centuries of oppression. Now finish the building and everything will look beautiful in its own place. This is all my plan. I am thoroughly convinced of this. Each nation has a main current in life. In India it is religion. Make it strong and the waters on either side must move along with it. This is one phase of my line of thought. In time, I hope to bring them all out, but at present I find I have a mission in this country (USA) also. Moreover, I expect help in this country and from here alone. But up to date I could not do anything except spreading my ideas. Now I want that a similar attempt be made in India.

Vol. 4, Writings: Prose and Poems, A Plan of Work for India, pp. 371–373

Do you not see—taking up this plea of Sattva, the country has been slowly and slowly drowned in the ocean of Tamas or dark ignorance? Where the most dull want to hide their stupidity by covering it with a false desire for the highest knowledge which is beyond all activities, either physical or mental; where one, born and bred in lifelong laziness, wants to throw the veil of renunciation over his own unfitness for work; where the most diabolical try to make their cruelty appear, under the cloak of austerity, as a part of religion; where no one has an eye upon his own incapacity, but everyone is ready to lay the whole blame on others; where knowledge consists only in getting some books by heart, genius consists in chewing the cud of others' thoughts, and the highest glory consists in taking the name of ancestors: do we require any other proof to show that that country is being day by day drowned in utter Tamas?

Therefore Sattva or absolute purity is now far away from us. Those amongst us who are not yet fit, but who hope to be fit, to reach to that absolutely pure Paramahamsa state—for them the acquirement of Rajas or intense activity is what is most beneficial now. Unless a man passes through Rajas, can he ever attain to that perfect Sattvika state? How can one expect Yoga or union with God, unless one has previously finished with his thirst for Bhoga or enjoyment? How can renunciation come where there is no Vairagya or dispassion for all the charms of enjoyment?

On the other hand, the quality of Rajas is apt to die down as soon as it comes up, like a fire of palm leaves. The presence of Sattva and the Nitya or Eternal Reality is almost in a state of juxtaposition—Sattva is nearly Nitya. Whereas the nation in which the quality of Rajas predominates is not so long-lived, but a nation with a preponderance of Sattva is, as it were, immortal. History is a witness to this fact.

In India, the quality of Rajas is almost absent; the same is the case with Sattva in the West. It is certain, therefore, that the real life of the Western world depends upon the influx, from India, of the current of Sattva or transcendentalism; and it is also certain that unless we overpower and submerge our Tamas by the opposite tide of Rajas, we shall never gain any worldly good or welfare in this life; and it is also equally certain that we shall meet many formidable obstacles in the path of realisation of those noble aspirations and ideals connected with our after-life.

Vol. 4, Translations of Writings: Prose and Poems, The Problem of Modern India and its Solution, pp. 405–406

It is an undoubted fact that if there had not been the advent of Kabir, Nanak, and Chaitanya in the Mohammedan period, and the establishment of the Brahmo Samaj and the Arya Samaj in our own day, then, by this time the Mohammedans and the Christians would have far outnumbered the Hindus of the present day in India.

As during the supremacy of the Brahmin and the Kshatriya there is a centralisation of learning and advancement of civilisation, so the result of the supremacy of the Vaishya is the accumulation of wealth [...] The Vaishya is always in fear lest the Brahmin swindles him out of this, his only possession, and lest the Kshatriya usurps it by virtue of his superior strength of arms. For self-preservation, the Vaishyas as a body are, therefore, of one mind. The Vaishya commands the money; the exorbitant interest that he can exact for its use by others, as with a lash in his hand, is his powerful weapon which strikes terror in the heart of all. By the power of his money, he is always busy curbing the royal power. That the royal power may not anyhow stand in the way of the inflow of his riches, the merchant is ever watchful. But, for all that, he has never the least wish that the power should pass on from the kingly to the Shudra class.

To what country does not the merchant go? Though himself ignorant, he carries on his trade and transplants the learning, wisdom, art, and science of one country to another. The wisdom, civilisation, and arts that accumulated in the heart of the social body during the Brahmin and the Kshatriya supremacies are being diffused in all directions by the arteries of commerce to the different marketplaces of the Vaishya. But for the rising of this Vaishya power, who would have carried today the culture, learning, acquirements, and articles of food and luxury of one end of the world to the other?

And where are they through whose physical labour only are possible the influence of the Brahmin, the prowess of the Kshatriya, and the fortune of the Vaishya? What is their history, who, being the real body of society, are designated at all times in all countries as 'base-born?'—for whom kind India prescribed the mild punishments, 'Cut out his tongue, chop off his flesh,' and others of like nature, for such a grave offence as any attempt on their part to gain a share of the knowledge and wisdom monopolised by her higher classes—those 'moving corpses' of India and the 'beasts of burden' of other countries—the Shudras, what is their lot in life? What shall I say of India? Let alone her Shudra class, her Brahmins to whom belonged the acquisition of scriptural knowledge are now the foreign professors, her Kshatriyas the ruling Englishmen, and Vaishyas too, the English in whose home and marrow is the instinct of trade, so that only the Shudra-ness, the beast of burdenness is now left with the Indians themselves.

A cloud of impenetrable darkness has at present equally enveloped us all. Now there is neither firmness of purpose nor boldness of enterprise, neither courage of heart nor strength of mind, neither aversion to maltreatment by others nor dislike for slavery, neither love in the heart nor hope nor manliness; but what we have in India are only deep-rooted envy and strong antipathy against one another, morbid desire to ruin by hook or by crook the weak, and to lick dog-like the feet of the strong. Now the highest satisfaction consists in the display of wealth and power, devotion in self-gratification, wisdom in the accumulation of transitory objects, Yoga in hideous diabolical practices, work in the slavery of others, civilisation in base imitation of foreign nations, eloquence in the use of abusive language, the merit of literature in extravagant flatteries of the rich or in the diffusion of ghastly obscenities! What to speak separately of the distinct Shudra class of such a land, where the whole population has come down to the level of the Shudra?

But a time will come when the Shudras of every country, with their inborn Shudra nature and habits—not becoming in essence Vaishya or Kshatriya, but remaining as Shudra—will gain absolute supremacy in every society. The first glow of the dawn of this new power has already begun to break slowly upon the Western world, and the thoughtful are at their wits' end to reflect upon the final issue of this fresh phenomenon. Socialism, Anarchism, Nihilism, and other like sects are the vanguard of the social revolution that is to follow. As the result of grinding pressure and tyranny, from time out of mind, the Shudras, as a rule, are either meanly servile, licking dog-like the feet of the higher class, or otherwise are as inhuman as brute beasts. Again, at all times their hopes and aspirations are baffled; hence a firmness of purpose and perseverance in action they have none.

In spite of the spread of education in the West, there is a great hindrance in the way of the rising of the Shudra class, and that is the recognition of caste as determined by the inherence of more or less good or bad qualities. By this very qualitative caste system which obtained in India in ancient days, the Shudra class was kept down, bound hand and foot. In the first place, scarcely any opportunity was given to the Shudra for the accumulation of wealth or the earning of proper knowledge and education; to add to this disadvantage, if ever a man of extraordinary parts and genius were born of the Shudra class, the influential higher sections of the society forthwith showered titular honours on him and lifted him up to their own circle. His wealth and the power of his wisdom were employed for the benefit of an alien caste—and his own caste-people reaped no benefits of his attainments; and not only so, the good-for-nothing people, the scum and refuse of the higher castes, were cast off and thrown into the Shudra class to swell their number. Vasishtha, Narada, Satyakama Jabala, Vyasa, Kripa, Drona, Karna, and others of questionable parentage were raised to the position of a Brahmin or a Kshatriya, in virtue of their superior learning or valour; but it remains to be seen how the prostitute, maidservant, fisherman, or the charioteer class was benefited by these upliftings. Again, on the other hand, the fallen from the Brahmin, the Kshatriya, or the Vaishya class were always brought down to fill the ranks of the Shudras.

In modern India, no one born of Shudra parents, be he a millionaire or a great Pandit, has ever the right to leave his own society, with the result that the power of his wealth, intellect, or wisdom, remaining confined within his own caste limits, is being employed for the betterment of his own community. This hereditary caste system of India, being thus unable to overstep its own bounds, is slowly but surely conducing to the advancement of the people moving within the same circle. The improvement of the lower classes of India will go on, in this way, so long as India will be under a government dealing with its subjects irrespective of their caste and position.

Whether the leadership of society be in the hands of those who monopolise learning or wield the power of riches or arms, the source of its power is always the subject masses. By so much as the class in power severs itself from this source, by so much is it sure to become weak. But such is the strange irony of fate, such is the queer working of Maya, that they from whom this power is directly or indirectly drawn, by fair means or foul—by deceit, stratagem, force, or by voluntary gift—they soon cease to be taken into account by the leading class.

On one side, new India is saying, 'If we only adopt Western ideas, Western language, Western food, Western dress, and Western manners, we shall be as strong and powerful as the Western nations;' on the other, old India is saying, 'Fools! By imitation, others' ideas never become one's own; nothing, unless earned, is your own. Does the ass in the lion's skin become the lion?

On one side, new India is saying, 'What the Western nations do is surely good, otherwise how did they become so great?' On the other side, old India is saying, 'The flash of lightning is intensely bright, but only for a moment; look out, boys, it is dazzling your eyes. Beware!'

Have we not then to learn anything from the West? Must we not needs try and exert ourselves for better things? Are we perfect? Is our society entirely spotless, without any flaw? There are many things to learn, we must struggle for new and higher things till we die—struggle is the end of human life. Shri Ramakrishna used to say, 'As long as I live, so long do I learn.' That man or that society which has nothing to learn is already in the jaws of death. Yes, learn we must many things from the West; but there are fears as well.

India, this is your terrible danger. The spell of imitating the West is getting such a strong hold upon you that what is good or what is bad is no longer decided by reason, judgment, discrimination or reference to the Shastras. Whatever ideas, whatever manners the white men praise or like are good; whatever things they dislike or censure are bad. Alas! What can be a more tangible proof of foolishness than this?

The Western ladies move freely everywhere, therefore that is good; they choose for themselves their husbands, therefore that is the highest step of advancement; the Westerners disapprove of our dress, decorations, food, and ways of living, therefore they must be very bad; the Westerners condemn image-worship as sinful, surely then, image-worship is the greatest sin, there is no doubt of it!

The Westerners say that worshipping a single Deity is fruitful of the highest spiritual good, therefore let us throw our gods and goddesses into the river Ganga! The Westerners hold caste distinctions to be obnoxious, therefore let all the different castes be jumbled into one! The Westerners say that child-marriage is the root of all evils, therefore that is also very bad, of a certainty it is!

We are not discussing here whether these customs deserve continuance or rejection; but if the mere disapproval of the Westerners be the measure of the abominableness of our manners and customs, then it is our duty to raise our emphatic protest against it.

The present writer has, to some extent, personal experience of Western society. His conviction resulting from such experience has been that there is such a wide divergence between the Western society and the Indian as regards the primary course and goal of each, that any sect in India framed after the Western model will miss the aim. We have not the least sympathy with those who, never having lived in Western society and, therefore, utterly ignorant of the rules and prohibitions regarding the association of men and women that obtain there, and which act as safeguards to preserve the purity of the Western women, allow a free rein to the unrestricted intermingling of men and women in our society.

India! With this mere echoing of others, with this case imitation of others, with this dependence on others, this slavish weakness, this vile detestable cruelty—wouldst thou, with these provisions only, scale the highest pinnacle of civilisation and greatness? Wouldst thou attain, by means of they disgraceful cowardice, that freedom deserved only by the brave and the heroic?

Vol. 4, Translations of Writings: Prose and Poems, Modern India, pp. 463–479

We have been slaves forever, i.e. it has never been given to the masses of India to express the inner light which is their inheritance.

The Indian people have not yet even the least faith in themselves, what to say of self-reliance. The faith in one's own Self, which is the basis of Vedanta, has not yet been even slightly carried into practice. It is for this reason that the Western method—i.e. first of all, discussion about the wished-for end, then the carrying it out by the combination of all the forces—is of no avail even now in this country; it is for this reason that we appear so greatly conservative under foreign rule. If this be true, then it is a vain attempt to do any great work by means of public discussion. 'There is no chance of a headache where there is no head'—where is the public? Besides, we are so devoid of strength that our whole energy is exhausted if we undertake to do anything, none is left for work. It is for this reason, I suppose, we observe in Bengal almost always—'Much cry but little wool.' Secondly, as I have written before, I do not expect anything from the rich people of India. It is best to work among the youth, in whom lies our hope—patiently, steadily, and without noise.

A nation is advanced in proportion as education and intelligence spread among the masses. The chief cause of India's ruin has been the monopolising of the whole education and intelligence of the land, by dint of pride and royal authority, among a handful of men. If we are to rise again, we shall have to do it in the same way, i.e. by spreading education among the masses. A great fuss has been made for half a century about social reform. Travelling through various places of India these last ten years, I observed the country full of social reform associations.

But I did not find one association for them by sucking whose blood the people known as 'gentlemen" have become and continue to be gentlemen? How many sepoys were brought by the Mussulmans? How many Englishmen are there? Where, except in India, can be had millions of men who will cut the throats of their own fathers and brothers for six rupees? Sixty millions of Mussulmans in seven hundred years of Mohammedan rule, and two millions of Christians in one hundred years of Christian rule—what makes it so? Why has originality entirely forsaken the country?

Education, education, education alone! Travelling through many cities of Europe and observing in them the comforts and education of even the poor people, there was brought to my mind the state of our own poor people, and I used to shed tears. What made the difference? Education was the answer I got. Through education comes faith in one's own Self, and through faith in one's own Self the inherent Brahman is waking up in them, while the Brahman in us is gradually becoming dormant.

The education that our boys receive is very negative. The schoolboy learns nothing, but has everything of his own broken down—want of Shraddha is the result. The Shraddha which is the keystone of the Veda and the Vedanta—the Shraddha which emboldened Nachiketa to face Yama and question him, through which Shraddha this world moves—the annihilation of that Shraddha [...] Therefore are we so near destruction. The remedy now is the spread of education. First of all, Self-knowledge. I do not mean thereby matted hair, staff, Kamandalu, and mountain caves which the word suggests. What do I mean then? Cannot the knowledge, by which is attained even freedom from the bondage of worldly existence, bring ordinary material prosperity? Certainly it can. Freedom, dispassion, renunciation—all these are the very highest ideals, but 'even a little of this Dharma saves one from the great fear (of birth and death).' Dualist, qualified-monist, monist, Shaiva, Vaishnava, Sakta, even the Buddhist and the Jain and others—whatever sects have arisen in India—are all at one in this respect that infinite power is latent in this Jivatman (individualised soul; from the ant to the perfect man there is the same Atman in all, the difference being only in manifestation [...] That power manifests as soon as it gets the opportunity and the right place and time. From the highest god to the meanest grass, the same power is present in all—whether manifested or not. We shall have to call forth that power by going from door to door.

Secondly along with this, education has to be imparted. That is easy to say, but how to reduce it into practice? There are thousands of unselfish, kind-hearted men in our country who have renounced everything. In the same way as they travel about and give religious instructions without any remuneration, so at least half of them can be trained as teachers or bearers of such education as we need most. For that, we want first of all a centre in the capital of each Presidency, from whence to spread slowly throughout the whole of India. Two centres have recently been started in Madras and Calcutta; there is hope of more soon. Then, the greater part of the education to the poor should be given orally; time is not yet ripe for schools. Gradually, in these main centres will be taught agriculture, industry etc. and workshops will be established for the furtherance of arts. To sell the manufactures of those workshops in Europe and America, associations will be started like those already in existence. It will be necessary to start centres for women, exactly like those for men. But you are aware how difficult that is in this country [...] the money required for these works would have to come from the West. And for that reason our religion should be preached in Europe and America.

Vol. 4, Translations of Writings: Prose and Poems, The Education that India Needs, pp. 481–485

Our motherland is a glowing example of the results and consequence of the eternal subjection of the individual to society and forced self-sacrifice by dint of institution and discipline. In this country men are born according to Shastric injunctions, they eat and drink by prescribed rules throughout life, they go through marriage and kindred functions in the same way; in short, they even die according to Shastric injunctions. The hard discipline, with the exception of one great good point, is fraught with evil. The good point is that men can do one or two things well with very little effort, having practised them every day through generations.

But all these things are done by people guided like lifeless machines. There is no mental activity, no unfoldment of the heart, no vibration of life, no flux of hope; there is no strong stimulation of the will, no experience of keen pleasure, nor the contact of intense sorrow; there is no stir of inventive genius, no desire for novelty, no appreciation of new things. Clouds never pass away from this mind; the radiant picture of the morning sun never charms this heart. It never even occurs to this mind if there is any better state than this. Where it does, it cannot convince. In the event of conviction, effort is lacking. And even where there is effort, lack of enthusiasm kills it out.

If living by rule alone ensures excellence, if it be virtue to follow strictly the rules and customs handed down through generations, say then, who is more virtuous than a tree, who is a greater devotee, a holier saint, than a railway train? Who has ever seen a piece of stone transgress a natural law? Who has ever known cattle to commit sin?

What is education? Is it book learning? No. Is it diverse knowledge? Not even that. The training by which the current and expression of will are brought under control and become fruitful is called education. Now consider, is that education as a result of which the will, being continuously choked by force through generations, is well-nigh killed out; is that education under whose sway even the old ideas, let alone the new ones, are disappearing one by one? Is that education which is slowly making man a machine? It is more blessed, in my opinion, even to go wrong, impelled by one's free will and intelligence than to be good as an automaton. Again, can that be called society which is formed by an aggregate of men who are like lumps of clay, like lifeless machines, like heaped up pebbles? How can such society fare well? Were good possible, then instead of being slaves for hundreds of years, we would have been the greatest nation on earth, and this soil of India, instead of being a mine of stupidity, would have been the eternal fountain-head of learning.

The truth is that in this country parents and relatives can ruthlessly sacrifice the best interests of their children and others for their own selfish ends to save themselves by compromise to society; and the teaching of generations rendering the mind callous has made it perfectly easy.

Vol. 4, Translations of Writings: Prose and Poems,
Our Present Social Problems, pp. 488–491

The Hindu mind was ever deductive and never synthetic or inductive. In all our philosophies, we always find hair splitting arguments, taking for granted some general proposition, but the proposition itself may be as childish as possible. Nobody ever asked or searched the truth of these general propositions. Therefore independent thought we have almost none to speak of, and hence the death of those sciences which are the result of observation and generalisation. And why was it thus? From two causes: the tremendous heat of the climate forcing us to love rest and contemplation better than activity, and the Brahmins as priests never undertaking journeys or voyages to distant lands. There were voyagers and people who travelled far; but they were almost always traders, i.e. people from whom priestcraft and their own sole love for gain had taken away all capacity for intellectual development. So their observations, instead of adding to the store of human knowledge, rather degenerated it; for their observations were bad and their accounts exaggerated and tortured into fantastical shapes, until they passed all recognition.

So you see, we must travel, we must go to foreign parts. We must see how the engine of society works in other countries, and keep free and open communication with what is going on in the minds of other nations, if we really want to be a nation again. And over and above all, we must cease to tyrannise.

Vol. 5, Epistles (First Series), II, pp. 4–5

The Hindu must not give up his religion, but must keep religion within its proper limits and give freedom to society to grow. All the reformers in India made the serious mistake of holding religion accountable for all the horrors of priestcraft and degeneration and went forthwith to pull down the indestructible structure, and what was the result? Failure! Beginning from Buddha down to Ram Mohan Roy, everyone made the mistake of holding caste to be a religious institution and tried to pull down religion and caste all together, and failed. But in spite of all the ravings of the priests, caste is simply a crystallised social institution, which after doing its service is now filling the atmosphere of India with its stench, and it can only be removed by giving back to the people their lost social individuality. Every man born here (USA) knows that he is a *man*. Every man born in India knows that he is a slave of society. Now, freedom is the only condition of growth; take that off, the result is degeneration. With the introduction of modern competition, see how caste is disappearing fast! No religion is now necessary to kill it. The Brahmana shopkeeper, shoemaker and wine-distiller are common in Northern India. And why? Because of competition. No man is prohibited from doing anything he pleases for his livelihood under the present Government, and the result is neck and neck competition, and thus thousands are seeking and finding the highest level they were born for, instead of vegetating at the bottom.

Vol. 5, Epistles (First Series), V, pp. 22–23

Act on the educated young men, bring them together, and organise them. Great things can be done by great sacrifices only. No selfishness, no name, no fame, yours or mine, nor my Master's even! Work, work the idea, the plan, my boys, my brave, noble, good souls—to the wheel, to the wheel put your shoulders! Stop not to look back for name, or fame, or any such nonsense. Throw self overboard and work. Remember, 'The grass when made into a rope by being joined together can even chain a mad elephant.' The Lord's blessings on you, all His power be in you all—as I believe it is *already*. 'Wake up, stop not until the goal is reached,' say the Vedas. Up, up, the long night is passing, the day is approaching, the wave has risen, nothing will be able to resist its tidal fury. The spirit, my boys, the spirit; the love, my children, the love; the faith, the belief; and fear not! The greatest sin is fear.

Try to get up a fund, buy some magic lanterns, maps, globes etc. and some chemicals. Get every evening a crowd of the poor and low, even the Pariahs, and lecture to them about religion first, and then teach them through the magic-lantern and other things, astronomy, geography, etc. in the dialect of the people. Train up a band of fiery young men. Put your fire in them and gradually increase the organisation, letting it widen and widen its circle. Do the best you can, do not wait to cross the river when the water has all run down. Printing magazines, papers etc. are good, no doubt, but actual work, my boys even if infinitesimal, is better than eternal scribbling and talking. Call a meeting at Bhattacharya's. Get a little money and buy those things I have just now stated, hire a hut, and buy those things I have just now stated, hire a hut, and go to work. Magazines are *secondary*, but this is primary. You must have a hold on the masses. Do not be afraid of a small beginning, great things come afterwards. Be courageous. Do not try to lead your brethren, but serve them. The brutal mania for leading has sunk many a great ship in the waters of life. Take care especially of that, i.e. be unselfish even unto death, and work.

Vol. 5, Epistles (First Series), X, pp. 34–36

You need not be sorry, my son, on account of the young men becoming Christians. What else can they be under the existing social bondages, especially in Madras? Liberty is the first condition of growth. Your ancestors gave every liberty to the soul, and religion grew. They put the body under every bondage, and society did not grow. The opposite is the case in the West—every liberty to society, none to religion. Now are falling off the shackles from the feet of Eastern society as from those of Western religion.

Each again will have its type; the religious or introspective in India, the scientific or out-seeing in the West. The West wants every bit of spirituality through social improvement. The East wants every bit of social power through spirituality. Thus it was that the modern reformers saw no way to reform but by first crushing out the religion of India. They tried, and they failed. Why? Because few of them ever studied their own religion, and not *one* ever *underwent* the training necessary to understand the *Mother of all religions.* I claim that no destruction of religion is necessary to improve the Hindu society, and that this state of society exists not on account of religion, but because religion has not been applied to society as it should have been. This I am ready to prove from our old books, every word of it. This is what I teach, and this is what we must struggle all our lives to carry out. But it will take time, a long time to study. Have patience and work—Save yourself by yourself.

P.S. The present Hindu society is organised only for spiritual men, and hopelessly crushes out everybody else. Why? Where shall they go who want to enjoy the world a little with its frivolities? Just as our religion takes in all, so should our society. This is to be worked out by first understanding the true principles of our religion and then applying them to society. This is the slow but sure work to be done.

Vol. 5, Epistles (First Series), XVIII, pp. 47–48

Talk of the Westerners? They have given me food, shelter, friendship, protection—even the most orthodox Christians! What do our people do when any of their priests go to India? You do not touch them even, they are MLECHCHHAS! No man, no nation, my son, can hate others and live; India's doom was sealed the very day they invented the world MLECHCHHA and stopped from communion with others. Take care how you foster that idea. It is good to talk glibly about the Vedanta, but how hard to carry out even its least precepts!

Vol. 5, Epistles (First Series), XXI, p. 52

What India wants is a new electric fire to stir up a fresh vigour in the national veins. This was ever, and always will be, slow work. Be content to work and, above all, be true to yourself. Be pure, staunch, and sincere to the very backbone, and everything will be all right!

Let each one of us pray day and night for the downtrodden millions in India who are held fast by poverty, priestcraft, and tyranny—pray day and night for them. I care more to preach religion to them than to the high and the rich.

So long as the millions live in hunger and ignorance, I hold every man a traitor who, having been educated at their expense, pays not the least heed to them.

Vol. 5, Epistles (First Series), XXV, pp. 57–58

You must always remember that every nation must save itself; so must every man; do not look to others for help. !

Vol. 5, Epistles (First Series), XXIX, p. 65

An organisation that will teach the Hindus mutual help and appreciation is absolutely necessary. Five thousand people attended that meeting that was held in Calcutta, and hundreds did the same in other places, to express an appreciation of my work here—well and good! But if you asked them each to give an anna, would they do it? The whole national character is one of childish dependence. They are all ready to enjoy food if it is brought to their mouth, and even some want it pushed down [...] You do not deserve to live if you cannot help yourselves.

I have given up at present my plan for the education of the masses. It will come by degrees. What I now want is a band of fiery missionaries. We must have a *College* in Madras to teach comparative religions, Sanskrit, the different schools of Vedanta, and some European languages; we must have a press, and papers printed in English and in the vernaculars. When this is done, then I shall know that you have accomplished something. Let the nation show that they are ready to *do*. If you cannot do anything of the kind in India, then let me alone. I have a message to give, let me give it to the people who appreciate it and who will work it out!

My name should not be made prominent; it is my ideas that I want to see realised. The disciples of all the prophets have always inextricably mixed up the ideas of the Master with the *person*, and at last killed the ideas for the *person*. The disciples of Shri Ramakrishna must guard against doing the same thing. Work for the *idea*, not the person. The Lord bless you.

Vol. 5, Epistles (First Series), XXX, pp. 67–68

I am so, so, sorry, Sister, that I cannot make myself sweet and accommodating to every black falsehood. But I cannot. I have essayed and essayed. But I cannot. At last I have given it up. The Lord is great. He will not allow me to become a hypocrite. Now let what is in come out. I have not found a way that will please all, and I cannot but be what I am, true to my own self.

I am too old to change now into milk and honey. Allow me to remain as I am.

I have no desire for wealth or name or fame or enjoyments—they are dust unto me. I wanted to help my brethren. I have not the *tact to earn money*, bless the Lord. What reason is there for me to conform to the vagaries of the world around me and not obey the voice of Truth within? The mind is still weak, Sister, it sometimes mechanically clutches at earthly help. But I am not afraid. Fear is the greatest sin my religion teaches.

I have a message to give, I have no time to be sweet to the world, and every attempt at sweetness makes me a hypocrite. I will die a thousand deaths rather than lead a jelly-fish like existence and yield to every requirement of this foolish world, no matter whether it be my own country or a foreign country. You are mistaken, utterly mistaken, if you think I have a work, as Mrs. Bull thinks; I have no *work* under or beyond the sun. I have a message, and I will give it after my own fashion. I will neither Hinduise my message, nor Christianise it, nor make it any 'ise' in the world. I will only my-ise it and that is all.

Come out if you can of this network of foolishness they call this *world*. Then I will call you indeed brave and free. If you cannot, cheer those that dare dash this false God, society, to the ground and trample on its unmitigated hypocrisy; if you cannot cheer them, pray be silent, but do not try to drag them down again into the mire with such false nonsense as *compromise* and becoming nice and sweet.

I hate this world, this dream, this horrible nightmare, with its churches and chicaneries, its books and blackguardism, its fair faces and false hearts, its howling righteousness on the surface and utter hollowness beneath, and above all its sanctified shopkeeping.

Vol. 5, Epistles (First Series), XXXII, pp. 71–73

Meddle not with so-called social reform, for there cannot be any reform without spiritual reform first. Who told you that I want social reform? Not I!

Vol. 5, Epistles (First Series), XXXIII, p. 74

Why should I waste my energies defending Hinduism if the Hindus all go to sleep? What are you three hundred millions of people doing there, especially those that are so proud of their learning etc.? Why do you not take up the fighting and leave me to teach and preach? Here am I struggling day and night in the midst of strangers [...] What help does India send? Did the world ever see a nation with less patriotism than the Indian? [...] If you could send and maintain for a few years a dozen well-educated strong men to preach in Europe and America, you would do immense service to India, both morally and politically. Every man who morally sympathises with India becomes a political friend. Many of the Western people think of you as a nation of half-naked savages, and therefore only fit to be whipped into civilisation. If you three hundred millions become cowed by the missionaries—you cowards—and dare not say a word, what can one man do in a far distant land? Even what I have done, you do not deserve.

Why do you not send your defences to the American magazines? What prevents you? You race of cowards—physical, moral, and spiritual! You animals fit to be treated as you are with two ideas before you—lust and money—you want to prod a Sannyasin to a life of constant fighting and you are afraid of the 'Saheb logs,' even missionaries! And you will do great things, pish! [...] Think that up to date every blackguard of a Hindu that had hitherto come to Western lands had too often criticised his own faith and country in order to get praise or money. You know that I did not come to seek name and fame; it was forced upon me. Why shall I go back to India? Who will help me? [...] You are children, you prattle you do not know what. Where are the men in Madras who will give up the world to preach religion? Worldliness and realisation of God cannot go together. I am the one man who dared defend his country, and I have given them such ideas as they never expected from a Hindu. There are many who are against me, but I will never be a coward like you. There are also thousands in the country who are my friends, and hundreds who would follow me unto death; every year they will increase, and if I live and work with them, my ideals of life and religion will be fulfilled. Do you see?

Vol. 5, Epistles (First Series), XXXIX, pp. 80–81

So long as you shriek at the missionary attempts and jump without being able to do anything, I laugh at you; you are little dollies, that is what you are [...] What can Swami do for old babies!!

I know, my son, I shall have to come and manufacture men out of you. I know that India is only inhabited by women and eunuchs. So do not fret. I will have to get means to work there. I do not put myself in the hands of imbeciles. You need not worry, do what little you can. I have to work alone from top to bottom. 'This Atman (Self) is not to be reached by cowards.' You need not be afraid of me. The Lord is with me, you defend yourselves only and show me you can do that; and I will be satisfied. Don't bother me any more with what any one says about me. I am not waiting to hear any fool's judgment of me. You babies, great results are attained only by great patience, great courage, and great attempts.

The brave alone do great things, not the cowards. Know once and for all, you faithless ones, that I am in the hands of the Lord. So long as I am pure and His servant, not a hair of my head will be touched [...] Do something for the nation, then they will help you, then the nation will be with you. Be brave, be brave! Man dies but once. My disciples must not be cowards. !

Vol. 5, Epistles (First Series), XLIII, pp. 86–87

I am surprised you take so seriously the missionaries' nonsense [...] If the people in India want me to keep strictly to my Hindu diet, please tell them to send me a cook and money enough to keep him. This silly *bossism* without a mite of real help makes me laugh. On the other hand, if the missionaries tell you that I have ever broken the two great vows of the Sannyasin—chastity and poverty—tell them that they are *big* liars. Please write to the missionary Hume asking him categorically to write you what misdemeanour he saw in me, or give you the names of his informants, and whether the information was *first hand or* not; that will settle the question and expose the whole thing [...]

As for me, mind you, I stand at nobody's dictation. I know my mission in life, and no chauvinism about me; I belong as much to India as to the world, no humbug about that. I have helped you all I could. You must now help yourselves. What country has any special claim on me? Am I any nation's slave? Don't talk any more silly nonsense, you faithless atheists.

I have worked hard and sent all the money I got to Calcutta and Madras, and then after doing all this, stand their silly dictation! Are you not ashamed? What do I owe to them? Do I care a fig for their praise or fear their blame? I am a singular man, my son, not even you can understand me yet [...] Do your work; if you cannot, stop; but do not try to 'boss' me with your nonsense. I see a greater Power than man, or God, or devil at my back. I require nobody's help. I have been all my life helping others [...] They cannot raise a few rupees to help the work of the greatest man their country ever produced [...] Ramakrishna Paramahamsa; and they talk nonsense and want to dictate to the man for whom they did nothing and who did everything he could for them! Such is the ungrateful world!

Do you mean to say I am born to live and die one of those caste-ridden, superstitious, merciless, hypocritical, atheistic *cowards* that you find only amongst the educated Hindus? I hate cowardice; I will have nothing to do with cowards or political nonsense. I do not believe in any politics. God and truth are the only politics in the world; everything else is trash.

Vol. 5, Epistles (First Series), LII, pp. 95–96

Several things are necessary. First there should be strict integrity. No that I even hint that any of you would digress from it, but the Hindus have a peculiar slovenliness in business matters, not being sufficiently methodical and strict in keeping accounts etc.

Secondly, entire devotion to the cause, knowing that your SALVATION depends upon making the *Brahmavadin* a success.

Let this paper be your Ishtadevata, and then you will see how success comes.

Remember that perfect purity, disinterestedness, and obedience to the Guru are the secret of all success [...]

Our countrymen must remember that in things of the Spirit we are the teachers, and not foreigners—but in things of the world we ought to learn from them.

Vol. 5, Epistles (First Series), LXIV, pp. 111–112

My child, what I want is muscles of iron and nerves of steel, inside which dwells a mind of the same material as that of which the thunderbolt is made. Strength, manhood, Kshatra-Virya + Brahma-Teja. Our beautiful hopeful boys—they have everything, only if they are not slaughtered by the millions at the altar of this brutality they call marriage. O lord, hear my wails! Madras will then awake when at least one hundred of its very heart's blood, in the form of its educated young men, will stand aside from the world, gird their loins, and be ready to fight the battle of truth, marching on from country to country. One blow struck outside of India is equal to a hundred thousand struck within. Well, all will come if the Lord wills it.

Vol. 5, Epistles (First Series), LXVIII, pp. 117–118

It has been for the good of India that religious preaching in the West has been and will be done. It has ever been my conviction that we shall not be able to rise unless the Western people come to our help. In this country no appreciation of merit can yet be found, no financial strength, and what is most lamentable of all, there is not a bit of practicality.

There are many things to be done, but means are wanting in this country. We have brains, but no hands. We have the doctrine of Vedanta, but we have not the power to reduce it into practice. In our books there is the doctrine of universal equality, but in work we make great distinctions. It was in India that unselfish and disinterested work of the most exalted type was preached; but in practice *we* are awfully cruel, awfully heartless—unable to think of anything besides our own mass-of-flesh bodies.

Yet it is only through the present state of things that it is possible to proceed to work. There is no other way.

I too believe that India will awake again if anyone could love with all his heart the people of the country—bereft of the grace of affluence, of blasted fortune, their discretion totally lost, downtrodden, ever-starved, quarrelsome, and envious. Then only will India awake, when hundreds of large-hearted men and women, giving up all desires of enjoying the luxuries of life, will long and exert themselves to their utmost for the well-being of the millions of their countrymen who are gradually sinking lower and lower in the vortex of destitution and ignorance. I have experienced even in my insignificant life that good motives, sincerity, and infinite love can conquer the world. One single soul possessed of these virtues can destroy the dark designs of millions of hypocrites and brutes.

My going to the West again is yet uncertain; if I go, know that too will be for India. Where is the strength of men in this country? Where is the strength of money? Many men and women of the West are ready to do good to India by serving even the lowest Chandalas, in the Indian way, and through the Indian religion. How many such are there in this country? And financial strength! To meet the expenses or my reception, the people of Calcutta made me deliver a lecture and sold tickets! [...] I do not blame nor censure anybody for this, I only want to show that our well-being is impossible without men and money coming from the West.

Vol. 5, Epistles (First Series), LXXIV, pp. 126–128

I do not propose any levelling of castes. Caste is a very good thing. Caste is the plan we want to follow. What caste really is, not one in a million understands. There is no country in the world without caste. In India, from caste we reach to the point where there is no caste. Caste is based throughout on that principle. The plan in India is to make everybody a Brahmin, the Brahmin being the ideal of humanity. If you read the history of India, you will find that attempts have always been made to raise the lower classes. Many are the classes that have been raised. Many more will follow till the whole will become Brahmin. That is the plan. We have only to raise them without bringing down anybody. And this has mostly to be done by the Brahmins themselves, because it is the duty of every aristocracy to dig its own grave; and the sooner it does so, the better for all. No time should be lost. Indian caste is better than the caste which prevails in Europe or America. I do not say it is absolutely good. Where would you be if there were no caste? Where would be your learning and other things if there were no caste? There would be nothing left for the Europeans to study if caste had never existed? The Mohammedans would have smashed everything to pieces. Where do you find the Indian society standing still? It is always on the move. Sometimes, as in the times of foreign invasions, the movement has been slow, at other times quicker. This is what I say to my countrymen. I do not condemn them. I look into their past. I find that under the circumstances no nation could do more glorious work. I tell them that they have done well. I only ask them to do better.

Caste is continually changing, rituals are continually changing, so are forms. It is the substance, the principle, that does not change. It is in the Vedas that we have to study our religion. With the exception of the Vedas every book must change. The authority of the Vedas is for all time to come; the authority of every one of our other books is for the time being. For instance, one Smriti is powerful for one age, another for another age. Great prophets are always coming and pointing the way to work. Some prophets worked for the lower classes, others like Madhva gave to women the right to study the Vedas. Caste should not go; but should only be readjusted occasionally. Within the old structure is to be found life enough for the building of two hundred thousand new ones. It is sheer nonsense to desire the abolition of caste. The new method is—evolution of the old.

We do stand in need of social reform. At times great men would evolve new ideas of progress, and kings would give them the sanction of law. Thus social improvements had been in the past made in India, and in modern times to effect such progressive reforms, we will have first to build up such an authoritative power. Kings having gone, the power is the people's. We have therefore to wait till the people are educated, till they understand their needs and are ready and able to solve their problems. The tyranny of the minority is the worst tyranny in the world. Therefore, instead of frittering away our energies on ideal reforms, which will never become practical, we had better go to the root of the evil and make a legislative body, that I to say, educate our people, so that they may be able to solve their own problems. Until that is done all these ideal reforms will remain ideals only. The new order of thing is the salvation of the people by the people, and it takes time to make it workable, especially in India, which has always in the past been governed by kings.

(Q: Do you think Hindu society can successfully adopt European social laws?)

No, not wholly. I would say, the combination of the Greek mind represented by the external European energy added to the Hindu spirituality would be an ideal society for India. For instance, it is absolutely necessary for you, instead of frittering away your energy and often talking of idle nonsense, to learn from the Englishman the idea of prompt obedience to leaders, the absence of jealousy, the indomitable perseverance and the undying faith in himself. As soon as he selects a leader for a work, the Englishman sticks to him through thick and thin and obeys him. Here in India, everybody wants to become a leader, and there is nobody to obey. Everyone should learn to obey before he can command. There is no end to our jealousies; and the more important the Hindu, the more jealous he is. Until this absence of jealousy and obedience to leaders are learnt by the Hindu, there will be no power of organisation. We shall have to remain the hopelessly confused mob that we are now, hoping and doing nothing. India has to learn from Europe the conquest of external nature, and Europe has to learn from India the conquest of internal nature. Then there will be neither Hindus nor Europeans—there will be the ideal humanity which has conquered both the natures, the external and the internal. We have developed one phase of humanity, and they another. It is the union of the two that is wanted. The word freedom which is the watchword of our religion really means freedom physically, mentally, and spiritually.

All along, in the history of the Hindu race, there never was any attempt at destruction, only construction. One sect wanted to destroy, and they were thrown out of India. They were the Buddhists. We have had a host of reformers—Shankara, Ramanuja, Madhva, and Chaitanya. These were great reformers, who always were constructive and built according to the circumstances of their time. All the modern reformers take to European destructive reformation, which will never do good to anyone and never did. Only once was a modern reformer mostly constructive, and that one was Raja Ram Mohan Roy. All history of Indian life is the struggle for the realisation of the ideal of the Vedanta through good or bad fortune. Whenever there was any reforming sect or religion which rejected the Vedantic ideal, it was smashed into nothing.

Vol. 5, Interviews, The Abroad and the Problems at Home, pp. 214–217

(Q: What made Your Holiness carry the mission of Hinduism to Western countries?)

I wanted to get experience. My idea as to the keynote of our national downfall is that we do not mix with other nations—that is the one and the sole cause. We never had opportunity to compare notes. We were Kupa-Mandukas (frogs in a well).

(Q: What do you intend doing for the regeneration of India?)

I consider the great national sin is the neglect of the masses, and that is one of the causes of our downfall. No amount of politics would be of any avail until the masses in India are once more well educated, well fed, and well cared for. They pay for our education, they build our temples, but in return they get kicks. They are practically our slaves. If we want to regenerate India, we must work for them.

My faith is in the younger generation, the modern generation, out of them will come my workers. They will work out the whole problem, like lions. I have formulated the idea and have given my life to it. If I do not achieve success, some better one will come after me to work it out, and I shall be content to struggle. The one problem you have is to give to the masses their rights. You have the greatest religion which the world ever saw, and you feed the masses with stuff and nonsense. You have the perennial fountain flowing, and you give them ditch-water.

The great thing is to have faith in oneself, even before faith in God; but the difficulty seems to be that we are losing faith in ourselves day by day. That is my objection against the reformers. The orthodox have more faith and more strength in themselves, in spite of their crudeness; but the reformers simply play into the hands of Europeans and pander to their vanity. Our masses are gods as compared with those of other countries. This is the only country where poverty is not a crime. They are mentally and physically handsome; but we hated and hated them till they have lost faith in themselves. They think they are born slaves. Give them their rights, and let them stand on their rights.

My idea of education is personal contact with the teacher—Gurugriha-Vasa. Without the personal life of a teacher there would be no education. Take your universities. What have they done during the fifty years of their existence? They have not produced one original man. They are merely an examining body.

Vol. 5, Interviews, The Missionary Work of the First Hindu Sannyasin to the West and his Plan of Regeneration of India, p. 220–224

(Q: And what do you consider to be the function of your movement as regards India?)

To find the common bases of Hinduism and awaken the national consciousness to them. At present there are three parties in India included under the term 'Hindu'—the orthodox, the reforming sects of the Mohammedan period, and the reforming sects of the present time. Hindus from North to south are only agreed on one point viz. on not eating beef.

(Q: Not in a common love for the Vedas?)

Certainly not. That is just what we want to reawaken.

(Q: With which of the three parties you name do you identify yourself, Swamiji?)

With all of them. We are orthodox Hindus, said the Swami, but, (he added suddenly with great earnestness and emphasis) we refuse entirely to identify ourselves with 'Don't touchism.' That is not Hinduism; it is in none of our books; it is an unorthodox superstition which has interfered with national efficiency all along the line.

Can you adduce any reason why India should lie in the ebb-tide of the Aryan nations? Is she inferior in intellect? Is she inferior in dexterity? Can you look at her art, at her mathematics, at her philosophy, and answer 'yes?' All that is needed is that she should de-hypnotise herself and wake up from her age-long sleep to take her true rank in the hierarchy of nations.

The national ideals of India are RENUNCIATION and SERVICE. Intensify her in those channels, and the rest will take care of itself.

Vol. 5, Interviews, Reawakening of Hinduism on a National Basis, pp. 226–228

They say there should be no caste. Even those who are in caste say it is not a very perfect institution. But they say, when you find us another and a better one, we will give it up. They say, what will you give us instead. Where is there no caste? In your nation (USA) you are struggling all the time to make a caste. As soon as a man gets a bag of dollars, he says, 'I am one of the 'Four Hundred.' We alone have succeeded in making a permanent caste. Other nations are struggling and do not succeed. We have superstitions and evils enough. Would taking the superstitions and evils from your country mend matters? It is owing to caste that three hundred millions of people can find a piece of bread to eat yet. It is an imperfect institution, no doubt. But if it had not been for caste, you would have had no Sanskrit books to study. This caste made walls, around which all sorts of invasions rolled and surged, but found impossible to break through. That necessity has not gone yet so caste remains. The caste we have now is not that of seven hundred years ago.

Vol. 5, Questions and Answers, I, pp. 307–308

We have had a negative education all along from our boyhood. We have only learnt that we are nobodies. Seldom are we given to understand that great men were ever born in our country. Nothing positive has been taught to us. We do not even know how to use our hands and feet! We master all the facts and figures concerning the ancestors of the English, but we are sadly unmindful about our own. We have learnt only weakness. Being a conquered race, we have brought ourselves to believe that we are weak and have no independence in anything. So, how can it be but that the Shraddha is lost? The idea of true Shraddha must be brought back once more to us, the faith in our own selves must be reawakened, and then only, all the problems which face our country will gradually be solved by ourselves.'

Vol. 5, Conversations and Dialogues (Recorded by Disciples), II, p.332

With [...] education women will solve their own problems. They have all the time been trained in helplessness, servile dependence on others, and so they are good only to weep their eyes out at the slightest approach of a mishap or danger. Along with other things they should acquire the spirit of valour and heroism. In the present day it has become necessary for them also to learn self-defence. See how grand was the Queen of Jhansi!

Vol. 5, Conversations and Dialogues (Recorded by Disciples), IV, p.342

How can the people of a country practise religion who do not get even sufficient food to appease their hunger? How can renunciation come to the people of a country in whose minds the desires for Bhoga (enjoyment) have not been in the least satisfied? For this reason, find out, first of all, the ways and means by which men may get enough to eat and have enough luxuries to enable them to enjoy life a little; and then gradually true Vairagya (dispassion) will come, and they will be fit and ready to realise religion in life.

We are a conquered race, and moreover there is nowhere in the world such a nation of mendicants as we are! The masses who comprise the lowest castes, through ages of constant tyranny of the higher castes and by being treated by them with blows and kicks at every step they took, have totally lost their manliness and become like professional beggars; and those who are removed one stage higher than these, having read a few pages of English, hang about the thresholds of public offices with petitions in their hands.

You go to England, but that is also in the garb of a beggar—praying for education. Some go, and what they do there at the most is, perchance, to applaud the Westerner's religion in some speeches and then come back. What an achievement, indeed! Why, have you nothing to give them? An inestimable treasure you have, which you can give—give them your religion, give them your philosophy! Study the history of the whole world, and you will see that every high ideal you meet with anywhere had its origin in India. From time immemorial India has been the mine of precious ideas to human society; giving birth to high ideas herself, she has freely distributed them broadcast over the whole world. The English are in India today, to gather those higher ideals, to acquire knowledge of the Vedanta, to penetrate into the deep mysteries of that eternal religion which is yours. Give those valuable gems in exchange for what you receive from them. The Lord took me to their country to remove this opprobrium of the beggar that is attributed by them to us. It is not right to go to England for the purpose of begging only. Why should they always give us alms? Does anyone do so forever? It is no the law of nature to be always taking gifts with outstretched hands like beggars. To give and take is the law of nature. Any individual or class or nation that does not obey this law never prospers in life. We also must follow that law. That is why I went to America.

Do you mean to say that I should go about from country to country, expatiating on your failings before the public? Should I not rather hold up before them the characteristic virtues that mark you as a nation? It is always good to tell a man his defects in a direct way and in a friendly spirit to make him convinced of them, so that he may correct himself—but you should trumpet forth his virtues before others. Shri Ramakrishna used to say that if you repeatedly tell a bad man that he is good, he turns in time to be good; similarly a good man becomes bad if he is incessantly called so. There, in the West, I have said enough to the people of their shortcomings. Mind, up to my time, all who went over to the West from our country have sung paeans to them in praise of their virtues and have trumpeted out only our blemishes to their ears. Consequently, it is no wonder that they have learnt to hate us. For this reason I have laid before them your virtues and pointed out to them their vices, just as I am now telling you of your weaknesses and their good points. However full of Tamas you may have become, something of the nature of the ancient Rishis, however little it may be, is undoubtedly in you still—at least the framework of it. But that does not show that one should be in a hurry to take up at once the role of a teacher of religion and go over to the West to preach it.

Vol. 5, Conversations and Dialogues (Recorded by Disciples), VI, pp. 353–357

(Q: What is your idea of educating our boys?)

Guru-griha-vasa—living with the Guru.

(Q: How?)

In the same way as of old. But with this education has to be combined modern Western science. Both these are necessary.

(Q: What is the defect in the present university system?)

It is almost wholly one of defects. Why, it is nothing but a perfect machine for turning out clerks. I would even thank my stars if that were all. But no! See how men are becoming destitute of Shraddha and faith. They assert that the Gita is only an interpolation, and that the Vedas are but rustic songs! They like to master every detail concerning things and nations outside of India, but if you ask them, they do not know even the names of their own forefathers up to the seventh generation, not to speak of the fourteenth!

(Q: But what does that matter? What if they do not know the names of their forefathers?)

A nation that has no history of its own has nothing in this world. Do you believe that one who has such faith and pride as to feel, 'I come of noble descent,' can ever turn out to be bad? How could that be? That faith in himself would curb his actions and feelings, so much so that he would rather die than commit wrong. So a national history keeps a nation well-restrained and does not allow it to sink so low. Oh, I know you will say, 'But we have not such a history!' No, there is not any, according to those who think like you. Neither is there any, according to your big university scholars; and so also think those who, having travelled through the West in one great rush, come back dressed in European style and assert, 'We have nothing, we are barbarians.' Of course, we have no history exactly like that of other countries [...] We have our own history exactly as it ought to have been for us. Will that history be made extinct by shutting your eyes and crying, 'Alas! We have no history!' Those who have eyes to see, find a luminous history there, and on the strength of that they know the nation is still alive. But that history has to be rewritten. It should be restated and suited to the understanding and ways of thinking which our men have acquired in the present age through Western education.

No one can teach anybody. The teacher spoils everything by thinking that he is teaching. Thus Vedanta says that within man is all knowledge—even in a boy it is so—and it requires only an awakening, and that much is the work of a teacher. We have to do only so much for the boys that they may learn to apply their own intellect to the proper use of their hands, legs, ears, eyes, etc. and finally everything will become easy. But the root is religion. Religion is as the rice, and everything else, like the curries. Taking only curries causes indigestion, and so is the case with taking rice alone. Our pedagogues are making parrots of our boys and ruining their brains by cramming a lot of subjects into them. Looking from one standpoint, you should rather be grateful to the Viceroy for his proposal of reforming the university system, which means practically abolishing higher education; the country will, at least, feel some relief by having breathing time. Goodness gracious! What a fuss and fury about graduating, and after a few days all cools down! And after all that, what is it they learn but that what religion and customs we have are all bad, and what the Westerners have are all good! At last, they cannot keep the wolf from the door! What does it matter if this higher education remains or goes? It would be better if the people got a little technical education, so that they might find work and earn their bread, instead of dawdling about and crying for service.

Does higher education mean mere study of material sciences and turning out things of everyday use by machinery? The use of higher education is to find out how to solve the problems of life, and this is what is engaging the profound thought of the modern civilised world, but it was solved in our country thousands of years ago.

All the soul-elevating ideas and the different branches of knowledge that exist in the world are found on proper investigation to have their roots in India.

What we need, you know, is to study, independent of foreign control, different branches of the knowledge that is our own, and with it the English language and Western science; we need technical education and all else that may develop industries so that men, instead of seeking for service, may earn enough to provide for themselves, and save something against a rainy day.

True education is gained by constant living in communion with nature. Knowledge should be acquired in that way, otherwise by educating yourself in the *tol* of a Pandit you will be only a human ape all your life. One should live from his very boyhood with one whose character is like a blazing fire and should have before him a living example of the highest teaching. Mere reading that it is a sin to tell a lie will be of no use. Every boy should be trained to practice absolute Brahmacharya and then, and then only, faith—Shraddha—will come. Otherwise, why will not one who has no Shraddha speak an untruth? In our country, the imparting of knowledge has always been through men of renunciation. Later, the Pandits, by monopolising all knowledge and restricting it to the *tols*, have only brought the country to the brink of ruin. India had all good prospects so long as Tyagis (men of renunciation) used to impart knowledge.

(Q: What do you mean, Maharaj? There are no Sannyasins in other countries, but see how by dint of their knowledge India is laid prostrate at their feet!)

Don't talk nonsense, my dear, hear what I say. India will have to carry others' shoes forever on her head if the charge of imparting knowledge to her sons does not again fall upon the shoulders of Tyagis. Don't you know how an illiterate boy, possessed of renunciation, turned the heads of your great old Pandits? Once at the Dakshineswar Temple the Brahmana who was in charge of the worship of Vishnu broke a leg of the image. Pandits were brought together at a meeting to give their opinions, and they, after consulting old books and manuscripts, declared that the worship of this broken image could not be sanctioned according to the Shastras and a new image would have to be consecrated. There was, consequently, a great stir. Shri Ramakrishna was called at last. He heard and asked, 'Does a wife forsake her husband in case he becomes lame?' What followed? The Pandits were struck dumb, all their Shastric commentaries and erudition could not withstand the force of this simple statement. If what you say was true, why should Shri Ramakrishna come down to this earth, and why should he discourage mere book-learning so much? That new life-force which he brought with him has to be instilled into learning and education, and then the real work will be done.

There are so many things left to be done for our country that thousands like you and me are needed. What will mere talk do? See to what a miserable condition the country is reduced; now do something! We haven't even got a single book well suited for the little boys [...] We must compose some books in Bengali as also in English with short stories from the Ramayana, the Mahabharata, the Upanishads, etc. in very easy and simple language, and these are to be given to our little boys to read.

If I can get some unmarried graduates, I may try to send them over to Japan and make arrangements for their technical education there, so that when they come back, they may turn their knowledge to the best account for India. What a good thing that would be! [...] In my opinion, if all our rich and educated men once go and see Japan, their eyes will be opened [...] There, in Japan, you find a fine assimilation of knowledge, and not its indigestion, as we have here. They have taken everything from the Europeans, but they remain Japanese all the same, and have not turned European; while in our country, the terrible mania of becoming Westernised has seized upon us like a plague [...] They are great as a nation because of their art. Don't you see they are Asians, as we are? And though we have lost almost everything, yet what we still have is wonderful. The very soul of the Asian is interwoven with art. The Asian never uses a thing unless there be art in it. Don't you know that art is, with us, a part of religion? How greatly is a lady admired, among us, who can nicely paint the floors and walls, on auspicious occasions, with the paste of rice powder? How great an artist was Shri Ramakrishna himself!

Alas, to such a state is our country reduced! The people will look upon their own gold as brass, while the brass of the foreigner is gold to them! This is, indeed, the magic wrought by modern education!

Vol. 5, Conversations and Dialogues (Recorded by Disciples), IX, pp. 364–373

As there are Sattva, Rajas and Tamas—one or other of these Gunas more or less—in every man, so the qualities which make a Brahmin, Kshatriya, Vaishya, or Shudra are inherent in every man, more or less. But at times one or other of these qualities predominates in him in varying degrees, and it is manifested accordingly. Take a man in his different pursuits, for example: when he is engaged in serving another for pay, he is in Shudhrahood; when he is busy transacting some piece of business for profit, on his own account, he is a Vaishya; when he fights to right wrongs, then the qualities of a Kshatriya come out in him; and when he meditates on God or passes his time in conversation about Him, then he is a Brahmin. Naturally, it is quite possible for one to be changed from one caste into another. Otherwise, how did Vishvamitra become a Brahmin and Parshurama a Kshatriya?

Vol. 5, Conversations and Dialogues (Recorded by Disciples), X, p. 377

(Q: How is it, Swamiji, that you do not lecture in this country? You have stirred Europe and America with your lectures, but coming back here you have kept silence)

In this country the ground should be prepared first; then if the seed is sown, the plant will come out best. The ground in the West, in Europe and America is very fertile and fit for sowing seeds. There, they have reached the climax of Bhoga (enjoyment). Being satiated with Bhoga to the full, their minds are not getting peace now even in those enjoyments, and they feel as if they wanted something else. In this country you have neither Bhoga nor Yoga (renunciation). When one is satiated with Bhoga, then it is that one will listen to and understand the teachings on Yoga. What good will lectures do in a country like India which has become the birthplace of disease, sorrow, and affliction, and men are emaciated through starvation, and weak in mind?

Now understand what religion means. The first thing required is the worship of the Kurma (tortoise) Incarnation, and the belly-god is this Kurma, as it were. Until you pacify this, no one will welcome your words about religion. India is restless with the thought of how to face this spectre of hunger. The draining of the best resources of the country by the foreigners, the unrestricted exports of merchandise, and, above all, the abominable jealousy natural to slaves are eating into the vitals of India. First of all, you must remove this evil of hunger and starvation, this constant anxiety for bare existence, from those to whom you want to preach religion; otherwise, lectures and such things will be of no benefit.

Vol. 5, Conversations and Dialogues (Recorded by Disciples), XI, pp. 379–380

The country has been flooded with dyspeptic Babajis living on vegetables only. That is no sign of Sattva, but of deep Tamas—the shadow of death. Brightness in the face, undaunted enthusiasm in the heart, and tremendous activity—these result from Sattva; whereas idleness, lethargy, inordinate attachment, and sleep are the signs of Tamas.

Rajas is badly needed just now! More than ninety per cent of those whom you now take to be men with the Sattva quality are only steeped in the deepest Tamas. Enough if you find one-sixteenth of them to be really Sattvika! What we want now is an immense awakening of Rajasika energy, for the whole country is wrapped in the shroud of Tamas. The people of this land must be fed and clothed—must be awakened—must be made more fully active. Otherwise they will become inert, as inert as trees and stones. So I say, eat large quantities of fish and meat, my boy!

All liking for fish and meat disappears when pure Sattva is highly developed, and these are the signs of its manifestation in a soul: sacrifice of everything for others, perfect non-attachment to lust and wealth, want of pride and egotism. The desire for animal food goes when these things are seen in a man. And where such indications are absent, and yet you find men siding with the non-killing party, know it for a certainty that here there is either hypocrisy or a show or religion. When you yourself come to that stage of pure Sattva, give up fish and meat, by all means.

Nowhere have I found the laws of the Rishis current in India, even when during my travels I searched carefully and thoroughly.

The blind and not unoften meaningless customs sanctioned by the people, local prejudices and ideas, and the usages and ceremonials prevalent amongst women, are what really govern society everywhere! How many care to read the Shastras or to lead society according to their ordinances after careful study?

Vol. 5, Conversations and Dialogues (Recorded by Disciples), XV, pp. 402–405

To such of our countrymen who go whimpering before foreigners—'We are very low, we are mean, we are degraded, everything we have is diabolical'—to them we say: 'Yes, that may be the truth, forsooth, because you profess to be truthful and we have no reason to disbelieve you; but why do you include the whole nation in that *We*? Pray, sirs, what sort of good manner is that?

First, we have to understand that there are not any good qualities which are the privileged monopoly of one nation only. Of course, as with individuals, so with nations, there may be a prevalence of certain good qualities, more or less in one nation than in another.

The fall of our country, of which we hear so much spoken, is due to the utter want of this Dharma. If the whole nation practises and follows the path of Moksha, that is well and good, but is that possible? Without enjoyment, renunciation can never come; first enjoy and then you can renounce. Otherwise, if the whole nation, all of a sudden, takes up Sannyasa, it does not gain what it desires, but it loses what it had into the bargain—the bird in the hand is fled, nor is that in the bush caught. When in the heyday of Buddhistic supremacy thousands of Sannyasins lived in every monastery, then it was that the country was just on the verge of its ruin!

Looking from outside, how are we to understand whether you are in a state wherein the Sattva or the Tamas prevails? Whether we are in the state of Sattvika calmness, beyond pleasure and pain, and past all work and activity, or whether we are in the lowest Tamasika state, lifeless, passive, dull as dead matter, and doing no work, because there is no power in us to do it, and are thus silently and by degrees getting rotten and corrupted within—I seriously ask you this question and demand an answer. Ask your own mind, and you shall know what the reality is. But what need to wait for the answer? The tree is known by its fruit. The Sattva prevailing, the man is inactive, he is calm, to be sure; but that inactivity is the outcome of the centralisation of great powers, that calmness is the mother of tremendous energy.

Those things which you see in pusillanimous, effeminate folk who speak in a nasal tone chewing every syllable, whose voice is as thin as of one who has been starving for a week, who are like a tattered wet rag, who never protest or are moved even if kicked by anybody—those are the signs of the lowest Tamas, those are the signs of death, not of Sattva—all corruption and stench. It is because Arjuna was going to fall into the ranks of these men that the Lord is explaining matters to him so elaborately in the Gita. Is that not the fact? Listen to the very first words that came out of the mouth of the Lord—'*Yield not to unmanliness, O Partha! Ill doth it befits thee!*' And then later—'*Therefore do thou arise and acquire fame.*' Coming under the influence of the Jains, Buddhas, and others, we have joined the lines of those Tamasika people.

Why is it that the English throne is so firmly established in India? Because it never touches the religion of the land in any way. The sapient Christian missionaries tried to tamper a little with this point, and the result was the Mutiny of 1857. So long as the English understand this thoroughly and act accordingly, their throne in India will remain unsullied and unshaken. The wise and far-seeing among the English also comprehend this and admit it—read Lord Roberts's *Forty-one Years in India*.

We have many things to learn from other nations [...] But one point to note here is that when we take anything from others, we must mould it after our own way. We shall add to our stock what others have to teach, but we must always be careful to keep intact what is essentially our own.

Vol. 5, Writings: Prose and Poems, The East and the West, Introduction, pp. 446–463

Too early religious advancement of the Hindus and that superfineness in everything which made them cling to higher alternatives, have reduced them to what they are. The Hindus have to learn a little bit of materialism from the West and teach them a little bit of spirituality.

I will tell you something for your guidance in life. Everything that comes from India take as true, until you find cogent reasons for disbelieving it. Everything that comes from Europe take as false, until you find cogent reasons for believing it. Do not be carried away by European fooleries. Think for yourselves. Only one thing is lacking: you are slaves; you follow what Europeans do. That is simply an impotent state of mind. Society may take up materials from any quarter but should grow in its own way.

Vol. 6, Notes of Class Talks and Lectures, Notes Taken Down in Madras 1892–93, pp. 115–123

The northern reaction of ritualism was followed by the fitful glory of the Malava empire. With the destruction of that in a short time, northern India went to sleep, as it were, for a long period, to be rudely awakened by the thundering onrush of Mohammedan cavalry across the passes of Afghanistan. In the south, however, the spiritual upheaval of Shankara and Ramanuja was followed by the usual India sequence of united races and powerful empires. It was the home of refuge of Indian religion and civilisation, when northern India from sea to sea lay bound at the feet of Central Asian conquerors. The Mohammedan tried for centuries to subjugate the south, but can scarcely be said to have got even a strong foothold; and when the strong and united empire of the Moguls was very near completing its conquest, the hills and plateaus of the south poured in their bands of fighting peasant horsemen, determined to die for the religion which Ramdas preached and Tuka sang; and in a short time the gigantic empire of the Moguls was only a name.

The movements in northern India during the Mohammedan period are characterised by their uniform attempt to hold the masses back from joining the religion of the conquerors—which brought in its train social and spiritual equality for all.

The friars of the orders founded by Ramananda, Kabir, Dadu, Chaitanya, or Nanak were all agreed in preaching the equality of man, however differing from each other in philosophy. Their energy was for the most part spent in checking the rapid conquest of Islam among the masses, and they had very little left to give birth to new thoughts and aspirations. Though evidently successful in their purpose of keeping the masses within the fold of the old religion, and tempering the fanaticism of the Mohammedans, they were mere apologists, struggling to obtain permission to live.

One great prophet, however, arose in the north, Govind Singh, the last Guru of the Sikhs, with creative genius; and the result of his spiritual work was followed by the well-known political organisation of the Sikhs. We have seen throughout the history of India, a spiritual upheaval is almost always succeeded by a political unity extending over more or less area of the continent, which in its turn helps to strengthen the spiritual aspiration that brings it into being. But the spiritual aspiration that preceded the rise of the Maratha or the Sikh empire was entirely reactionary. We seek in vain to find in the court of Poona or Lahore even a ray of reflection of the intellectual glory which surrounded the courts of the Mughals, much less the brilliance of Malava or Vidyanagara. It was intellectually the darkest period of Indian history; and both these meteoric empires, representing the upheaval of mass-fanaticism and hating culture with all their hearts, lost all their motive power as soon as they had succeeded in destroying the rule of the hated Mohammedans.

Then there came again a period of confusion. Friends and foes, the Mogul empire and its destroyers, and the till then peaceful foreign traders, French and English, all joined in a melee of fight. For more than half a century there was nothing but war and pillage and destruction. And when the smoke and dust cleared, England was stalking victorious over the rest. There has been half a century of peace and law and order under the sway of Britain. Time alone will prove if it is the order of progress or not.

There have been a few religious movements amongst the Indian people during the British rule, following the same line that was taken up by northern Indian sects during the sway of the empire of Delhi. They are the voices of the dead or the dying—the feeble tones of a terrorised people, pleading for permission to live. They are ever eager to adjust their spiritual or social surroundings according to the tastes of the conquerors—if they are only left the right to live, especially the sects under the English domination, in which social differences with the conquering race are more glaring than the spiritual. The Hindu sects of the century seem to have set one ideal of truth before them—the approval of their English masters. No wonder that these sects have mushroom lives to live. The vast body of the Indian people religiously hold aloof from them, and the only popular recognition they get is the jubilation of the people when they die. But, possibly for some time yet, it cannot be otherwise.

Vol. 6, Writings: Prose and Poems, Historical Evolution of India, pp. 165–167

Social laws and customs likewise, being based on this Karma-kanda, have been changing and will continue to change hereafter. Minor social usages also will be recognised and accepted when they are compatible with the spirit of the true scriptures and the conduct and example of holy sages. But blind allegiance only to usages such as are repugnant to the spirit of the Shastras and the conduct of holy sages has been one of the main causes of the downfall of the Aryan race.

Vol. 6, Writings: Prose and Poems, Hinduism and Shri Ramakrishna, p. 182

A country where millions of people live on flowers of the Mohua plant, and a million or two of Sadhus and a hundred million or so of Brahmins suck the blood out of these poor people, without even the least effort for their amelioration—is that a country or hell? Is that a religion, or the devil's dance? My brother, here is one thing for you to understand fully—I have travelled all over India, and seen this country too—can there be an effect without cause? Can there be punishment without sin?

'Amidst all the scriptures and Purana, know this statement of Vyasa to be true, that doing good to others conduces to merit, and doing harm to them leads to sin.' Isn't it true?

My brother, in view of all this, specially of the poverty and ignorance, I had no sleep. At Cape Comorin sitting in Mother Kumari's temple, sitting on the last bit of Indian rock—I hit upon a plan: We are so many Sannyasins wandering about, and teaching the people metaphysics—it is all madness. Did not our Gurudeva use to say, 'An empty stomach is no good for religion?' That those poor people are leading the life of brutes is simply due to ignorance. We have for all ages been sucking their blood and trampling them underfoot. Suppose some disinterested Sannyasins, bent on doing good to others, go from village to village, disseminating education and seeking in various ways to better the condition of all down to the Chandala, through oral teaching, and by means of maps, cameras, globes and such other accessories—can't that bring forth good in time? All these plans I cannot write out in this short letter. The long and the short of it is—if the mountain does not come to Mohammed, Mohammed must go to the mountain. The poor are too poor to come to schools and Pathashalas, and they will gain nothing by reading poetry and all that sort of thing. We, as a nation, have lost our individuality, and that is the cause of all mischief in India. We have to give back to the nation its lost individuality and *raise the masses.* The Hindu, the Mohammedan, the Christian, all have trampled them underfoot. Again the force to raise them must come from inside, that is, from the orthodox Hindus. In every country the evils exist not with, but against, religion. Religion therefore is not to blame, but men.

To effect this, the first thing we need is men, and the next is funds. Through the grace of our Guru I was sure to get from ten to fifteen men in every town. I next travelled in search of funds, but do you think the people of India were going to spend money! [...] Selfishness personified—are they to spend anything? Therefore I have come to America, to earn money myself, and then return to my country and devote the rest of my days to the realisation of this one aim of my life.

We cannot give up jealousy and rally together. That is our national sin!! It is not to be met with in this country (USA), and this is what has made them so great.

Nowhere in the world have I come across such 'frogs-in-the-well' as we are. Let anything come from some foreign country, and Americans will be the first to accept it. But we? Oh, there are none like us in the world, we men of Aryan blood!! Where that heredity really expresses itself, I do not see [...] Yet they are descendants of the Aryans?

Vol. 6, Epistles (Second Series), XLI, pp. 254–256

There is no hope for our nation. Not one original idea crosses anyone's brains, all fighting over the same old, threadbare rug—that Ramakrishna Paramahansa was such and such—and cock-and-bull stories—stories having neither head nor tail. My God! Won't you do something to show that you are in any way removed from the common run of men!—Only indulging in madness! [...] Today you have your bell, tomorrow you add a horn, and follow suit with a chowry the day after; or you introduce a cot today, and tomorrow you have its legs silver-mounted, and people help themselves to a rice-porridge, and you spin out two thousand cock-and-bull stories—in short, nothing but external ceremonials. This is called in English imbecility. Those into whose heads nothing but that sort of silliness enters are called imbecile. Those whose heads have a tendency to be troubled day and night over such questions as whether the bell should ring on the right or on the left, whether the sandal-paste mark should be put on the head or anywhere else, whether the light should be waved twice or four times—simply deserve the name of wretches, and it is owing to that sort of notion that we are the outcastes of Fortune, kicked and spurned at, while the people of the West are masters of the whole world [...] There is an ocean of difference between idleness and renunciation.

If you want any good to come, just throw your ceremonials overboard and worship the Living God, the Man-God—every being that wears a human form—God in His universal as well as individual aspect. The universal aspect of God means this world, and worshipping it means serving it—this indeed is work, not indulging in ceremonials. Neither is it work to cogitate as to whether the rice-plate should be place in front of the God for ten minutes or for half an hour—that is called lunacy. Millions of rupees have been spent only that the temple-doors at Varanasi or Vrindaban may play at opening and shutting all day long! Now the Lord is having His toilet, now He is taking His meals, now He is busy on something else we know not what [...] and all this, while the Living God is dying for want of food, for want of education! The banias of Bombay are erecting hospitals for bugs—while they would do nothing for men even if they die! You have not the brain to understand this simple thing—that it is a plague with our country, and lunatic asylums are rife all over [...] Let some of you spread like fire, and preach this worship of the universal aspect of the Godhead—a thing that was never undertaken before in our country. No quarrelling with people, we must be friends with all [...]

Vol. 6, Epistles (Second Series), XLV, pp. 263–264

The present religion of the Hindus is not in the Vedas, nor in the Puranas, nor in Bhakti, nor in Mukti—religion has entered into the cooking pot. The present religion of the Hindus is neither the path of knowledge nor that of reason—it is 'Don't touchism.' 'Don't touch me!' 'Don't touch me!'—that exhausts its description. See that you do not lose your lives in this dire irreligion of 'Don't touchism. Must the teaching 'Looking upon all beings as your own self' be confined to books alone? How will they grant salvation who cannot feed a hungry mouth with a crumb of bread? How will those who become impure at the mere breath of others purify others? Don't touchism is a form of mental disease. Beware!

Vol. 6, Epistles (Second Series), LXXI, pp. 319–320

Our nation is totally lacking in the faculty of organisation. It is this one drawback which produces all sorts of evil. We are altogether averse to making a common cause for anything. The first requisite for organisation is obedience.

Vol. 6, Epistles (Second Series), LXXII, p. 321

Human society is [...] governed by the four castes—the priests, soldiers, the traders, and the labourers. Each state has its glories as well as its defects. When the priest (Brahmin) rules, there is a tremendous exclusivity on hereditary grounds; the persons of the priests and their descendants are hemmed in with all sorts of safeguards—none but they have any knowledge—none but they have the right to impart that knowledge. Its glory is that at this period is laid the foundation of sciences. The priests cultivate the mind, for through the mind they govern.

The military (Kshatriya) rule is tyrannical and cruel, but they are not exclusive; and during that period arts and social culture attain their height.

The commercial (Vaishya) rule comes next. It is awful in its silent crushing and blood-sucking power. Its advantage is, as the trader himself goes everywhere, he is a good disseminator of ideas collected during the two previous states. They are still less exclusive than the military, but culture begins to decay.

Last will come the labourer (Shudra) rule. Its advantages will be the distribution of physical comforts—its disadvantages, (perhaps) the lowering of culture. There will be a great distribution of ordinary education, but extraordinary geniuses will be less and less.

If it is possible to form a state in which the knowledge of the priest period, the culture of the military, the distributive spirit of the commercial, and the ideal of equality of the last can all be kept intact, minus their evils, it will be an ideal state. But is it possible?

Yet the first three have had their day. Now is the time for the last—they must have it—none can resist it. I do not know all the difficulties about the gold or silver standards (nobody seems to know much as to that), but this much I see that the gold standard has been making the poor poorer, and the rich richer. Bryan was right when he said, 'We refuse to be crucified on a cross of gold.' The silver standard will give the poor a better chance in this unequal fight. I am a socialist not because I think it is a perfect system, but half a loaf is better than no bread.

The other systems have been tried and found wanting. Let this one be tried—if for nothing else, for the novelty of the thing. A redistribution of pain and pleasure is better than always the same persons having pains and pleasures. The sum total of good and evil in the world remains ever the same. The yoke will be lifted from shoulder to shoulder by new systems, that is all.

Let every dog have his day in this miserable world, so that

after this experience of so-called happiness they may all come to the Lord and give up this vanity of a world and governments and all other botherations.

Vol. 6, Epistles (Second Series), CXII, pp. 380–382

It is only a few that understand the language of the brain, but everyone, from the Creator down to a clump of grass, understands the language that comes from the heart. But then, in our country, it is a case of rousing men that are, as it were, dead. It will take time, but if you have infinite patience and perseverance, success is bound to come. No mistake in that.

How are the English officials to blame? Is the family, of whose unnatural cruelty you have written, an isolated one in India? Or are there plenty of such? It is the same story all over the country. But then, it is not as a result of pure wickedness that the selfishness commonly met with in our country has come. This bestial selfishness is the outcome of centuries of failure and repression. It is not real selfishness, but deep-rooted despair. It will be cured at the first inkling of success. It is only this that the English officials are noticing all round; so how can they have faith at the very outset? But tell me, do they not sympathise with any real work that they meet with?

Vol. 6, Epistles (Second Series), CLIV, pp. 425–426

It is only you who are in this world lying prostrate today like inert matter. You have been hypnotised. From very old times, others have been telling you that you are weak, that you have no power, and you also, accepting that, have for about a thousand years gone on thinking, 'We are wretched, we are good for nothing.' (Pointing to his body): This body also is born of the soil of your country, but I never thought like that. And hence you see how, through His will, even those who always think us low and weak, have done and are still doing me divine honour. If you can think that infinite power, infinite knowledge and indomitable energy lie within you, and if you can bring out that power, you also can become like me.

Vol. 6, Conversations and Dialogues, II, p. 454

How can there be any progress of the country without the spread of education, the dawning of knowledge? Even no real effort or exertion in the cause is visible among the few in your country who are the promise of the future, you who have received the blessings of education. But know for certain that absolutely nothing can be done to improve the state of things, unless there is spread of education first among the women and the masses [...] But the whole work must be done in the style of our own country. Just as centres have to be started for men, so also centres have to be started for teaching women.

Brahmacharinis of education and character should take up the task of teaching at these different centres. History and the Puranas, housekeeping and the arts, the duties of home-life and principles that make for the development of an ideal character have to be taught with the help of modern science, and the women students must be trained up in ethical and spiritual life. We must see to their growing up as ideal matrons of home in time. The children of such mothers will make further progress in the virtues that distinguish their mothers. It is only in the homes of educated and pious mothers that great men are born. And you have reduced your women to something like manufacturing machines; alas, for heaven's sake, is this the outcome of your education? The uplift of the women, the awakening of the masses must come first, and then only can any real good come about for the country, for India.

Religion, arts, science, housekeeping, cooking, sewing, hygiene—the simple essential points in these subjects ought to be taught to our women. It is not good to let them touch novels and fiction. The Mahakali Pathashala is to a great extent moving in the right direction. But only teaching rites of worship won't do; their education must be an eye-opener in all matters. Ideal characters must always be presented before the view of the girls to imbue them with a devotion to lofty principles of selflessness. The noble examples of Sita, Savitri, Damayanti, Lilavati, Khana, and Mira should be brought home to their minds, and they should be inspired to mould their own lives in the light of these.

Vol. 6, Conversations and Dialogues, VIII, pp. 489–494

Guru Govind made it understood everywhere that the men of his age, be they Hindus or Mussulmans, were living under a regime of profound injustice and oppression. He did not create any common interest; he only pointed it out to the masses. And so both Hindus and Mussulmans followed him. He was a great worshipper of Shakti. Yes, in Indian history, such an example is indeed very rare.

Vol. 6, Conversations and Dialogues, XII, pp. 514–515

From the earliest times in India the Brahmin caste have held themselves beyond all law; they claim to be gods. They are poor, but their weakness is that they seek power. Here are about sixty millions of people who are good and moral and hold no property, and they are what they are because from their birth they are taught that they are above law, above punishment. They feel themselves to be 'twice-born,' to be sons of God.

Vol. 7, Inspired Talks, 27 July 1895, p. 72

The wicked pay the price of the great soul's holiness. Think of that when you see a wicked man. Just as the poor man's labour pays for the rich man's luxury, so is it in the spiritual world. The terrible degradation of the masses in India is the price nature pays for the production of great souls like Mirabai, Buddha etc.

Vol. 7, Inspired Talks, 31 July 1895, p. 81

What nonsense are you talking? Within you lies indomitable power. Only thinking, 'I am nothing, I am nothing,' you have become powerless. Why you alone? The whole race has become so. Go round the world once, and you will find how vigorously the life-current of other nations is flowing. And what are you doing? Even after learning so much, you go about the doors of others, crying, 'Give me employment.' Trampled under others' feet, doing slavery for others, are you men any more? You are not worth a pin's head. In this fertile country with abundant water supply, where nature produces wealth and harvest a thousand times more than in others, you have no food for your stomach, no clothes to cover your body! In this country of abundance, the produce of which has been the cause of the spread of civilisation in other countries, you are reduced to such straits! Your condition is even worse than that of a dog. And you glory in your Vedas and Vedanta! A nation that cannot provide for its simple food and clothing, which always depends on others for its subsistence—what is there for it to vaunt about? Throw your religious observances overboard for the present and be first prepared for the struggle for existence. People of foreign countries are turning out such golden results from the raw materials produced in your country, and you, like asses of burden, are only carrying their load. The people of foreign countries import Indian raw goods, manufacture various commodities by bringing their intelligence to bear upon them, and become great; whereas you have locked up your intelligence, thrown away your inherited wealth to others, and roam about crying piteously for food.

That is what I say, my son, you have no Shraddha—no faith in yourselves. What will you achieve? You will have neither material nor spiritual advancement. Either put forth your energy in the way I have suggested and be successful in life, or give up all and take to the path we have chosen. Serve the people of all countries through spiritual instruction—then only will you get your dole of food like us. If there is no mutual exchange, do you think anybody cares for anybody else? You observe in our case that because we give the householders some spiritual instructions, they in return give us some morsels of food. If you do nothing, why will they give you food? You observe so much misery in mere service and slavery of others, still you are not waking up; and so your misery also is never at an end. This is certainly the delusive power of Maya! In the West I found that those who are in the employment of others have their seats fixed in the back rows in the Parliament, while the front seats are reserved for those who have made themselves famous by self-exertion, or education, or intelligence. In Western countries there is no botheration of caste. Those on whom Fortune smiles for their industry and exertion are alone regarded as leaders of the country and the controllers of its destiny. Whereas in your country, you are simply vaunting your superiority in caste, till at last you cannot even get a morsel of food! You have not the capacity to manufacture a needle, and you dare to criticise the English! Fools! Sit at their feet and learn from them the arts, industries, and the practicality necessary for the struggle for existence. You will be esteemed once more when you will become fit. Then they too will pay heed to your words. Without the necessary preparation, what will mere shouting in the Congress avail?

You consider a man as educated if only he can pass some examinations and deliver good lectures. The education which does not help the common mass of people to equip themselves for the struggle for life, which does not bring out strength of character, a spirit of philanthropy, and the courage of a lion—is it worth the name? Real education is that which enables one to stand on one's own legs. The education that you are receiving now in schools and colleges is only making you a race of dyspeptics. You are working like machines merely, and living a jellyfish existence.

Set yourselves to the task of spreading education among masses. Tell them and make them understand. 'You are our brothers—a part and parcel of our bodies, and we love you and never hate you.' If they receive this sympathy from you, their enthusiasm for work will be increased a hundredfold. Kindle their knowledge with the help of modern science. Teach them history, geography, science, literature, and along with these the profound truths of religion. In exchange for that teaching, the poverty of the teachers will also disappear. By mutual exchange both parties will become friendly to each other.

(Q: To bring the higher classes to sympathise with the lower seems to be a difficult affair in India)

But without that there is no wellbeing for your upper classes. You will be destroyed by internecine quarrels and fights—which you have been having so long. When the masses will wake up, they will come to understand your oppression of them, and by a puff of their mouth you will be entirely blown away! It is they who have introduced civilisation amongst you; and it is they who will then pull it down. Think how at the hands of the Gauls the mighty ancient Roman civilisation crumbled into dust! Therefore I say, try to rouse these lower classes from slumber by imparting learning and culture to them. When they will awaken—and awaken one day they must—they also will not forget your good services to them and will remain grateful to you.

Vol. 7, Conversations and Dialogues, VII, pp. 144–150

You priest-class never let the non-Brahmin classes read the Vedas and Vedanta and all such weighty Shastras—never touch them even. You have only kept them down. It is you who have always done like that through selfishness. It was the Brahmins who made a monopoly of the religious books and kept the question of sanction and prohibition in their own hands. And repeatedly calling the other races of India low and vile, they put this belief into their heads that they were really such.

The Brahmins, in fact, gradually took a course of gross immorality and oppression. Through selfishness they introduced a large number of strange, non-Vedic, immoral, and unreasonable doctrines—simply to keep intact their own prestige. And the fruits of that they are reaping forthwith.

It is simply due to your having despised the masses of India that you have now been living a life of slavery for the last thousand years; it is therefore that you are objects of hatred in the eyes of foreigners and are looked upon with indifference by your countrymen.

I have travelled the whole of India, and everywhere I have found society to be guided by local usages which are condemned by the Shrutis and Smritis. Popular customs, local usages, and observances prevalent among women only—have not these taken the place of the Smritis everywhere? Who obeys, and whom? If you can but spend enough money, the priest-class is ready to write out whatever sanctions or prohibitions you want! How many of them read the Vedic Kalpa (Ritual), Grihya and Shrauta Sutras?

Vol. 7, Conversations and Dialogues, XI, pp. 172–173

Going round the whole world, I find that people of this country are immersed in great Tamas (inactivity), compared with people of other countries. On the outside, there is a simulation of the Sattvika (calm and balanced) state, but inside, downright inertness like that of sticks and stones—what work will be done in the world by such people? How long can such an inactive, lazy, and sensual people live in the world? First travel in Western countries, then contradict my words. How much of enterprise and devotion to work, how much enthusiasm and manifestation of Rajas are there in the lives of the Western people! While, in your country, it is as if the blood has become congealed in the heart, so that it cannot circulate in the veins—as if paralysis has overtaken the body and it has become languid. So my idea is first to make the people active by developing their Rajas, and thus make them fit for the struggle for existence. With no strength in the body, no enthusiasm at heart, and no originality in the brain, what will they do—these lumps of dead matter! By stimulating them I want to bring life into them—to this I have dedicated my life. I will rouse them through the infallible power of Vedic Mantras. I am born to proclaim to them that fearless message—'Arise, Awake!' Be you my helpers in this work! Go from village to village, from one portion of the country to another, and preach this message of fearlessness to all, from the Brahmin to the Chandala. Tell each and all that infinite power resides within them, that they are the sharers of immoral Bliss. Thus rouse up the Rajas within them—make them fit for the struggle for existence, and then speak to them about salvation. First make the people of the country stand on their legs by rousing their inner power, first let them learn to have good food and clothes and plenty of enjoyment—then tell them how to be free from this bondage of enjoyment.

Laziness, meanness and hypocrisy have covered the whole length and breadth of the country. Can an intelligent man look on all this and remain quiet? Does it not bring tears to the eyes? Madras, Bombay, Punjab, Bengal—whichever way I look, I see no signs of life. You are thinking yourselves highly educated. What nonsense have you learnt? Getting by heart the thoughts of others in a foreign language, and stuffing our brain with them and taking some university degrees, you consider yourselves educated! Fie upon you! Is this education? What is the goal of your education? Either a clerkship, or being a roguish lawyer, or at the most a Deputy Magistracy, which is another form of clerkship—isn't that all? What good will it do you or the country at large? Open your eyes and see what a piteous cry for food is rising in the land of Bharata, proverbial for its wealth! Will your education fulfil this want? Never. With the help of Western science set yourselves to dig the earth and produce foodstuffs—not by means of mean servitude of others—but by discovering new avenues to production, by your own exertions aided by Western science. Therefore I teach the people of this country to be full of activities, so as to be able to produce food and clothing for themselves. For want of food and clothing and plunged in anxiety for it, the country has come to ruin—what are you doing to remedy this? Throw aside your scriptures in the Ganga and teach the people first the means of procuring their food and clothing, and then you will find time to read to them the scriptures. If their material wants are not removed by the rousing of intense activity, none will listen to words of spirituality. Therefore I say, first rouse the inherent power of the Atman within you, then, rousing the faith of the general people in that power a much as you can, teach them first of all to make provision for food, and then teach them religion. There is no time to sit idle—who knows when death will overtake one?

Vol. 7, Conversations and Dialogues, XII, pp. 181–183

Now it won't do to merely quote the authority of our ancient books. The tidal wave of Western civilisation is now rushing over the length and breadth of the country. It won't do now simply to sit in meditation on mountaintops without realising in the least its usefulness. Now is wanted—as said in the Gita by the Lord—intense Karma-yoga, with unbounded courage and indomitable strength in the heart. Then only will the people of the country be roused, otherwise they will continue to be as much in the dark as you are.

Vol. 7, Conversations and Dialogues, XIII, p. 185

Though outwardly there may be difference between men and women, in their real nature there is none. Hence, if a man can be a knower of Brahman, why cannot a woman attain to the same knowledge? Therefore, I was saying that if even one amongst the women became a knower of Brahman, then by the radiance of her personality thousands of women would be inspired and awakened to truth, and great well-being of the country and society would ensue.

We have seen in Shri Ramakrishna how he had this idea of divine motherhood in every woman, of whatever caste she might be, or whatever might be her worth. It is because I have seen this that I ask you all so earnestly to do likewise and open girls' schools in every village and try to uplift them. If the women are raised, then their children will by their noble actions glorify the name of the country—then will culture, knowledge, power and devotion awaken in the land.

Female education is to be spread with religion as its centre. All other training should be secondary to religion. Religious training, the formation of character and observance of the vow of celibacy—these should be attended to. In the female education which has obtained up till now in India, it is religion that has been made a secondary concern, hence those defects you were speaking of have crept in. But no blame attaches therefore to the women. Reformers having proceeded to start female education without being Brahmacharins themselves have stumbled like that.

Vol. 7, Conversations and Dialogues, XVIII, pp. 219–221

My hope of the future lies in the youths of character—intelligent, renouncing all for the service of others, and obedient—who can sacrifice their lives in working out my ideas and thereby do good to themselves and the country at large. Otherwise, boys of the common run are coming in groups and will come. Dullness is written on their faces—their hearts are devoid of energy, their bodies feeble and unfit for work, and minds devoid of courage. What work will be done by these? If I get ten or twelve boys with the faith of Nachiketa, I can turn the thoughts and pursuits of this country in a new channel.

Among those who appear to me to be of good calibre, some have bound themselves by matrimony; some have sold themselves for the acquisition of worldly name, fame or wealth; while some are of feeble bodies. The rest, who form the majority, are unable to receive any high idea.

Playing on the Khol and Kartal and dancing in the frenzy of Krishna has degenerated the whole people. They are, in the first place, a race of dyspeptics—and if in addition to this they dance and jump in that way, how can they bear the strain? In trying to imitate the highest Sadhana, the preliminary qualification for which is absolute purity, they have been swallowed in dire Tamas. In every district and village you may visit, you will find only the sound of the Khol and Kartal! Are not drums made in the country? Are not trumpets and kettle-drums available in India? Make the boys hear the deep-toned sound of these instruments. Hearing from boyhood the sound of these effeminate forms of music and listening to the kirtana, the country is well-nigh converted into a country of women. What more degradation can you expect? Even the poet's imagination fails to draw the picture! The Damaru and horn have to be sounded, drums are to be beaten so as to raise the deep and martial notes, and with 'Mahavira, Mahavira' on your lips and shouting 'Hara, Hara, Vyom, Vyom,' the quarters are to be reverberated. The music which awakens only the softer feelings of man is to be stopped now for some time. Stopping the light tunes such as Kheal and Tappa for some time, the people are to be accustomed to hear the Dhrupad music. Through the thunder-roll of the dignified Vedic hymns, life is to be brought back into the country. In everything the austere spirit of heroic manhood is to be revived. In following such an ideal lies the good of the people and the country. If you can build your character after such an ideal, then a thousand others will follow. But take care that you do not swerve an inch from the ideal. Never lose heart. In eating, dressing, or lying, in singing or playing, in enjoyment or disease, always manifest the highest moral courage. Then only will you attain the grace of Mahashakti, the Divine Mother.

Vol. 7, Conversations and Dialogues, XXI, pp. 230–233

The Brahmo Samaj [...] spread in Calcutta for a certain time and then died out. I am not sorry, neither glad that it died. It has done its work viz. social reform. Its religion was not worth a cent, and so it must die out [...] I am even now a great sympathiser of its reforms; but the 'booby' religion could not hold its own against the old 'Vedanta.'

Vol. 7, Epistles (Third Series), XXI, pp. 468–469

In these modern days there is a greater impetus towards higher education on the European lines, and the trend of opinion is strong towards women getting this higher education. Of course, there are some people in India who do not want it, but those who do want it carried the day. It is a strange fact that Oxford and Cambridge are closed to women today, as are Harvard and Yale; but Calcutta University opened its doors to women more than twenty years ago. I remember that the year I graduated, several girls came out and graduated—the same standard, the same course, the same in everything as the boys; and they did very well indeed. And our religion does not prevent a woman being educated at all. In this way the girl should be educated; even thus she should be trained; and in the old books we find that the universities were equally resorted to by both girls and boys, but later the education of the whole nation was neglected. What can you expect under foreign rule? The foreign conqueror is not there to do good to us; he wants his money. I studied hard for twelve years and became a graduate of Calcutta University; now I can scarcely make $5.00 a month in my country. Would you believe it? It is actually a fact. So these educational institutions of foreigners are simply to get a lot of useful, practical slaves for a little money—to turn out a host of clerks, postmasters, telegraph operators, and so on. There it is.

Vol. 8, Women of India, pp. 69–70

I am not a very great believer in monastic systems. They have great merits, and also great defects. There should be a perfect balance between the monastics and the householders. But monasticism has absorbed all the power in India. We represent the greatest power. The monk is greater than the prince. There is no reigning sovereign in India who dares to sit down when the 'yellow cloth' is there. He gives up his seat and stands. Now that is bad, so much power, even in the hands of good men—although these monastics have been the bulwark of the people. They stand between the priestcraft and knowledge. They are the centres of knowledge and reform. They are just what the prophets were among the Jews. The prophets were always preaching against the priests, trying to throw out superstitions. So are they in India. But all the same so much power is not good there; better methods should be worked out. But you can only work in the line of least resistance. The whole national soul there is upon monasticism. You go to India and preach any religion as a householder; the Hindu people will turn back and go out. If you have given up the world, however, they say, 'He is good, he has given up the world. He is a sincere man, he wants to do what he preaches.' What I mean to say is this that it represents a tremendous power. What can we do is just to transform it, give it another form. This tremendous power in the hands of the roving Sannyasins of India has got to be transformed, and it will raise the masses up.

Vol. 8, Lectures and Discourses, My Life and Mission, pp. 89–90

Hundreds of castes! If one man touches another man's food, he cries out, 'Lord help me, I am polluted!' When I returned to India after my visit to the West, several orthodox Hindus raised a howl against my association with Western people and my breaking the rules of orthodoxy. They did not like me to teach the truths of the Vedas to the people of the West.

But how can there be these distinctions and differences? How can the rich man turn up his nose at the poor man, and the learned at the ignorant, if we are all spirit and all the same? Unless society changes, how can such a religion as Vedanta prevail? It will take thousands of years to have large numbers of truly rational human beings. It is very hard to show men new things, to give them great ideas. It is harder still to knock off old superstitions, very hard; they do not die easily. With all his education, even the learned man becomes frightened in the dark—the nursery tales come into his mind, and he sees ghosts.

Vol. 8, Lectures and Discourse, Is Vedanta the Future Religion?, p. 136

Hitherto the great fault of our Indian religion has lain in its knowing only two words: renunciation and Mukti. Only Mukti here! Nothing for the householder! But these are the very people whom I want to help. For are not all souls of the same quality? Is not the goal of all the same? And so strength must come to the nation through education.

Vol. 8, Sayings and Utterances, 23, p. 267

The less you read, the better. Read the Gita and other good works on Vedanta. That is all you need. The present system of education is all wrong. The mind is crammed with facts before it knows how to think. Control of the mind should be taught first. If I had my education to get over again and had any voice in the matter, I would learn to master my mind first, and then gather facts if I wanted them. It takes people a long time to learn things because they can't concentrate their minds at will.

P.S. One thing that I am very sorry to notice in these parts (Bombay) is the thorough want of Sanskrit and other learning. The people of this part of the country have for their religion a certain bundle of local superstitions about eating, drinking, and bathing, and that is about the whole of their religion.

Vol. 8, Sayings and Utterances, 57, p. 280

Poor fellows! Whatever the rascally and wily priests teach them—all sorts of mummery and tomfoolery as the very gist of the Vedas and Hinduism (mind you, neither these rascals of priests nor their forefathers have so much as *seen* a volume of the Vedas for the last 400 generations—they follow and degrade themselves. Lord help them from the Rakshasas in the shape of the Brahmins of the Kaliyuga.

Vol. 8, Epistles (Fourth Series), IX, p. 290

On the one hand, my vision of the future of Indian religion and that of the whole world, my love for the millions of beings sinking down and down for ages with nobody to help them, nay, nobody with even a thought for them; on the other hand, making those who are nearest and dearest to me miserable; I choose the former. 'Lord will do the rest.' He is with me, I am sure of that if of anything. So long as I am sincere, nothing can resist me, because He will be my help. Many and many in India could not understand me; and how could they, poor men? Their thoughts never strayed beyond the everyday routine business of eating and drinking [...] But appreciation or no appreciation, I am born to organize these young men; nay, hundreds more in every city are ready to join me; and I want to send them rolling like irresistible waves over India, bringing comfort, morality, religion, education to the doors of the meanest and the most downtrodden. And this I will do or die.

Our people have no idea, no appreciation. On the other hand, that horrible jealousy and suspicious nature which is the natural outcome of a thousand years of slavery make them stand as enemies to every new idea. Still the Lord is great.

Three things are necessary to make every man great, every nation great: (1) Conviction of the powers of goodness; (2) Absence of jealousy and suspicion; (3) Helping all who are trying to be and do good. Why should the Hindu nation with all its wonderful intelligence and other things have gone to pieces? I would answer you, *jealousy*. Never were there people more wretchedly jealous of one another, more envious of one another's fame and name than this wretched Hindu race.

Vol. 8, Epistles (Fourth Series), XV, pp. 297–299

The whole difference between the West and the East is in this: They are nations, we are not, i.e. civilisation, education here is general, it penetrates into the masses. The higher classes in India and America are the same, but the distance is infinite between the lower classes of the two countries. Why was it so easy for the English to conquer India? It was because they are a nation; we are not. When one of our great men dies, we must sit for centuries to have another; they can produce them as fast as they die.

A nation of 300 millions has the smallest field of recruiting its great ones compared with nations of thirty, forty, or sixty millions, because the number of educated men and women in those nations is so great. Now do not mistake me, my kind friend, this is the great defect in our nation and must be removed.

Educate and raise the masses, and thus alone a nation is possible. Our reformers do not see where the wound is, they want: save the nation by marrying the widows; do you think that a nation is saved by the number of husbands its widows get? Nor is our religion to blame, for an idol more or less makes no difference. The whole defect is here: the real nation who live in cottage have forgotten their manhood, their individuality. Trodden under the foot of the Hindu, Mussulman, or Christian, they have come to think that they are born to be trodden under the foot of everybody who has money enough in his pocket. They are to be given back their lost individuality. They are to be educated. Whether idols will remain or not, whether widows will have husbands enough or not, whether caste is good or bad, I do not bother myself with such questions. Everyone must work out his own salvation. Our duty is to put the chemicals together, the crystallisation will come through God's laws. Let us put ideas into their heads, and they will do the rest. Now this means educating the masses. Here are these difficulties. A pauper government cannot, will not, do anything; so no help from that quarter.

Even supposing we are in a position to open schools in each village free, still the poor boys would rather go to the plough to earn their living than come to your school. Neither have we the money, nor can we make them come to education. The problem seems hopeless. I have found a way out. It is this. If the mountain does not come to Mohammed, Mohammed must go to the mountain. If the poor cannot come to education, education must reach them at the plough, in the factory, everywhere. How? You have seen my brethren. Now I can get hundreds of such, all over India, unselfish, good and educated. Let these men go from village to village bringing not only religion to the door of everyone but also education. So I have a nucleus of organising the widows also as instructors to our women.

The old Hinduism can only be reformed through Hinduism, and not through the new-fangled reform movements. At the same time the reformers must be able to unite in themselves the culture of both the East and the West. Now do you not think that you have already seen the nucleus of such a great movement (to reform Hinduism), that you have heard the low rumblings of the coming tidal wave? That centre, that God-man to lead was born in India. He was the great Ramakrishna Paramahamsa, and round him this band is slowly gathering. They will do the work. Now, Diwanji Maharaj, this requires an organisation, money—a little at least to set the wheel in motion. Who would have given us money in India? So, Diwanji Maharaj, I crossed over to America. You may remember I begged all the money from the poor, and the offers of the rich I would not accept because they could not understand my ideas. Now lecturing for a year in this country (USA), I could not succeed at all (of course I have no wants for myself) in my plan for raising some funds for setting up my work. First, this year is a very bad year in America; thousands of their poor are without work. Secondly, the missionaries and the Brahmo Samajists try to thwart all my views. Thirdly, a year has rolled by, and our countrymen could not even do so much for me as to say to the American people that I was a real Sannyasin and no cheat, and that I represented the Hindu religion. Even this much, the expenditure of a few words, they could not do! Bravo, my countrymen!

You are at liberty, my friend, to think that I am a dreamer, a visionary; but believe at least that I am sincerely to the backbone, and my greatest fault is that I love my country only too, too well.

Vol. 8, Epistles (Fourth Series), XX, pp. 306–309

On the whole, the Americans are a million times nobler than the Hindus, and I can work more good here than in the country of the ingrate and the heartless. After all, I must work my Karma out.

It was my foolishness—the forgetting for a moment that we Hindus have not yet become human beings, and giving up for a moment my self-reliance and relying upon the Hindus—that I came to grief. Every moment I expected something from India. No, it never came. Last two months especially I was in torture at every moment. No, not even a newspaper from India! My friends waited—waited month after month; nothing came, not a voice. Many consequently grew cold and at last gave me up. But it is the punishment for relying upon man and upon brutes, for our countrymen are not men as yet. They are ready to be praised, but when their turn comes even to say a word, they are nowhere.

America is the best field in the world to carry on any idea; so I do not think of leaving America soon. And why? Here I have food and drink and clothes, and everybody so kind, and all this for a few good words! Why should I give up such a noble nation to go to the land of brutes and ingrates and the brainless boobies held in eternal thralldom of superstitious, merciless, pitiless wretches? So good-bye again.

I am not pleased with myself. I committed a terrible error—of calculating upon others' help—once in my life—and I have paid for it. It was my fault and not theirs. Lord bless all the Madras people. They are at least far superior to the Bengalis, who are simply fools and have no souls, no stamina at all. Good-bye, good-bye. I have launched my boat in the waves, come what may. Regarding my brutal criticisms, I have really no right to make them. You have done for me infinitely more than I deserve. I must bear my own Karma, and that without a murmur. Lord bless you all.

Vol. 8, Epistles (Fourth Series), XXI, pp. 312–314

I am the same here as in India, only here in this highly cultural land there is an appreciation, a sympathy which our ignorant fools never dream of. There our people grudge us monks a crumb of bread, here they are ready to pay one thousand rupees a lecture and remain grateful for the instructions forever.

I am appreciated by these strangers more than I was ever in India. I can, if I will, live here all my life in the greatest luxury; but I am a Sannyasin, and 'India, with all thy faults I love thee still.' So I am coming back after some months, and go on sowing the seeds of religion and progress from city to city as I was doing so long, although amongst a people who know not what appreciation and gratefulness are.

I am ashamed of my own nation when I compare their beggarly, selfish, unappreciative, ignorant ungratefulness with the help, hospitality, sympathy, and respect which the Americans have shown to me, a representative of a foreign religion. Therefore come out of the country, see others, and compare.

Vol. 8, Epistles (Fourth Series), XXXIII, pp. 327–328

Why amongst the poor of India so many are Mohammedans? It is nonsense to say they were converted by the sword. It was to gain their liberty from the [...] zamindars and from the [...] priest, and as a consequence you find in Bengal there are more Mohammedans than Hindus among the cultivators, because there were so many zamindars there.

Vol. 8, Epistles (Fourth Series), XXXIV, p. 330

British rule in modern India has only one redeeming feature, though unconscious; it has brought India out once more on the stage of the world; it has forced upon it the contact of the outside world. If it had been done with an eye to the good of the people concerned, as circumstances favoured Japan with, the results could have been more wonderful for India. No good can be done when the main idea is bloodsucking. On the whole the old regime was better for the people, as it *did not* take away everything they had, and there was some justice, some liberty.

A few hundred, modernised, half-educated and denationalised men are all the show of modern India—*nothing else*. The Hindus were 600 million in number according to Ferishta, the Mohammedan historian, in the 12th century—now less than 200 million.

In spite of the centuries of anarchy that reigned during the struggles of the English to conquer, the terrible massacre the English perpetrated in 1857 and 1858, and the still more terrible famines that have become the inevitable consequence of British rule (there never is a famine in a native state), and that take off millions, there has been a good increase of population, but not yet what it was when the country was entirely independent—that is, before the Mohammedan rule. Indian labour and produce can support five times as many people as there are now in India with comfort, if the whole thing is not taken off from them.

This is the state of things—even education will no more be permitted to spread; freedom of the press stopped already, (of course we have been disarmed long ago), the bit of self-government granted to them for some years is being quickly taken off. We are watching what next! For writing a few words of innocent criticism, men are being hurried to *transportation for* life, others imprisoned without *any* trial; and nobody knows when his head will be off.

There has been a reign of terror in India for some years. English soldiers are killing our men and outraging our women—

only to be sent home with passage and pension at our expense. We are in a *terrible* gloom—where is the Lord? Mary, you can afford to be optimistic, can I? Suppose you simply publish this letter—the law just passed in India will allow the English Government in India to drag me from here to India and kill me without trial. And I know all your Christian governments will only rejoice, because we are heathens. Shall I also go to sleep and become optimistic? Nero was the greatest optimistic person! They don't think it worth while to write these terrible things as news items even! If necessary, the news agent of *Reuter* gives the exactly opposite news fabricated to order! Heathen-murdering is only a legitimate pastime for the Christians! Your missionaries go to preach God and dare not speak a word of truth for fear of the English, who will kick them out the next day.

All property and lands granted by the previous governments for supporting education have been swallowed up, and the present Government spends even less than Russia in education. And what education? The least show of originality is throttled.

Mary, it is hopeless with us, unless there really is a God who is the father of all, who is not afraid of the strong to protect the weak, and who is not bribed by wealth. Is there such a God? Time will show.

PS: As for religious sects—the Brahmo Samaj, the Arya Samaj, and other sects have been useless mixtures; they were only voices of apology to our English masters to allow us to live! We have started a *new India—a growth* waiting to see what comes. We believe in new ideas only when the nation wants them, and what will be true for us. The test of truth for this Brahmo Samaj is 'what our masters approve;' with us, what the Indian reasoning and experience approves. The struggle has begun—not between the Brahmo Samaj and us, for they are gone already, but a harder, deeper, and more terrible one.

Vol. 8, Epistles (Fourth Series), CXLV, pp. 475–477

”

NOTES